Jobs and Economic Development in Minority Communities

Jobs and Economic Development in Minority Communities

Edited by
PAUL ONG AND
ANASTASIA LOUKAITOU-SIDERIS

 TEMPLE UNIVERSITY PRESS
Philadelphia

PAUL ONG is Director of the Ralph and Goldy Lewis Center for Regional Policy Studies at the University of California, Los Angeles. He is co-editor of *The New Asian Immigration in Los Angeles and Global Restructuring* (Temple).

ANASTASIA LOUKAITOU-SIDERIS is Professor and Chair of Urban Planning in the School of Public Affairs at the University of California, Los Angeles. She is co-author of *Urban Design Downtown: Poetics and Politics of Form.*

Temple University Press
1601 North Broad Street
Philadelphia PA 19122
www.temple.edu/tempress

♾ The paper used in this publication meets the requirements of the American National Standard for Information Sciences—Permanence of Paper for Printed Library Materials, ANSI Z39.48-1992

Library of Congress Cataloging-in-Publication Data
Jobs and economic development in minority communities / edited by
    Paul Ong and Anastasia Loukaitou-Sideris.
        p.   cm.
    Includes bibliographical references and index.
        ISBN 1-59213-409-2 (cloth : alk. paper)—ISBN 1-59213-410-6 (pbk. : alk. paper)
    1. Community development, Urban—United States.   2. Minorities—
United States—Economic conditions.   3. Minorities—Employment—United States.
I. Ong. Paul M.   II. Loukaitou-Sideris, Anastasia, 1958–

    HN90.C6J63   2006
    331.60973—dc22   2005055939

2   4   6   8   9   7   5   3   1

Contents

owth of the Latino and Asian population requires that CED strategies e more sensitive to issues of language, assimilation, and citizenship. Immigrant neighborhoods face many of the same daily struggles for survival as traditional inner-city communities but may have their own cultural and institutional support systems. These realities require different approaches, and this diversity presents a risk of fragmenting the CED movement. Worse, immigrants are at times pitted against other poor ethnic and native minority groups for the same very small piece of the economic pie.

Despite these differences, there is still a common thread, the struggle to improve economic and employment opportunities. Given the new realities, answers to the economic shortfalls have been elusive. The challenge is made more difficult by the fact that many solutions are constrained by a lack of political will, a tendency to "blame the victims," and an inadequacy of resources. Despite the magnitude of the problems and the plethora of hurdles, or perhaps because of them, we need to renew the goal of enhancing employment opportunities as central to community economic development. For the overwhelming majority of poor neighborhoods, the single largest source of income comes from paid work. Unfortunately, wages are low, benefits are scarce, and work is unstable. What is critically needed is a rethinking and reformulation of community economic development that takes into account the particularities of different minority groups. For a problem so pervasive and deep as structural unemployment and underemployment, we cannot hope to devise a panacea or a solution that "fits all." We need innovative strategies to respond to the new challenges, but we must be careful not to change just for change's sake.

Charting a new course for CED requires not only action but also thoughtful reflection, discussion, and debate. This book contributes to the evolving literature by adopting a multipronged perspective to examine specific case studies of economic development and job creation in different physical and social settings. The book contains work by leading scholars who seek to forge a new agenda for community economic development in minority neighborhoods.

The book is divided into four parts. The first part, "The Context," examines some of the larger demographic, economic, social, and physical issues as well as policies that determine or influence the characteristics and problems of low-income minority neighborhoods. These communities are marginalized but not completely insulated from developments beyond their borders. The second part, "Labor Market Development," discusses factors and forces that shape labor demand and supply, including strategies, policies, and practices of workforce development. The focus is on understanding the impacts on minority communities from multiple perspectives. The third part, "Business Development," examines what has been traditionally viewed as a way to create jobs. This section concentrates on the opportunities and barriers encountered by minority-owned businesses and investigates the role and contributions of ethnic entrepreneurs in minority communities. The last part, "Complementary Strategies," explores the connections with other community development strategies. This includes

Introduction
Jobs and Economic Development in Minority Communities
Realities, Challenges, and Innovation

PAUL ONG AND ANASTASIA LOUKAITOU-SIDERIS

COMMUNITY ECONOMIC DEVELOPMENT (CED) offers a promise of improving economic and employment opportunities for low-income minority communities. Impoverished neighborhoods of color are inherent to our nation, rooted in fundamental failings of the postindustrial economy. The shift to a service economy and the decline of traditional manufacturing has disproportionately impacted such communities by undercutting their employment bases. The concomitant spatial restructuring, with the increasing geographic separation of people and jobs, has added to their woes. Economic globalization has boosted the profits of multinational corporations by depressing labor wages within the United States and exporting jobs overseas to lower-wage and nonunionized environments. All these have contributed to structural unemployment, poverty, and welfare dependency, a process most pronounced for the residents of minority neighborhoods.

But the plight of minority neighborhoods is not merely an outcome of economic restructuring or globalization. Caught in a vicious circle, disadvantaged communities concentrate poverty and accentuate inequality as they segregate and isolate poor people of color. Their location often denies residents access to employment and business opportunities and may hinder civic and political participation. Their existence serves as a mechanism that infects and distorts basic social services, such as public education and health care, creating a two-tier system of citizens. These neighborhoods have emerged as the dumping grounds for environmental ills. Many of today's ghettos, ethnic enclaves, barrios, and reservations are the visible manifestations of America's festering domestic shortcomings, which should not be hidden or ignored.

Efforts to address the plight of poor neighborhoods are not new. A systematic response to poverty as a matter of public policy dates back to President Lyndon B. Johnson's War on Poverty (1964–1968). There is considerable debate about the effectiveness and long-term accomplishments of this effort. Some have argued that little has been achieved because poverty has not been eliminated or even reduced. Indeed, the poverty rate in 2003 was 12.5 percent, not much different from 1968's 12.8 percent. This simple yardstick, however, ignores some important positive legacies, such as the dramatic decrease of poverty of the elderly (from 28.5 percent in 1968 to 10.2 percent in 2003) and the important benefits supplied by Medicare. While the effort to address youth poverty has been less effective (from 15.3 percent in 1968 to 17.2 percent in 2003), there is no doubt that the War on Poverty has left a legacy of policies seeking to respond to the structural issue of poverty in systematic and concerted ways.

One such legacy is community development, which was a key ingredient to fighting neighborhood problems during the 1960s. The economic part of community development, that is, CED, remains central to efforts to address the myriad of employment problems blighting many low-income minority communities. There are, of course, social, cultural, and political issues that should be addressed by community development, but improving economic and employment opportunities is critical to the material well-being of any community. Moreover, it is far easier to address the noneconomic aspects of community development when residents are not overwhelmed by a daily struggle to pay the rent, buy food, and cover the other necessities of everyday life. The core challenge for CED today is the same as it was two generations ago—developing effective strategies that are economically sound and incorporate social, cultural, and political realities.

While the core challenge for CED remains unchanged, the realities have altered dramatically since the late 1960s. The five most relevant are the restructuring of the economy, the increase in foreign competition in product markets, a shift in the ethnic composition of the population, a reconfiguration of the urban spatial structure, and a transformation of social policy. These phenomena are interdependent, overlapping, and mutually reinforcing and affect all corners of our society. Nonetheless, the impacts are more pronounced for those at the lower end of the economic ladder both because the forces at work are disproportionately felt there and because the people in that segment are the least able to successfully adjust to change. While the impacts of some of these transformations are discussed in the following chapters, it is useful to provide a summary of how they affect low-income minority communities.

The key feature of the restructuring of the economy is deindustrialization, or the declining importance of manufacturing. In the mid-1960s, the production of durable and nondurable goods accounted for about 27 percent of all value added in the United States. In the last few years, the percentage has fallen to about 13 percent. This decline translated into a corresponding decline in what was once a major source of well-paying jobs for those with limited education. For low-income minority communities, this resulted in a displacement of workers and a subsequent downward mobility. Many of the jobs that have replaced production jobs require more education because of technological change and therefore do not offer the same opportunities for advancement for those without more schooling. The constriction on the avenues of upward mobility has made it more difficult for those at the bottom to work their way out of poverty.

The driving source behind two of the changes comes from beyond the borders of the United States. The increase in foreign competition in the

product market, referred to as the globalization of th[...] g[...] contributed to deindustrialization. In the early 1960s impo[...] a[...] equal to about 4 percent of gross domestic product; by [...] n[...] climbed to 15 percent. Many of the imports come from dev[...] t[...] tries with labor-intensive industries that utilize low-wage [...] workers. This has created an enormous downward wage pr[...] American industries that rely disproportionately on minority w[...] international movement of people, the other face of globalizati[...] affected low-income minorities. Unequal development at the g[...] and the demand for low-wage workers within the United States[...] respond to growing foreign competition, have contributed to a r[...] large scale immigration to the United States. While in 1970, only [...] of the total population were foreign born, by 2004 this share [...] 12 percent. Because the primary sending countries are located in A[...] Latin America, the ethnic composition of the total population h[...] changed. In 1970, Asians and Latinos comprised less than 6 percent [...] total population, but by 2004, they comprised over 18 percent. [...] proportionate number of the new immigrants have limited skills and [...] ited English language ability, and these factors have contributed to [...] concentration in low-income neighborhoods.

The last two transformations are domestic. Over the last few decades, [...] urban landscape has been spatially reconfigured as freeways and increas[...] automobile usage facilitated the dispersion of people and employmen[...] creating an increased geographic separation of places of residence from [...] places of work. While this phenomenon has affected the whole urban population, the impact on low-income minorities has taken on the form of a "spatial mismatch." Because of housing discrimination and a lack of affordable housing in many suburbs, many disadvantaged minorities are trapped in the inner city and have limited transportation resources to access the more adequate job opportunities in the outlying areas. The problems created by this spatial mismatch are compounded by the second domestic change, the transformation of social policy. A part of the change has taken on the form of a retreat from civil rights, including dismantling affirmative action programs and ending forced school integration. The former restricts the immediate economic and employment opportunities for low-income minorities, while the latter diminishes the long-term prospects for their children. In some states, the movement against race-based policies and programs has taken on an anti-immigrant spin. The other part of the policy change is a radical shift in the programs for the poor from income support to moving people into employment. The latter can potentially generate positive outcomes, but this can only come about with adequate support (e.g., job training, transportation, child care services, etc.) to give workers an opportunity to move beyond wages that fail to lift them and their families out of poverty.

The five changes outlined above have not only created new realities and hurdles for community economic development but have also necessitated new approaches. The demographic recomposition brought about by the social and survival networks, affordable housing, and social services. These approaches complement economic strategies by addressing the complex daily realities of workers.

Part 1 starts with Evelyn Blumenberg's examination of the recent changes in the demographic and spatial structure of U.S. metropolitan areas, which in turn have changed the characteristics of neighborhoods (Chapter 1). Over the last few decades, renewed large-scale immigration has driven population growth and increased ethnic diversity. Immigrants and their children have reshaped the urban landscape by transforming many central-city neighborhoods and older suburbs. Despite overall growth, the pattern within metropolitan areas has been very uneven. Suburbs have grown in population, but the populations of many central cities have declined. Another feature of the new urban configuration is the spatial mismatch discussed earlier. For residents trapped in low-income neighborhoods in the inner city, the dispersion of employment has created a geographic barrier to economic opportunities. While all metropolitan areas have been affected by demographic and economic changes, there is nonetheless diversity in outcomes. Although poverty is still concentrated in central-city neighborhoods, many inner-ring suburbs have become blighted while the cores of some cities are prosperous. Because of the diversity in spatial configuration and population composition among and within metropolitan areas, community economic developers must tailor strategies and programs to meeting the needs of the residents of the neighborhoods in which they work.

Public policy determines how governmental resources and power are used to address the problems of low-income people, and one of the most important is the dramatic shift in social policy mentioned earlier. Welfare reform ended income entitlements for the poor and replaced them with tax credits for the working poor. But has this shift eliminated poverty and welfare dependency? Chapter 2 by Douglas Houston and Paul Ong explores the impacts of welfare reform's "new policy regime" on poor neighborhoods in the nation's three largest metropolitan areas: New York, Los Angeles, and Chicago. They find a mixed picture, with a decline in rolls and concentrated poverty, but progress being very uneven across regions and across communities within regions. Even under the best conditions, many have not been able to escape poverty and have moved only from depending on welfare to being a part of the working poor. The authors conclude with a discussion of the implication of these findings for community economic development.

Low-income minority communities have often been pictured as islands, cut off from the job opportunities, services, resources, and amenities of the rest of the metropolitan area. Manuel Pastor, Chris Benner, and Martha Matsuoka explore the opportunities presented and the challenges faced by "community-based regionalism," the marriage of community concerns with regional perspectives (Chapter 3). This concept is premised on the idea that by engaging in regional strategies, ethnic community-based organizations (CBOS) can identify new opportunities, connect to new allies, and affect policies that structure their local environment. The authors try to take a "realistic look" at the potential of community-based regionalism to affect community economic development for minority communities by drawing on the experiences of CBOS in the San Francisco Bay Area. They conclude that community regionalism as a strategy for local economic development may benefit some groups, but not others. They propose a "regional audit," a framework by which communities can identify if regionalism might be a good match for them.

Given this book's focus on employment outcomes, we clearly need to understand how the labor market functions with respect to minority neighborhoods. This is addressed in Part 2, which discusses labor force development policies in the United States that aim to enhance the employment earnings of low-income, low-skilled workers. Such policies have met with mixed success. This is partly the outcome of the programs' inability to train workers in skills that employers demand, with a resulting mismatch between jobs and available skills. The challenges of mounting successful workforce development programs are further compounded in low-income and minority communities because of the economic conditions there. Residents of such neighborhoods lack the resources to extend their job search to outlying areas. Travel to areas where jobs are more abundant presents economic and logistical challenges. Drawing from empirical data, with some concrete examples from Los Angeles, Michael Stoll gives a detailed account of how low-skill labor markets function (Chapter 4). He also examines best practices in workforce development and explores a variety of potential policies that can lead to a better matching of low-skilled workers in minority communities to jobs.

Overcoming the geographic barriers that separate low-income workers from employment opportunities is the focus of Chapter 5 by Michela Zonta. The phenomenon of spatial mismatch has been widely used to explain poor labor-market outcomes. Most of the studies on this topic examine job search from the supply side, focusing on the characteristics of job seekers. Zonta's chapter takes an alternative approach. Focusing on the demand side, she examines the effects of firm location on job applicant rates among minorities. Her study discusses the employment patterns and practices of over one thousand firms in New York, Philadelphia, Atlanta, and Los Angeles. Her findings confirm the spatial mismatch hypothesis, as firms closer to minority communities tend to have more Latino and African American job seekers. She suggests that a key component of economic development strategies for minority communities is the lowering of spatial barriers.

While the working poor face common struggles to survive, contingent workers employed by the informal economy represent a significant and extremely disadvantaged subsegment of the immigrant labor force. In Chapter 6, Abel Valenzuela sheds light on the complex characteristics and special needs of Latino contingent workers. Contingent workers exist at the very margins of the economy and have little formal and ongoing relationship with those who use their labor. In many ways they are independent contractors, but they lack the benefits and freedom enjoyed by contractors in professional fields. Valenzuela identifies three key areas that economic development strategists should consider to improve the economic status of this group, including promoting small-scale entrepreneurship. The first is a place-based strategy that emphasizes the role of community institutions, ethnic networks, businesses, churches, and civic organizations. Second is the need for specialized training programs with a clearly defined market niche. Finally, Valenzuela highlights the importance of accountability. Contingent workers are particularly vulnerable to exploitation, and strategies like living wage ordinances and campaigns to expose unduly harsh and illegal working conditions can greatly improve their plight.

One way to enhance employment opportunities is to revitalize the economic base of minority communities, and Part 3 contains three examples of the potentials and limitations of this approach. While most revitalization strategies view job generation as a critical component, few have focused on the role of minority businesses. Chapter 7 by Thomas Boston fills this gap by examining the contribution of minority-owned businesses to community development. Using Atlanta as a case study, he demonstrates the employment impact of such businesses when they are fully integrated in the development process. About half of the planning, design, and construction contracts in Atlanta's revitalization effort have gone to minority-owned firms. In examining black-owned contracting companies, Boston finds that they tend to hire more minority employees than firms owned by non-minorities and often offer better employment conditions as well. He concludes that the promotion of minority business involvement in communities with high concentrations of minority populations is a sound economic development strategy.

Minority-owned businesses in ethnic economies are often small family businesses. While these businesses create employment opportunities for workers of the same ethnicity, they usually operate with limited resources and are very vulnerable to external circumstances. In Chapter 8, Tarry Hum examines the challenges faced by the Chinese immigrant economy in New York City in the aftermath of September 11, 2001. The impacts of the tragedy on Manhattan's Chinatown economy have been devastating. While focusing on the impacted immigrant economy, Hum also outlines the components of an economic development strategy that transcends the narrow boundaries of the ethnic enclave and promotes linkages to the regional economy.

Not all business development for minority communities is situated in urban settings, and this is particularly true for American Indians. In the last few decades Indian gaming emerged as a significant, albeit controversial, strategy of ethnic entrepreneurship among many Indian tribes. Since Congress passed the Indian Self-Determination Act of 1975, a number of tribes have departed significantly from self-reliant development strategies, which drew primarily on local tribal government resources, and have instead pursued gaming enterprises, which encourage interaction and economic alliances with outsiders. Chapter 9 by Ted Jojola and Paul Ong examines the economic impacts of Indian gaming on eleven Native American tribes residing within a fifty-mile radius from the city of Albuquerque. They carefully document the effects of gaming on the quality of life of Native Americans, their economic well-being, and the leverage they have to influence their everyday landscape.

While the narrow focus of economic development strategies is to increase employment opportunities and wages for workers, a broader definition should also incorporate complementary strategies. Part 4 examines three approaches that complement economic strategies for low-income, minority workers.

One of the most important lessons learned over the last decade is the importance of networks. What is it about neighborhoods and reciprocity that enhances economic development? What types of social networks and ties exist in ethnic communities, and do they lead people to "get by" or "get ahead?" These are the questions addressed in Chapter 10 by Anastasia Loukaitou-Sideris and Judith Hutchinson. Focusing on the Pico Union neighborhood of Los Angeles, the authors illuminate the activities, alliances, and collaborations among different Latino groups in the area. They find that Latinos in Pico Union engage in multiple informal associations revolving around the family, the school, the church, and the recreation center. Such associations serve more as survival networks to help people get by than as venues for major economic advancement. Nevertheless, the emotional and practical support they provide often allows individuals to enter the job market. The authors also identify different strategies for economic advancement followed by two different ethnic groups in the neighborhood, the Oaxacans and the Salvadorans. They conclude that policy responses for economic development strategies may differ significantly from one ethnic group to another and should be tailored to the particularities of needs, cultural norms, and circumstances.

Because the working poor spend more on housing than any other major item, a lack of affordable housing can make a bad financial situation worse. Jacqueline Leavitt asserts the importance and interdependence of strategies for economic development with efforts to ensure affordable housing (Chapter 11). Campaigns for a living wage ordinance go hand in hand with efforts to preserve the existing housing stock in the community, as activists see housing and economic development as two sides of the same coin. Leavitt details a new tool for community economic development, the community benefits agreement, as exercised by the Figueroa Corridor Coalition, an alliance of unions, community-based organizations, clergy, businesses, and neighborhood groups that strives for economic development, business improvement, and affordable housing in Los Angeles.

Low-income communities of color are often dependent on social service agencies to provide basic needs, such as food, child care, health care, and transportation. Lois Takahashi argues that effective community economic development strategies must not only seek to match the job skills of individuals and households with appropriate jobs but also should consider their need to access social services at the same time they are seeking and maintaining employment (Chapter 12). She uses data from an empirical study of minority populations in Orange County, California, to show that sustainable participation in the labor force by low-income minority households requires an effective system of flexible social services to counteract rising living costs, low wages, and lack of health care benefits. She argues that the social service delivery system should "synchronize more closely with the complex and dynamic daily routines of working persons of color."

This book does not pretend to offer a magic recipe that will end chronic unemployment and underemployment in communities of color. Collectively, however, the chapters, which cover diverse communities and practices, send several unambiguous messages. While the broader goal remains to improve employment opportunities through community economic development, a single strategy that "fits all" is impossible. Concrete policies, programs, and practices must be tailor-made, taking into account the particularities, needs, and skills of individuals and their communities. *Access* and *linkages* emerge as key words for the economic development of minority communities. Access to education, training programs, housing, and social services are essential for workforce development and for finding and maintaining decent jobs. Linkages, in the form of alliances to and collaborations with the wider community and region, the labor movement and unions, and other inner-city and suburban groups, can counteract the historic tendencies of isolation and segregation experienced by communities of color. Finally, the promise for economic development lies with complementary strategies that, depending on the context, may incorporate aspects of both the formal and informal economy and ensure access to affordable housing and social services.

These lessons are central to today's community economic development, but they are also pivotal to success in the future. The same structural factors and underlying dynamics that create impoverished minority neighborhoods now are likely to become even more powerful in the future. The twenty-first century will witness a heightening, deepening, and intensifying of globalization, economic and spatial restructuring, and the ethnic recomposition of the population. In this book, we have covered some of the new paths that CED must follow, but much more reflection, discussion, and debate will be needed to help formulate the requisite innovations to address old and emerging problems.

NOTE

We would like to thank Margaret Johnson and Lucy Tran for helping prepare the manuscript for submission and Mike Manville for his copyediting skills. We should also acknowledge the Ralph and Goldy Lewis Center for its support of this book project and the UCLA Department of Urban Planning for supporting the initial seminar on the topic of economic development in minority communities. We also want to acknowledge the John Randolph Haynes and Dora Haynes Foundation for its support of research on disadvantaged neighborhoods. Finally, we wish to express our gratitude to the anonymous reviewers for their constructive comments and to the staff of Temple University Press for their ample and efficient help during the different stages of the book's production.

I   THE CONTEXT

COMMUNITY ECONOMIC DEVELOPMENT affects people and places and in turn is affected by specific political and economic circumstances. Part One of this book contains three chapters that craft the all-important backdrop for economic and jobs development in minority communities. This is nothing less but the social, economic, policy, and physical landscape of urban America. Evelyn Blumenberg's chapter documents the considerable changes experienced by U.S. cities over the last couple of decades. Population diversity has increased with the rise in the number of Latino and Asian immigrants, who have partially offset the decline due to white flight from the urban core. Uneven growth has certainly affected the spatial layout of the American metropolis. As geographers have informed us, many metropolitan areas have witnessed a simultaneous recentralization and decentralization in the last decade. While central cities grew by attracting a deluge of new immigrants and at times middle-class gentrifiers, the most significant expansion took place in the suburbs and urban periphery. Indeed, the 1990s experienced an unprecedented urban sprawl, with new communities pushing outward the boundaries of metropolitan areas.

Some residents of minority neighborhoods, who for the first part of the century could only find shelter and jobs in the ghettos, barrios, and ethnic enclaves of the central city, discovered the path to the suburbs. Many more, however, remained locked in disadvantaged communities of the central city. Nevertheless, the perception of "white suburbs—colored central city" started becoming rather blurred in the 1990s. While it is true that central cities remained the ports of entry for new immigrants, second- and third-generation immigrants fled to the suburbs. As a result, many suburbs acquired their own ethnic parts, and suburban ethnic communities started dotting the metropolitan landscape. Significantly, and as a result of municipal revitalization efforts, some downtown areas witnessed a renaissance that brought new middle-class, white-collar residents back to the central city. Where it happened, this return of the wealthy may have brought vibrancy to downtowns but has also contributed to an increase of land values and rents for downtown housing.

The policy landscape has also changed, and one of the most dramatic changes is welfare reform, which has tossed aside a long-standing policy of income entitlement in favor of work requirements for the poor. This approach has been complemented by the Earned Income Tax Credit for those who work. As Douglas Houston and Paul Ong show, this drastic change in social policy coupled with the economic boom of the 1990s is generally favored as the explanation for the substantial decline in minority poverty and the relative closing of the gap between white and minority poverty that took place in the 1990s. Most metropolitan areas witnessed a decrease in concentrated poverty across racial and ethnic groups from the previous decades. Unfortunately, the success of the new policies has not been universal and has certainly not cut across all regions of the country, or even across communities within the same region, equally. Many of those who left welfare moved into unstable, minimum-wage jobs; poverty remains a problem in even the neighborhoods that have experienced the "best" results; and the gap between white and minority poverty rates remained high.

While the new policy regime emphasizes work, many of the better jobs are inaccessible to the poor. The post-Fordist restructuring and globalized out-sourcing have eliminated a significant share of the better-paid jobs in man-ufacturing. The geographic separation of employment opportunities has also occurred at the regional level: domestically, jobs seemed to follow the trend to the suburbs, which proved to be the most dynamic part of the metropolitan landscape in terms of new job development. A large number of minority households are unable to capitalize from these "outlying" jobs, suffering from what is known as spatial mismatch of jobs and places of residence. The central city poor have been most hurt by this phenomenon. Manuel Pastor, Chris Benner, and Martha Matsuoka address this problem and offer a solu-tion in the form of community-based regionalism.

1 Metropolitan Dispersion and Diversity
Implications for Community Economic Development

EVELYN BLUMENBERG

INTRODUCTION

The image of blighted central-city neighborhoods surrounded by white, affluent suburbs is one that continues to dominate the literature on urban poverty and community development. While this image has merit, recent changes in the composition and spatial structure of U.S. metropolitan areas suggest that it is also overly simplistic. The structure of metropolitan areas has become increasingly complex, defying most generalizations across U.S. metropolitan areas and defying simple dichotomous central city—suburban characterizations as well.

Metropolitan areas are diverse. They differ with respect to population and employment dynamics, ethnic and racial composition, the extent of central-city decline and the concentration of poverty, their levels of employment growth, and the locations where that growth takes place. When almost 50 percent of the poor live in the suburbs, it is no longer acceptable to simply contrast poor, central-city neighborhoods with their more affluent suburbs. Although poverty is still concentrated in central-city neighborhoods, it is also increasingly a suburban problem, particularly in older, inner-ring suburbs. Nor are central cities necessarily synonymous with blight. New York and San Francisco are very prosperous inner cities, and revitalized urban neighborhoods can be found in metropolitan areas across the country.

As diverse as metropolitan areas are, however, in one way they are all similar: all are dispersing. The outward movement of both people and employment from the city center is one seemingly universal feature of metropolitan areas. "Sprawl," as this phenomenon has been termed, has taken the blame for urban decline. Critics of urban sprawl have long argued that it exacerbates social inequities and increases the spatial isolation of the poor (Duany, Plater-Zyberk, and Speck 2000). The data, however, do not support these conclusions. It is the underlying factors that accompany urban growth—and not sprawl itself—that have contributed to urban decline and spatial inequities. And while equity arguments have helped buttress efforts to slow sprawl, efforts to curtail sprawl have not necessarily led to greater equity; measures designed to stem decentralization have done little to improve the economic opportunities of low-income families and their communities.

To address the underlying problems facing the urban poor, community economic developers must go beyond simple, uniform explanations for poverty and address some of the more subtle dynamics that perpetuate economic inequality. These include the lack of affordable housing, racial discrimination, spatial isolation, and the absence of adequate transportation. Moreover, community developers must recognize that metropolitan diversity requires the consideration of local context in developing effective programs and policies.

POPULATION GROWTH, DECLINE, AND LOCATION

Since the turn of the previous century, the U.S. population has grown steadily. While population growth—the percentage increase in the population— was certainly higher in the early 1900s than it is today, the absolute number of new people added was at an all-time high during the 1990s, when the United States added an additional 33 million people to its population.

The 1990s marked the first time in U.S. history that every state gained population. But not all regions of the country, nor all neighborhoods within metropolitan areas, experienced this population growth equally. The South and the West accounted for nearly two-thirds of the U.S. population increase since 1900, pushing the mean center of the U.S. population westward (Hobbs and Stoops 2002). Of this increase, one third can be attributed to four states—California, Texas, Florida, and New York, all of which have populations of over 15 million. (New York, of course, is neither southern nor western, making it a bit of an anomaly.) California, with almost 34 million people, has the largest population, followed by Texas (20.9 million), New York (19 million), and Florida (16 million).

These trends also have contributed to the restructuring of U.S. urban centers. Over the course of the twentieth century, the U.S. population became metropolitan, with the vast majority of the population living in dense urban areas.[1] Where in 1910 less than 30 percent of the U.S. population lived in metropolitan areas, by 1950 a majority of the U.S. population was metropolitan, and by 2000 the percentage had jumped to over 80 percent (see Figure 1.1). These figures represent continued population growth in large urban centers like New York and Chicago and rampant population growth in smaller urban areas such as Phoenix and Las Vegas—areas that, over time, grew large enough to achieve metropolitan status.

The biggest changes, however, have occurred in the suburbs of metropolitan areas. America became not just metropolitan but suburban. Although the central-city population has increased over time, in each decade the percentage increase in the suburban population has far surpassed that of the central city. The percentage of the U.S. population living in the central city grew during the first few decades of the twentieth century, but has since remained steady at approximately 30 percent of the population. While some central cities have continued to grow, albeit at a slower rate than their suburbs, others have suffered large population losses; from 1970 to 2000, more than 100 central cities experienced a net decline in population. These

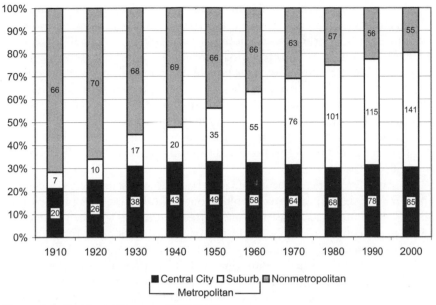

FIGURE 1.1. Residential Location, 1910–2000.
Source: U.S. Census Bureau, decennial census of population, 1910 to 2000. Labels are in millions.

losses were greatest in the metropolitan areas of the Midwest and Northeast, where employment in heavy manufacturing industries like auto and steel declined and took with them the economic base of their communities.[2] In contrast, the percentage of the population living in the suburbs has continued to expand rapidly, growing from less than 10 percent of the population in 1910 to more than half in 2000. Sixty-two percent of the metropolitan population—almost two-thirds—now lives in the suburbs.

Historically, higher-income central-city residents have moved to the suburbs to enhance the quality of their lives through larger homes and lot sizes (at lower prices), better schools and infrastructure, plentiful open space, and other amenities associated with a suburban lifestyle (Jackson 1987). They also fled from declining inner-city neighborhoods and thereby contributed to the plight of the places they were abandoning. The movement of higher-income residents to the suburbs continues. Between 1979 and 1999, the proportion of households with high incomes declined in 79 of the 100 largest U.S. cities (Berube and Thacher 2004).

Not all families have been able to participate in the migration out of the central city. Poverty and discrimination have limited the residential mobility of low-income and minority families, and they remain disproportionately concentrated in low-income, central-city neighborhoods. From the late 1960s through the 1980s, poverty became increasingly concentrated in inner-city neighborhoods (Quillian 1999; Kingsley and Pettit 2003)—contributing to a set of associated problems such as blight, crime, welfare dependency, and joblessness (Wilson 1987). In the 1980s, the percentage of metropolitan poor living in extreme poverty neighborhoods (census tracts with poverty rates of 40 percent or more) grew from 13 to 17 percent; and the percentage living in high poverty neighborhoods (census tracts with poverty rates of 30 percent or more) grew from 25 to 31 percent (Kingsley and Pettit 2003). From 1980 to 1990, the absolute number of poor people living in high poverty neighborhoods almost doubled, from 4.9 to 7.1 million people (Jargowsky 2003; Kingsley and Pettit 2003). The concentration of poverty in the central city has also been accompanied by a growth in the physical size of blighted central-city areas (Jargowsky 2003) contributing to the "doughnut and hole" portrayal of metropolitan areas—hollowed-out urban cores surrounded by more affluent suburbs.

But white flight and concentrated poverty—although still occurring—are by no means the only story to be told about central cities. The problems of central cities and the residents living in them are quite varied. During the 1990s most central cities grew, and some became increasingly vibrant places in and of themselves, even if their suburbs grew more rapidly. Much of this central-city growth occurred in the Sun Belt, and particularly in states—such as California, Florida, and Texas—that have rapidly growing Hispanic populations. However, the population in other eastern cities—Boston, Chicago, and New York—also expanded during the 1990s. For example, during the 1980s the population of central-city Chicago declined by almost 6 percent, but in the 1990s this trend was more than reversed, and the central-city population grew by almost 7 percent.

The 1990s also brought a decrease in concentrated poverty. Overall, the share of the poor living in extreme poverty neighborhoods fell to 12 percent in 2000 (Kingsley and Pettit 2003), and during the 1990s the absolute number of people living in extreme-poverty neighborhoods decreased by 24 percent, or 2.5 million people (Jargowsky 2003). Concentrated poverty declined across all racial and ethnic groups, particularly among African Americans (Jargowsky 2003). Detroit (MI), San Antonio (TX), Flint (MI), Columbus (OH), and Lafayette (LA) were among the metropolitan areas experiencing the greatest percentage reductions in the population living in extreme poverty neighborhoods.

Although these trends are promising, some caveats are necessary. Most of the central-city population growth (60 percent) occurred in outer-ring neighborhoods close to the city edge and adjacent to inner-ring suburbs (Berube and Forman 2002). Most inner-city neighborhoods continued to decline and captured only 11 percent of the central-city population growth (Berube and Forman 2002). The one exception to this pattern is the increase in the population living in "downtowns," neighborhoods defined by their location within the city's central business district. Between 1990 and 2000 two-thirds of all downtown census tracts gained population (Berube and Forman 2002). And in an analysis of population trends in downtowns from 1990 to 2000, Sohmer and Lang (2001) find that three-quarters of the 24 downtowns in their study gained population, 6 of which grew even as their cities lost population. Much of the downtown population growth was fueled by a resurgence of white downtown residents, a trend that defies the typical pattern of white-out migration. Although symbolically important as an indicator of urban revitalization, downtown population growth is a relatively small contributor to overall citywide population dynamics.

DEMOGRAPHIC DYNAMISM AND DIVERSITY

The character of U.S. metropolitan areas has also been fundamentally shaped by decades of demographic dynamism. As a consequence of immigration coupled with ethnic variation in birthrates (African Americans and especially Hispanics have higher birth rates than the general population), U.S. metropolitan areas have become increasingly ethnically and racially diverse. Ethnic and racial diversity is more pronounced in central-city neighborhoods, which are both the traditional ports of entry for immigrants and the location of 52 percent of African Americans (U.S. Census Bureau 2003b). However, decades of demographic dynamism have also transformed suburbs, many of which no longer look and feel like the suburbs of the 1950s. Lily-white, middle-class enclaves of suburban stereotypes might still exist in neighborhoods located on the urban periphery, but they stand in sharp contrast to many of today's suburban neighborhoods, which are increasingly diverse both racially and ethnically and share many of the problems traditionally associated with the inner city.

Demographic change has been driven, first and foremost, by immigration, the foundation upon which the United States was established. Figure 1.2 presents two different, but important, patterns: legal immigration to the United States, and, on the secondary y axis, the foreign born as a percentage

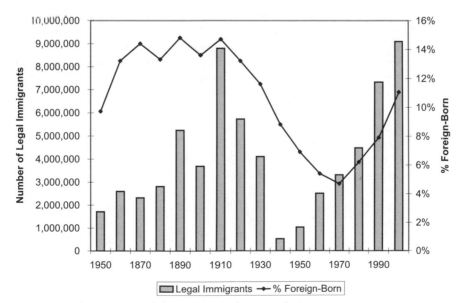

FIGURE 1.2. Immigration and the U.S. foreign-born population.
Source: Gibson and Lennon, 1999; U.S. Census Bureau, 2003; Office of Immigration Statistics, 2003.

of the U.S. population. As the graph shows, the United States experienced high levels of immigration during the early 1900s as immigrants fled the famine- and war-torn countries of Europe, among them Austria, Hungary, Italy, and Russia. This early immigration was responsible for the dramatic growth in U.S. cities during the first part of the twentieth century. Cities' difficulties in accommodating this growth fueled a host of urban problems, including overcrowding, poor sanitary conditions, and the prevalence of slum housing.

Immigration slowed during the Second World War but subsequently increased, and in the 1990s it reached levels exceeding those of any previous decade. The composition of the immigrant population, however, has changed substantially. Today immigrants are largely from Latin America (37 percent) and Asia (31 percent), while Europeans, once the dominant group, comprise less than 15 percent of all immigrants to the United States. Of the foreign-born population, over 70 percent lives in 6 gateway states (California, Florida, Illinois, New Jersey, New York, and Texas), which in turn house only 39 percent of all U.S. residents (Schmidley 2001). In California, the state with the highest percentage of immigrants, more than one quarter of the population is foreign born. However, one of the more recent trends is the dispersion of foreign-born immigrants away from these six magnet states to Sun Belt states such as Arizona, Georgia, Nevada, and North Carolina, whose growing employment opportunities are fueled in part by domestic migration (Frey 2002). Cities such as Atlanta, Dallas, Seattle, and the Twin Cities have emerged as new or reemerging gateway communities and cities such as Salt Lake City (UT) and Raleigh-Durham (NC) are now "preemerging" gateway communities, communities that are about to experience large increases in foreign-born residents (Singer 2004).

Relative to the total population, the foreign-born population is more likely to reside in metropolitan areas. Ninety-five percent of immigrants live in metropolitan areas, with the greatest concentration of foreign born (45 percent) settling in 3 regions—Southern California (Los Angeles, Riverside, and Orange Counties), New York (New York, New Jersey, and Long Island) and South Florida (Miami and Fort Lauderdale). The concentration of immigrants in a few gateway metropolitan areas greatly affects the composition of these areas. Table 1.1 shows the 10 metropolitan areas with the highest percentages of foreign born. Miami–Fort Lauderdale and Southern California are areas at the top of the list.

Years of immigration have led to greater overall racial and ethnic diversity. Data from the 2000 census show that approximately one-third of the U.S. population is minority, with Hispanics now the largest and fastest growing ethnic group—a result of both immigration and higher than average fertility rates.[3] As of 2000, less than half of all metropolitan areas were predominantly white (with "predominantly white" meaning that at least 80 percent of the population was white, and that no minority group represented more than 10 percent of the population), and 5 percent, or 15 metropolitan areas, was predominantly minority (having at least 50 percent of their population of one minority group, and with no other minority group

TABLE 1.1. Metropolitan areas with the highest percentage of foreign born

Area	State	Percentage Foreign Born
Miami–Fort Lauderdale (CMSA)	Florida	40%
Los Angeles–Riverside–Orange County (CMSA)	California	31%
McAllen-Edinburg-Mission (MSA)	Texas	30%
Laredo (MSA)	Texas	29%
Salinas (MSA)	California	29%
El Paso (MSA)	Texas	27%
San Francisco–Oakland–San Jose (CMSA)	California	27%
Brownsville–Harlingen–San Benito (MSA)	Texas	26%
Merced (MSA)	California	25%
New York–Northern New Jersey–Long Island (CMSA)	New York–New Jersey– Connecticut–Pennsylvania	24%

representing more than 10 percent of the population). But more than half of all metropolitan areas were mixed-race, where minority groups comprised a sizeable percentage of the population (between 10 and 50 percent).[4]

Within metropolitan areas, minorities and foreign born are disproportionately concentrated in central cities. Over 60 percent of African Americans, over half of Hispanics, and close to half of both Asians and foreign born reside in the central city, compared to less than 30 percent of non-Hispanic whites. As a consequence, approximately 50 percent of central-city residents are nonwhite and 17 percent of central city residents are foreign born. This is not to say, however, that minority and foreign-born families have not suburbanized. They have, albeit at lower rates than non-Hispanic white families. For the foreign-born population, the rate of suburbanization tends to vary with assimilation as measured by length of time in the United States. Thirty-three percent of immigrants who arrived prior to 1970 live in the central city, compared to 48 percent of more recent immigrants.

Despite overall racial and ethnic diversity, residential segregation remains a prominent feature of metropolitan life, particularly in metropolitan areas with large nonwhite populations. Over the last twenty years residential segregation has declined for African Americans but has remained relatively unchanged for both Hispanics and Asians (Iceland, Weinberg, and Steinmetz 2002; Logan, Stults, and Reynolds 2004). These trends suggest progress, but also mask other, more disconcerting findings. One positive trend for African Americans is that black/nonblack residential segregation is at its lowest point since 1920 (Glaeser and Vigdor 2001). Further, the reduction in residential segregation for African Americans during the 1990s was almost universally positive across U.S. metropolitan areas with all but 19 metropolitan areas more integrated in 2000 than they had been in 1990. These trends are due predominantly to African Americans' moving out of overwhelmingly African American neighborhoods and into previously all-white neighborhoods (Glaeser and Vigdor 2001). Finally, suburbs are associated with lower levels of reductions in residential separation, particularly in immigrant gateway cities (Alba, Logan, and Stults 2000; Clark and Blue 2004), which may be evidence that status or income trumps racial and ethnic considerations (Hwang and Murdock 1998).

Yet despite these encouraging trends, residential segregation among African Americans remains high, and significantly higher than segregation among Hispanics and Asians (Iceland and Weinberg 2002; Logan, Stults, and Reynolds 2004). Sixty-four percent of African Americans would have to change residences for African Americans and whites to be evenly distributed across metropolitan neighborhoods; this percentage—termed the dissimilarity index—is 51 percent for Hispanics and 41 percent among Asians (Iceland and Weinberg 2002). Moreover, the decline in residential segregation across metropolitan areas—for all three major racial/ethnic groups—can be explained in part by greater integration in metropolitan areas that had small minority populations (Glaeser and Vigdor 2001; Logan and Stults 2001). Many of the largest and most racially and ethnically diverse U.S. metropolitan areas, in other words, remain highly segregated. For example, Detroit has the highest white/black segregation index of any metropolitan area in the country, followed closely by Chicago. In both of these metropolitan areas, more than 80 percent of African Americans would have to move in order to bring about racial integration. Although less segregated than African Americans, Hispanics are highly segregated in Los Angeles and Asians in San Francisco.[5]

Finally, many immigrants also live in segregated communities or immigrant enclaves—thought, by some scholars, to allow new arrivals to better assimilate to conditions in the United States (Logan, Alba, and Zhang 2002). Many higher-income immigrants also prefer to live in ethnic neighborhoods (Logan, Alba, and Zhang 2002). This desire may have contributed to the development of suburban ethnic enclaves, particularly in metropolitan areas with sizeable Hispanic and Asian populations (Logan 2001).[6] For example, Chinese "ethnoburbs" have developed in the San Gabriel Valley, an area in eastern Los Angeles County that by 1990 had the largest suburban concentration of Chinese in the nation (Li 1998). Also in Los Angeles (approximately 9 miles from downtown Los Angeles), the city of Glendale has emerged as the third most heavily immigrant large city in the United States (Rodriguez 2003). To be sure, older ethnic enclaves, such as the Lower East Side in New York City or San Francisco's Chinatown, remain and continue to provide a home for recent immigrants to the United States. But current population and housing trends suggest that immigrants, like other demographic groups, increasingly reside in suburban communities, perhaps enticed by and, at the same time, contributing to the growth of suburban ethnic enclaves.

JOBS AND JOB SPRAWL

The employment landscape in metropolitan areas is characterized by the rapid growth of the service economy and the dispersion of employment from central business districts. Employment in the service sector fueled the job

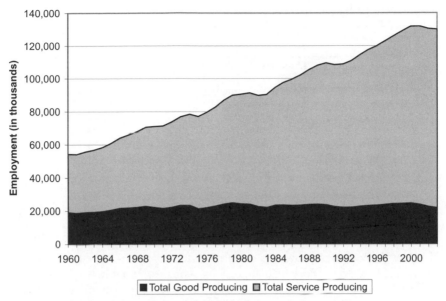

FIGURE 1.3. Employment in Goods- and Service-Producing Sectors, 1960–2003.
Source: U.S. Department of Labor, Employment and Earnings, Historical Tables
(Washington, DC: Bureau of Labor Statistics).

growth of the 1990s, as manufacturing employment continued its decline as
a percentage of total employment. However, manufacturing jobs are not,
contrary to the conventional wisdom, disappearing; total manufacturing
employment has been remarkably stable over time, and in fact there are
slightly more manufacturing jobs today than there were in 1960 (Figure 1.3).
Nor is manufacturing declining in productivity. Productivity growth in the
manufacturing sector has been tremendous, but because much of this growth
is owed to improved technology and capital goods, it has not resulted in a
corresponding surge in employment. Output has increased without an expansion in hiring (Congressional Budget Office 2004).

Manufacturing is in decline not because of its failure to grow but because
its meager rate of growth has been swamped by the dramatic expansion of
employment in the service sector, which has grown by over 200 percent since
1960. The steady increase in service-sector employment has been accompanied by a growth in low-wage jobs, many of which offer few benefits and
are part time. As of August 2004, average weekly earnings for production
workers (nonsupervisory employees) in the manufacturing sector were $659,
compared to $502 in the private service-producing sector; service workers,
in other words, earned on average only three-quarters what manufacturing
employees did (Bureau of Labor Statistics 2004). Approximately one-third
of all low-wage workers work in service sector occupations, compared to
only 16 percent of all workers (Schochet and Rangarajan 2004). Low-wage
workers in smaller firms and those in the retail trade and services are typically paid lower wages and have higher turnover rates, even controlling for

TABLE 1.2. Employment change from 1990 to 2003—9 top metropolitan areas

State	Area	Percentage Change in Employment
Nevada	Las Vegas	98.0%
Texas	Austin	81.2%
Arkansas	Fayetteville-Springdale	76.1%
Texas	Mcallen-Edinburg-Mission	74.7%
Idaho	Boise City	72.9%
Utah	Provo-Orem	63.9%
Texas	Laredo	63.4%
Florida	Sarasota	61.2%
Arizona	Phoenix	61.0%

the individual characteristics of the workers (Andersson, Holzer, and Lane 2003).

The location of employment, like the location of the population, also is shifting. Although employment remains concentrated in large metropolitan areas such as New York, Chicago, Los Angeles, Washington D.C., and Philadelphia (Bureau of Labor Statistics 2003), employment growth has been more rapid in some smaller metropolitan areas. Table 1.2 lists the 9 metropolitan areas that experienced the largest percentage change in total private employment from 1990 to 2003. Las Vegas stands out with an almost 100-percent increase in total employment; the other areas listed had growth rates exceeding 60 percent.

Change has also occurred within metropolitan areas as jobs—again like the population—have dispersed. No longer are downtowns the locations of the vast majority of metropolitan employment; outlying areas have long since surpassed the central business district. Amongst the 100 largest metropolitan

TABLE 1.3. Densest and most decentralized metropolitan areas

	3-mile Employment Share	10+ mile Employment Share
Densest Employment Metropolitan Areas		
Honolulu, HI MSA	59%	13%
Lexington, KY MSA	49%	26%
New York, NY PMSA	45%	23%
Providence–Fall River–Warwick, RI-MA, MSA	45%	20%
San Francisco, CA PMSA	45%	39%
Extremely Decentralized Employment Metropolitan Areas		
Baton Rouge, LA MSA	5%	20%
Detroit, MI PMSA	5%	78%
Tampa–St Petersburg–Clearwater, FL MSA	6%	75%
West Palm Beach–Boca Raton, FL MSA	7%	59%
Los Angeles–Long Beach, CA PMSA	7%	62%

Source: Glaeser and Kahn (2001). Used by permission of the Brookings Institution, Metropolitan Policy Program, http://www.brookings.edu/metro.

areas in the United States, only 22 percent of the population works within 3 miles of the city center, while over a third (35 percent) work more than 10 miles away from it (Glaeser, Kahn, and Chu 2001). Table 1.3 shows the 5 most dense and the 5 most decentralized metropolitan areas according to the percentage of employment located within a 3-mile buffer from the city center. In general, metropolitan areas in the Northeast have the least job sprawl, and those in the South the most. There are some exceptions, however. Some western metropolitan areas, for example—including San Francisco (CA), Portland (OR-WA), Salt Lake City (UT), and Fresno (CA)—are quite centralized and would appear on a slightly longer list of dense metropolitan areas.

These figures reflect the rapid growth of suburban employment. Between 1992 and 1997, central cities increased their employment by 8.5 percent; suburban employment grew at over twice that rate (U.S. Department of Housing and Urban Development 2000). By 1990 a plurality of metropolitan residents (40 percent) both lived and worked in the suburbs; growth in suburb-to-suburb trips comprised 58 percent of the growth in commuting between 1980 and 1990 (Pisarski 1996), and although figures are not yet available for 1990 to 2000, the suburb-to-suburb share is expected to have increased even more.[7]

METROPOLITAN DISPERSION AND LOW-INCOME FAMILIES

What are the implications of dispersion for the poor? Overall, studies show that sprawl benefits low-income families if they are able to take advantage of its opportunities—such as lower-cost housing. Not all families can do this, however, and while dispersion itself cannot be blamed for economic inequality or urban decline, other underlying factors exclude many low-income families from the opportunities associated with the suburbs. Ultimately, for these families, metropolitan change can be economically debilitating.

Sprawl and Equity

Advocates of creating more compact urban environments argue that sprawl increases inequality by depleting central-city resources, concentrating poverty in the inner city, and separating central-city residents from available suburban job opportunities (Duany, Plater-Zyberk, and Speck 2000). The evidence, however, suggests just the opposite; economic opportunity increases—not decreases—with sprawl. Downs (1999) used 1980 and 1990 data on 162 urbanized areas to examine whether urban decline is related to suburban sprawl and found, to his surprise, no statistical relationship between the two. More recently, Foster-Bey (2002) examined the relationship between economic opportunity and sprawl in 34 metropolitan areas for 1980 and the change in economic opportunity from 1980 to 1990.[8] He found a positive relationship between the two. Metropolitan areas with the most compact growth—areas such as Portland or Minneapolis-St. Paul— experienced less sprawl but also less economic opportunity (Foster-Bey

2002). Finally, Pendall and Carruthers (2003) examine the relationship between density and income segregation in U.S. metropolitan areas from 1980 to 2000 and find that income segregation first rises and then falls as densities increase. They conclude that "sprawl—at least in its low-density manifestation—is neither directly associated with nor causes income segregation" (Pendall and Carruthers 2003:581). Urban growth and residential dispersion may actually increase the availability of affordable homes, allowing low-income households opportunities to move out of the central city.

Moreover, there is a positive association between suburban living and a number of economic and social measures. Data from the 1997 American Housing Survey show that black households living in more sprawling metropolitan areas consume larger housing units and are more likely to own their homes than black households living in less sprawling areas (Kahn 2001). And in some metropolitan areas—Dallas, Los Angeles, New York, and Washington—a suburban residential location increases the employment probability of blacks (Cooke 1996). Moreover, evaluations of housing mobility programs—programs that enable low-income families to move from high-poverty, central-city neighborhoods to the suburbs—show a number of positive outcomes for participants who successfully relocate to the suburbs. These outcomes include reductions in welfare usage, higher employment rates, health status improvements, better educational outcomes, and lower rates of youth criminal offenses (Johnson, Ladd, and Ludwig 2002).[9]

But even if urban poverty and decline cannot be attributed to metropolitan dispersion, they exist and are reproduced as part of the overall metropolitan development process. Community economic development must, therefore, address the underlying factors that exclude some low-income families from the emerging economic opportunities within metropolitan areas, whether these opportunities lie in the central city or the suburbs. These underlying issues include the lack of affordable housing, housing and employment discrimination, the changing nature of employment, and the negative consequences of gentrification.

The Affordable-Housing Crisis

In many metropolitan areas a rapidly growing population has contributed to rising real estate markets and, consequently, to increasing rents. These trends—combined with both the imminent expiration of subsidies and contracts on much of the nation's publicly regulated housing and suburban zoning and development restrictions—have resulted in a severe shortage of affordable housing, and have diminished the effects of policies aimed at increasing housing mobility.

Since 1993, multifamily housing construction has barely kept up with housing stock losses. Although 1.8 million new rentals were added over this period, the housing stock expanded by only 100,000 (Joint Center for Housing Studies 2003). As a consequence, housing remains unaffordable for many families. In 2001 renters in the bottom income quintile outnumbered the supply of low-cost housing units by 2 million, a figure that expands to 4.7

million when you account for the fact that high-income households occupied 2.7 million of the affordable units (Joint Center for Housing Studies 2003).

The affordable housing shortage is most pronounced in metropolitan areas located along the two coasts—on the west coast in San Francisco, San Jose, and Orange Counties (California) and on the east coast in Nassau-Suffolk and Westchester Counties, both in New York (Low Income Housing Coalition 2003). Within metropolitan areas, the shortage is most acute in the suburbs where land use and development restrictions have limited the construction of multifamily housing (Belsky and Lambert 2001; Glaeser and Gyourko 2002; Ihlanfeldt 2004; Joint Center for Housing Studies 2003).[10] Data from the 1999 American Housing Survey show that there are 1.7 very-low-income households for every affordable unit in the central city, compared to 2 very-low-income households for every affordable unit in the suburbs (Belsky and Lambert 2001).[11] And these calculations underestimate the mismatch between supply and demand, for two reasons: first, many of the residents of affordable units have incomes higher than the low-income cutoff and second, there is a mismatch in location as well as in absolute quantity—the supply is often lowest in places where the demand may be highest. For example, some residents living in the central city would prefer housing located in the suburbs.[12]

The housing affordability crisis has many repercussions. Three out of ten families who find rental units experience affordability problems, meaning they spend more than 30 percent of their incomes on housing (Joint Center for Housing Studies 2003). High housing expenses put pressure on household budgets, making it difficult for families to manage other household expenses, such as those for transportation, food, and clothing. The affordable housing shortage also forces some households into inadequate units; over 9,000,000 households live in units that are either overcrowded or physically inadequate (Joint Center for Housing Studies 2003).

The lack of affordable housing also limits the benefits of residential mobility programs—tenant-based rental subsidies that, in theory, enable low-income families to move to more affluent suburban neighborhoods. While residential mobility programs have helped some participants successfully relocate, "lease up rates" have varied substantially across programs, from as low as 19 percent to as high as 60 percent (Johnson, Ladd, and Ludwig 2002). In all cases, some families were prevented from successfully leasing units in more advantaged neighborhoods. Among families that successfully find units in suburban neighborhoods, many locate in low-income suburban neighborhoods with high proportions of minorities; it is these suburban neighborhoods that typically have higher concentrations of rental units (Hartung and Hening 1997; McClure 2004; Pendall 2000).

Housing and Employment Discrimination

Overlapping with the lack of affordable housing are housing and employment discrimination that, combined, also limit access to suburban opportunities. Ample evidence confirms the prevalence of housing discrimination with respect to both homeownership as well as housing rentals, although the extent of this discrimination has declined over time (Turner et al. 2002). Household wealth is the largest determinant of home ownership; however, minority homebuyers are more likely to have their loan applications rejected compared to comparable white buyers (Charles and Hurst 2002; Wyly 2002).[13] When minorities do obtain loans, discrimination often limits the geographic location of their purchases to segregated neighborhoods in the central city. Although illegal under the Fair Housing Act, "steering," the process by which real estate agents steer minority homebuyers toward segregated neighborhoods and less actively marketed properties in white neighborhoods, continues to exist and appears to be increasing (Ondrich, Ross, and Yinger 2003; Turner et al. 2002). Although their primary constraint is the lack of affordable rental units in more affluent suburban neighborhoods, minority renters face similar discrimination. Landlords discriminate against minority renters by restricting their access to certain types of units and by engaging in actions that aid or hinder the rental of units (Ondrich, Stricker, and Yinger 1999). For example, white renters are both consistently more likely to receive information about available housing units and have greater opportunities to inspect units than minority renters (Turner et al. 2002).

Housing discrimination may prevent some minority families from finding homes in the suburbs. At the same time, employment discrimination reduces the likelihood of their being hired by suburban firms. Some studies suggest that suburban employers discriminate against African American applicants. Black applicants, particularly less-educated black men, are less likely to be hired in suburban establishments than in central-city firms (Holzer and Reaser 2000). In a study of Cleveland, Gottlieb and Lentnek (2001) found that residents of a black Cleveland suburb had longer commutes than residents of a similar white suburb, despite the fact that the black suburb was accessible to more "skill-matched" jobs. They found that many more black residents commuted into the central city, suggesting, perhaps, suburban "hiring discrimination or industry sector preferences." These findings might result from the relationship between the racial composition of an establishment's customers and the race of who gets hired, particularly in jobs that involve direct contact with customers (Holzer and Ihlanfeldt 1998).

In contrast, Zenou (2002) finds that employers discriminate not explicitly by race but by distance. He argues that because workers commuting longer distances provide lower effort levels than those residing closer to jobs, firms are less likely to hire them. Therefore, if nonwhite or low-income workers are more likely to live in the central city, they—by the nature of their residential location—would be less likely to be hired by suburban firms.

Geographic Isolation and the Lack of Adequate Transportation

Therefore, some low-income families—both in the central city and in the suburbs—remain isolated from employment, and the distance between these families and employment opportunities is frequently amplified by a lack of adequate transportation.

For low-income, central-city residents, geographic access to employment can vary depending on the metropolitan area, the particular neighborhood within the metropolitan area, and the household's access to reliable transportation. In some metropolitan areas, the movement of low-wage jobs away from inner-city neighborhoods, the lack of affordable suburban housing, and housing discrimination have created a spatial mismatch between low-income residents and suburban employment opportunities (Holzer, Ihlanfelt, and Sjoquist 1994; Ihlanfeldt and Sjoquist 1998; Kain 1968; Raphael 1998; Stoll 1999). The effects of the spatial mismatch are particularly relevant in larger metropolitan areas where distances between central-city and suburban neighborhoods can be lengthy (Blumenberg and Shiki 2004; Cooke 1996; Ihlanfeldt and Sjoquist 1998; Weinberg 2004).

But the rapid increase of employment in the suburbs does not necessarily indicate that entry-level jobs no longer exist in central cities; nor does it mean that all central-city residents have limited geographic access to jobs. In contrast to many older metropolitan areas of the Northeast and Midwest, metropolitan areas such as Atlanta, Las Vegas, and Boston have experienced strong central-city job growth (U.S. Department of Housing and Urban Development 2000). Much of this growth can be attributed to the strength of the economy during the late 1990s.

Further, care must be taken to distinguish between net new job growth and turnover in existing jobs. There is plentiful evidence suggesting that job turnover rates in metropolitan areas can actually exceed the rate of suburban job growth. In other words, in some metropolitan areas, there may be *more* entry-level job vacancies in the central city than there are in its suburbs (Shen 2001). Also, central-city residents often have greater job proximity than families living in the suburbs where employment is typically dispersed across large land areas (Boardman and Field 2002; Gottlieb and Lentnek 2001; Shen 2001; Wang 2003). But the relevant issue is not simply the sheer number of jobs but rather the relative ratio between job openings and the number of potential applicants. In aggregate the studies show that for households living in job-poor neighborhoods—whether they reside in the central city or the suburbs—travel time to employment may be lengthy and overall access to employment opportunities limited (Blumenberg and Hess 2003; Blumenberg and Ong 2001; Boardman and Field 2002; Kawabata 2003; Shen 1998; Shen 2001; Taylor and Ong 1995; Wyly 1998).

The problems associated with spatial isolation are compounded by the lack of adequate transportation. While most low-income households own at least one automobile, auto ownership is still not universal. According to data from the 2001 National Household Travel Survey, 92 percent of all households have at least one vehicle, but only 73.5 percent of households with incomes less than $20,000 do (Pucher and Renne 2003). Therefore, more than a quarter of all low-income, residents suffer from a *modal* mismatch, a drastic divergence in the relative advantage between those who have access to automobiles and those who do not (Blumenberg and Hess 2003, Blumenberg and Ong 2001, Kawabata 2003; Shen 1998; Taylor and Ong 1995; Wyly 1998). The lack of an automobile can have negative economic consequences since automobiles are pivotal to improving employment rates and earnings among the poor (Cervero, Sandoval, and Landis 2002; Ong 1996; Ong 2002; Taylor and Ong 1995).

Those individuals who do not have access to automobiles are reliant on public transit. However, the same forces that have dispersed employment—suburbanization and deindustrialization—have created serious challenges for transit agencies, which have had to contend with expanded service areas, decreasing ridership (Pucher and Renne 2003), and an emerging work/residence pattern in which the dominant commute is now from suburb to suburb (Pisarski 1996). Public transportation systems have been designed for middle-class suburban riders heading inbound to downtown areas, and not for those traveling within the suburbs or heading outbound from the central city. Transit clearly works best in the inner city, where there are dense clusters of jobs and residents, and where employment is frequently located adjacent to transit stops (Levinson 1992). In the suburbs, the opposite exists. Employment typically is dispersed and often distant from transit stops (Bania, Coulton, and Leete 1999; Ihlanfeldt and Young 1996).

These difficulties explain the weak statistical relationship between access to public transportation and employment rates among low-income adults. Sanchez et al. find no statistical relationship between the two (Sanchez, Shen, and Peng 2004). However, a few studies show the positive effects of public transit on economic outcomes for low-income adults. For example, among low-income adults without household cars, improved access to public transit appears to increase employment rates "moderately" (Ong and Houston 2002). In another study, 36 percent of the difference in the racial composition of suburban employment was attributed to the fact that suburban firms are less frequently served by public transit (Ihlanfeldt and Young 1996); and, more recently, the expansion of heavy rail to a San Francisco Bay Area suburb resulted in a sizable increase in the hiring of Latinos, but not blacks, near newly opened stations (Holzer, Quigley, and Raphael 2003).

Economic Insecurity

Even if low-income adults overcome housing and transportation barriers, many have difficulty finding jobs that pay livable wages and, ultimately rely, at least in part, on public benefits. Finding employment—whether in the central city or the suburbs—is no longer a guarantee of economic security. Numerous adults work full-time year-round, only to have earnings that leave them well below the poverty line. As of 2000, almost 5 percent of persons in the labor market for 27 weeks or more (or 6.4 million people) had incomes below the poverty line (Bureau of Labor Statistics 2002). More troublesome than the sheer presence of low-wage work, however, are two related trends—the reduction in employment security and the decline in economic mobility. These trends leave many low-income families economically vulnerable and trapped in jobs that offer few, if any, avenues for advancement.

The problem of the working poor is often attributed to the rise of the service economy and the concomitant proliferation of low-wage jobs. However, the shift in employment toward lower-paying industries is only one of a number of factors influencing income. Wage inequality is also affected by the change in the size and composition of the workforce and would, for example, increase with the rise in the percentage of less-skilled workers. The introduction of new production technologies that require a more skilled workforce also benefits more highly educated workers and increases inequality. Finally, low-skilled central-city residents could suffer from a skills mismatch as manufacturing jobs leave the central city and are replaced by firms seeking higher-skilled professional employees (Burtless and Mishel 1993). In combination, these trends contribute to the growth in the proportion of the low-wage workforce and to rising wage inequality.

Low-wage jobs, by themselves, are not necessarily a sign of a labor market gone awry. Low-wage employment always has been a part of the U.S. economy providing immigrants, youth, and other newcomers inroads into the economy, and low-wage workers have contributed to the vitality of labor-intensive industries. However, employees in today's labor market have much less job security and fewer opportunities for advancement than in previous years. During the postwar period, employees tended to have careers in large organizations, where they would work their way up well-defined career ladders. Employers benefited from these internal labor markets by reducing their recruitment and training costs; at the same time, employees received lifetime job security and opportunities for occupational advancement within the firm. In recent years, however, this career structure has collapsed contributing to declining tenure, increasing job turnover and layoff rates, and declining occupational and earnings mobility (Osterman 1999).

Moreover, public education may also contribute to this problem. While public schools are not "turning out worse workers now than twenty-five years ago," many have not adjusted to the increasing and changing skill requirements demanded by today's jobs (Blank 1997:65). Further, residential segregation and the concentration of minority children in low-achieving, inner-city schools perpetuate the achievement gap among racial and ethnic groups (Kain 2004) and disproportionately limit the job prospects and mobility of minority, central-city residents.

Gentrification

Finally, what about gentrification? Gentrification is a topic that has received substantial attention from scholars and the media as evidence of revitalization in blighted, central-city neighborhoods. At the same time, gentrification has sparked concern by residents, scholars, and planners that reinvestment in the inner city, while worthwhile, can increase property values, displace existing residents, increase racial and class selectivity in the housing market, and intensify racial and ethnic discrimination. Although a popular issue premised on the rebirth of the city's urban core, gentrification and its consequences are somewhat limited relative to overall patterns of metropolitan development.

Data on mortgage lending show that suburban home loans—one measure of investment—have outpaced loans in gentrified inner-city neighborhoods (Wyly and Hammel 2004). Gentrification occurs, but in relatively few neighborhoods. The growth of home purchase loans in gentrified neighborhoods has increased more than twice the suburban rate (Wyly and Hammel 2004). Some core districts, such as neighborhoods in Boston, Philadelphia, Baltimore, Chicago, and San Francisco, have experienced substantial recentralization; even higher rates can be found in smaller gentrifying neighborhoods in Fort Worth, Milwaukee, New Orleans, and San Jose. Newer gentrifying areas, areas that are in the early stages of gentrification, can be found in some older cities of the Northeast and Midwest.

There are many benefits of gentrification, some of which can, both directly and indirectly, improve the quality of life for low-income families. Cash-strapped cities can benefit from increased property and retail tax revenues that they then can reinvest in urban areas. Working-class homeowners who remain in gentrifying neighborhoods may benefit directly from urban revitalization through improved employment opportunities, greater retail and cultural services, lower levels of concentrated poverty, better infrastructure (e.g., schools), and greater socioeconomic and racial integration. Other working-class homeowners may capitalize on the increase in their property values by selling their homes and moving elsewhere, perhaps to the suburbs. Cashing out allows other middle-class families to move into the neighborhood and, consequently, perpetuates the gentrification process (Hamnett 2003).

For renters, however, the outcome is more uncertain. Gentrification may not result in displacement but rather may be associated with lower propensities of low-income families to move, perhaps because residents in these neighborhoods experience improved satisfaction with their neighborhoods (Freeman and Braconi 2004; Vigdor 2002). So how do neighborhoods gentrify? As families move out of these neighborhoods through the normal succession process, higher-income families move in and take up residence slowly changing the character of the neighborhood. Hence, gentrification appears to limit the opportunities of low-income families in two ways: lower-income residents are less likely than higher-income families to move into gentrifying neighborhoods (Freeman and Braconi 2004), and low-income families who leave gentrifying neighborhoods through the normal succession process are more likely to move into less desirable neighborhoods due to their lack of resources, the shortage of affordable housing, and housing discrimination.

METROPOLITAN CHANGE AND COMMUNITY DEVELOPMENT

Metropolitan areas are both similar to and different from each other in ways that have significant implications for community economic development. As the data show, metropolitan areas are dynamic, experiencing cycles of growth and decline spurred in part by fluctuations in the economy and by demographic change. It would be natural to expect a lag in response to these new conditions as planners and community developers adjust to new sets of opportunities and constraints. However, much can be learned from metropolitan areas that have reversed their fortunes after periods of decline. For example, numerous scholars have written on revitalization efforts in old industrialized metropolitan areas. These studies are related to the literature on efforts to increase downtown development through tourism and large-scale investments in projects such as sports arenas, convention centers, entertainment districts, and malls (Fainstein and Stokes 1998). Finally, other scholars have focused on the role of urban containment in motivating central-city reinvestment such as the creation of urban growth boundaries (Nelson et al. 2004). For community economic developers, of course, the empirical question is to what extent these strategies or combinations of strategies benefit low-income, minority residents.

The centerpiece of these revitalization efforts typically is the central city with the goal of bringing back the urban core and, at the same time, curtailing sprawl. However, as the numbers show, metropolitan areas—regardless of their size or density—have dispersed. A focus, therefore, on the central city, while important, is too narrow. Almost half of all low-income families now live in the suburbs and would benefit only indirectly from central-city urban revitalization efforts. Many other low-income families are hurt because they are cut off from opportunities—jobs, better schools, open space, and so on—increasingly located in the suburbs. Therefore, policies and programs to increase central-city residents' access to suburban housing and employment are essential, as are efforts to improve economic opportunities in suburban neighborhoods—particularly older, inner-ring suburbs. Further, policies to slow sprawl may have the unintended consequence of increasing land values and therefore pricing low-income families out of the housing market. With appropriate institutional interventions, this effect can be mitigated (Nelson 2002).

Most metropolitan areas also share a similar demographic trend—increasing racial and ethnic diversity. Major metropolitan areas such as Los Angeles, New York, and Miami continue to serve as gateway communities, ports of entry for immigrants arriving primarily from Latin America and Asia. Other metropolitan areas are diversifying through secondary migration as immigrant families resettle in search of improved opportunities. In contrast, most central-city revitalization strategies—particularly in large metropolitan areas—focus on extracting resources from upper-income white residents. These strategies include enticing young singles to live in downtown neighborhoods or attracting affluent suburban residents into the central city to frequent museums, concert halls, and sports facilities. Revitalization efforts can also take another path by supporting and enhancing existing minority, immigrant, and low-income communities. For example, immigrants have transformed many historically neglected and abandoned neighborhoods into thriving, vibrant ethnic communities and economies (Lin 1998). In some areas, housing developers have worked successfully to deconcentrate the poor and increase moderate-income homeownership, simultaneously revitalizing the neighborhood while benefiting working- and middle-class minority families (Newman and Ashton 2004).

Although metropolitan areas share many of these underlying trends, they also vary substantially—by size, demographic composition, and economic character and vitality. Within metropolitan areas, neighborhoods are diverse, and this diversity defies simple geographic categorizations such as central city/ suburb. The image of blighted central city and resource-rich suburb, while certainly valid in some neighborhoods, does not begin to capture the enormous variation within both the central city and the suburbs. For example, some central-city neighborhoods are job-poor; others are proximate to numerous employment opportunities. Some suburban neighborhoods are comprised primarily of white, affluent homeowners while others are ethnic enclaves. Therefore, community economic developers must put aside generalizations about metropolitan areas and tailor their strategies and programs to meeting the needs of the residents of the neighborhoods in which they work.

NOTES

1. The United States Office of Management and Budget defines a metropolitan statistical area (MSA) as "a core area containing a substantial population nucleus, together with adjacent communities having a high degree of economic and social integration with that core" (U.S. Census Bureau 2003a).

2. Data from the State of the Cities Data Systems of the U.S. Department of Housing and Urban Development show the following metropolitan areas sustained the largest percentage of decline in their central-city populations from 1970 to 2000: Johnstown (PA), Gary (IN), Youngstown-Warren (OH), Buffalo–Niagara Falls (NY), St. Louis (MO-IL), Pittsburgh (PA), Flint (MI), Wheeling (WV-OH), Detroit (MI), Utica-Rome (NY). All ten of these central cities continued to sustain large population losses into the 1990s.

3. The fertility rate—live births per 1,000 women aged 15 to 44 years—is 65.3 for all races, 68 for African Americans, 64 for Asians, and 96 for Hispanics (U.S. Department of Health and Human Services 2004).

4. This typology of metropolitan areas is based on that developed by Fasenfest, Booza, and Metzger (2004) for their analysis of neighborhoods.

5. The indices of dissimilarity for the four metropolitan areas are the following: African Americans in Detroit and Chicago, 85.5 and 81; Hispanics in Los Angeles 63; and Asians in San Francisco, 50.7 (These data are from the Racial Residential Segregation Measurement Project produced by the Population Studies Center, University of Michigan, http://enceladus.isr.umich.edu/race/racestart.asp.)

6. Data from the 2000 census shows that the foreign-born population comprises over one quarter of the population in Miami (FL); Laredo, El Paso, and McAllen (TX); Yuma (AZ); and Visalia, Los Angeles, Salinas, and Merced (CA); and Honolulu (HI). In six of these areas (Laredo, El Paso, McAllen, Yuma, Visalia, Merced), the percentage of foreign born in the suburbs exceeds that in the central city.

7. Central city to central city commutes comprised approximately 27 percent of all metropolitan commutes; central city to suburb commutes comprised just over 6 percent of all commutes, suburb to central city commutes comprised 17 percent of all commutes, and the remainder began or ended in another metropolitan area (Pisarski 1996).

8. To create the measures of economic opportunity, Foster-Bey (2002) incorporated the following measures: the poverty rate, the spatial concentration of poverty, living wage employment, the proportion of less-educated African American males employed and earning a wage high enough to keep a family out of poverty, and the gap in living wage employment between white and black less-educated males.

9. Johnson, Ladd, and Ludwig (2002) review the benefits and costs of residential mobility programs for the poor.

10. Publicly subsidized suburban housing is also limited. Rohe and Freeman (2001) find that during the 1980s, publicly assisted housing continued to be built in neighborhoods with high percentages of minority households, despite regulations discouraging this practice.

11. Very-low-income households are defined as households with incomes greater than or equal to 50 percent of the area median income.

12. In a study of participants in Chicago's Moving to Opportunity Demonstration project, over 20 percent of the sample indicated a preference for moving to the suburbs (Rosenbaum and Harris 2001). In a study of Section 8 housing voucher and certificate participants in Alameda County, California, 13 percent of movers opted for suburban housing authority jurisdictions (Lahr and Gibbs 2002).

13. When, for example, blacks purchase homes, they are also more likely to pay more for these homes—approximately 10 percent—than comparable white home-buyers (Myers 2004).

REFERENCES

Alba, Richard D., John R. Logan, and Brian J. Stults 2000. The changing neighborhood contexts of the immigrant metropolis. *Social Forces* 79(2):587–621

Andersson, Fredric, Harry J. Holzer, and Julia Lane. 2003. *Worker Advancement in the Low-Wage Labor Market: The Importance of 'Good Jobs.'* Washington, DC: The Brookings Institution.

Bania, Neil, Claudia Coulton, and Laura Leete. 1999. Welfare reform and access to job opportunities in the Cleveland metropolitan area. Working Paper of the Center for Urban Poverty and Social Change. Cleveland, OH: Case Western Reserve University.

Belsky, Eric S., and Matthew Lambert. 2001. Where will they live: Metropolitan dimensions of affordable housing problems, W01–9. Cambridge: Joint Center for Housing Studies, Harvard University.

Berube, Alan, and Benjamin Forman. 2002. Living on the edge: Decentralization within cities in the 1990s. Washington, DC: Brookings Institution, Center on Urban and Metropolitan Policy, October.

Berube, Alan, and Tiffany Thacher. 2004. The shape of the curve: Household income distributions in U.S. cities, 1979–1999. Washington, DC: Brookings Institution.

Blank, Rebecca. 1997. *It Takes a Nation: A New Agenda for Fighting Poverty.* New York: Russell Sage Foundation.

Blumenberg, Evelyn, and Daniel Baldwin Hess. 2003. Measuring the role of transportation in facilitating the welfare-to-work transition: Evidence from three California counties. *Journal of the Transportation Research Board* 1859: 93–101.

Blumenberg, Evelyn, and Paul Ong. 2001. Cars, buses, and jobs: Welfare recipients and employment access in Los Angeles. *Journal of the Transportation Research Board* 1756:22–31.

Jackson, Kenneth T. 1987. *Crabgrass Frontier: The Suburbanization of the United States*. Oxford: Oxford University Press.

Jargowsky, Paul A. 2003. *Stunning Progress, Hidden Problems: The Dramatic Decline of Concentrated Poverty in the 1990s*. Washington DC: Brookings Institution.

Johnson, Michael P., Helen F. Ladd, and Jens Ludwig. 2002. The benefits and costs of residential mobility programmes for the poor. *Housing Studies* 17(1): 125–138.

Joint Center for Housing Studies 2003. *The State of the Nation's Housing, 2003*. Cambridge: Harvard University.

Kahn, Matthew E. 2001. Does sprawl reduce the black/white housing consumption gap? *Housing Policy Debate* 12(1):77–86.

Kain, John F. 1968. Housing segregation, negro employment, and metropolitan decentralization. *Quarterly Journal of Economics* 82:175–197.

———. 2004. A pioneer's perspective on the spatial mismatch literature. *Urban Studies* 41(1):7–32.

Kawabata, Mizuki. 2003. Job accessibility and employment outcomes for low-skilled autoless workers in US metropolitan areas. *Environment and Planning A* 35(9):1651–1668.

G. Thomas Kingsley, and Kathryn Pettit. 2003. *Concentrated Poverty: A Change in Course*. Washington, DC: The Urban Institute.

Lahr, Michael L, and Robert M. Gibbs. 2002. Mobility of Section 8 families in Alameda County. *Journal of Housing Economics* 11(3):187–213.

Larsen, Luke J. 2004. The foreign-born population in the U.S.: 2003. Current Population Reports, P20–551, Washington, DC: U.S. Census Bureau.

Levinson, Herbert S. 1992. "System and Service Planning," in *Public Transportation* (second edition). George E. Gray and Lester A. Hoel, eds. Englewood Cliffs, NJ: Prentice Hall.

Li, Wei. 1998. Anatomy of a new ethnic settlement: The Chinese Ethnoburb in Los Angeles. *Urban Studies* 35(3):479–501.

Lin, Jan 1998. Globalization and the revalorizing of ethnic places in immigration gateway cities. *Urban Affairs Review* 34(2):313–339.

Logan, John R. 2001. *The New Ethnic Enclaves in America's Suburbs*. New York: University at Albany, Lewis Mumford Center for Comparative Urban and Regional Research.

Logan, John R., Richard D. Alba, and Wenquan Zhang. 2002. Immigrant enclaves and ethnic communities in New York and Los Angeles. *American Sociological Review* 67(2):299–322.

Logan, John R., Brian J. Stults, and Reynolds Farley. 2004. Segregation of minorities in the metropolis: Two decades of change. *Demography* 41(1):1–22.

Logan, John, and Brian Stults. 2001. *Ethnic Diversity Grows, Neighborhood Integration Lags*. New York: University at Albany, Lewis Mumford Center for Comparative Urban and Regional Research.

Low Income Housing Coalition 2003. *Out of Reach 2003: America's Housing Wage Climbs*. Washington, DC: Low Income Housing Coalition.

McClure, Kirk. 2004. Section 8 and movement to job opportunity: Experience after welfare reform in Kansas City. *Housing Policy Debate* 5(1):99–131.

Myers, Caitlin Knowles. 2004. "Discrimination and neighborhood effects: Understanding racial differentials in U.S. housing prices." *Journal of Urban Economics*, 56(2):279–302.

Nelson, Arthur C. 2002. Comment on Anthony Downs's "Have housing prices risen faster in Portland than elsewhere?" *Housing Policy Debate* 13(1): 33–42.

Nelson, Arthur C., Raymond J. Burby, Edward Feser, Casey J. Dawkins., Emil E. Malizia, and Roberto Quercia. 2004. Urban containment and central-city revitalization. *Journal of the American Planning Association* 70(4):411–425.

Newman, Kathe, and Philip Aston. 2004. Neoliberal urban policy and new paths of neighborhood change in the American inner city. *Environment and Planning A* 36(7):1151–1172.

Office of Immigration Statistics. 2003. 2002 Yearbook of Immigration Statistics, Office of Management, Department of Homeland Security. Washington, DC: U.S. Government Printing Office.

Ondrich Jordan, Stephen Ross, and John Yinger. 2003. Now you see it, now you don't: Why do real estate agents withhold available houses from black customers? *Review of Economics and Statistics* 85(4):854–873.

Ondrich, Jan, Alice Stricker, and John Yinger. 1999. Do Landlords Discriminate. The Incidence and Causes of Racial Discrimination in Rental Housing Markets, *Journal of Housing Economics*, 8(3):185–204.

Ong, Paul M., Douglas Houston. 2002. Transit, employment, and women on welfare, *Urban Geography* 23 (4):344–364.

Ong, Paul. 1996. Work and car ownership among welfare recipients. *Social Work Research* 2(4):255–262.

Ong, Paul M. 2002. Car ownership and welfare-to-work. *Journal of Policy Analysis and Management* 21(2):239–252.

Osterman, Paul. 1999. *Securing Prosperity. The American Labor Market: How it has Changed and What to Do about it*. Princeton: Princeton University Press.

Pendall, Rolf. 2000. Why voucher and certificate users live in distressed neighborhoods. *Housing Policy Debate* 11 (4):881–910.

Pendall, Rolf, and John I. Carruthers. 2003. Does density exacerbate income segregation? Evidence from US metropolitan areas, 1980 to 2000. *Housing Policy Debate* 14(4):541–589.

Pisarski, Alan E. 1996. *Commuting in America II*. Lansdowne, VA: Eno Transportation Foundation.

Pucher, John, and John L. Renne. 2003. Socioeconomics of urban travel: Evidence from the 2001 NHTS. *Transportation Quarterly* 57(3):49–77.

Quillian, Lincoln. 1999. Migration patterns and the growth of high-poverty neighborhoods, 1970–1990. *American Journal of Sociology* 105(1):1–37.

Raphael, Steven. 1998. The spatial mismatch hypothesis and black youth joblessness: Evidence from the San Francisco Bay Area. *Journal of Urban Economics* 43, 1:79–111.

Rodriguez, Gregory 2003. Suburbia gains an accent. *Los Angeles Times*, December 28.

Rohe, William M., and Lance Freeman. 2001. Assisted housing and residential segregation—The role of race and ethnicity in the siting of assisted housing developments. *Journal of the American Planning Association* 67(3):279–292.

Rosenbaum, Emily, and Laura E. Harris. 2001. "Residential mobility and opportunities: Early impacts of the moving to Opportunity Demonstration Program in Chicago." *Housing Policy Debate*, 12(2):321–346.

Sanchez, Thomas W., Qing Shen, and Zhong-Ren Peng. 2004. Transit mobility, job access and low-income labour participation in US metropolitan areas. *Urban Studies* 41(7):1313–1331.

Schmidley, A. Dianne. 2001. *Profiles of the Foreign-Born Population in the United States: 2000*. U.S. Census Bureau, Current Population Reports, Series P23–206. Washington, DC: U.S. Government Printing Office.

Schochet, Peter, and Anu Rangarajan. 2004. *Characteristics of Low-Wage Workers and Their Labor Market Experiences: Evidence from the Mid-to Late 1990s. Final Report*. Princeton, NJ: Mathematica Policy Research Inc.

Shen, Qing. 1998. Location characteristics of inner-city neighborhoods and employment accessibility of low-wage workers. *Environment and Planning B* 25(3): 345–365.

———. 2001. A spatial analysis of job openings and access in a U.S. metropolitan area. *Journal of the American Planning Association* 67(1):53–68.

Singer, Audrey, 2004. *The Rise of New Immigrant Gateways*. Center on Urban and Metropolitan Policy. Washington, DC: Brookings Institution.

Sohmer, Rebecca, and Robert E. Lang. 2001. Downtown rebound. Washington, DC: Fannie Mae Foundation and Brookings Institution Center on Urban and Metropolitan Policy. Census Note.

Stoll, Michael A. 1999. Spatial mismatch, discrimination, and male youth employment in the Washington, DC area: Implications for residential mobility policies. *Journal of Policy Analysis and Management* 18(1):77–98.

Taylor, Brian, and Paul Ong. 1995. Spatial mismatch or automobile mismatch? An examination of race, residence, and commuting in U.S. metropolitan areas. *Urban Studies* 32(9):1453–1473.

Turner, Margery Austin, Stephen L. Ross, George Galster, and John Yinger. 2002. Discrimination in metropolitan housing markets: National results from phase I HDS 2000. Washington, DC: U.S. Department of Housing and Urban Development.

U.S. Census Bureau. 2003a. About metropolitan and micropolitan statistical areas. Population Division, Population Distribution Branch. Washington, DC: U.S. Census Bureau.

U.S. Census Bureau. 2003b. The black population in the U.S.: March 2002. Current population reports, Table 21. Washington, DC: Current Population Survey, Racial Statistics Branch, Population Division. http://www.census.gov/population/socdemo/race/black/ppl-164/tab21.pdf. April 25, 2003.

U.S. Census Bureau. 2004. Current population survey, 2003. Annual Social and Economic Supplement. Immigration Statistics Staff, Population Division. Washington, DC.

U.S. Department of Health and Human Services. 2003. Revised birth and fertility rates for the 1990s and new rates for Hispanic populations. *National Vital Statistics Reports* 51(12). Washington, DC: National Center for Health Statistics.

U.S. Department of Housing and Urban Development. 2000. *The state of the cities 2000. Megaforces shaping the future of the nation's cities*. Washington, DC: HUD Office of Policy Development and Research.

Vigdor, Jacob 2002. Does gentrification harm the poor? *Brookings-Wharton Papers on Urban Affairs: 2002*, ed. Janet Rothenberg Pack. Washington, DC: Brookings Institution.

Wang, Fahui H. 2003. Job proximity and accessibility for workers of various wage groups. *Urban Geography* 24(3):253–271.

Weinberg, Bruce A. 2004. Testing the spatial mismatch hypothesis using inter-city variations in industrial composition. *Regional Science and Urban Economics* 34(5):505–532.

Wilson, William Julius. 1987. *The Truly Disadvantaged*. Chicago: University of Chicago Press.

Wyly, Elvin. 1998. Containment and mismatch: Gender differences in commuting in metropolitan labor markets. *Urban Geography* 19:395–430.

Wyly, Elvin. 2002. Mortgaged metropolis: Evolving urban geographies of residential lending. *Urban Geography* 23(1):3–30.

Wyly, Elvin K., and Daniel J. Hammel. 2004. Gentrification, segregation, and discrimination in the American urban system. *Environment and Planning A* 36: 1215–1241.

Zenou, Yves. 2002. How do firms redline workers? *Journal of Urban Economics* 52(3):391–408.

2 Impacts of the New Social Policy Regime

DOUGLAS HOUSTON AND PAUL ONG

INTRODUCTION

Poor urban neighborhoods changed substantially in the 1990s. One manifestation of this has been a reversal in the concentration of poverty. Although the percentage of the urban poor living in high-poverty areas increased from 1970 to 1990, the last decade witnessed a deconcentration in most metropolitan areas (Jargowsky 1997, 2003). This meant that many poor urban neighborhoods became less poor. The dispersal of poverty has profound implications for community development in minority neighborhoods, which have historically been plagued by disinvestment, declining property values, deteriorated housing, limited business opportunities, insurance redlining, and poor schools (Jaret, Reid, and Adelman 2003; Pettit, Kingsley, and Coulton 2003; Ong 2002; Squires 2003). Declines in concentrated poverty could signal substantial neighborhood socioeconomic transformations and changes in community needs and priorities.

The neighborhood-level changes in poverty in the 1990s coincided with a major restructuring of national social policy, which moved from income entitlements for the poor to income supports for the working poor. President Clinton captured the frustration over soaring welfare rolls as well as the growing convergence between political parties on the question of poverty when in his 1993 State of the Union address he said "we will offer a plan to end welfare as we know it," and followed that statement with another: "if you work full time, you should not be poor." These points encapsulated the new social agenda for the poor—an end to welfare checks and an emphasis instead on financial support tied to employment. The first charge of this agenda was a major transformation of the nation's welfare program. Enacted in 1996, the Personal Responsibility and Work Opportunity Reconciliation Act (PRWORA) replaced the Aid to Families with Dependent Children (AFDC) benefit entitlement program with TANF (Transitional Assistance for Needy Families), which embraced a "work-first" approach that promoted transitioning from public assistance into the labor force as soon as possible. A simultaneous expansion of the Earned Income Tax Credit (EITC) was aimed at enabling low-income working families with children to rise above the federal poverty level. These changes, along with a robust economy, are credited with drastic declines in welfare caseloads nationwide and a substantial increase in the number of working families taking advantage of the EITC as a form of income support.

This chapter explores how these shifts in social policy impacted low-income minority communities. Trends at the national level are consistent with the goals of the new social policy regime. Welfare usage declined, EITC usage increased, and poverty declined. Unfortunately, some were left behind. Many former welfare recipients were unable to find employment, and many that did get jobs had tenuous relationships with the labor market and were unable to climb from poverty.

This mixed picture and the potential limitations of the new policy regime become more apparent when we look at the geographic variability in outcomes across regions. We analyze local-level differences by examining poor neighborhoods in the nation's three largest metropolitan areas: New York, Los Angeles and Chicago.[1] The welfare caseloads in these regions, historically the largest in the nation, shrank dramatically in the 1990s. Simultaneously, working families in these areas received more annual EITC tax dollars than any other metropolitan area. The socioeconomic trends of these regions provide a context for understanding the community-level responses to shift from transfer payments to earnings.

While all three of the study areas have been affected by the change in social policy, Chicago's outcomes were most consistent with the expressed goals of the new policy regime. Outcomes in Los Angeles were the most problematic, while the changes in New York fell between these extremes. Within each metropolitan area, there were considerable differences across communities, with some experiencing economic upswings and others experiencing economic declines.

The remainder of this chapter is organized into three parts. The first provides a political and historical overview of the shift away from entitlements and toward income support in the 1990s and discusses corresponding nationwide declines in the welfare caseload, the expansion of EITC usage, and the declines in minority poverty rates. The second part discusses these trends at a regional level for the Chicago, Los Angeles, and New York metropolitan areas. The third part analyzes the community-level implications of policy changes on poverty rates, welfare usage, employment levels, and earned income tax usage, with particular attention on the outcomes of poor and very poor areas. Finally, we broadly discuss the implications of these trends for community development activities.

THE NEW POLICY CONTEXT—NATIONAL TRENDS

Welfare Reform

> [O]ur goal must be to liberate people and lift them from dependence to independence, from welfare to work, from mere childbearing to responsible parenting. Our goal should not be to punish them because they happen to be poor.
>
> —President Bill Clinton, 1995 State of the Union Address

Calls for welfare reform are not new. The American welfare state has historically been categorical in nature with separate relief programs for quickly as possible. PRWORA established a system of block grants in which states were no longer obligated to provide assistance to poor families. It ended federal entitlements, established new regulations to limit cash support, established a lifetime limit on benefits, and mandated strong work requirements.

PRWORA's "work-first" approach stressed rapid entry into the labor force through short-term training in immediate job search activities and "soft skills" such as dress, punctuality, and workplace expectations. Whereas previous job-training programs under the Job Training and Partnership Act stressed skill development and completion of high school or its equivalency, "work-first" programs encourage immediate job placement under the assumption that on-the-job training and immediate work experience were more important than skills development for their success in the labor market.

It is this shift in national welfare policy, combined with the robust economy that is credited with cutting welfare rolls by half during the late 1990s. The decline began before the federal implementation of PRWORA at the national level in 1996, in part because of the state-based welfare-to-work experiments using federal "waivers." State and national studies suggest that over 60 percent of those who left welfare after PRWORA worked at some point during the year they left. This connection to the labor force was tenuous, though, given that only about 40 percent worked consistently throughout the year, and most earned very low wages and often remained below the federal poverty level. Another 40 percent of those who left welfare were not employed; these former recipients were more likely to have limited education or work experience, or other barriers to employment (Bernstein and Greenberg 2001; Work, Welfare, and Families and the Chicago Urban League 2000; Grogger, Karoly, and Klerman 2002; Children's Defense Fund 2000). Handler and Hasenfeld (1997) suggest that welfare reform is misdirected and that the problem is not welfare, but poverty. They propose measures, including job creation and an expansion of the EITC, that reform the low-wage job market and ensure that every person who wants to work can find a job.

The Earned Income Tax Credit

By expanding the Earned Income Tax Credit, we will make history: We will help reward work for millions of working poor Americans. Our new direction aims to realize a principle as powerful as it is simple: If you work full time, you should not be poor.

—President Bill Clinton, 1993 State of the Union Address

The EITC became an important policy mechanism for encouraging labor market participation among the poor as PRWORA and TANF took effect in the late 1990s. Policy debates in the 1960s and early 1970s had explored ways of using the tax system as a mechanism to remove individuals from poverty and keep them from turning to welfare. The EITC was established in

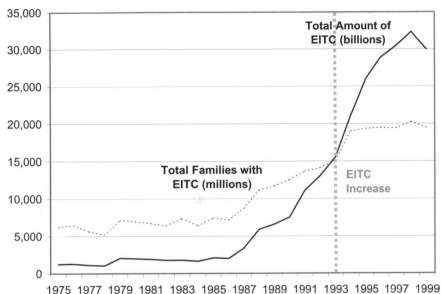

FIGURE 2.2. EITC amount and participation, 1975–1999.[4]

1975 to encourage employment, to reduce the unemployment rate, and to reduce welfare rolls while keeping would-be claimants in the labor force. The program remained relatively small until the early 1990s, when it was greatly expanded with bipartisan support (Figure 2.2).[3] President George Bush initiated the 1990 expansion, and in 1993 Bill Clinton initiated a second expansion to "make work pay" (Ventry 2000). Clinton's expansion raised the maximum credit for families with three or more children by five hundred dollars and expanded the credit for married, double-income families.[4] Between 1993 and 1999 the maximum credit nearly tripled, an increase of two thousand dollars for multiple-child families (Grogger 2003).

The program provides a credit against federal income tax liability for working families who have children and whose earnings is less than double the federal poverty line. Unlike other tax credits, EITC is refundable: if the credit amount exceeds the amount of taxes owed, the taxpayer receives the difference from the Internal Revenue Service (IRS). The EITC thus has the potential to be a negative tax, or essentially a tax-based form of welfare—poor families can collect an IRS check for working, rather than pay into the IRS out of their earnings. The credit amount increases with the amount of earned income under the maximum allowed credit. In 2000, a family with one child could receive a maximum credit of about $2,300 while a family with two children could receive a maximum of about $3,800. Once a household's income rises above $12,000, the credit phased out to zero by about $30,000 (Berube and Tiffany 2004). For a minimum-wage worker with two children, the EITC means a 40 percent increase in annual earnings (Jencks 2002).

The tax credit played an important role in "making work pay" by effectively raising the income level of many poor families above the federal poverty level. In 1999, almost 19.5 million impoverished families received over $31 billion in EITC payments (Hotz, Mullin, and Scholz 1999).

The expansion of EITC made a substantial impact on the labor market participation of single women with children. Meyer and Rosenbaum (1999) estimate that changes to EITC account for 37 percent of the increase in the employment rate of single women with children from 1992 to 1996. Grogger (2003) ties EITC to the decrease in welfare use and the increase in employment, labor supply, and earnings. Ellwood (2000) suggests that "20 percent of the growth in work can be traced to the economy, perhaps another 50 percent is linked to welfare reform, and the remaining 30 percent can be traced to the EITC and other work supports." Hotz, Mullin, and Scholz (1999) examined the effects of the EITC in helping former recipients to work and found that EITC played an important role in increasing the employment rates among low-skilled workers, particularly among those who received public assistance.

Although these findings suggest the EITC may have had its desired policy impact, little is known about its geographic implications. We don't know whether poor mothers with children leaving welfare in high-poverty areas are taking advantage of the tax credit. Furthermore, rates of leaving welfare for work are sensitive to the business cycle (Fitzgerald 1995; Blank 2001); a survey of employers in the largest cities in Michigan suggests that the demand for workers leaving welfare varied and was highly dependent on the business cycle (Holzer 1999). Former welfare recipients already occupy a disadvantaged position in urban labor markets and could be particularly vulnerable in a recession, especially if they live in distressed areas with limited job access, high unemployment, and weak job-related social networks (Coulton 2003; Danziger et al. 2000).

National Poverty Trends

The shift from entitlements to tax credits corresponded with a substantial decline in minority poverty in the late 1990s. Nationwide, the poverty rate among blacks fell from about 33 percent to 22 percent, while among Hispanics it declined from about 30 percent to 21 percent. While the minority rates remained substantially higher than the 8 percent poverty rate for non-Hispanic whites in 2000, the difference between minority and non-Hispanic white poverty was reduced significantly.[5]

The Federal Poverty Level (FPL) provides a standard national measure tracking poverty over time but may underestimate poverty, especially in urban areas with a high cost of living. The FPL was developed in the 1960s and is set at three times the "breadbasket," the minimum acceptable level of food for a particular family size and composition, and is adjusted annually based on inflation. The 1999 FPL for a family of four was an annual income of $16,700. This index of poverty is the primary indicator used to measure changes in the size of the poor population and is a fundamental policy indicator. Although adjusted annually for inflation, the FPL is not geographically adjusted. Thus in relatively expensive areas such as Chicago, Los Angeles, and New York, estimates of the poverty level using the FPL likely underestimate the size of the poor population. Despite continued controversy over whether the level is too low, the federal poverty guidelines provide a nationwide standard for tracking changes for low-income populations over time and across different population groups.

National poverty rates fluctuate with the business cycle, so it is not surprising that poverty rates declined with the unemployment level in the late 1990s. Policy changes could also have played an important role in the national decline of poverty. Many former welfare recipients responded to new limits on welfare usage by successfully transitioning into steady jobs that lifted their households above the FPL. Even some facing barriers to steady employment may have increased their labor market participation substantially. In addition, tax credits could have raised the annual household income for many former welfare and other poor families to just over the poverty level.

REGIONAL PATTERNS

This section investigates how the robust economy and the overhaul of social programs for the poor in the late 1990s impacted minority communities in the three regions with historically high rates of concentrated poverty and welfare usage: Chicago, Los Angeles, and New York. The section begins with a consideration of the regional impacts of welfare reform on public assistance, household income and labor force participation followed by a discussion of EITC usage rates. Finally, we discuss regional declines in poverty within these regions.

Regional Welfare

Welfare usage in the three study regions mirrored national patterns. Usage dramatically increased in the early 1990s, peaked in the mid-1990s, and began a sharp decline by 1996 when welfare reform was passed at the federal level. The decline continued into the late 1990s as state and regional implementation of welfare reform became a reality. The State of Illinois and the Chicago area experienced the most dramatic decline from a combined average monthly caseload of about 638,000 in 1990 to about 293,000 in 2000. New York had the highest overall number of welfare recipients into the mid-1990s, with over one million persons on welfare in an average month, but the number of persons on public assistance declined substantially in the late 1990s and by 2000 had reached a monthly average of about 573,000, a level comparable to Los Angeles. Los Angeles, which had a swollen monthly caseload just over 850,000 in the mid-1990s, experienced a much slower decline to about 553,000 in 2000. The region had roughly the same number on public assistance in 2000 as it had in 1990. Its welfare rolls continued to fall after 2000, however.[6]

Table 2.1. Regional public assistance, all households and households under 200 percent of federal poverty level

	Chicago		Los Angeles		New York	
	1990	2000	1990	2000	1990	2000
Percentage of households receiving public assistance						
All households	5	3	5	5	6	5
Poor households[a]	15	8	12	11	15	11
Per household public assistance[b]						
All households	$167	$84	$269	$252	$797	$575
Poor households[a]	$581	$225	$290	$186	$807	$439
Percentage of female-headed households						
All households	15	14	13	14	17	18
Poor households[a]	27	26	21	21	28	28

[a]Includes households under 200 percent of the federal poverty line.
[b]Amounts in 1999 dollars.
Source: Census (1990 & 2000 Public Use Micro Sample).

The public assistance rates of these regions tell a similar story (Table 2.1).[7] Between 1990 and 2000, Chicago experienced the largest drop in public assistance followed by New York, which experienced a lesser decline. Using 1990 and 2000 as guideposts, Los Angeles did not experience a net decline. Likewise, the dollar amount of public assistance divided by the number of regional households declined by about 50 percent in Chicago and by over 60 percent in New York.[8]

We see similar patterns when we consider the subset of households within each region that have an income below 200 percent of the FPL. In Chicago, the rate of public assistance of these households decreased by roughly half, while New York had a more modest decline and Los Angeles only a minimal decline. Noticeably, the overall amount of public assistance received by poor households in Los Angeles declined between 1990 and 2000, although not as much as in Chicago and New York.

The work requirements of welfare reform could have the consequence of pressuring single mothers into marriage or household partnerships in order to bolster household income. However, we do not see substantial regionwide changes in the percentage of female-headed households, which suggests that welfare reform has not resulted in widespread restructuring of households.

Given welfare reform's stress on employment as a means toward financial self-sufficiency, we expect the labor force participation rate to increase, particularly among the poor who could be significantly impacted by welfare reform.[9] Surprisingly, the percentage of the working-age population working or looking for work dropped in the study regions, with the largest decline being in Los Angeles (Table 2.2). Despite this decline, there was a modest increase in the per capita earnings in Chicago while the per capita earning levels in New York and Los Angeles remained fairly constant. This pattern held for households under 200 percent of the FPL, with the exception of poor households in Los Angeles that experienced a slight increase in per capita earnings.[10]

TABLE 2.2. Regional labor force participation and earnings of the total population, and persons in households under 200 percent of federal poverty level

	Chicago		Los Angeles		New York	
	1990	2000	1990	2000	1990	2000
Labor force participation rate						
Total population	80%	77%	78%	71%	76%	71%
Poor population[a]	61%	56%	64%	56%	54%	52%
Per capita earnings[b]						
Total population	$18,391	$20,190	$17,492	$16,916	$19,074	$19,635
Poor population[a]	$3,785	$4,036	$4,269	$4,323	$3,565	$3,708

[a]Includes households under 200 percent of the federal poverty line.
[b]Amounts in 1999 dollars.
Source: Census (1990 & 2000 Public Use Micro Sample).

Earned Income Tax Credit

In the 1990s, the study regions received more EITC tax dollars than any other metropolitan areas. Residents of Los Angeles in 1998 received the most EITC tax dollars,—just under $1.3 million—followed by New York with about $1.2 million and Chicago with over $700,000.[11] Although Los Angeles had a lower rate of tax return filings than the other study regions, persons filing a return had a higher rate of claiming EITC in Los Angeles than Chicago or New York (Table 2.3). Since 200 percent poverty is the cutoff line below which working families qualify for filing EITC, we examine EITC claim rates as a percentage of total persons under 200 percent poverty. This rate is over 20 percent for all three metropolitan areas and the EITC claim amount is over $340 per person under 200 percent poverty. This indicates that although Chicago and New York seem to have a lower overall rate of claiming the credit based on total returns, poor households in these regions have an equal or slightly higher rate of claiming EITC than Los Angeles.[12]

These regional differences are consistent with findings that EITC usage rates vary by geographic regions of the country, especially in relation to the

TABLE 2.3. Regional usage of the Earned Income Tax Credit (EITC), 1998

	Chicago	Los Angeles	New York
Total population			
Percentage of tax returns claiming EITC	14	21	19
Per-return EITC amount	$225	$359	$305
Percentage of persons filing returns	45	38	40
Poor population			
Percentage of poor population claiming EITC	24	20	22
Per capita EITC amount	$382	$343	$345

Sources: 1998 Internal Revenue Service zip code level data and 2000 Census SF3 ZCTA-level data.

Table 2.4. Regional poverty rates and minority poverty rates of the total population, & persons in households under 200 percent poverty

	Chicago		Los Angeles		New York	
	1989	1999	1989	1999	1989	1999
Poverty Rate						
Total population	14%	12%	17%	18%	19%	19%
Population <200 percent FPL	52%	41%	47%	42%	57%	49%
Minority Poverty Rate						
Total population	25%	20%	21%	22%	26%	25%
Population <200 percent FPL	56%	46%	45%	43%	57%	51%
Non-Hispanic Black Poverty Rate						
Total population	29%	25%	21%	23%	23%	23%
Population <200 percent FPL	58%	52%	47%	51%	52%	52%
Hispanic Poverty Rate						
Total Population	20%	17%	23%	24%	31%	29%
Population <200					56%	52%
percent FPL	41%	38%	40%	42%		

Source: Census (1990 & 2000 Public Use Micro Sample).

concentration of working poor within regions (Berube and Foreman 2001; Berube and Tiffany 2004).

Regional Poverty

The overall poverty rate was lower in Chicago than in New York and Los Angeles (Table 2.4). Of the three regions, Chicago also experienced the largest reduction in poverty between 1990 and 2000. Although minorities in all areas had a higher poverty rate than that of the general population, the minority poverty rate in Chicago declined by five percentage points. Although the poverty level in New York was steady between 1990 and 2000, Hispanics experienced a slight decline. The general population and minorities in Los Angeles had a slight increase in poverty.

Examining households below 200 percent poverty is instructive since this income level is roughly the cutoff for claiming the EITC. It also provides insight into the concentration of families near the FPL (Table 2.4). For instance, although 52 percent of households under 200 percent poverty in Chicago were under 100 percent poverty in 1990, only 41 percent of these households were under 100 percent poverty in 2000. This trend holds for New York and Los Angeles as well, suggesting that while the shift from entitlements to credits helped a large percentage of the poorest households earn enough to lift themselves above the FPL, they were not able to escape this higher, arguably more realistic, threshold of poverty. For most purposes these families remained poor, albeit now "working poor" and no longer classified as poor by the federal government. Of those families that did

TABLE 2.5. Poverty rates of central cities and non-central cities, 1981–1999

	Chicago	Los Angeles	New York
Central City—Average Poverty Rate			
1981–1991	26%	20%	23%
1992–1999	21%	24%	24%
Non–Central City—Average Poverty Rate			
1981–1991	5%	12%	6%
1992–1999	6%	14%	7%
Central City to Non–Central City—Ratio			
1981–1991	5.1	1.6	4.2
1992–1999	3.8	1.7	3.5

Source: Current Population Survey, U.S. Bureau of labor Statistics and the Bureau of the Census.

remain under both the FPL and the 200 percent poverty threshold, a disproportionate share were minorities. While a fair percentage of poor minority families moved slightly above the poverty line, Hispanic and black families in Los Angeles fell farther under it. The poverty distribution of black families in New York remained constant.

The "snapshot" poverty rates provided by census data for 1989 and 1999 do not capture the substantial fluctuation in poverty levels in the 1990s. Los Angeles experienced the highest poverty rate of the three regions in the 1990s, which ranged from around 15 percent to 20 percent. New York's overall poverty rate fluctuated near 15 percent in the mid-1990s with a slight drop by 2000. Chicago experienced the smallest rise in poverty in the early 1990s with the greatest decline to about 10 percent by 2000.[13]

Regional poverty comparisons obscure the different rates of poverty *within* regions. The percentage of persons in poverty in each region varies greatly between central city and non–central city areas (Table 2.5). Between 20 to 26 percent of the residents of central cities were in poverty, compared to 5 percent to 14 percent in non–central cities. The greatest discrepancies were in Chicago, where the poverty rate in the central city was 4 to 5 times more than the poverty rate outside it. New York experienced a similar differential, while the central city poverty rate in Los Angeles was less than twice the poverty rate of non–central city areas—suggesting that the poor in Los Angeles have a stronger presence in non–central city areas.

LOCAL PATTERNS

Although the "gap" between central city poverty and non–central city poverty closed somewhat in Chicago and New York, socioeconomic differences persist at the subregional level. The policy shift from entitlements toward work-based credits could detrimentally impact high-poverty areas, particularly since high-poverty minority neighborhoods are often plagued by disinvestment, declining property values, deteriorated housing, limited business opportunities, insurance redlining, and poor schools (Jaret, Reid, and Adelman 2003; Pettit, Kingsley, and Coulton 2003; Ong 2002; Squires 2003). William Wilson (1987) suggests that larger structural forces contribute to the high rates of public assistance and unemployment in distressed minority neighborhoods. For instance, the movement of middle-class African American residents from inner-city, mixed-income neighborhoods in the 1970s contributed to the concentration of poverty by leaving behind disadvantaged segments of the black population in inner-city neighborhoods that are far from suburban job opportunities.

Given these subregional structural forces, communities represent important geographic contexts for understanding the impact of the social policy changes of the 1990s. Claudia Coulton (2003) suggests that "inequities within cities, metropolitan labor markets, and neighborhoods are an important context for understanding the effects of welfare reform and for promoting the welfare-to-work transition." Recent findings for Los Angeles suggest that the severity of business cycle effects in the 1990s varied across neighborhoods in the region and that the safety net for the poor does not increase in relation to increased need in poor neighborhoods during economic downturns (Ong et al. 2003).

This section investigates subregional patterns of public assistance, labor force participation, earnings, and EITC usage across communities by their poverty status. Geographic distinctions between central city and non–central city areas may not adequately distinguish between poor and nonpoor areas given the historic residential patterns of these regions, especially given the uneven growth patterns in Los Angeles. Therefore, we conduct analysis based on communities defined by their poverty status. We approximate communities in the study regions using census-based Public Use Microsample Areas (PUMAS), a census-based level of geography that contains a minimum of 100,000 people.[14] The Census Bureau defines poor areas as communities with over 20 percent of persons in poverty. Research and literature on urban underclass and neighborhoods define high-poverty areas as communities with over 40 percent of persons in poverty. Drawing from both definitions, we define communities with between 20 percent to 40 percent of residents below the FPL as poor, communities with over 40 percent poverty as very poor, and those with less than 20 percent poverty as not poor. For the purpose of analysis, we classify communities based on their 1990 poverty status in order to examine the impact of policy changes on poor neighborhoods.[15]

The large majority of residents in each region live in nonpoor areas (Table 2.6). Roughly 30 percent of the population lives in poor or very poor neighborhoods. Poor communities in Los Angeles are concentrated in the central and south portions of the region and stretch from the downtown area through South Los Angeles, Compton, and Long Beach. In New York, poor communities are spread through Brooklyn, Queens, upper Manhattan, and the Bronx. Poor neighborhoods in Chicago stretch toward Cicero west of downtown and south into the South Side. Minority populations in all three regions experienced growth in the 1990s. Although they remained roughly 40 percent of the population of poor or very poor areas, this percentage

TABLE 2.6. Population and minority distribution by 1990 community poverty status

	Total Population		Minority		Non-Hispanic Black		Hispanic	
	1990	2000	1990	2000	1990	2000	1990	2000
Chicago								
Very poor	5%	5%	13%	9%	19%	15%	4%	3%
Poor	24%	23%	49%	39%	54%	48%	48%	35%
Not poor	71%	72%	38%	52%	27%	37%	48%	62%
Los Angeles								
Very poor	4%	4%	7%	6%	11%	8%	7%	7%
Poor	31%	28%	41%	35%	49%	44%	42%	36%
Not poor	65%	67%	52%	59%	40%	48%	51%	57%
New York								
Very poor	11%	11%	20%	18%	22%	19%	24%	22%
Poor	23%	22%	31%	28%	28%	25%	36%	33%
Not poor	66%	67%	49%	55%	50%	55%	40%	45%

Source: Census (1990 & 2000 Public Use Micro Sample).

declined in the 1990s, suggesting that minorities became more dispersed in these regions, whether by overall growth or by residential mobility.

Public Assistance and Labor Force Participation

Public assistance rates declined most substantially in poor and very poor neighborhoods in Chicago, followed by poor and very poor neighborhoods in New York (Table 2.7). Comparable areas in Los Angeles experienced no decrease or only a slight decrease in public assistance. The public assistance dollars received per household in these areas declined along the same lines as the overall public assistance rates, with poor and very poor neighborhoods in Chicago experiencing the greatest declines, followed by New York. The amount of per household public assistance remained highest in Los Angeles, where declines were modest. Among households that continued to receive public assistance in 2000, the amount they received fell, particularly in Chicago and New York. The percentage of female-headed households declined in very poor neighborhoods in Los Angeles and New York suggesting that some families may have reorganized in light of the increased pressure toward employment in the 1990s.

The pressure of welfare reform to transition from public assistance to the labor market may have affected the labor force participation of residents in poor and nonpoor areas. As discussed above, the overall labor force participation rate declined in all three regions among all working-age persons and those in poverty (Table 2.2). Even though there was an overall decline in labor force participation, the gap between the rate of participation in nonpoor and very poor areas declined in Chicago and New York (Table 2.8). In Chicago, where this gap decreased the most, earnings increased in poor and very poor areas. The earnings in very poor neighborhoods in New York and Los Angeles increased to a lesser degree.

TABLE 2.7. Public assistance by 1990 community poverty status

	Percentage of Public Assistance Households		Percentage of Female-Headed Households		Public Assistance Amount per Household[a]		Public Assistance Amount per Public Assistance Household	
	1990	2000	1990	2000	1990	2000	1990	2000
Chicago								
Very poor	20	11	35	34	$767	$288	$3,764	$2,532
Poor	11	6	23	22	$371	$181	$3,441	$3,072
Not poor	2	1	10	11	$62	$43	$3,212	$3,077
Los Angeles								
Very poor	16	14	27	22	$949	$765	$5,950	$5,325
Poor	7	7	16	17	$413	$379	$5,689	$5,273
Not poor	4	3	11	13	$172	$178	$4,712	$5,228
New York								
Very poor	22	15	40	37	$1,066	$587	$4,917	$3,952
Poor	10	8	23	23	$498	$317	$4,912	$4,214
Not poor	3	2	12	13	$116	$89	$4,361	$4,104

[a]In 1999 dollars.
Source: Census (1990 & 2000 Public Use Micro Sample).

TABLE 2.8. Regional labor force participation and earnings by 1990 community poverty status

	Labor Force Participation Rate		Per capita earnings	
	1990	2000	1990	2000
Chicago				
Very poor	63%	63%	$8,601	$10,683
Poor	75%	70%	$12,626	$14,964
Not poor	83%	79%	$21,059	$22,446
Los Angeles				
Very poor	65%	57%	$6,453	$6,762
Poor	75%	67%	$12,844	$12,431
Not poor	80%	74%	$20,453	$19,452
New York				
Very poor	59%	57%	$7,762	$8,179
Poor	70%	66%	$12,791	$12,807
Not poor	80%	75%	$23,153	$23,791

Source: Census (1990 & 2000 Public Use Micro Sample).

Neighborhood-Level Earned Income Tax Credits

Not surprisingly, the percentage of people claiming EITC is higher in poor and very poor communities, in part because poor working families who qualify for the tax credit are more concentrated in poor areas where the cost of living is lower (Table 2.9).[16] The number of EITC claims as a percentage of the number of persons under 200 percent poverty suggests that working

TABLE 2.9. Usage of the Earned Income Tax Credit by 1990 community poverty status

	Percentage Claiming EITC of Tax Returns	EITC Amount per Tax Return	Percentage of Persons Filing a Tax Return	Percentage Claiming EITC of Persons Under 200 Percent Poverty	EITC Amount per Persons Under 200 Percent Poverty
Chicago					
Very poor	53	$953	29	23	$410
Poor	33	$569	35	23	$402
Not poor	10	$147	47	25	$366
Los Angeles					
Very poor	47	$893	24	15	$291
Poor	34	$613	32	19	$345
Not poor	15	$235	43	22	$348
New York					
Very poor	46	$822	29	20	$357
Poor	31	$518	35	21	$352
Not poor	12	$183	44	23	$333

Source: 1998 Internal Revenue Service zip code level data and 2000 census SF3 ZCTA-level data.

families in nonpoor areas have a slightly higher rate of claiming. Noticeably, this higher rate of claiming EITC in nonpoor areas did not necessarily translate into a higher amount of credits per person. The rate of filing a tax return varies by community poverty status. Persons in nonpoor areas are more likely to file a tax return than residents of poor and very poor communities. As discussed in the conclusion, the success of EITC in poor neighborhoods could be hampered by the low rate of persons filing tax returns.

Local-Level Poverty

The fall in Chicago's poverty rate occurred in both poor and very poor communities (Table 2.10). The declines in overall poverty in New York and Los Angeles, by contrast, were mainly concentrated in very poor communities. Minorities, again, are more concentrated in poor and very poor communities compared to the whole population in the three regions. Minority poverty rates in Chicago declined in all community types. The poverty rate among Hispanics in Los Angeles rose, particularly in very poor communities. The poverty rate among blacks in poor and nonpoor areas rose in both Los Angeles and New York.

These findings suggest that the rate of poverty among minorities as a whole declined or held constant in poor and very poor areas of Chicago and New York, while it increased slightly in poor and very poor areas of Los Angeles. Jargowsky's (2003) analysis of concentrated poverty provides further context for understanding the regional differences in outcomes. While the concentration of the poor in urban neighborhoods doubled from 1970 to 1990, this trend was reversed in the 1990s in most metropolitan

TABLE 2.10. Poverty rates and minority poverty rates by 1990 community poverty status

	Poverty Rate		Minority Poverty Rate		Non-Hispanic Black Poverty Rate		Hispanic Poverty Rate	
	1990	2000	1990	2000	1990	2000	1990	2000
Chicago								
Very Poor	45%	35%	45%	37%	46%	38%	34%	30%
Poor	27%	23%	29%	26%	30%	28%	26%	24%
Not poor	7%	7%	14%	13%	16%	15%	13%	13%
Los Angeles								
Very poor	40%	38%	37%	39%	41%	41%	34%	39%
Poor	25%	25%	26%	27%	21%	26%	28%	29%
Not poor	12%	13%	15%	17%	14%	18%	17%	19%
New York								
Very poor	47%	39%	44%	39%	37%	36%	49%	42%
Poor	29%	28%	31%	31%	26%	28%	34%	33%
Not poor	11%	12%	15%	17%	14%	17%	17%	20%

Source: Census (1990 & 2000 Public Use Micro Sample).

areas, including Chicago and New York. In these regions, a smaller percentage of poor blacks and Hispanics lived in poor neighborhoods in 2000 than in 1900. In Los Angeles the opposite was true: a higher percentage of Blacks and Hispanics lived in poor neighborhoods (McConville and Ong 2003).

Subregional trends suggest that the impact of welfare reform and the expansion of EITC have affected communities differently across Chicago, New York and Los Angeles. In many ways neighborhoods in Chicago and to a lesser degree New York experienced outcomes consistent with the goals of these programs. Although Los Angeles began the decade with lower welfare and poverty rates in the poorest areas, the region's gains on these counts were generally less dramatic compared to those of Chicago and New York.

CONCLUSION AND DISCUSSION

The national restructuring of American social policy in the late 1990s occurred in the midst of a national economic boom. Previous attempts to integrate work requirements into the nation's welfare system had failed to substantially reduce welfare rolls despite favorable economic conditions. Although many who left welfare during the recent wave of reform face barriers to self-sufficiency and a tenuous relationship with the labor force, the policy changes were the first in recent history to dramatically reduce soaring welfare rolls. This policy shift from public entitlements corresponded with extensive tax credits for low-income working families that have enabled many families to rise above the federal poverty level.

Our analysis of the three regions with the highest historic welfare caseloads suggests there were regional discrepancies in how policy changes and economic forces impacted low-income minority communities in the 1990s.

Chicago experienced the most sizeable reduction in welfare usage and poverty; these changes were experienced in both poor and very poor areas. The reduction in public assistance and poverty in New York was more tempered, but was most pronounced in the poorest neighborhoods. The welfare rate in Los Angeles, the region that experienced the greatest spike in the welfare rolls in the mid-1990s, by 2000 fell to the level it was at the start of the decade.

In all three regions, overall earnings increased modestly or held even as the amount of public assistance dropped. Chicago had the greatest gain in per capita earnings in both poor and very poor communities. Per capita earnings remained fairly constant in poor communities in New York and Los Angeles between 1990 and 2000. Chicago also experienced the most sizeable decrease in the gap between the labor force participation in nonpoor and very-poor neighborhoods. Low-income residents seem to be taking advantage of EITC; very poor communities receive the largest per-return credits.

These results suggest that while the policy changes aimed at reducing welfare dependency succeeded on many levels, their impact varied across regions. Regional differences may persist for multiple reasons, including community-level job availability, transportation access, and housing markets. Some scholars, including Popkin et al. (2004), have documented the large-scale demolition of public housing in Chicago under the federal HOPE VI program, which may help explain the decline of concentrated poverty in that region. HOPE VI represented a dramatic shift from physically deteriorated public housing to less-dense mixed-income communities carried out under the assumption that the interaction between unemployed public housing residents and working adults would promote greater access to job networks and labor market connection for the poor. This approach resulted in a net loss of public housing units and the relocation of many poor families in Chicago to less poor areas throughout the region. Although many of the displaced residents relocated to communities with lower poverty levels, the program had little impact on racial segregation, since most moved to areas that were predominantly minority. Despite substantial relocation assistance, many dislocated residents faced a tight rental market and unwillingness by some landlords to accept vouchers.

The community-level declining welfare participation and increasing EITC usage described in this chapter should be understood in the context of similar regional and community-level forces. In the case of Chicago, the large-scale geographic reorganization of poverty within the region and changes to welfare and EITC may have helped low-income residents rise out of poverty and away from welfare dependency. While this may be the success story of many families, it also may be that the economic struggles of lower-income families are masked by the community-level results presented in this chapter. That is, as these families became more dispersed within the region and their former neighborhoods became more mixed-income, their experience becomes "washed out" by their increased dispersion among families with higher income levels.

Regional and community-level differences in the reduction of welfare and increase in EITC usage may be also due to differences in the implementation of policy changes within the study regions. In fact, difference may persist in EITC usage in part because of local outreach and administration. In 1999, Chicago launched the first large-scale municipal campaign to promote EITC usage among working poor families, which may help explain why the number of EITC claimants had risen faster in Chicago than comparable cities. Such campaigns are important given that many eligible families are not aware of the credit. In addition, some fear they will owe taxes and don't file or fear they will lose eligibility for other benefits if they claim the EITC. Results in this chapter suggesting families in high-poverty areas are less likely to file a tax return reinforce the need to strengthen outreach efforts. Currently, about 100 cities have EITC campaigns, including Los Angeles and New York and the number of EITC filers nationally continues to grow (Berube 2004). Such campaigns often provide important tax preparation resources through volunteer sites that give information often not provided by commercial tax preparers. This is an important service for low-income taxpayers that are more likely to use tax preparation services and to purchase a refund anticipation loan. The use of such volunteer sites has increased nationwide.

While the shift from welfare entitlements to tax credits has not solved the ongoing problem of poverty, the changes were instrumental in helping many families embrace the labor market and climb from poverty. But given the tenuous nature of the low-wage labor market, it remains unclear whether the gains of many poor families in the late 1990s will provide adequate support in leaner economic times. Many may find increased difficulty retaining employment and may once again seek public assistance. Some families may intermittently return to welfare in their transition to the labor force. Other poor families may rely heavily on public assistance given that they face substantial barriers to employment. Public assistance may be insufficient to help low-income households through lean economic times since many will hit their lifetime limit on welfare assistance under welfare reform and will no longer be able to receive benefits.

Community-based organizations, policy makers, and practitioners can pursue a number of strategies that help low-income families avoid or overcome periods of unemployment, especially since tax credits only benefit households with an employed adult. The job training programs advocated in Chapter 4 are critical for assisting less-skilled workers. Increasing the number of businesses and jobs in low-income minority communities as advocated in Chapter 7 can help residents in their transition from public assistance to tax-based income supports. At the same time, renewed efforts are needed to help residents overcome the geographic barriers to employment identified in Chapter 7. While these strategies are not new within community economic development, they take on a greater importance within the new policy regime.

Many states, including Illinois and New York, have taken important steps to expand support for low-income families by implementing EITC programs. State-based tax credits provide an important mechanism to increase the overall level of income retained within low-income communities and provide an additional incentive for participation in the labor market. Community-based organizations can help raise awareness about tax credits in low-income communities and help facilitate tax preparation for households that previously felt little incentive to prepare a tax return. Tax-based income support fails to address the needs of low-wage workers in the informal labor market since their work and contribution to the economy is unreported. While some may argue that these workers should not benefit from public support or credits since they do not pay taxes, community-based organizations and antipoverty strategies must recognize that these workers comprise a sizeable source of income for many poor minority communities.

The increased poverty levels among blacks and Hispanics in New York and Los Angeles and the lower use of tax credits in high-poverty communities suggest that the success of the new policy regime has not been universally successful despite the widespread gains of the late 1990s. Now that these initial gains have been realized, it is important that policy makers and practitioners understand and address the distinct needs and realities of particular communities if low-income minority families are to overcome the remaining limitations of the new policy regime.

NOTES

We would like to acknowledge the John Randolph Haynes and Dora Haynes Foundation for its support of research on disadvantaged neighborhoods, which partly supported the development of the data and methods used in this chapter. We would also like to thank the UCLA Ralph and Goldy Lewis Center for Regional Policy Studies for data and computing support.

1. The Los Angeles and New York metropolitan areas correspond with boundaries of Metropolitan Statistical Areas as defined by the United States Office of Budget and Management. The Chicago metropolitan area corresponds with Cook County and Du Page County.

2. U.S. House of Representatives, Committee on Ways and Means, 2000 Green Book: Background Material and Data on Programs within the Jurisdiction of the Committee on Ways and Means, aspe.hhs.gov/2000gb/sec7.txt.

3. U.S. House of Representatives, Committee on Ways and Means, 2000 Green Book: Background Material and Data on Programs within the Jurisdiction of the Committee on Ways and Means, aspe.hhs.gov/2000gb/sec7.txt.

4. Represents proposed amounts.

5. Based on tabulations from the Current Population Survey.

6. Caseload information for the study areas were derived from the Illinois Department of Human Services, the California Department of Social Services, and the City of New York. Summary statistics on Chicago were not available. The majority of welfare recipients in Illinois have been historically concentrated within the city of Chicago.

7. For consistent definition of public assistance between 1990 and 2000 Public Use Micro Sample (PUMs) data, we define a household receiving public assistance as a household that had income from public assistance or supplemental security income

and had a child in the household. Since having a child is a condition of receiving AFDC/TANF, this definition allows us to estimate households for which this income is received as AFDC/TANF-based support rather than income supports such as General Relief or disability payments.

8. Original analysis of PUMS data and IRS data for this chapter define Chicago as Cook and Dupage counties. We define Los Angeles as Los Angeles County and New York as Kings, New York, Queens, Richmond, Rockland, and Westchester counties.

9. The Labor Force Participation Rate represents the percentage of the population between 18 and 65 who were not enrolled in school and who were in the labor force. That is, they were employed or were actively looking for work.

10. Analysis of the growth or fluctuation of economic sectors and jobs in the study regions could provide useful context for understanding the employment patterns and earnings of low-wage workers. Such analysis is not included in this chapter since the classification of industries in 1990 PUMS data, based on the Standard Industrial Classification, does not correspond directly with classification of industries in 1990 PUMS data, based on the North American Industry Classification System.

11. Although analysis of tax data from the early 1990s could provide useful insight into the changes in EITC usage before and after the expansion of the program, analysis in this chapter is based on 1998 IRS data since earlier data were not available.

12. EITC and tax return analysis is conducted at the zip code–Zip Code Tabulation Area (ZCTA) level since IRS data were not available at the PUMA level. Therefore, the very poor, poor, and nonpoor communities are not directly comparable with communities defined by PUMA boundaries.

13. Based on tabulations from the Current Population Survey.

14. The PUMA geographic level represents the lowest level of census geography for which we are able to derive a consistent definition of public assistance between 1990 and 2000 for the purposes of this analysis. PUMA boundaries are the lowest level of aggregation possible using 1990 and 2000 PUMS data, which represent a sample of individual-level responses to the census long form, including sources of household income. As described earlier, these data were required for our analysis in order to derive a common definition of public assistance between 1990 and 2000. Tract-level data released by the census contains different definitions of public assistance for 1990 and 2000.

15. In some cases, PUMA boundaries changed from 1990 to 2000. These changes were largely inconsequential to the summary classifications used here. In instances where boundary changes occurred on the border of area classifications, we ensured that the impact of boundary changes were minimal to reported statistics. We also normalize reported statistics to avoid inflating patterns.

16. EITC and tax return analysis is conducted at the zip code–ZCTA level since IRS data were not available at the PUMA level. Therefore, the very poor, poor, and nonpoor communities are not directly comparable with communities defined by PUMA boundaries.

REFERENCES

Bernstein, Jared, and Mark Greenberg. 2001. Reforming welfare reform. *The American Prospect* 12(1). http://www.prospect.org/web/page.ww?section=root&name=viewprint&articleID=4583. [Accessed December 2005].

Berube, Alan. 2004. EITC Outreach Campaigns. Presentation to the EITC Funders Network, June 21, 2004. Washington, DC: Brookings Institution. http://www. brookings.edu/metro/speeches/20040621_eitc.htm. Accessed August 2004.

Berube, Alan, and Thacher Tiffany. 2004. The "State" of Low-Wage Workers: How the EITC Benefits Urban and Rural Communities in the 50 States. Washington, DC: Brookings Institution.

Berube, Alan, and Benjamin Forman. 2001. A Local Ladder for the Working Poor: The Impact of the Earned Income Tax Credit in U.S. Metropolitan Areas. Washington, DC: Brookings Institution.

Blank, Rebecca M. 2001. What causes public assistance caseloads to grow? Journal of Human Resources 36(1):85–118.

Children's Defense Fund. 2000. Families Struggling to Make It in the Workforce: A Post Welfare Report. Washington, DC: Children's Defense Fund.

Coulton, Claudia J. 2003. Metropolitan inequities and the ecology of work: Implications for welfare reform. Social Service Review 77:159–160.

Danziger, Sandra, Mary Corcoran, Sheldon Danziger, and Collee M. Helfin. 2000. Work, income, and material hardship after welfare. Journal of Consumer Affairs 43(1):6–30.

Ellwood, David T. 2000. The impact of the Earned Income Tax Credit and social policy reforms on work, marriage, and living arrangements. National Tax Journal 53(4):1063–1106.

Fitzgerald, John M. 1995. Local labor markets and local area effects on welfare duration. Journal of Policy Analysis and Management 14(1):43–67.

Freedman, Stephen, Daniel Friedlander, and James Riccio. 1994. GAIN: Benefits, Costs, and Three-Year Impacts of a Welfare-to-Work Program. New York: Manpower Demonstration Research Corporation.

Grogger, Jeffrey, Lynn Karoly, and Jacob Klerman. 2002. Conflicting benefits; Trade-offs in welfare reform. Rand Review 26(3). http://www.rand.org/publications/ randreview/issues/rr.12.02/benefits.html. [Accessed December 2005].

Grogger, Jeffrey. 2003. The effects of time limits, the EITC, and other policy changes on welfare use, work, and income among female-headed families. Review of Economics and Statistics 85:394–408.

Handler, Joel F., and Yehsekel Hasenfeld. 1997. We the Poor People: Work Poverty, & Welfare. New Haven: Yale.

Holzer, Harry J. 1999. Will employers hire welfare recipients? Recent survey evidence from Michigan. Journal of Policy Analysis & Management 18(3):449–472.

Hotz, V. Joseph, Charles H. Mullin, and John Karl Scholz. 1999. The Earned Income Tax Credit and labor market participation of families on welfare. In The Incentives of Government Programs and the Well-Being of Families, ed. Bruce Mayer and Greg Duncan, pages 97–143. Chicago, IL: Joint Center for Poverty Research.

Jaret, C., L. Reid, and R. Adelman. 2003. Black-white income inequality and metropolitan socioeconomic structure. Journal of Urban Affairs 25(3):305–333.

Jargowsky, Paul. 1997. Poverty and Place: Ghettos, Barrios, and the American City. New York: Russell Sage Foundation.

Jargowsky, Paul. 2003. The Stunning Progress, Hidden Problems: The Dramatic Decline of Concentrated Poverty in the 1990s. Washington, DC: Brookings Institution.

Jencks, Christopher. 2002. Liberal lessons from welfare reform. The American Prospect 13(13). http://www.prospect.org/web/page.ww?section=root&name= viewprint&articleID=6376. [Accessed December 2005].

McConville, Shannon, and Paul Ong. 2003. *The Trajectory of Poor Neighborhoods in Southern California, 1970–2000*. Washington, DC: Brookings Institution.

Mead, Lawrence. 1986. *Beyond Entitlement: The Social Obligations of Citizens*. New York: Free Press.

Meyer, Bruce D., and Dan T. Rosenbaum. 1999. *Welfare, the Earned Income Tax Credit and the Labor Supply of Single Mothers*. National Bureau of Economic Research working paper 7363. Washington, DC: National Bureau of Economic Research, September 1999.

Ong, Paul. 2002. Car ownership and welfare-to-work. *Journal of Policy Analysis and Management* 21(2):255–268.

Ong, Paul, James Spencer, Michela Zonta, Todd Nelson, Douglas Miller, and Julia Heintz-Mackoff. 2003. Economic cycles and Los Angeles neighborhoods, 1987–2001. Report to the John Randolph Haynes and Dora Haynes Foundation.

Pettit, Kathryn L. S., G. Thomas Kingsley, and Claudia J. Coulton. 2003. *Neighborhoods and Health: Building Evidence for Local Policy*. Washington, DC: The Urban Institute.

Piven, Frances Fox, and Richard A. Cloward. 1971. *Regulating the Poor: The Functions of Public Welfare*. New York: Pantheon.

Popkin, Susan J., Bruce Katz, Mary K. Cunningham, Karen D. Brown, Jeremy Gustafson, and Margery Austin Turner. *A Decade of HOPE VI; Research Findings and Policy Challenges*. The Urban Institute and the Brookings Institution.

Squires, D. G. 2003. Racial profiling, insurance style: Insurance redlining and the uneven development of metropolitan areas. *Journal of Urban Affairs* 25(4):391–410.

United States General Accounting Office. 1994. Welfare to Work: Current AFDC program not sufficiently focused on employment. GAO/HEHS-95–28. Washington, DC: United States General Accounting Office.

United States General Accounting Office. 1996. Welfare waiver implementation: States work to change welfare culture, community involvement, and service delivery. GAO/HEHS-96–105. Washington, DC: United States General Accounting Office.

Ventry, Dennis. 2000. The collision of tax and welfare politics: The political history of the Earned Income Tax Credit, 1969–99. *National Tax Journal* 53(4).

Wilson, William. 1987. *The Truly Disadvantaged*. Chicago: University of Chicago Press.

Work, Welfare, and Families and the Chicago Urban League. 2000. *Living with Welfare Reform: A Survey of Low-Income Families in Illinois*. Chicago, IL: Work, Welfare, and Families.

3   The Regional Nexus

*The Promise and Risk of Community-Based
Approaches to Metropolitan Equity*

Manuel Pastor, Chris Benner,
and Martha Matsuoka

Introduction

In recent years, community-based organizations (cbos) have sought to broaden their economic development activities by adding a regional component to their work. The fundamental rationale is simple: regional strategies that complement neighborhood-based approaches can help community-based organizations recognize new opportunities, connect to new resources and allies, and affect broad policies that structure the environment for all their activities. In the Delaware Valley around Philadelphia, for example, community leaders developed a regional Reinvestment Fund, which has provided valuable financing for affordable housing, community service, and workforce development programs in the region. In Milwaukee in the late 1990s, labor and community groups developed a regional plan that included a living wage ordinance, redirected transportation funds to central city workers to access regional job opportunities, and helped establish the Milwaukee Jobs Initiative, which over its first 6 years resulted in 1,400 residents gaining full-time employment in living wage jobs. In Los Angeles, a coalition of churches, labor organizations, and community organizations won a Community Benefits Agreement related to the expansion of a regional attraction—the Staples Convention Center—that included $1 million worth of parks improvement, $100,000 in seed funding to create job training programs through community organizations, local hiring, and the construction of 160 affordable housing units.

While the results seem impressive, engaging in these regionally oriented strategies also creates its own set of difficulties for community groups. It requires developing a whole new set of capacities beyond those required for neighborhood-based organizing and economic development. It means engaging with people with significantly different agendas and working to resolve the emerging conflicts without losing sight of one's own agenda. Indeed, one risk of regionalism is that it can take energy and focus away from other activities more directly linked to neighborhoods. Being effective at developing regional strategies thus requires a careful assessment of both the possibilities and challenges involved.

This chapter tries to take a realistic look at community-based regionalism's potential to affect community development and particularly community economic development in low-income and working poor urban neighborhoods. We begin with a discussion of why regionalism has become a new focus of both urban affairs literature and some policy practioners. We then focus on the promise this holds for those interested in promoting equity and community development, elaborating along the way on several different approaches to metropolitan equity, including a municipality-based approach that focuses on jurisdictional equity; a labor-based approach that considers new strategies for improving workers' outcomes; and a "community-based regionalism" (CBR) that has at its center community-based organizations in specific geographies. In this section of the chapter, we also offer specific examples of the successful application of such strategies; most of the analysis that follows takes this promise as a premise and so instead emphasizes the challenges involved in community adoption and implementation.

Given this emphasis on implementation issues, we then highlight the experience of one group of communities in the San Francisco Bay Area. All have been engaged in a foundation-sponsored set of "comprehensive community initiatives" or CCIS that seek to marry project-based community development with social network and citizen engagement approaches of community building. Each of these CCIS added a regional component to their work sometime in the development of their planning, providing an interesting set of experiments with different communities and different approaches, all within the same larger region. The communities include West Oakland, a large swath of East Palo Alto, and the Mayfair neighborhood in East San Jose. We believe that these cases may offer several interesting lessons for other community-based regional initiatives around the country, particularly those that focus on community economic development efforts.

We conclude the chapter by lifting up two of those lessons. The first is that CBR is not one-size-fits-all: for some neighborhoods interested in community development, CBR might make great sense; others may find themselves unable to agree on a regional agenda or preoccupied with internal issues of self-organization. The second main lesson we draw from both our cases and national practice is that CBR should not be thought of as development per se but rather as advocacy to affect development possibilities. The problem for CCIS is that this can draw organizations into sharp political conflicts, something that may run against the intersectoral collaboration emphasis typical of such initiatives.

Despite these complications, we argue that CBR, with its political/policy emphasis and its focus on scaling networks up to the region, actually reflects a return to some of the original purposes and activities of the community development field. Moreover, CBR is consistent with ongoing developments in the regional economy as well as increasing regional organizing by business interests, municipal actors, environmental advocates, and planning authorities. Therefore, getting into the regionalist game early in its arrival (or, some say, revival) might therefore be of great utility for those worried about the constraints America's urban landscape has placed on community development in many communities of color.

Why Regionalism?

One of the most important recent developments in the United States in the field of urban affairs is the emergence of the "new regionalism"—a framework that stresses the importance of the region as a fundamental scale for understanding and addressing urban problems (see Dreier, Mollenkopf, and Swanstrom 2001, chapter 6; Henton, Melville, and Walesh 1997; Bullard 1998, Katz 2000, Pastor et al. 2000). The economic argument for a regional approach is partly derived from a scale argument about government services, many of which might be more efficiently delivered on a regional basis. Consolidating services could also level the regional playing field, reducing the hassles many businesses experience when grappling with multiple jurisdictions and regulations.

But this scale argument itself derives from an underlying notion that the regional economy is an increasingly important scale of economic organization: it is where businesses clusters and investments stick. No longer limited to industrial manufacturing industries, the driving industrial clusters of today are more likely to be in information- and knowledge-driven sectors, including computer technology, telecommunications, pharmaceuticals, entertainment, finance, or advanced business services. Success in these "cluster" industries is often driven again not directly by global competition, but instead by the skill level of the local workforce, the quality of life in the region (which attracts more talented labor), and the nature of regional physical and institutional infrastructure, with the latter running the gamut from transportation systems to the community college and regional university systems. Partly as a result, a wide range of business organizations, such as the Silicon Valley Manufacturing Group and Chicago Metropolis 2020, have taken the lead in promoting regional investments in transportation and affordable housing, while other business organizations, such as Joint Venture: Silicon Valley Network and the Hampton Roads Partnership around the Norfolk, Virginia area, have worked to encourage regional business clusters and development strategies (FutureWorks 2004; Lampe, Parr, and Woodward 2004).

The focus on the regional economy has also led to new efforts and dimension in workforce development. Groups representing both employers and employees have recognized that industrial clusters are often defined by the regional commute shed for workers and have begun to work together to provide the sort of job training efforts that can keep labor skilled and businesses rooted. The result has been the emergence of numerous innovative workforce intermediaries, including the Wisconsin Regional Training Partnership, a joint effort by employers and unions that started with training incumbent workers to help manufacturing firms stay competitive and has since gone on to train entry-level workers. Many of these regional workforce intermediary efforts have also been useful at addressing issues of low wages and job loss, including efforts by Project QUEST in San Antonio, Texas, to train displaced workers for new jobs in the health sector and by Cleveland's WIRE-Net to train unemployed residents for positions in precision manufacturing (Benner et al. 2001; Bernhardt et al. 2001; Giloth 2004; Kazis 2004).

The regional level has also captured the interest of people working to address persistent poverty in inner-city neighborhoods, particularly neighborhoods of color (Barron 2003). Regional and racial inequalities are, after all, inextricably linked, as institutionalized racism reflected in a range of local, state, and federal government policies have contributed to the creation of racially and economically segregated space (Wilson 1996; Pastor 2001a; Chapter 1 in this volume). Discriminatory housing lending policies based on race, for example, offered metropolitan mobility to some but locked others into designated inner-city areas (powell 1998). Exclusionary zoning practices, including the prohibition of multifamily housing in upscale neighborhoods, created additional obstacles for poor families in search of affordable housing in white suburban communities (Powell 1998). Racial disparities, then, are frozen into the regional landscape of opportunity—and in the view of Powell and others, a regional approach will be necessary to reverse the trend.

Noting the relationship between inner-city decline and suburban sprawl, some have argued that "Smart Growth"—with attention to redirecting growth to central cities in order to prevent the consumption of open space and farmland—could be part of a recipe for poverty reduction and racial equity (PolicyLink 2002). Others have suggested that the metropolitan agenda could also help both theorists and practioners move past the place versus people debate so prevalent in community development—that is, the concern that fragmented approaches to improving conditions in poorer communities (for example, separate efforts at housing and workforce development) will lead to economic and social imbalance, with successful housing development chasing out poor residents, or successful job placement via workforce intermediaries leading some to abandon old neighborhoods. Regionalism offers the possibility to think about both people and place, trying to simultaneously raise living standards by connecting to employment anywhere in a region *and* improving local livability to retain successful residents.

However, regionalism also challenges community development thinking itself. Many past approaches to such development tend to be inward-looking, focused on neighborhood problems and assets, even when major decisions about jobs, housing, and transportation are made at a regional level. David Rusk (1999) in *Inside Game, Outside Game* argues this position forcefully. In a striking analysis of poor neighborhoods, Rusk finds that locally focused community development efforts generally have quite modest economic impacts (compared to the effects of overarching regional forces such as the state of the metro economy) and instead suggests that the route to development relies on a regional focus. A similar position is taken by Jeremy Nowak (1997:7), who argues that the "future of a more effective community development requires an explicit emphasis on poverty alleviation, which in turn requires linking the possibilities of the inner city to the regional economy." Certainly, the workforce development efforts briefly reviewed above are all about making the connections for individual workers to the broader economy.

But the key question for community developers goes beyond individual fortunes: can an equity-oriented regional approach can really help poor neighborhoods? Even if Rusk, Nowak, and others overstate the case about the limits to community development and the advantages of a regional strategy, the emphasis on regional levers and levels may offer a useful counterbalance to the traditional approach. Before we explore these strategies further, we need to more clearly specify community-based regionalism and its relationship to community development.

WHAT IS COMMUNITY-BASED REGIONALISM?

Community-based regionalism is a subset of a broader category of equity-oriented regionalism. One variant of this equity-oriented regionalism is focused on the relationship between cities and suburbs, stressing the key role of municipal authorities as regional actors. This perspective itself has two strands. The first emphasizes the possible mutual gain from recognizing the common fortunes of all those situated in a region (see, for example, Voith 1992 and Pastor et al. 2000). Another strand of this perspective is less concerned about widespread mutual gain and instead focuses on the common interests of inner cities and lower-income inner-ring suburbs *vis-à-vis* outlying and more recent suburbs. In his seminal book *Metropolitics*, Myron Orfield (1997) notes that older inner-ring suburbs are suffering from economic dislocations and experiencing a rising presence of poor and minority residents; as such, their dilemmas have become more connected to the cities many of their residents once sought to escape. Orfield suggest that the best way to address this dilemma is through regional tax-sharing to redistribute funds to central cities and more distressed suburbs.

But alliance building between municipalities is difficult: older, problem-ridden inner-ring suburbs are faced with the choice of striking a deal with their often minority central cities or seeking alliances with the whiter ex-burbs, where many inner-ring residents wish eventually to escape. Moreover, the implications for community development of municipal equity are somewhat unclear: fiscal balance between cities and suburbs, a key tenet of this "municipal-based regionalism," holds the promise of improvement for central cities, but there is no guarantee that this will translate to development opportunities in the poorest areas of the central city.

A second broad variant of equity-oriented regionalism is rooted in the labor movement. Recent years have seen the revitalization of central labor councils, federations of local unions organized at the level of regional labor markets (Ness and Eimer 2001). This "metro union" approach combines a bit of carrot and a bit of stick: there are attempts to work with employers to raise skill levels and retain "good jobs" even as there are strategies to raise the floor for the lowest-skilled workers (AFL-CIO Human Resources Development Institute 1998; Luria and Rogers 1997). Some of these efforts focus on workforce development, such as the previously mentioned Wisconsin Regional Training Partnership. What concerns us here is when regional union-allied institutions go beyond workforce per se and begin to address broader issues of community development and planning.

One of the most sophisticated examples of this sort of approach is the South Bay Labor Council and its affiliated policy research arm, Working Partnerships USA (WPUSA), in San Jose, California. The council rose up partly to counter the influence of several business-oriented regional initiatives to stir economic recovery, including the efforts of Joint Venture: Silicon Valley Network. One of its initial policy successes was a typical "bread and butter" labor issue: the 1998 passage of a Living Wage law in San Jose that at the time gave the city the highest wage level of any such ordinance in the country. But both the labor council and WPUSA quickly went well beyond Living Wages per se, participating in debates about smart growth, suggesting new approaches to affordable housing (see Bhargava et al. 2001), and pushing for a broad array of community benefits from redevelopment efforts (see Muller et al. 2003).

While there is much to be said for this approach, particularly its ability to improve outcomes for broad groups of workers within a region, the tie to community development in minority communities can sometimes be tentative. The best of the union efforts are rooted in the emerging workforce, including immigrant workers, and eschew the racial exclusivity of past union practices (see Vargas and Ong in this volume). Yet community wariness about unions remains, particularly given the estrangement of many minorities from unions in the past, and the very strength of unions—at least, relative to poor inner-city communities—makes some community organizers concerned that their specific development and neighborhood interests will get downplayed in any coalition.

A third variant of equity-oriented regionalism has emerged from both the earlier principles of the community development field and some frustrations with how it has evolved over time. This approach, emerging from the activities of a range of community-based actors around the country, represents a distinct new way to address problems of persistent poverty in poor neighborhoods. The emergence of different types of community development organizations—community-based organizations (CBOs), community development corporations (CDCs), and comprehensive community initiatives (CCIs)—reflect political and economic trends and changes.

Though there is obviously a long history of community-based activity in this country, community-based organizations saw a significant resurgence in the late 1950s and 1960s. In the context of opposition to urban renewal, the civil rights movement, the urban crisis and the social upheaval of the era, CBOs emerged as specific attempts to improve the social and economic circumstances of residents of poor, primarily inner-city neighborhoods. With organic ties to social movements both large and small, CBOs during this period tended to be strongly focused on mobilization of community residents, frequently advocating not only for specific services and projects that would benefit neighborhood residents but also for changes in local and federal urban policies, with an explicit goal of transforming power relations in society.[1] Over time, however, many CDCs became primarily focused on more concrete services such as building affordable housing, providing meaningful job training, and promoting neighborhood business districts.

The narrowing of the community development movement to this "bricks and mortar" approach received significant criticism in the early 1990s, as the U.S. urban crisis deepened and the inability of narrow CDC-based approaches to transform conditions in poor neighborhoods became readily apparent. As a result, the community development movement has begun to pay more attention to broadening the focus of community development efforts, particularly paying more attention to the social dimensions of urban poverty and the importance of consolidating community voice as part of a strategy for confronting persistent urban poverty (Walsh 1997). As part of this attempt to return to the roots of community development in community organizing, foundations around the country began developing CCIs, place-based strategies that integrate social network approaches to project-based development approaches.

What does this trinity of CBOs, CDCs, and CCIs imply for community-based regionalism (CBR)? In our view, CBR takes as its starting point the need to understand, challenge, and work with outside forces in the process of community development. It recognizes that the lack of development in inner-city minority neighborhoods is not merely the result of a failure to invest in the local neighborhood, which often results in the escape of both consumer dollars (due to a lack of retail amenities) and the middle-class consumers themselves. It is also the result of isolation from positive regional economic trends, and the only way to secure appropriate regional support for local issues may be to fight for attention, a task that takes advantage of the traditional strength in organizing and conflict of CBOs.

Why would CDCs and CCIs, both of which are so spatially or geographically focused, want to purse CBR? It is partly because the CBR perspective appropriately complicates the notion that the answer for neighborhood poverty lies primarily in the attraction of business back to the central city in order to overcome the spatial mismatch induced by the suburbanization of employment (see Pastor 2001b; Wilson 1996; Chapter 5 this volume). CBR instead notes that highly successful neighborhoods, particularly those that are higher income, are often quite jobs-scarce; they are, however, rich in amenities, available transportation, and networks to employment. As Nowak (1997:9) argues, "Strong neighborhoods are destination places and incubators; they are healthy, not because they are self-contained or self-sufficient but because their residents are appropriately linked to non-neighorhood opportunities." In this view, the task of workforce development is to prepare people for available opportunities, the task of community development is to make communities livable so that residents do not depart, and the task of CBR is crafting the connective tissue and supportive policies that will make this possible.

Examples of Community-Based Regionalism

What are the strategies of CBR? In general, CBR includes linkage efforts that connect low-income residents to dynamic growth sectors in the regional economy; advocacy initiatives that try to make equity more central in regional policy decisions such as transportation, environment, and workforce development; strategies that seek to place affordable housing in suburban areas with higher accessibility to employment or to improve indigenous home ownership in low-income neighborhoods on the edge of gentrification; and economic reform initiatives that target the quality of jobs being created in the regional economy and seeking to promote economic and workforce development that better serves the needs of low-income residents (PolicyLink 2002). The potential effectiveness of these strategies can be seen in the work of a range of groups around the country.

In South Los Angeles, for example, a locally based group of organizers under the banner of a grassroots organizing project named AGENDA sought to challenge the decision of the City of Los Angeles to award a $70 million subsidy to persuade the Dreamworks Studio to locate in West Los Angeles. Rather than what might be thought of as the usual neighborhood approach—either kill the subsidy to redistribute the funds to local needs, or insist that the place of employment be situated in South Los Angeles—AGENDA instead catalyzed and anchored the Metropolitan Alliance, a coalition of community, labor, social service providers, and churches to fight for a commitment to train young students from inner-city communities of color for jobs in this powerful (and persistent) regional industry.

Faced with a local problem of development, AGENDA had targeted a regional industry and adopted a regionalist approach to job training: its focus was not on bringing jobs near workers—as it was highly unlikely that Hollywood would suddenly build studios in South Los Angeles—but rather on generating accessible training opportunities that would, in turn, allow job seekers to gain a foothold in a growing and regionally rooted "cluster" industry. Both the workforce perspective and the political organizing to make this happen had to occur on a regional scale, with alliances needed between AGENDA's grassroots membership in South L.A. and progressive efforts in other parts of the Los Angeles landscape. The result, one brought about in conjunction with the efforts of sympathetic public officials, was a multimillion-dollar program involving the community college system that has since morphed into a larger program involving multiple studios called Workplace Hollywood (see Pastor et al. 2000; Pastor 2001a; Soja 2000; PolicyLink 2000.)

One of the CBR examples most rooted in the community development world itself has occurred in Chicago's West Garfield Park.[2] There, members of the small Bethel Lutheran Church began in 1979 trying to fight the poverty and hopelessness that characterized the neighborhood. Over the next twenty years, Bethel New Life, Inc., has grown to be a nationally recognized, innovative CDC with over 300 employees and has created over

1,000 new housing units, placed over 7,000 people in living wage jobs, and brought $110 million into its community.

Bethel's regional perspective first emerged in the group's efforts to re-develop the Garfield Park Conservatory, a once nationally renowned attraction that had fallen into disrepair. Arguing that this local resource was an underused regional attraction, Bethel worked with the Chicago Park District to renovate the site and to host a Dale Chihuly glass exhibit that drew over 500,000 visitors in the first nine months. The park and conservatory is now a vibrant site for multiple cultural events and exhibits throughout the year, and brings significant numbers of visitors to the neighborhood.

A more far-reaching example of Bethel's regional perspective emerged in 1992, when the Green Line, a rail line that ran through the neighborhood, was threatened with closure due to low ridership. The CDC recognized that closure would damage the ability of neighborhood residents to reach suburban areas where lower-skill employment was growing. But Bethel's leadership also recognized that suburban residents further out on the Green Line had a common interest in maintaining the route, because they used it to access downtown employment. As a result, the CDC was able to form an unusual alliance of city and suburb. The two eventually convinced the Chicago Transit Authority not only to maintain the line but also to make $300 million in capital improvements and upgrade its service. The Lake-Pulsaski station in the neighborhood has now become the hub of Bethel's transit-oriented development strategy, with a 23,000-square-foot commercial center that will house a day care facility, commercial enterprises, a clinic, employment services, and job training.

The notion of unusual alliances also lies at the heart of the work of the Northwest Indiana Federation of Interfaith Organizations.[3] The effort began in 1994 when three neighborhoods in the greater Gary, Indiana, region, with the help of the Gamaliel Foundation, formed a regional federation of churches to begin tackling the shared conditions facing the urban core. Their first campaign, "Operation Holy Ground," sought to rid their neighborhoods of drug houses. In the wake of progress in this arena, however, the federation realized that no matter how many abandoned buildings were removed, the systemic causes of concentrated poverty still remained.

The federation thus began focusing on regional transportation as a strategy to ensure that residents had access to jobs and basic goods and services, and organizers and leaders began to call for regional transportation that would link urban core residents to outlying opportunities. They soon realized that an efficient regional transportation system was being hindered by the fragmentation of local transportation systems, which were often designed to make access to white suburban areas more difficult for central-city blacks. This fragmentation, however, also inconvenienced city-bound suburban commuters, whose treks to higher-paying downtown employment were made more difficult by the transit system's inefficiency.

Recognizing that the issues and voices of the predominantly white suburban communities were also ignored through the fragmented transit authorities, the Interfaith Federation reframed its transportation program and redesigned its organizing and advocacy strategy to work in coalition with these suburban interests. The result: establishment of a regional community-based coalition with enough influence and power over elected officials to direct establishment of a single transportation authority that meets the needs of the region, including and particularly the urban core.

The positive impacts of these regional strategies communities are clear. What is murkier is how we go from "here" to "there." How can minority communities already under economic stress effectively engage regionally, build coalitions, and bring the real benefits of regional development to their areas? Which neighborhoods are more or less ripe for taking on a regional view? What difference does it make if the actor is involved in a CCI trying to combine elements from both the CBO and CDC models—and what difference does it make that many CCIs are foundation-sponsored place-based initiative? We take up these questions below in the context of a specific set of cases in the Bay Area.

CBR AND CCIS IN THE SAN FRANCISCO BAY AREA

In this section, we consider the experience of three comprehensive community initiatives grappling with a regional perspective in the San Francisco Bay Area. Each of the CCIs considered was part of an effort funded and supported by the Hewlett Foundation's Neighborhood Improvement Initiative. These Hewlett-sponsored CCIs emerged just as several other foundation-sponsored CCI efforts were sprouting in other parts of the United States, including Los Angeles, Atlanta, and Baltimore. The foundation made its first planning investment in the Mayfair neighborhood of East San Jose in 1996, when it funded the Mayfair Improvement Initiative (MII). It later made investments in West Oakland's 7th Street/McClymonds Corridor in 1998, which led to the establishment of the 7th Street/McClymonds Initiative organization (also known as 7th Street), and in a section of East Palo Alto in 1999 which led to the creation of a group called One East Palo Alto, or OEPA (see Figure 3.1 for a map; basic demographics and other data for the three are shown in Table 3.1, with comparison made to the counties of which they are a part).

Initially, connecting the neighborhoods to regional dynamics was not an explicit part of the early programming. The "new regionalism"—new in that it incorporates equity and economic competitiveness as well as administrative efficiency and an antisprawl environmental agenda—was just emerging as a refined concept in the mid-1990s. Newer still was the movement for CBR. However, the element was added to the CCI programming and the sites had varying experiences. The MII became actively engaged in regional discussions and explicitly incorporated regionalism into their agenda. The 7th Street Initiative, which had a significant presence of community organizers, went regional early in its thinking and alliance building, but did not fully attend to local tensions and was thus unsustainable as a CCI. OEPA struggled to gain significant traction on the regional level

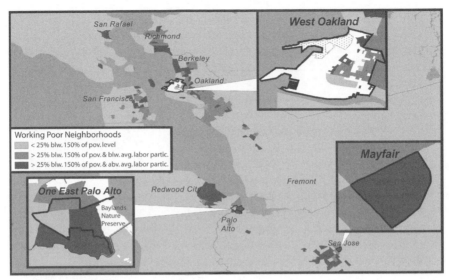

FIGURE 3.1. Neighborhood improvement initiatives in the San Francisco Bay Area mapped against tract-level poverty and labor force participation. Note: Blank area in West Oakland contains no persons. Dotted area is lightly populated and not included in analysis.

although it eventually became a key part of its strategic thinking; while this had something to do with its internal evolution as a program, a striking challenge was that the internal dynamics of the site actually led to different regionalist interests. We develop these points further below.[4]

Seeing the Bay

The CCIs began in the midst of a period in which the Bay Area was seen as the heart not only of the New Economy but of the world economy. At the center of the region's economic engine was the Silicon Valley: its tech industry—the manufacture of computer components, software engineering, and eventually web design—comprised a full 27.3 percent of private employment in the San Jose metro area in the 1998–2001 period, well above the state share of 7.1 percent in the same era.[5] This proved to be a great boon to growth—but it has also meant the region suffered disproportionately in the subsequent downturn, as business investment plunged and the tech and telecommunication sectors began a sharp collapse in early 2001.

It was, however, not simply rapid economic growth—with its more abundant fiscal resources, clearer reasons to connect to employment, and upward pressures on housing prices, even in neglected areas—that set the context. Equally important was a strong regional consciousness that had emerged in the Bay Area. There were, of course, precedents for regional business and social organization in the Bay Area. Public officials in the 9-county area have long been brought together under the rubric of the Association of Bay Area Governments (ABAG), and the Bay Area Council, a group of private-sector leaders across the region, has been in operation since

TABLE 3.1. Comparing the nIIs to the counties

	One East Palo Alto	San Mateo County	Mayfair	Santa Clara County	West Oakland	Alameda County
Population	13,855	707,161	8,349	1,682,585	14,127	1,443,741
Anglo	3.1%	49.7%	2.9%	44.0%	5.6%	40.8%
Latino	61.6%	21.8%	79.8%	24.0%	17.3%	19.0%
African American	25.1%	3.3%	1.8%	2.5%	65.7%	14.4%
Asian Pacific Islander	7.9%	21.1%	13.6%	25.7%	7.9%	20.8%
Other	2.3%	4.1%	2.0%	3.7%	3.5%	5.0%
Foreign born	43.2%	32.3%	59.2%	34.1%	16.9%	27.2%
Noncitizen	34.1%	16.5%	42.2%	20.0%	10.6%	15.4%
Foreign born, entered in 1990s	44.8%	36.5%	50.2%	46.3%	34.7%	42.3%
Foreign born, entered in 1980s	34.0%	29.5%	33.2%	29.8%	48.8%	32.1%
Foreign born, entered early	21.2%	33.9%	16.6%	23.9%	16.5%	25.6%
Median age of population	25.3	36.8	26.6	34.0	29.3	34.5
Median age of African Americans	37.3	37.4	33.0	32.3	30.5	33.5
Median age of Latinos	21.8	27.3	24.7	26.1	24.1	26.3
Median household income	$53,056	$70,819	$53,833	$74,335	$22,073	$55,946
Median family income	$50,929	$80,737	$51,685	$81,717	$23,360	$65,857
Per capita income	$13,391	$36,045	$12,233	$32,795	$12,996	$26,680
Total households	2,784	254,103	1,711	565,863	4,874	523,366
Single-person households	10.8%	24.6%	11.6%	21.4%	30.8%	26.0%
Married-couple households	55.1%	53.0%	58.6%	54.9%	21.1%	47.0%
Households with a single male head	8.0%	4.3%	9.9%	4.9%	7.3%	4.9%
Households with a single female head	22.0%	10.1%	15.7%	10.0%	32.7%	13.0%
Nonfamily households	4.0%	8.0%	4.2%	8.7%	8.1%	9.2%
Households with children	1,460	78,959	898	197,245	1,706	170,762
Married-couple households with children	72.8%	79.3%	75.8%	79.7%	34.2%	72.1%
Single-male-headed households with children	6.6%	5.6%	7.5%	5.8%	9.0%	6.4%
Single-female-headed households with children	20.5%	15.1%	16.7%	14.5%	56.9%	21.5%
Housing tenure: owners	59.3%	61.4%	40.2%	59.8%	22.7%	54.7%
Housing tenure: renters	40.7%	38.6%	59.8%	40.2%	77.3%	45.3%

1945. The South Bay has had its own set of organizations, including the Santa Clara Valley (now Silicon Valley) Manufacturing Group, an organization founded by David Packard that has long lobbied for improvements in regional infrastructure and been willing to persuade both business and consumers to pay increased taxes to foot the bill.

But the slump of the early 1990s, induced by defense spending cutbacks and a tech slowdown, created the conditions for a new business-led organization called Joint Venture: Silicon Valley Network (JV:SVN). JV:SVN developed a regional indicators project, promoted economic clusters based on network models, and developed the notion that firms and cities in the region should "collaborate to compete." It was soon celebrated as the archetype for a new set of approaches that were eventually encouraged throughout the state by an Irvine Foundation–sponsored project to incubate "civic entrepreneurs."

In short, regionalism was in the air. But critics also rightly noted that a rising regional tide was not lifting all boats. San Jose's WPUSA, the labor-affiliated think tank arm of the South Bay Central Labor Council, documented growing disparities in its own Silicon Valley backyard, warned of the growth of temporary work and volatile work lives, and pursued such issues as a living wage ordinance, housing policy, and community benefits agreements. Urban Habitat, an Oakland-based group long focused on issues of environmental justice, began to identify issues of gentrification as critical to community stability, issued an important report calling for regional tax-sharing, and organized a Social Equity Caucus to bring together various community leaders who were concerned about the region's evolution.

The business sector, at least in the heady days of the 1990s boom, became increasingly sympathetic to the calls for change. The motivation behind this sympathy was, in part, purely economic: with demand high and land scarce, developers were interested in the economic development of areas they might once have passed by. Business leaders were also interested in improving the general level of human capital in the Bay Area, noting that the labor shortages of the 1990s might be addressed not only by importing immigrant engineers but also by developing "home-grown" talent (Joint Venture, 2002). But it was more than just crass economic interest—the policy orientation and style of the business groups had shifted as well. The business-dominated Bay Area Council began working with community organizations and a series of important intermediaries—including the National Economic Development and Law Center and PolicyLink in Oakland—to develop a Community Capital Investment Initiative designed to spur private investment in distressed areas. Joint Venture: Silicon Valley revised its signature Annual Index of Silicon Valley to include measures of poverty, income distribution, and human capital.

Other business groups teamed up with housing advocates to lobby for affordable housing in communities that were willing to take on in-fill housing and higher density. This was of special interest to communities like West Oakland, East Palo Alto, and East San Jose, all of whom felt the sting of rising housing prices. Displacement of current residents became a particular worry as longer and more painful traffic jams—caused by the region's explosive growth and the failure of its housing production to keep pace—led some newly wealthy young workers to buy property in inner-city areas. While housing prices in Mayfair were about 60 percent of the Santa Clara County average during 1996–1997, they rose to seventy percent by 2001–2002. West Oakland also saw a dramatic rise in relative prices, from around 30 percent of the Alameda County average to nearly 60 percent over the same period. But the most important and displacing surge took place in East Palo Alto; here the ratio of local prices to the county average rose from 55 percent in 1996–1997 to nearly 80 percent in 2001–2002.[6]

This, then, was the scenario facing the three CCIs as they began their various journeys: a robust economy, a business sector beginning to think regionally, an increasingly vibrant set of progressive regional intermediaries and advocates, pressures on housing stock and hence community stability, and even some interest by businesses boxed out of other areas by over-development and more open to investment opportunities in poorer neighborhoods. In short, there seemed to be a real possibility for neighborhood initiatives to hook up with sympathetic regional actors and even market forces and finally leverage the region to make a difference in their communities.

Taking up the Torch

Were the CCIs able to pick up the regional torch? One fact to keep in mind in any assessment is that the Bay Area economy collapsed as 2001 dawned, a slowdown driven mainly by the sharp decline in the technology sector and its affiliates in telecommunications and web design. Like any first-mover, the earliest CCI organization out the door, the MII, already had ties to business and regional leaders before its attention was diverted to overall recuperation, giving this case a special edge compared to the others.

But the fact that these ties were built at all speaks volumes: early on in its process, Mayfair staff developed a regional advisory board to keep the CCI in touch with broader trends. It also had a singular consciousness-raising experience when it combined its local organizing around health education in the community with an effort led by local unions and community-based networks to lobby county and city authorities to use dollars from a tobacco tax settlement to extend health insurance to all children regardless of documentation status. The resulting victory had especially positive impacts in the highly immigrant Mayfair neighborhood—and it illustrated the power of complementing a local approach with a regional alliance.

The power of combining local organizing and a regional perspective was also seen when the MII decided to participate in the Strong Neighborhoods Initiative (SNI) launched in 2000 by the City of San Jose and its Redevelopment Agency. SNI stemmed from a city commitment to use redevelopment money to help neighborhoods after years of supporting downtown development; because MII was highly organized and understood the larger context, it was able to quickly form a neighborhood advisory council for the SNI and consequently became one of the largest recipients of SNI aid.

Thus, as MII prepared to wean itself off Hewlett Foundation funding, it went through a strategic planning exercise in which a regional scan was one of the prominent elements. As a result, MII shifted from a relative smorgasbord of projects to three focus areas: employment, housing, and education. It also came to a clearer idea of its role—that of an intermediary linking regional resources and local needs—and Mayfair staff began to participate actively in activities organized by one of the CBR umbrellas for the Bay, Urban Habitat. Mayfair, in short, had caught the regionalist bug.

West Oakland would seem to have been uniquely positioned to take advantage of a regionalist strategy. The East Bay itself was on a special economic lift-off as the 7th Street Initiative came online, partly because development opportunities on the peninsula were being exhausted. A new mayor, Jerry Brown, came to power in 1998 with an agenda aimed at revitalizing the downtown so proximate to West Oakland. West Oakland itself is very near the Port of Oakland, a place where employment was slated to grow and local authorities were open to the creation of opportunities for nearby residents.

The 7th Street Initiative did develop some regional momentum. Several of the early board members were disposed toward a regionalist approach, including one who received a special leadership award from the Bay Area Transportation and Land Use Coalition for his work on a project launched by ABAG, the area's regional council of governments. The first executive director had also been involved in the environmental justice movement, a framework that lends itself to regional thinking, and several leaders in the neighborhood passed through a leadership training program organized by Urban Habitat that was viewed as the precursor to the creation of a new community-based cadre for progressive regionalism.

Unfortunately, board and staff turnover meant that those interested in regionalism were soon looking for other venues for their political and community commitments. The first executive director left and the organization proved itself unable to find and agree on a replacement. For a complex set of reasons, the Hewlett Foundation made a decision to pull the plug, and the 7th Street Initiative was disbanded. Interestingly, this did not end regionalist impulses; as it turns out, many of the initiative's leaders participated in a special summit of community-based regionalists in the Bay Area entitled "Bridging the Bay" organized by Urban Habitat. Without the base of the CCI organization itself, however, this stands as a tale of separation of the CCI from the local constituency rather than a regional-local link.

The third story unfolded in East Palo Alto. The newest of the initiatives, it was still getting its sea legs on a community plan when it was presented with a regional challenge: the discount retail chain IKEA announced its desire to place a store in East Palo Alto, which the company saw as a valuable crossroads of regional transportation networks and one of the few areas in the region with readily developable land. The city and some advocates painted IKEA as a potential source of sales tax revenue and generator of entry-level positions. However, IKEA was also viewed as a potential disruption to the local community, primarily because it would add to a traffic problem already exacerbated by commuters who passed through East Palo Alto on their way to jobs in the Silicon Valley. IKEA, according to these critics, was an external imposition: in criticizing the idea, one resident suggested that "IKEA will serve the Bay Area, not East Palo Alto."[7]

This was, of course, exactly the point: attracting a branch of this home furnishing chain was supposed to capture retail dollars that were being spent elsewhere in the region and thereby address some of the fiscal disparities plaguing East Palo Alto. Despite being a pressing issue through 2001–2002 and one in which the regional-community connection was clear, OEPA, the Hewlett funded CCI, took no explicit or implicit position in a crucial election in which the issue was decided by the voters. Caution on the regional front remained characteristic of OEPA for some time. While this reflected the fact that OEPA was a new organization focused on the initial steps of building community, the caution also stemmed from some sharp differences within the community that resulted in different regional interests. These differences could not be easily negotiated or resolved, an issue we highlight below.

In 2003, however, OEPA became increasingly interested in the regional dimension, with recent organizational goals including the capacity to broker regional resources and develop leadership to advocate for policy change in the areas of economic independence, education, and neighborhood safety. This suggests the importance of phasing: OEPA required significant internal work before its leadership and staff could look outward.

Analyzing the Patterns

In these three neighborhood initiatives we have one CCI that became deeply engaged in regional processes relatively early and saw that as a way to accomplish local goals, one CCI which sought engagement but found itself vulnerable at home, and one CCI which was very preoccupied with internal affairs and thus eschewed early action when directly presented with a regional opportunity. What explains the pattern, particularly given that these were all in the same broad political economy and were, in fact, part of a family of comprehensive initiatives funded and guided by the same foundation?

First, the nature of poverty seems to matter. Much of the thinking around community-based regionalism assumes that poorer neighborhoods suffer from a problem of isolation, particularly economic isolation, and that the main tasks are to devise employment programs to connect employees and employers, create transportation programs to insure that workers can get to jobs, and attract business investors into the areas to take advantage of a workforce that is ready and willing (Pastor 2001b). Regional workforce intermediaries can help the process along, particularly the sort that provide training to both equip employees with better skills and help regional industries upgrade their competitiveness (Giloth 2004). However, when jobs are out of reach for other reasons, such as child care needs, disability, lack of basic education, and other issues, it may matter little that regional opportunities are available.

Glancing at Table 3.1, note that of the three sites, West Oakland had the highest rate of individuals living below the poverty line but the lowest rate of those living between 150 and 200 percent line, a usual marker of the working poor. Indeed, West Oakland's share in that category was not far off that of its host county, while both Mayfair and OEPA diverged sharply from their respective counties in this measure. This is further seen in Figure 3.1, which shows those Bay Area census tracts where the percent of those above the 150 percent poverty cut-off exceeds 25 percent and the male labor force participation rates exceeds the regional average for such poor tracts. Note that Mayfair falls entirely into this category, while most of OEPA and a significant portion of an adjoining neighborhood is working poor.[8] West Oakland, by contrast, tends more to the nonworking poor, with an extraordinarily high rate of employment disability and rates of female-headed households with children twice as high (at about twenty percent of all households) as in Mayfair or OEPA. Thus, we would expect regionalism to be a harder immediate fit with West Oakland, even though a broad group of activists were interested.

Second, the size of the neighborhood relative to its immediate jurisdiction seems to matter. Mayfair is a small neighborhood in the third largest city in California; even thinking about local authorities requires a pseudo-regionalist framework simply because of the scale of the municipality. OEPA was about half of the city of East Palo Alto, and residents were therefore able to act at the scale of the city itself; but since East Palo Alto is a small city, this led to more inward-looking thought and action. West Oakland is a distressed neighborhood in a medium-sized city, a seemingly perfect fit for engaging on a higher scale *and* forming alliances with other neighborhoods. The problem for the area is that other Oakland neighborhoods, such as Fruitvale and San Antonio, were already attracting city, foundation, and regional attention and having great success at understanding regional opportunities (such as Fruitvale's decision to turn a rapid transit station into an opportunity for local economic and retail development). West Oakland was thus less prominent.

Third, the three neighborhoods seem to have faced different opportunity structures and experienced different comfort levels with regard to drawing upon external resources. Mayfair was a poor area in one of the most dynamic economies in the state, and, as such, it attracted the attention of business and civic leaders, for whom it represented both a significant contradiction to the image of regional prosperity and a significant opportunity to do better. The city of San Jose was also under considerable pressure to do better by its neighborhoods after decades of redevelopment activity focused on its downtown. Thus, Mayfair found itself with ready allies, including city officials.

West Oakland, by contrast, faced a less dynamic business sector—the East Bay was still limping forward in the 1990s even as the Silicon Valley turned into an economic dynamo—and the attention of its new mayor was focused on the central business district. As for OEPA, San Mateo business had a less distinct personality: important tech companies are there but they seem to draw their geographic identity from Silicon Valley to the south and the San Francisco financial center to the north.

With regard to external resources, Mayfair was the only one of the three CCIs to sustain an advisory board of prominent officials, policy makers, and private sector actors. Mayfair was more used to outsiders in general: while many of the leaders of the MII were long-time residents, this was also an area that had traditionally been an immigrant portal. The 2000 census indicated that about 48 percent of residents above the age five had been living in the same house for five years, three percentage points lower than that for the county as a whole. By contrast, 57 percent of residents in OEPA had been living in their homes for at least five years, slightly higher than that for the county in which the neighborhood is situated.

Fourth, the areas also had different populations and tensions around identifying regional issues and strategies. Mayfair was predominantly Latino and largely low-income but working, hence there were broad commonalities around getting access to health insurance, improving basic adult education, and other such measures. Tensions did exist between native born and more recent immigrants, but the history of the local area as an immigrant gateway meant that even native-born residents were aware of and somewhat comfortable with addressing the needs of the immigrant population.[9]

West Oakland is largely African American and actually has a level of foreign-born residents that is below the county average, a contrast to the relatively high immigrant presence in the rest of the NIIs; partly as a result, West Oakland was slightly out of touch with immigrant empowerment dynamics occurring elsewhere in the region and tended to be more reflective of the perspective and needs of its overwhelmingly African American community. Moreover, as noted above, West Oakland is not ranked in the Bay Area census tracts we have deemed working poor and it is also predominantly renters rather than home owners; these two facts gave the community common ground in maintaining social welfare programs and resisting gentrification.

OEPA was the most complex of the sites. First, consider home ownership: glancing back at the data in Table 3.1, we see a startling fact: nearly 60 percent of homes were owned in OEPA, essentially the same as in San Mateo County as a whole and much higher than the figures for Mayfair and West Oakland.[10] What this meant was that the pressure of rising housing prices that led many in the other sites to worry about the regional influence of gentrification was also giving some locals in OEPA a reason to celebrate: assets held for years through tougher times were finally coming up in value. Renters and homeowners had potentially very different interests.

This difference in renting and ownership was complicated by demographics. While all the areas had experienced an influx of Latinos, particularly immigrants, during the 1990s, East Palo Alto had experienced the most massive demographic shift, with a 32 percent decline in the African American population (from 9,727 to 6,641) and a doubling of the Latino population (from 8,527 to 17,346).[11] Interestingly, the home ownership rates for African Americans and the burgeoning Latino population were divergent but

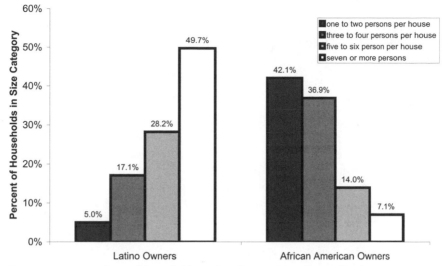

FIGURE 3.2. Ownership and household size by ethnicity in one East Palo Alto

not wildly so: 66 percent of black households in the OEPA area were owners versus 50 percent of Latino households. What was truly different was how each group got to realizing this part of the American dream. Latino households seemed to be stretching to ownership through resource pooling: if one glances at Figure 3.2, one can see that nearly 50 percent of Latino-owned households have 7 or more members; by contrast, 42 percent of black-owned households had 1 to 2 members. Looked at another way, around 80 percent of Latino-owned households had 5 or more members; 80 percent of black-owned households had four or fewer members.

The Latino statistics imply that both ends of the households may be stretched: older adults, often family members, pooling resources and the younger children that were attached to primary and other families. The African American statistics suggest a different story: older, often solo, residents hanging on after decades of residency. The pattern is reflected in the results for median age, 37.3 for African Americans and 21.8 for Latinos, a gap of 15.5 years that far exceeds the statewide gap between these two ethnic groups of only about 6.5 years. This large age gap played out in regionalist agendas: older African Americans had fresher memories of a history of exclusion by regional actors, were therefore wary of regionalist agendas, and tended to be more interested in quality of life issues; Latinos had a blanker historical slate and also had interests that were more clearly focused on jobs and development, even at the cost of further clogging traffic corridors.

Regionalist agendas around housing and transportation, in short, were complicated by internal considerations and diverging interests. In that light, it is unsurprising that OEPA was not eager to quickly pick up the regionalist banner, at least until its leadership had built internal unity of purpose. Rightly so, they focused more on internal planning, interethnic communications, and improving local schools and safety. As noted above,

OEPA is now more engaged in the regional dimension, with the organization now aiming to broker regional resources and develop leadership to advocate for policy change in the areas of economic independence, education, and neighborhood safety.

CONCLUSION: WAITING FOR REGIONALISM

Excitement about community-based regionalism seems to be building around the country. Many organizations have adopted the mantra, as demonstrated by the over 600 participants, the vast majority working with communities of color—who attended a National Summit on Regional Equity organized by PolicyLink and the Funders Network on Smart Growth and Livable Communities in Los Angeles in November 2002.[12] Supporting the movement are a growing number of examples how local community groups have tried "thinking and linking" to the region, and found new ways to achieve their traditional goals of community development and empowerment. Community-based regionalism also opens up the way to new common ground, particularly since business leaders may share an interest in workforce development for low-income residents while progressive environmentalists may be happy to find new allies in the struggle to curtail sprawl and protect open space.

We share the excitement about regionalism's potential. However, the analysis we offer here suggests that when regionalism hits the ground, it can stumble as easily as succeed.

We offer two central lessons. The first is that regionalism may not fit all communities, and it is not likely to be the first thing on a community development agenda. As we have noted, an in-depth analysis can help reveal the degree of fit: we think that CBR is an easier match when working poverty is an important factor, when the neighborhood is in a larger area and used to working at a larger scale, and when interests *within* the community are more closely aligned. More of this sort of pre-preparation—analysis and selection—may be necessary as CBR becomes a more common approach (see Pastor, Benner, and Rosner 2003 for one effort at just such a "regional audit").

However, even under the best of circumstances, it is important to let the regional component of community development strategies evolve at its own pace. CBR requires new capacities for analysis and coalition building, and it also requires the credibility that comes from first demonstrating that one is targeting and meeting local needs. CBR is essentially asking neighbors to make a leap of faith, believing that regional levers can move local solutions and that the organization is strong enough to not lose sight of its own interests on that larger playing field. Mayfair was able to make the connection, West Oakland lost its local base (at least in the CCI form), and OEPA was still trying to establish itself before branching out and away.

Our second and more complex lesson involves which sort of local community strategies are necessary for regional engagement. The striking fact is that rather than focusing primarily on specific projects and services provided within poor neighborhoods, CBR involves communities searching for opportunities that exist within broader regional political and economic processes. Sometimes these opportunities represent potential mutual gains, as when regional workforce intermediaries solve labor market problems for both job seekers and struggling employers. But getting what neighborhoods need from regional decision makers, as with the challenges Bethel New Life launched against the Chicago Transit Authority or the Community Benefits fight during the expansion of the Los Angeles Staples Center, can be a resolutely political process—and many CDCs, focused on local projects and worried about funders and government allies, have found this perspective a harder sell than their sometimes more policy-oriented and politically oriented colleagues in CBOs.

CCIs may have more potential to move the agenda. CCI organizations have multiple purposes—they are supposed to both make deals and empower residents, which puts them somewhere between the practical focus of CDCs and the political purpose of many CBOs. CBOs face fewer political constraints (but often more economic constraints since they may not have the property assets CDCs may control). CBOs, in fact, can thrive by enhancing their scale, impact, and perceived level of power. It is little wonder that CBOs dominate in the community-oriented part of equity regionalism (as reflected in the presence of various organizing federations that themselves are regional in scope) or that these groups see the regional policy agenda as a way to pursue organizing that is consistent with the interconnections they are trying to promote.[13]

This more political organizing strategy, however uncomfortable a fit with community development, may be necessary. Our experience with CBR clarifies the ongoing debate within the broad community development field between project-based community development and "power-based community development" by lifting up the necessity of political activism and community-based agenda setting as an important factor for community development and community-based regionalism.[14] Indeed, Reverend Cheryl Rivera, executive director of the Northwest Indiana Interfaith Federation, has argued that: "Metropolitan organizing is about changing the rules of the game so that those who have not, will have. ... Metropolitan organizing is the new civil rights movement, and we must be persistent."[15]

Casting the phenomenon in that light may be instructive: as with civil rights, any new movement must be prepared to challenge both itself and its allies. But it is also a characterization that can fill one with hope. Progress, however imperfect and incomplete, was made in America as a result of the civil rights generation. Perhaps regionalist thinking and action can help further the field of minority community economic development as well.

NOTES

The authors thank the William and Flora Hewlett Foundation as well as the Ford Foundation for funding the research behind this work. We thank Paul Ong and two anonymous reviewers for comments on earlier drafts and acknowledge the able research support of Javier Huizar, Julie Jacobs, Rachel Rosner, and Justin Scoggins. Finally, we thank the leaders in the movement for regional equity, particularly those in the Bay Area neighborhoods we describe here, for pointing the way to a new approach to community development and empowerment.

1. Labor organizing campaigns of the 1930s and 1940s also provided early models for community organizing and set the context for Alinsky's community-based organizing efforts in Chicago. Labor union and worker organizing as well efforts by faith-based institutions are highly visible in community-based regionalism organizing and coalition building strategies.

2. Presentation by Mary Nelson, President, Bethel New Life at the Fourth Annual Cross-site Retreat of the Hewlett Neighborhood Investment Initiative, November 15–17, 2002, Milpitas, California. See www.bethelnewlife.org for organizational history and campaign background. See also PolicyLink 2000; and Nelson 2000.

3. See also www.interfaithfederation.org. Information from Cheryl Rivera, keynote address for Bridging the Bay, a conference organized by the Social Equity Caucus, Santa Cruz, California, April, 2003.

4. For a longer analysis, see Pastor et al. 2004.

5. Employment data taken from the Labor Market Information Division of California's Employment Development Department.

6. Housing data is not available at the tract level. Hence, the data for East Palo Alto is for the city as a whole while the Mayfair and West Oakland figures are for the zip codes that include those areas. As such, these are similar to but not exactly the prices in the neighborhoods themselves. Data come from statistics maintained by the Rand Corporation which were originally derived from data collected by the California Association of Realtors.

7. Reported in Nalepa 2001.

8. The geographic areas mapped are tracts, with an overlay of the NII boundaries and a block-level shape to determine potential areas where there are no residents. It is the latter procedure that allows us to determine the low number of people in the working poor area in the north of West Oakland.

9. Indeed, in 2003, the Mayfair neighborhood took the initiative, along with OEPA, in organizing a conference, "From Shadows to Strategies: A Symposium on Undocumented Labor, Workforce Development, and Community Improvement," which considered how best to incorporated undocumented workers into local development.

10. Home ownership in the OEPA footprint was also much higher than the average 43 percent for the City of East Palo Alto as a whole, suggesting some potential differences from the rest of the city as well.

11. The data on demographic change are for East Palo Alto as a whole while all other figures and data are constrained to the "footprint" or subset of the city (that is. the OEPA service area). We did this to ensure maximum consistency between the geographies over the two census years when calculating change.

12. Over 1,200 people participated in a follow-up summit in May 2005 in Philadelphia, signally growing interest in the field.

13. See the discussion of the Gamaliel approach in Rusk (1999:333–335), and the description of the Industrial Areas Foundation experience with a regional strategy in one part of California in Pastor, Benner, and Rosner (2003).

14. See Callahan, Mayer, et al. (1999) and Hess (1999).

15. Quote is taken from a keynote address by Cheryl Rivera for Bridging the Bay, a conference organized by the Social Equity Caucus, Santa Cruz, California, April, 2003.

REFERENCES

AFL-CIO Human Resources Development Institute. 1998. *Economic Development: A Union Guide to the High Road.* Washington, DC: AFL-CIO Working for America Institute.

Barron, David J. 2003. The community economic development movement: A metropolitan perspective. *Stanford Law Review* 56(3):701–740.

Benner, Chris, Bob Brownstein, Laura Dresser, and Laura Leete. 2001. Staircases and treadmills: The role of labor market intermediaries in placing workers and fostering upward mobility. In *Proceedings of the 53rd Annual Meeting of the Industrial Relations Research Association, January 5–7, 2001, New Orleans,* ed. Paula Voos, 34–46. Champaign, IL: IRRA.

Bernhardt, Annette, Manuel Pastor, Erin Hatton, and Sarah Zimmerman. 2001. Moving the demand side: Intermediaries in a changing labor market. In *Proceedings of the 53rd Annual Meeting of the Industrial Relations Research Association, January 5–7, 2001, New Orleans,* ed. Paula Voos, 26–33. Champaign, IL: IRRA.

Bhargava, Shalinia, Bob Brownstein, Amy Dean, and Sarah Zimmerman. 2001. *Everyone's Valley: Inclusion and Affordable Housing in Silicon Valley.* San Jose: Working Partnerships.

Bullard, Robert D. 1998. *Sprawl Atlanta: Social Equity Dimensions of Uneven Growth and Development.* Atlanta: Environmental Justice Resource Center, Clark Atlanta University.

Callahan, Steve, Neil Mayer, Kris Palmer, and Larry Ferlazzo. 1999. "Rowing the Boat with Two Oars." Paper presented on COMM-ORG: The On-Line Conference on Community Organizing and Development. http://comm-org.wisc.edu/papers99/callahan.htm. Originally published in Neighborhood Funders Group (NFG) Reports 5, no. 3, 1998.

Dreier, Peter, John Mollenkopf, and Todd Swanstrom. 2001. *Place Matters: Metropolitics for the Twenty-first Century.* Kansas City: University of Kansas Press.

FutureWorks. 2004. *Imagine a Region.* http://www.metrobusinessnet.net/assets/Downloads/Imagine_A_Region.pdf. Arlington, Mass.: FutureWorks.

Giloth, Robert P. 2004. Introduction: A case for workforce intermediaries. In *Workforce Intermediaries for the Twenty-first Century,* ed. Robert P. Giloth, 3–30. Philadelphia: Temple University Press.

Henton, Douglas, John Melville, and Kimberly Walesh. 1997. *Grassroots Leaders for a New Economy: How Civic Entrepreneurs are Building Prosperous Communities.* San Francisco, CA: Jossey-Bass Publishers.

Hess, Daniel R. 1999. "Community Organizing, Building and Developing: Their Relationship to Comprehensive Community Initiatives." Presented on COMM-ORG: The On-Line Conference on Community Organizing and Development. http://comm-org.wisc.edu/papers99/hesscontents.htm.

Joint Venture: Silicon Valley Network. 2002. *2002 Workforce Study: Connecting Today's Youth with Tomorrow's Technology Careers.* San Jose, CA: Joint Venture: Silicon Valley Network (http://www.jointventure.org/PDF/2002workforcestudy.pdf).

Katz, Bruce, ed. 2000. *Reflections on Regionalism.* Washington, DC: Brookings Institution.

Kazis, Richard. 2004. What do workforce intermediaries do? In *Workforce Intermediaries for the Twenty-first Century,* ed. Robert P. Giloth, 73–92. Philadelphia: Temple University Press.

Lampe, David, John Parr, and Scott Woodward. 2004. *Regional Business Civic Organizations: Creating New Agendas for Metropolitan Competitiveness*. Monograph No. 9, October. Denver, CO: Alliance for Regional Stewardship (www. regionalstewardship.org).

Luria, Daniel D., and Joel Rogers. 1997. New urban agenda. *Boston Review* February/March, vol. XXII, no. 1. http://bostonreview.net/BR22.1/luria.html.

Muller, Sarah, Sarah Zimmerman, Bob Brownstein, Amy B. Dean, and Phaedra Ellis-Lamkins. 2003. *Shared Prosperity and Inclusion: The Future of Economic Development Strategies in Silicon Valley*. San Jose, CA: Working Partnerships USA.

Naelpa, Michael. 2001. IKEA bid on life support, but still breathing; see http:// www.stanford.edu/class/comm177/nalepa8.html.

Nelson, Mary. 2000. We build as we travel, *Shelterforce Online* 110, March/April, www.nhiorg.online/issues/110/nelson.html.

Ness, Immanuel, and Stuart Eimer, eds. 2001. *Central Labor Councils and the Revival of American Unionism*. New York: ME Sharpe.

Nowak, Jeremy. 1997. Neighborhood initiative and the regional economy. *Economic Development Quarterly* 11(1):3–10.

Orfield, Myron. 2002. *American Metropolitics: The New Suburban Reality*. Washington, DC: Brookings Institution Press.

Pastor, Manuel Jr. 2001a. Geography and opportunity. In *America Becoming: Racial Trends and Their Consequences*, ed. Neil Smelser, William Julius Wilson, and Faith Mitchell, Vol. 1 of the National Research Council Commission on Behavioral and Social Sciences and Education. Washington, DC: National Academy Press.

Pastor, Manuel Jr. 2001b. Common ground at ground zero? The new economy and the new organizing in Los Angeles. *Antipode* 33(2):260–289.

Pastor, Manuel Jr., Chris Benner, and Rachel Rosner. 2003. "An option for the poor": A Research audit for community-based regionalism in California's central coast. *Economic Development Quarterly* 17(2):175–192.

Pastor, Manuel Jr., Chris Benner, Martha Matsuoka, Rachel Rosner, and Julie Jacobs. 2004. *Connecting for the Common Good: Regionalism and Comprehensive Community Development in the Bay Area*. Santa Cruz, CA: University of California, Center for Justice, Tolerance, and Community.

Pastor, Manuel Jr., Peter Dreier, Eugene Grigsby, and Marta López Garza. 2000. *Regions That Work: How Cities and Suburbs Can Grow Together*. Minneapolis: University of Minnesota Press.

PolicyLink. 2000. *Briefing Book: Strategies and Examples of Community-Based Approaches to Equity and Smart Growth-A Working Document*. Oakland, CA: PolicyLink.

PolicyLink. 2002. *Promoting Regional Equity: A Framing Paper*. Oakland, CA: PolicyLink.

Powell, John A. 1998. "Race and Space: What Really Drives Metropolitan Growth." *Brookings Review* 16(4):20–22.

Rusk, David. 1999. *Inside Game, Outside Game: Winning Strategies for Saving Urban America*. Washington, DC: The Brookings Institution.

Soja, Edward W. 2000. *Postmetropolis: Critical Studies of Cities and Regions*. Oxford and Malden, MA: Blackwell Publishers.

Voith, R. 1992. City and suburban growth: Substitutes or complements? *Business Review* September/October:21–33.

Walsh, Joan. 1997. *Stories of Renewal: Community Building and the Future of Urban America*. New York: Rockefeller Foundation.

Wilson, William Julius. 1996. *When Work Disappears: The World of the New Urban Poor*. New York: Alfred A. Knopf.

II   LABOR MARKET DEVELOPMENT

As SHOWN IN the previous three chapters, the lack of meaningful employment is at the core of the economic problem facing low-income minority neighborhoods. Labor market development is arguably the most significant aspect of community economic development because the single largest component of household income comes from employment. This is even true for low-income neighborhoods. The residents of poor minority communities, however, face a number of hurdles in finding employment that generates enough income to lift them into the middle class. Training the labor force to acquire timely, relevant, and job-appropriate skills is an absolute prerequisite for economic development. Michael Stoll addresses some of the challenges in improving the stock of human capital. In contrast to more affluent communities, poor minority communities have lower levels of education and higher school dropout rates. Residents of immigrant communities may also lack English language skills and references that can testify to their prior work experiences. At a time when skill requirements for even entry-level jobs are increasing, low levels of human capital have negative consequences for the employment efforts of minority residents. The American workplace has experienced significant computerization in recent decades. Having less access to educational resources and computers, minority workers find themselves handicapped when competing for jobs.

The hurdles are not just limited education and skills. Some lie in the lack of appropriate social networks that can give information about existing jobs and link job seekers to appropriate job networks. Members of ethnic communities may have strong social capital within the compounds of their neighborhoods but often lack the bridging capital that can effectively connect them to the resources of the outside world. By relying exclusively on neighborhood-based social networks of friends and family, many inner-city residents have poor knowledge of job opportunities that exist in the broader metropolitan area. Other hurdles are structural. Racism and employer prejudice often determine a firm's hiring behavior. Employers are typically more likely to hire employees of similar racial backgrounds and can perceive as unreliable or even threatening job applicants from other races. Fearing discrimination, minority job seekers are also more likely to apply for jobs in firms characterized by a racial diversity of their labor pool. Both weak social networks and discrimination contribute to the difficulty for residents of low-income minority neighborhoods of finding jobs in the larger regional labor market. But even for less-skilled jobs, these residents are disadvantaged. Michela Zonta examines how spatial mismatch works from the demand side.

Perhaps the most disadvantaged segment of the minority population is those who are here illegally. Because of immigration restrictions, millions have entered this country without proper documents. As Abel Valenzuela discusses, undocumented workers must work in the shadow of the economy, in what is known as the informal sector. By their very clandestine nature, this population is extremely difficult to study. Being invisible, however, is not the same as being insignificant. Undocumented immigrants work hard and contribute to the economy, and their plight tells us much about how the poor are exploited. One does not have to be undocumented to be trapped in unstable low-wage jobs with little or no benefits.

4   Workforce Development in Minority Communities

Michael A. Stoll

Introduction

Workforce development policy and programs in the United States have aimed to enhance the employment and earnings of disadvantaged workers, including less-educated workers in low-income minority communities.[1] But most evaluations of these programs have shown mixed to limited success. In these situations, policy attention usually remains focused on efforts to improve the effectiveness of such programs, particularly if the labor market difficulties of less-educated workers remain part of the public policy agenda.

This focus may have attenuated during the economic boom of the 1990s. Over this period, the economic fortunes of the less educated improved on many counts. Poverty declined sharply, so much that its deepening concentration in minority communities—a pattern throughout the 1970s and 1980s—slowed and in most cases reversed (Jargowsky 2003). Black unemployment reached a 30-year low (7 percent) in 2000, while real wages for the less educated rose for the first time in almost two decades (Bureau of Labor Statistics 2003). Coupled with historic lows in interest rates, these developments increased housing demand among minority households, and as a consequence minority homeownership rates also increased (U.S. Census 2005). These developments led to slightly greater minority representation in inner-suburban communities (Lewis Mumford Center 2001), which contributed to modest improvements in minorities' physical access to jobs over the 1990s (Raphael and Stoll 2002). Of course, key policy changes over this period, such as the expansion of the earned income tax credit, could have contributed to these developments as well.

Despite these successes, other trends suggested that not all was well in the 1990s. In contrast to other young adults, young black men experienced declines in employment over this period (Holzer and Offner 2001). Similarly counter to national trends, neighborhood poverty grew significantly in California (the state with the largest population in the country), and especially within its Latino communities (Jargowsky 2003). Moreover, while the growth in job development that accompanied the economic boom slowed and in most cases reversed the 20-year trend of central-city job loss, little of this growth occurred in inner-city minority communities (Rosen, Kim, and Patel 2003).

The economic bust that occurred right after the boom probably accelerated these disturbing trends and brought other pain as well. Poverty and unemployment rates rose sharply, with Latinos and blacks suffering disproportionately from these increases. Indeed, the black unemployment rate rose faster than other groups over this period and topped 10 percent in 2003, over 5 percentage points higher than the rate for whites (Bureau of Labor Statistics 2003).

No doubt these events will raise questions once again about the need for and effectiveness of policies designed to improve the labor market outcomes of less-skilled groups, and particularly minority groups. This paper addresses these questions by critically examining workforce development policies that aim to enhance the employability and earnings of low-skilled, low-income minorities. In order to do this effectively, an examination of how low-skill labor markets function, and of the unique challenges that less-educated minority workers face, is also warranted. The paper argues that the challenges of mounting successful workforce development programs are compounded in minority communities because of the economic conditions there. Many minority communities, particularly those that are African American, suffer from significant job shortages, and travel to areas where jobs are more abundant is difficult for a variety of reasons. Moreover, many minority communities are located in or near central-city areas, where the skill requirements of jobs are greater. These features, in addition to persistent discrimination, require workforce development policies and programs that take into consideration the spatial dimensions of employment, and that engage in effective skill enhancement practices. But in order to do the latter effectively, newly identified best practices in employment and training must be incorporated as key features of workforce development policy design.

The remainder of the paper proceeds as follows. Section II discusses the labor market for less-skilled workers more generally, paying particular attention to the spatial and skills issues relevant to minority communities. Section III discusses various policies that address the labor market difficulties of those residing in jobs-poor neighborhoods. Section IV and V examine the record of employment and training policy, and looks at practices in employment and training that are likely to be effective in improving employment and wage outcomes of less-educated minority workers. Section VI concludes the paper.

THE LABOR MARKET FOR LESS-SKILLED WORKERS

Employer Hiring Behavior in Low-Wage Labor Markets

Before considering practices and policies that might improve the effectiveness of workforce development programs on the employment and earnings of those in minority communities, it is useful to provide some context by reviewing some general facts about employer hiring behavior more broadly in the low-wage labor market.

The following generalizations can be made about employer hiring behavior in low-wage and low-skill labor markets[2]:

- Virtually all employers seek basic "work-readiness" in prospective employees, while many seek additional "hard" and "soft" skills, even in low-wage markets;
- Since most skills are not directly observable at the time of hiring, employers generally seek applicants with certain credentials that signal employability and skill and tend to avoid those with certain stigmas, such as ex-felons and others with criminal records;
- Employers vary in the amounts of resources they can apply to hiring and compensation decisions, as well as in their information and expertise on these matters;
- Recruiting and screening choices (as well as compensation, promotion, and retention decisions) are often made informally and can reflect employer prejudices, perceptions, and experiences;
- Employers' access to a reliable and steady pool of applicants is also affected by their physical proximity to various neighborhoods and groups, their employee networks, and the tightness of both the local and national labor markets.

The basic work-readiness that virtually all employers seek involves personal qualities such as honesty and reliability, an inclination to arrive at work on time every day, a positive attitude towards work, and so on. Avoidance of problems that might be associated with high absenteeism and poor work performance, such as drug abuse or physical or mental health difficulties, is often viewed as critical (Holzer 1996; Moss and Tilly 2001).

Beyond these, even low-wage jobs require basic cognitive skills such as reading and writing, arithmetic skills (for tasks like making change), and often the rudimentary use of a computer. The relevant "soft" skills frequently include the ability to interact with customers or coworkers. Of course, the exact requirements vary greatly with the occupation and industry under consideration, and many unskilled blue-collar or service jobs in construction or manufacturing require fewer such skills than those in the retail trade and some parts of the service sectors (Holzer 1996). Even some service-sector jobs (such as cleaning and maintenance of buildings and grounds or food preparation and service) require many fewer of these skills than others.

Since many of the desirable qualities and skills can not be directly observed, employers use "credentials"—such as attainment of a high school diploma, previous work experience, and references—to gain such information. In a minority of cases, drug tests and a variety of background checks are also used. Skill tests are even more rare. Many employers make inferences regarding basic skills on the basis of the quality of writing on the application as well as the interview, though these judgments are notoriously unreliable. Employers avoid applicants with criminal records, as they consider prior criminality a signal of poor skills or reliability.

Small and medium-sized employers without human resources departments often lack the time, staff, or financial resources to invest in more-formal recruitment and screening techniques, so they are more likely to make their selections informally. They may post "help-wanted" signs or seek referrals from their current employees when recruiting, and they often rely on simple written applications or verbal interviews for screening. While larger and more experienced employers may increasingly use Internet-based searches, temporary agencies, or other private firms to perform their human resource functions, these strategies remain relatively rare among small retail trade or service employers in the low-wage market.

Accordingly, the personal experiences and perceptions of employers will play a comparatively larger role in smaller establishments in hiring, and the potential for discriminatory judgments rises there as well (Holzer 1998). Discrimination might arise out of the employers' own biases, the perceived biases of their customers or existing employees (Holzer and Ihlanfeldt 1998), or simply their lack of information about individual qualities and attributes among their applicants and therefore a reliance on group characteristics.

Employers seem most reluctant to hire young and less-educated black men, whom they often see as threatening, either generally or on the basis of perceived criminality (Holzer, Raphael, and Stoll 2002b; Kirschenman and Neckerman 1991). In contrast, immigrants are frequently perceived as being reliable and having good work attitudes and are therefore preferred, particularly in jobs where cognitive skill or language demands are minimal. Indeed, some low-wage employers make use of ethnic "niches" by obtaining workers whom current employees recommend and who are therefore deemed trustworthy.

Many employers, including smaller ones, can also access a steady stream of desirable applicants by virtue of their geographic location and can similarly avoid applicants whom they do not want to consider (Holzer and Ihlanfeldt 1996). All else equal, however, smaller firms are much less likely to hire minorities, especially blacks, and are more likely to engage in statistical discrimination against black men on the basis of perceived criminality (Holzer, Raphael, and Stoll 2002b).

Still, the ability of employers to generate sufficient numbers of applicants through these largely informal practices depends in part on the tightness of labor markets, both locally and nationally. During the late 1990s, when unemployment rates sank to 30-year lows, job vacancy rates climbed and many employers had difficulty attracting (or retaining) employees through their traditional sources. Accordingly, employers seemed relatively open to hiring welfare recipients (Holzer and Stoll 2001a) and other groups they might otherwise have largely avoided. It is quite possible that racially discriminatory hiring patterns could have diminished, as they had in previous boom periods (Freeman and Rodgers 2000). If so, the positive effects of the boom on the employment prospects of minorities and the disadvantaged could have been long term had the attitudes or behaviors of employers been changed by any positive experiences they had in hiring minorities during that time. Recent evidence on black unemployment rates after the boom casts doubt on this possibility, however; black unemployment rates rose dramatically relative to those of whites and Latinos during the immediate years after the boom (Bureau of Labor Statistics 2003).

The Space Issue

Despite this, proximity to public transit and poor neighborhoods has large effects on the applicant pools employers face. Indeed, the quality of applicants desired appears to influence employer locational decisions (Moss and Tilly 2001), and outer suburban areas have had the highest rates of employer location and job growth over the past few decades. In combination with the existence of racial residential segregation in which blacks, and to a lesser extent Latinos, are concentrated in the central cities and whites in the suburbs, these factors tend to generate a "spatial mismatch" between the inner-city neighborhoods in which many poor minorities live and the outlying suburbs in which most low-wage jobs are found (Holzer and Ihlanfeldt 1996; Stoll, Holzer, and Ihlanfeldt 2000).[3]

Geographic isolation from areas with skill-appropriate jobs can increase workers' costs in several ways and thereby reduce their employment opportunities. First, search costs, such as the additional time and out-of-pocket costs of an extra mile of travel while looking for work, vary with the distance one is from job-rich areas. For example, each additional mile of private auto travel during search requires more out-of-pocket costs for items like gas, while traffic congestion and the use of public transportation increase time costs.[4] Thus workers who live far from areas with skill-appropriate jobs must travel farther and pay more to access opportunities for work. Second, it is harder for workers who live far from skill-appropriate jobs to even find out about those jobs; they have to exert more effort to learn about openings and other opportunities, and the time costs of gathering this information are high.

Table 4.1 presents some recent evidence on the spatial unevenness of minorities and jobs in Los Angeles. This table uses employer data from the Los Angeles portion of the 1992–94 Multi-City Study of Employers (MCES)[5] and the 2001 Los Angles Survey of Employers (LASE)[6] as well as population data from the 2000 U.S. Census. The employer data are used to examine the spatial distribution of all jobs and low-skill jobs[7] across areas within the central city and suburbs that are characterized by the racial residential concentration of these areas.[8] The population data (ages 25 to 65) are used to define areas within the central city and suburbs by their racial residential concentration and to examine the spatial distribution of people over these areas.[9] These areas include the central business district (CBD), black central city, Latino central city, white central city, black suburbs, integrated suburbs, and white suburbs.[10] Firms in the employer databases were geocoded to one of these seven submetropolitan areas based on their business location.

Table 4.1 also shows the spatial distributions of recently filled noncollege jobs and people (total and by race) across the 7 submetropolitan areas in Los Angeles.[11] In the early 1990s the central city had 41.0 percent of all newly filled jobs and 38.6 percent of the people, while the suburbs had 59.0 percent of the jobs and 61.5 percent of the people. Thus people in central cities, considered as a whole, had about the same proximity to newly filled jobs as

TABLE 4.1. Distributions of jobs and people across submetropolitan areas of Los Angeles

	Total Central City	Black Central City	Latino Central City	White Central City	Central Business District	Total Suburbs	Black Suburbs	Integrated Suburbs	White Suburbs	Total
Jobs 2001										
All jobs[a]	28.2	5.4	13.2	6.6	3.0	71.9	1.8	26.4	43.7	607
Low-skill jobs[a]	27.7	4.5	13.3	5.9	4.0	72.3	2.0	23.1	47.3	147
1992–94										
All jobs[b]	41.0	6.9	27.1	4.9	2.1	59.0	0.7	25.0	33.3	828
Low-skill jobs[b]	39.7	5.3	19.0	6.3	9.1	60.4	2.5	25.4	32.5	144
People[c] (age 25 to 65)										
All people										
White	21.0	1.6	7.5	10.9	1.0	79.0	0.6	25.5	52.9	2,927,362
Black	66.4	54.7	4.8	5.8	1.1	33.8	1.0	15.6	17.2	499,747
Latino	55.1	9.8	34.0	8.0	3.3	44.9	0.5	23.7	20.7	1,929,751
Total	38.6	9.3	19.8	7.6	1.9	61.5	0.7	24.0	36.8	5,882,948
High school dropouts										
White	39.4	4.1	8.8	24.5	2.0	60.7	0.6	26.8	33.3	654,100
Black	76.6	65.3	3.5	6.5	1.3	23.4	1.0	10.4	12.0	129,424
Latino	63.6	12.8	38.0	8.4	4.4	36.4	0.4	19.8	16.2	821,418
Total	57.4	13.7	31.6	8.4	3.7	42.6	0.5	21.2	20.9	2,174,589

[a]2001 Los Angeles Survey of Employers.
[b]1992–94 Multi-City Employer Survey.
[c]2000 U.S. Census.

people in the suburbs, considered as a whole. By 2001, however, the spatial distribution of jobs in Los Angeles shifted towards the suburbs. In 2001, 28.2 percent of all newly filled jobs and 38.6 percent of the people were in the central city, while the suburban share of jobs had increased to 71.9 percent, while 61.5 percent of the people were in the suburbs. Of course, the continuing decentralization of metropolitan areas could explain part of this pattern, but so too could the timing of the employer surveys. The 1992–94 employer survey was taken during Los Angeles's emergence from the recession of the early 1990s, when both central cities and suburbs had already been affected by the downturn, while the 2001 survey was conducted at the beginning of the 2001 recession—when central-city, relative to suburban, employment was likely hit particularly hard.

Still, when we look within cities and suburbs we find not only that people and recently filled jobs are not evenly distributed, but also that they weren't evenly distributed in the early 1990s either. For example, the share of people residing in black central cities (9.3 percent) is significantly greater than the share of jobs located in this submetropolitan area (6.9 percent). On the other hand, the share of jobs is greater than the share of people in the white suburbs, black suburbs, and the CBD. By 2001, these patterns became even more extreme, and even those residing in Latino central cities began experiencing severe relative job shortages.

The spatial distributions shown in Table 4.1 suggest that at the general level residents of black central cities have an employment disadvantage when compared to residents of white suburban areas, because of the black residents' relatively worse physical proximity to jobs.[12] Furthermore, though there appear to be jobs in the CBD that are spatially accessible for blacks and Latinos, many of these jobs may be inaccessible for other, nonspatial reasons. CBD jobs tend to be highly competitive (Stoll 2000), and data from MCES show that a high percentage of them require a college degree, while the percentage of residents who are high school dropouts is greatest in the black and Latino central cities.

Low-Skill Jobs and Less-Educated People

Table 4.1 also shows the spatial distributions of recently filled low-skill jobs and people (total and by race) and high school dropouts (total and by race) in Los Angeles. The spatial distribution of low-skill jobs across the submetropolitan areas is very similar to that of all jobs for both years, except that low-skill jobs are slightly more decentralized, a finding consistent with national trends and previous research (Glaeser and Kahn 2001). At the broadest geographic comparison (i.e., central city versus total suburbs), in the early 1990s, 60.4 percent of the Los Angeles area's lowest-skilled jobs were in the suburbs, but only 42.6 percent of the least-educated people (i.e., those with no high school degree) were located there. These patterns remained as stark in 2001. But at a more disaggregated level—looking at the seven submetropolitan areas—the spatial disparity between jobs and people is worse. Consider two areas—white suburbs and black central city. The former contains 32.5 and 47.3 percent of the lowest-skilled jobs in 1992–94 and 2001, respectively, but only 20.9 percent of the least-educated people. The latter holds 5.3 and 4.5 percent of these jobs in 1992–94 and 2001, respectively, relative to 13.7 percent of the least-educated people. In 2001, this imbalance relative to white suburbs was even more extreme for those residing in Latino central-city areas.

These comparisons suggest that job proximity, as measured by the number of nearby jobs available per resident, is markedly higher in the area where most of the least-educated whites reside in comparison to the area where most of the least-educated blacks and Latinos reside. But these patterns are not unique to Los Angeles, even though urban scholars and policymakers often consider Los Angeles unique in its economic geography. Indeed, the patterns shown here also appear across very different metropolitan areas, such as Atlanta, Boston, and Detroit (Stoll, Holzer, and Ihlanfeldt 2000).

These geographic imbalances between minorities and jobs, especially low-skill jobs, are magnified by minorities' relative lack of access to cars. As noted earlier, mode of transit, in addition to location, is a major factor influencing geographic job search. Blacks, and to a lesser extent Latinos, are significantly less likely than whites to have access to cars, and these differences are greater for the less educated (Raphael and Stoll 2001; Holzer, Ihlanfeldt, and Sjoquist 1994). For example, in the mid-1990s for those with a high school degree or less in the United States, the car ownership rates for whites, blacks, and Latinos were 74.2 percent, 47.0 percent, and 48.0 percent, respectively. Moreover, these patterns were similar despite alternative definitions of car access, such as presence of a car in the household, and were similar across all large metropolitan areas (Raphael and Stoll 2001). To be sure, the problem could be circular: the relative lack of car access for blacks and Latinos could be influenced by their lack of income—without which they cannot support car payments, insurance, and maintenance—and their lack of income could be because they are more likely to live in job-poor areas where employability is difficult without a car.

Still, lack of access to a car for those living in such neighborhoods diminishes their employment prospects for a number of reasons. Because they own fewer cars, blacks and Latinos are much more likely to travel by public transportation, which increases their search costs in a number of ways. Commuting times on public transit are considerably longer than those for private travel. Moreover, "reverse commutes" from central cities to suburbs are difficult via transit because transit is often designed to carry riders into city workplaces, not bring city riders out to dispersed suburban location sites. Transit, and particularly rail routes, that serves suburban workplaces is sparse (Wachs and Taylor 1998), and suburban firms are more physically distant from public transit stops than are central-city firms, making many suburban employment opportunities that much more inaccessible (Holzer and Ihlanfeldt 1996). In the mid-1990s, nearly half of all low-skill jobs in white suburbs were inaccessible by public transportation (defined as being over a quarter-mile away from the nearest public transit stop), while the

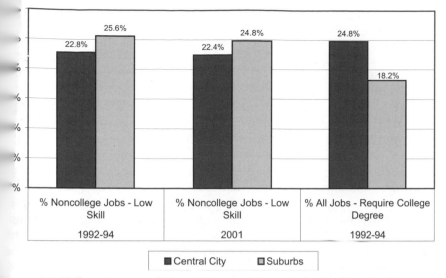

IGURE 4.1. Skill requirements of jobs within central city and suburbs of Los Angeles

mplies that the employment challenges of less-skilled central-city minority workers are compounded by the skill composition of jobs there.

As a corollary to this, there is currently a debate about whether skill requirements of jobs are rising over time and climbing beyond the skill attainment of workers, especially in central cities. The growing wage inequality between those with a college degree and high school diploma is usually cited as evidence of the rising skill requirements of jobs (Levy and Murnane 1992; Katz and Murphy 1992). In general, there seems to be a consensus that on some measures, such as use of computers, skill requirements are increasing, albeit modestly (Holzer 1998). Some evidence on this question is provided in Kasarda (1995), who shows in most large metropolitan areas from 1970 to 1990, the percentage of jobs in the central city that required a college degree was much higher than the share of residents with a college degree. Kasarda also finds that the percentage of jobs in the central city requiring a college degree rose dramatically from 1970 to 1990, much faster than central-city residents who attained college degrees over the same period.

The problem is of particular importance to the employment and earnings of Latino workers, especially those of Mexican decent. Mexican Americans represent the majority of Latino workers in the United States and also one of the nation's most economically disadvantaged groups. Mexican Americans have also accumulated the least human capital of most racial and ethnic groups in the United States, though much of this is accounted for by recent Mexican immigrants who arrive with very limited education. The education/ human capital deficit of workers of Mexican descent is the principal reason why they earn less than other U.S. workers (Grogger and Trejo 2002). Thus,

comparable figure for low-skill jobs in the central city was   30
(Stoll, Holzer, and Ihlanfeldt 2000). These difficulties are
the greater likelihood relative to other workers that low   25
workers will working nonstandard hours, such as the gra
morning shifts (Beers 2000), when public transit often doe: 20
far less frequently.
The preceding analysis suggests that though employmei   1!
appear relatively greater in suburban areas, there are a numl
that prevent central-city minority workers from attaining   1
of these challenges, central-city minorities are likely to limit 1
travel to work to areas near their residential locations rathe
with the additional travel costs imposed on them by geogra
and limited vehicle availability. Indeed, recent research s
search and travel costs limit the geographic distance workers
able to travel to work, and this results in differences in the ge
searched by whites, blacks, and Latinos. Whites search for woi
areas where job growth is relatively strong, and blacks in cen
where job growth has been relatively weak, with Latinos :
between (Stoll and Raphael 2000). Blacks, however, search
graphic radius (Stoll 1999).

The Skills Issue

Limiting job search to the central city hurts minority workers
yond the relative shortage of jobs there. Jobs and industries
more skill are more centralized than less skill-intensive industri
earlier, since the postwar period, metropolitan areas have l
tralizing in part as a result of the reduced costs of transportatioi
land prices on the suburban periphery (Glaeser and Kahn 2001; N
However, this pattern of decentralization is less true of industri
that are more skill intensive—as measured by either the average
level of workers or the extent of computer use across industries (C
Kahn 2001). Some argue that this pattern is explained by the in
externalities of proximity, as dense urban areas facilitate the spee
of ideas. If this is the case, then idea-intensive industries such as cc
banking and high services would be much more likely than others
manufacturing—to centralize. This hypothesis is supported by the
research (Glaeser and Kahn 2001; Glaeser 2000).
Jobs in central cities are likely to have higher skill requirements tl
in the suburbs, even though central cities may account for a smaller
of the metropolitan areas' jobs as a result of decentralization. Fi;
provides evidence on this question for Los Angeles using data fro
and LAES. The first two pairs of columns show that in both 1992-
2001 the percentage of noncollege jobs (jobs that do not require a
degree) that are low skill is higher in the suburbs than central city.
over, the column to the far right indicates that the percentage of j
quiring a college degree is higher in the central city and suburbs.

the problem of rising skill requirements of jobs is likely to hit the Latino community particularly hard.

Much of the rise in skill requirements can be attributed to the increasing computerization of the workplace (Autor, Katz, and Krueger 1998; Autor, Levy, and Murnane 2003). The relationship between computers and skills is not one-way, however, and not as straightforward as it might appear. Computerization can lead to both the downskilling and upskilling of work, depending on how the technology is used and introduced (Cappelli 1996). For example, computers can substitute for certain skilled clerks at a workplace, but the computer tasks may only involve basic data input, which results in the downskilling of that job. On the other hand, the increasing demand for such computers is also likely to result in increased demand for software programmers, network administrators and consultants, and computer design makers, which results in the upskilling of work more generally. Much of the research suggests that though computerization leads to both of these outcomes, more upskilling of work appears to be taking place than downskilling, with the result being rising skill requirements of jobs on average (Autor, Levy, and Murnane 2003).

The rise of computerization and its attendant skills has raised questions about the information-technology (IT) economy's impact on less-educated workers. ("Information technology" is defined as "the infrastructure and knowledge that is necessary to market information readily available" [U.S. Department of Commerce 1999:3]).[14] In 1984 about 25.1 percent of all workers in the United States used a computer at work (Autor, Katz, and Krueger 1998); by 2000 this had risen to 68 percent, representing a 170 percent increase (Heldrich Center for Workforce Development 2000). Many jobs that use computers are in IT occupations and concentrated in high-technology industries. But they are not *exclusively* in high-tech sectors: IT occupations and skills are now integrated into most parts of the economy and are particularly prevalent in the financial and health industries (U.S. Department of Commerce 2000).

The skill requirements of these jobs change rapidly, so workers that lack familiarity with the computer are at a distinct disadvantage in competing for them. The racial disparities in computer access in the United States thus compound the skill barriers already facing less-educated minorities. It is estimated that 55 and 47 percent of Asians and whites, respectively, have computer access at home, compared to 26 and 23 percent of Latinos and blacks, respectively. These gaps are slightly larger in the central city and also larger for the less educated. Similar differences exist with respect to internet access, and there is evidence that these gaps widened over the 1990s (U.S. Department of Commerce 1999). Community Technology Centers (CTCs), which provide computing and Internet access and training in mostly minority, underserved communities (and are sponsored and financed by a wide range of actors including the federal government, nonprofits, and foundations), are growing rapidly, but their effect on closing the racial digital divide is unclear.

Potential Policy Approaches

Traditionally, there have been two main approaches to addressing the employment challenges of less-educated workers in mostly job-poor, inner-city minority communities. These can be distinguished as "place-based" and "people-based" policies. Place-based policies concentrate resources in economically distressed areas as a revitalization strategy, while people-based policies target resources to disadvantaged individuals irrespective of where they are. A variant of these is "people-place polices," which focus attention on disadvantaged individuals in disadvantaged communities.

In the United States, a major place-based policy is the enterprise zone, which was originally conceived in England but embraced in the United States, especially under the Regan and first Bush administrations. Enterprise zones evolved, under President Clinton, into empowerment zones. Enterprise zones use tax and other financial incentives—such as job creation and wage credits, employer income tax credits, selective hiring credits, and investment and property tax credits—to encourage firms to locate or expand in particular areas, usually distressed urban communities (Erickson and Friedman 1991; Green 1991).

The results of this strategy have been largely disappointing. Enterprise policies generate few jobs and instead simply induce firms to move into designated areas from nearby locations (Ladd 1994). If the goal is to increase minority employment more generally in distressed areas, then the zones may be viewed as a benefit. But research has also shown that zone residents' employability remains largely unchanged. Another concern is that zone policies are expensive; each new job created in a zone costs between $40,000 and $60,000 (Ladd 1994). Whether Clinton's empowerment version of enterprise zones shows different outcomes remains to be seen; however, the empowerment zone's focus on community building and its more stringent enforcement of hiring zone residents suggest that it may prove more beneficial.

Alternatively, job growth in disadvantaged minority communities has also been pursued through macroeconomic growth policies stimulated by either fiscal or monetary intervention at the federal level. The depth and length of national economic growth has a large influence on job growth in disadvantaged and particularly inner-city minority communities. The economic boom the late 1990s brought with it tremendous economic and employment growth, so much so that the hemorrhaging of jobs from the central city, which ran unabated for the previous four decades, slowed and in some cases reversed (U.S. Department of Housing and Urban Development 1997). But even then, amidst the largest period of postwar economic growth, employment rose only modestly in distressed urban areas. In fact, had blacks not moved out of their segregated neighborhoods to the extent that they did over the 1990s, their geographic isolation from jobs would likely have gotten significantly worse, not better, during the boom (Raphael and Stoll 2002). This is not to say, however, that national economic growth is of no help to disadvantaged minorities. Growth, even if it is not directly beneficial, is likely to complement other policy approaches, some of which are described here, and may even be a necessary condition for their success.

Two general people-place approaches are available to increase minority residents' physical access to jobs. The first is residential mobility, which aims to increase minority access to suburban housing. Residential mobility policies, such as the Gautreaux or the "Moving to Opportunity" programs, often provide incentives and supports for low-income, mostly minority residents living in high-poverty areas to move to low-poverty suburban neighborhoods. The Gautreaux program, implemented in the 1970s in Chicago, appears to have had some success in improving the economic and social outcomes of the adults and children it helped move (Rosenbaum and Popkin 1991). The results have been mixed for "Moving to Opportunity," a demonstration mobility program implemented by the U.S. Department of Housing and Urban Development (HUD) in 5 large metropolitan areas (Katz, Kling, and Liebman 1997; Johnson, Ladd, and Ludwig 2002).[15]

A major concern with residential mobility is the problem of going to scale. Suburban housing discrimination and the limited availability of low-income housing in nonpoor suburban areas may limit the extent to which the minority poor can move there. Mobility policies, then, would affect few people relative to the number of people who are spatially disadvantaged in the labor market. Such programs are also likely to be politically controversial and costly, both in economic and social terms (Briggs 1997; Haar 1996). Leaving family, friends, and other neighborhood social institutions can be difficult and potentially costly. In spite of the incentives offered in the "Moving to Opportunity" program demonstration, only about 50 percent of the treatment group actually moved, perhaps for all the reasons just mentioned (Katz, Kling, and Liebman 1997; Johnson, Ladd, and Ludwig 2002). Still, it is clear that even without these policies, residential mobility could occur; if the federal government strengthened and enforced the Fair Housing Act of 1988, suburban housing market discrimination and mortgage lending discrimination could be greatly reduced (Yinger 1995). Likewise, increased development of suburban low-income housing would offer more spaces for mobility-minded residents of distressed urban areas. Each of these tactics, of course, faces its own economic and political challenges.

The second people-place approach takes residential location as given and attempts to improve physical access to suburbs instead—by subsidizing commutes, providing vanpools, or improving public transportation connections between the central city and suburban areas. An example of this kind of program is HUD's "Bridges to Work" initiative, which emphasizes job placement and transportation assistance (i.e., reverse commute) programs. These policies are generally less costly per participant and less politically controversial than residential mobility programs. However, they do not address the potentially negative effects of residing in areas of segregation or concentrated poverty.

Transportation-based programs have other limitations as well. They will have limited success if the wage benefits gained from suburban jobs are not sufficient to compensate for the additional travel costs of a long commute. In

Relevant and Timely Skills Training

Given the rising skill requirements of jobs and the rate of computerization of work, relevant and timely skills training seems mandatory to successfully link and retain low-skilled workers to jobs. But training in relevant skills has historically been absent in previous employment and training models, especially those that follow "work first" strategies. Employer involvement in training will help agencies overcome this absence. Another way to accomplish it is to contract with other training agencies that have proven track records of successfully training workers in relevant and timely skills. For example, in the Casey Foundation's St. Louis Jobs Initiative, the Better Family Life (BFL) community-based organization (CBO), which was responsible for coordinating training efforts, approached the local community college to conduct its training because the community college had larger facilities, better equipment, and past success in worker training. The CBO/college partnership led to the creation of the WorkLink program, whereby BFL concentrates on "soft" skill and other preemployment training, while the community college trains the "hard" skills set (Annie E. Casey Foundation 2000).

The establishment of standardized curriculums for various skill sets is another way to effectively train workers in relevant skills. Mature occupations are usually defined by skills standards, which are used to establish consistent information about the requirements of particular jobs. The National Skills Standards Board defines these standards as "performance specifications that identify the knowledge, skills and abilities an individual needs to succeed in the workplace" (Northwest Center for Emerging Technologies 1999:4). Once established, standards allow job trainers to develop curricula that train workers in specific skills, and by definition such training should produce somewhat consistent skill outcomes across different training sites. This consistency of training allows programs to certify their program graduates, which plays two roles. It provides employers certainty about the bundle of skills that the potential worker possesses and provides the potential worker with a marketable credential.

The timing of skills training is also an important factor to consider. The literature indicates that training in "hard," in addition to "soft," skill training *before* job placement produces the greatest positive effect on job retention. For example, San Francisco Works found that instruction in "hard skills" such as computer training for jobs in the financial/banking sector before employment or internship placements produced longer job retention rates for participants than when it occurred simultaneously (Bliss 2000). Presumably, training before placement in employment or internships led to greater familiarity with computer skills and components, which in turn led to greater confidence and ability on the subsequent job.

Mixed Approach to Training

"Work first" employment programs clearly indicate that assistance in job search and training in workplace norms and customs is an important component of training, particularly for participants who have been out of the labor force for significant periods of time. A 1995 study by the General Accounting Office suggested that successful training programs include "soft" skills training in addition to job-specific "hard" skills (U.S. Department of Labor 1995). The Casey Foundation's New Orleans Jobs Initiative follows this strategy and has had positive preliminary program results. Participants receive technical skills training and preemployment and "soft" skills training, which focus on teaching workplace codes (Annie E. Casey Foundation 2000). Welfare-to-work programs such as Riverside, California's GAIN program, Florida's Family Transition Program, and the Baltimore OPTIONS program also follow this balanced approach and have shown signs of success (Strawn 1998).

Networking and Collaboration Among Training Providers

No single organization usually has the internal capacity (in size, resources, equipment, facilities, access to clients, expertise) to complete the training process from beginning to end, and thus collaboration is important for training success. Moreover, collaboration may be effective when organizations appear to be encroaching on other's "territory," in either geographic or program area (Harrison and Weiss 1998). Indeed, recent evidence supports the hypothesis that networking makes a positive difference for organizational and participant outcomes, though networks with other job development intermediaries seem more effective than collaborations with government or social service agencies (Falcon, Melendez, and de Montrichard 2003).

There are a number of examples that illustrate these points. In both the St. Louis Jobs Initiative and the New Orleans Jobs Initiative, CBOs and community colleges partner to accomplish their training goals. In both initiatives, community colleges conduct the "hard" skills training because often the CBOs do not have the expertise, capacity, or resources and equipment to conduct the training themselves. However, the community colleges gain from these partnerships as well because they benefit from the additional participants they receive from referrals from these CBOs, which usually have deep roots in disadvantaged communities, and from the additional "soft" skill training that CBOs conduct (Annie E. Casey Foundation 2000).

These kinds of partnerships are also likely to benefit community technology centers (CTCs). Many CTCs are moving into more formal technical job training by partnering with larger training institutions, such as community colleges, because of their size and expertise (Chapple et al. 2000). As these programs evolve and as the goals for their training programs grow to include "soft" skills training, many CTCs will most likely need to look to partner with other nonprofits that have expertise in conducting such training.

Post-Employment Assistance

Finally, post-employment assistance can help participants learn new skills quickly and continuously, which is important given the rise and changes in task requirements of jobs and the growing concern over job retention. Recent research indicates that postemployment programs are particularly effective when they are developed in conjunction with employers and when the programs are sensitive to specific workplace dynamics (Bliss 2000). Some examples of postemployment assistance include skill enhancement— such as continued on-the-job training or formal apprenticeship programs— in which employers provide continued instruction in job skills. For example, the Cooperative Health Care Network provides continued in-service training and career upgrading programs for its graduates (Strawn 1998). The objectives of these programs are to strengthen or update skills for the current job or to facilitate career advancement.

Postemployment assistance is most effective when it addresses the range of issues that confront disadvantaged workers. Indeed, these forms of assistance are particularly important for reducing absenteeism and job retention. Recent research indicates that well over half of the absenteeism problems of welfare recipients at work are due to child-care and transportation problems (Holzer and Stoll 2001a). To address these kinds of issues, the Chicago Commons Employment and Training Center provides comprehensive on-site support services, transportation assistance, and child care for their program graduates (Strawn 1998).

Conclusion

Though difficult, improving the employment and earnings prospects for disadvantaged workers, especially less-educated workers in low-income minority communities, can be accomplished through careful public policy. To start, deliberate, expansionary monetary policy—the type that contributed the strong economic conditions that we witnessed over the 1990s— is likely to help. The economic boom of the late 1990s brought with it increased employment opportunities and therefore better economic fortunes for the disadvantaged in low-income minority communities. With employers facing significant job shortages, their willingness to hire those that historically had been marginalized increased, and the employment and earnings of these workers rose as well, after having declined or been stagnant for the past two decades. Moreover, there was a sense that if the boom were to continue on, secular changes in employer attitudes concerning minority groups, especially blacks, would occur, and the long-term employment prospects for these groups would greatly improve. But with the economic bust coming suddenly and minority economic losses rising disproportionately in the aftermath, it is clear that this was not to be the case.

This is not to say that macroeconomic conditions and therefore monetary policies don't matter for the labor market prospects of disadvantaged workers. They do. It is much easier for less-educated minority workers to get jobs during economic growth periods than during economic busts. But it is difficult to maintain strong economic conditions over the long run, and even when this does occur there are no guarantees that strong employment growth will follow. The recovery following the economic bust of 2000, for example, was a "jobless" one. Minority employment and wages didn't rise during this period, even though growth took place, because few jobs were generated (National Urban League 2004). Thus, economic growth alone may not be sufficient to overcome the persistent joblessness and poverty that characterize many low-income minority communities.

As a result, additional policies and programs must be pursued, especially those that better link less-educated minority workers to jobs for which they qualify and which increase their competitiveness in local labor markets. To accomplish this, targeted public policies that focus on the unique problems associated with these communities, such as spatial and skill barriers to employment and persistent discrimination, are necessary. Policies that reduce the spatial divide of work, such as those that foster car ownership; that raise the skills of such workers, such as through effective employment and training programs that incorporate "best practices" in the field; and those that lessen discriminatory practices of employers are likely to be particularly effective. Moreover, these interventions are likely to be that much more effective when the economy is strong and labor markets tight.

Nonprofits in the employment and training business and foundation-supported jobs initiatives have provided particularly good models on how to raise the employment and earnings of less-educated minority workers through innovative "best practice" methods. But the combined efforts of these actors are not enough to meet the employment and training needs of these groups. There is still a need for a federal role in employment and training. Though past federal efforts in this regard have been met with limited success, the restructuring of employment and training services and programs embodied in the WIA and that include many of the "best practices" identified here offer some hope that the effectiveness of these efforts will improve. The systematic cutbacks in funding for federal employment and training programs that have occurred over the past decade, however, temper this optimism. But if evaluations of the WIA indicate that such changes in employment and training policies and programs have been successful, usually as measured by whether the benefits of the program exceed the costs, then surely a case can be made that expansion of the WIA is warranted and needed.

NOTES

1. The term *workforce development* is used here to describe those public policies and programs, such as the federal government's Job Training and Partnership Act (JTPA) and now the Workforce Development Investment Act (WIA) and other residential or transportation mobility programs, that aim to improve the skills or employment access of disadvantaged workers in the United States, such as the less educated, welfare recipients, dislocated workers, disadvantaged youth, and so on. While much of the coordination of workforce development has historically emanated from federal government efforts, increasingly states, local governments, and private foundations, among others, are helping to shape workforce development in the United States. Moreover, the design and implementation of many of these are increasingly being done by nonprofit institutions, such as community-based organizations, other not-for-profits and community colleges.

2. The basis of this discussion was developed in Holzer, Raphael, and Stoll (2002a).

3. This issue applies to other disadvantaged groups such as welfare recipients. See Ong and Blumenberg (1998) and Holzer and Stoll (2001b) for more.

4. The basis of this discussion is developed in Stoll (1999). Stoll shows that average distance from search areas, as well as the absence of vehicle availability, is negatively related to the number of areas searched and to the distance searched by workers. Thus, distance from search areas and lack of access to cars imposes high search costs (in both time and money) on workers and limits the extent of geographic job search.

5. The Multi-City Employer Survey (MCES) was developed by Harry J. Holzer and successfully completed telephone interviews with 3,220 employers between 1992 and 1994 in four cities (approximately 800 per city): Atlanta, Boston, Detroit, and Los Angeles. Questions focused on overall employer and employee character- istics, for example, establishment size, recent hiring behavior, composition of current employees by race and gender, and the numbers and characteristics of all currently vacant jobs and recently filled jobs and of the last worker hired into that job. The sample of firms was drawn from two sources: a random sample of firms and their phone numbers stratified by establishment size and the employers of respondents in the MCSUI household survey. The random samples were drawn across establishment size categories to reproduce the distribution of employment across these categories in the work force; the household-generated sample implicitly weights firms in the same way. The sample of recently filled jobs at these firms reasonably represents the universe of new jobs that are currently available to job seekers. There were few differences in response rates across observable categories, for example, establishment size, industry, and location, suggesting little if any sample selection bias. In addition, comparison of industries and size of firm with the *County Business Patterns Data* and with U.S. Census data on occupations verified the representativeness of the sample. See Holzer (1996) for more discussion on the method and sampling of MCES.

6. By and large, the LAES sampling frame and data collection methods were identical to those of the MCES, except for the data collection date, and thus are comparable over time. LAES data were collected between May 2001 and November 2001 from a 20-minute telephone survey administered to 619 establishments in Los Angeles. One difference in the surveys is that the LAES sampled only noncollege jobs, or those jobs that do not require a college degree, while MCES sampled all jobs.

7. Both the MCES and LASE asked a representative sample of employers in Los Angeles the same questions about the hiring requirements (education, experience, and training) of and tasks involved in the last filled job in the firm, thus allowing for different skill definitions of jobs that may be more accurate than other, more universally used measures based upon occupation or industry. These jobs may better represent those for which new low-skilled labor market entrants are qualified. Definitions of low-skill jobs were pursued based upon the tasks performed and the experience, training or educational levels required by employers. Following recent research, the low-skill job category presented in Table 4.1 is the union of jobs that involve no reading, writing, or math tasks and require no experience, training, or high school diploma, and those that require no high school degree, experience, or training.

8. Due to the unique spatial character of the Los Angeles region, we deviated somewhat from official central city/suburban boundaries. There, boundaries define areas that are atypical central-city and suburban places. The low population and employment densities of some central-city areas, in particular the San Fernando

Valley, are more analogous to those in the suburbs, while some close-in areas, in particular East Los Angeles, have densities that match or exceed those in the central city. Thus, in Los Angeles, we include the San Fernando Valley, a central-city area that looks more like a suburban area, as part of the suburbs, and East Los Angeles, a suburban area that looks like a central-city area, as part of the central city in the analysis.

9. Geographic Information Systems and 2000 U.S. Census data were used to examine the racial/ethnic residential composition of census tracts and define seven types of submetropolitan areas within Los Angeles: the central business district (CBD), black central city, Latino central city, white central city, black suburbs, integrated suburbs, and white suburbs. Except for the CBD, the submetropolitan areas are defined by racial/ethnic composition and central city/suburban boundaries. The CBD is defined by the U.S. Census Bureau and is that area within the central city commonly referred to as downtown. The black (Latino) central city is defined as that area within the central city with contiguous census tracts of blacks (Latinos) representing 50 percent or more of the population. Because of the population diversity in Los Angeles, the white central-city area is as those contiguous census tracts where whites represent the plurality of the population. The black suburban area is defined as that area within the suburbs with contiguous census tracts of blacks representing at least 30 percent of the population. The white suburban area is defined as that area within the suburbs with contiguous census tracts of whites representing 80 percent of the population. Finally, the remaining suburban census tracts are defined as integrated suburban areas. In Los Angeles, the integrated area is racially mixed (Asians, Latinos, whites and blacks) and is represented by census tracts where no one group is the majority. See Stoll, Holzer, and Ihlanfeldt (2000) for a justification of these definitions, their sensitivity to different definitions, and a more through discussion of them more generally.

10. Since we compare data on jobs over time, we also examined whether the areas defined by racial residential concentration would change using the 1990 U.S. Census data and whether the distributions of people (total and by race) would change as well. We found that the areas defined by racial residential concentration defined above and the spatial distributions of people were strikingly similar across the two time periods, so we use only data from 2000.

11. In this table for both years, all jobs refer to those jobs that do not require a college degree to make the MCES and LAES exactly comparable.

12. Of course, two major assumptions are being made here. First, the analysis focuses only on the *relative* availability of jobs to different groups of people by geographic location. To the extent that the *absolute* number of jobs available to low-skilled workers may be insufficient for all to become employed (e.g., Holzer and Danziger 2000), these results may understate their employment problems. Furthermore, it is assumed that job proximity is more heterogeneous across submetropolitan areas than within them. This assumption may not always hold; in particular, due to the geographic expanse of the white suburban area, physical job accessibility may display important variability within this area.

13. MCES also contains this information for Atlanta, Boston, and Detroit and finds that the percent of jobs that require a college degree is higher in the central city than suburbs in Atlanta and Detroit and about identical in Boston.

14. IT positions range from technical support, network administration, Web page design, software development, 3-D animation, and digital video editing and mapping, to hardware repair and maintenance and database management and design.

15. The Moving-to-Opportunity program is also partly motivated by the notion of "neighborhood effects," where the concentration of low-income minorities in poor neighborhoods leads to their social isolation from other groups and compounds the various disadvantages that they face (see, for instance, Wilson 1987).

16. To be sure, the skills issue also became prominent because the program administers a clientele with weaker skills than they expected as a result of the booming economy in the late 1990s that adsorbed many unemployed workers that were more job ready.

17. The characterization of workforce development models into basic education and "work first" has also been noted in other studies (see, for example, Strawn 1998; U.S. Department of Labor 1995; Grubb 1995).

18. These ideas were in part influenced by the development of human capital theory in economics (see, for example, Becker 1964, for a discussion of these ideas).

19. In reviewing this literature, a broad base of training organizations were examined and included, among others, CBOs, community technology centers (CTCs), community colleges, and public- and private-sponsored initiatives and training intermediaries. This discussion highlights a number of promising practices. However, this section should not be viewed as exhaustive but rather representative of some of the more important training practices. Moreover, these practices should not be viewed as mutually exclusive in the sense that some practices may serve dual purposes and because many organizations incorporate more than one practice into their training programs and strategies.

20. Employers spend a nontrivial amount of money to keep any one low-skill job filled, particularly when one factors in the high turnover rates that are characteristic of these jobs. Research indicates that employers' search costs for low-skilled to semiskilled workers are on average between $300 and $1,500, depending on how difficult it is to find appropriate labor, and that training costs for these workers range from $700 to $3,000, depending on the type of training required (Frazis, Gittleman, Horrigan, and Jovce 1998; Bishop 1994).

REFERENCES

Annie E. Casey Foundation. 2000. *Stronger links: New ways to connect low-skill workers to better jobs*. Baltimore, MD: Annie E. Casey Foundation.

Autor, David, Lawrence Katz, and Alan Krueger. 1998. Computing inequality: Have computers changed the labor market? *Quarterly Journal of Economics* 113(4):1169–1214.

Autor, David, Frank Levy, and Richard Murnane. 2003. The skill content of recent technological change: An empirical exploration. *Quarterly Journal of Economics* 118(4):1279–1333.

Becker, Gary. 1964. *Human capital: A theoretical and empirical analysis with special reference to education*. Chicago: The University of Chicago Press.

Beers, Thomas M. 2000. Flexible schedules and shift work: Replacing the "9-to-5" workday? *Monthly Labor Review* 123(6):33–40.

Bishop, John. 1994. The incidence of and payoff to employer training. Working paper 94–17, Cornell University, Center for Advanced Human Resource Studies.

Blank, Rebecca M. 1997. *It takes a nation: A new agenda for fighting poverty*. New York and Princeton, NJ: Russell Sage Foundation and Princeton University Press.

Bureau of Labor Statistics. 2003. *Employment and earnings*. Washington, DC: U.S. Department of Labor.

Bliss, Steven. 2000. *San Francisco works: Toward an employer-led approach to welfare reform and workforce development.* New York: Manpower Demonstration Research Corporation.

Briggs, X. 1997. Moving up versus moving out: Neighborhood effects in housing mobility programs. *Housing Policy Debate* 8:195–234.

Buck, Maria. 2002. *Charting New Territory: Early Implementation of the Workforce Investment Act,* New York: Public/Private Ventures.

Cappelli, Peter. 1996. Technology and skill requirements: Implications for establishment wage structure. *New England Economic Review* May/June:139–156.

Chapple, Karen, Matthew Zook, Radhida Kunamneni, AnnaLee Sazenian, Steven Weber, and Beverly Crawford. 2000. *From promising practices to promising futures: Job training in information technology.* New York and Oakland, CA: Ford Foundation and PolicyLink.

Elliot, Mark, B. Palubinsky, and Joseph Tierney. 1999. *Overcoming roadblocks on the way to work.* Philadelphia: Public/Private Ventures.

Erickson, Rodney A., and Susan W. Friedman. 1991. Comparative dimensions of state enterprise zone policies. In *Enterprise Zones: New Directions on Economic Development,* ed. Roy Green, 136–154. Newbury Park, CA: Sage Publications.

Falcon, Luis, Edwin Melendez, and Alexandra de Montrichard. 2003. The role of partnerships and collaborations for workforce development providers serving the disadvantaged in Boston. Paper prepared for the Networking and Best Practices in Workforce Development Conference, June, New York: Ford Foundation.

Frazis, H., M. Gittleman, M. Horrigan, and M. Jovce. 1998. Results from the 1995 survey of employer-provided training. *Monthly Labor Review* 121:3–13.

Freeman, Richard, and William M. Rodgers III. 2000. Area economic conditions and the labor market outcomes of young men in the 1990's expansion. In *Prosperity for All? The Economic Boom and African Americans,* ed. Robert Cherry and William M. Rodgers III, 50–87. New York: Russell Sage Foundation.

Friedlander, Daniel, and Gary Burtless. 1995. *Five years after: The long-term effects of welfare-to-work programs.* New York: Russell Sage Foundation.

Glaeser, Edward. 2000. The future of urban research: Non-market interactions. *Brookings-Wharton Papers on Urban Affairs* 1:101–150.

Glaeser, Edward, and Kahn, Matthew. 2001. Decentralized employment and the transformation of the American city. *Brookings-Wharton Papers on Urban Affairs* 2:1–64.

Green, Roy, ed. 1991. *Enterprise zones: New directions on economic development.* Newbury Park, CA: Sage Publications.

Grogger Jeff, and Stephen J. Trejo. 2002. *Falling behind or moving up? The intergenerational progress of Mexican Americans.* San Francisco: Public Policy Institute of California.

Grubb, W. Norton. 1995. *Evaluating job training programs in the United States: Evidence and explanations.* Berkeley, CA: National Center for the Study of Vocational Education.

Haar, Charles M. 1996. *Suburbs under siege: Race, space and audacious judges.* Princeton, NJ: Princeton University Press.

Harrison, Bennett, and Marcus Weiss. 1998. *Workforce development networks: Community-based organizations and regional alliances.* Thousands Oaks, CA: Sage Publications.

Heldrich Center for Workforce Development at Rutgers University and Center for Survey Research and Analysis at the University of Connecticut. 2000. *Nothing but net: American workers and the information economy.* Newark, NJ: Rutgers University.

Holzer, Harry J. 1996. *What employers want.* New York: Russell Sage Foundation.

————. 1998. Employer skill demands and labor market outcomes of blacks and women. *Industrial and Labor Relations Review* 52(1):82–98.

Holzer, Harry J., and Sheldon Danziger. 2000. Are jobs available for disadvantaged groups in urban areas? In *The Changing Face of Urban Inequality in America,* ed. Lawrence Bobo, Alice O'Connor, and Chris Tilly, 496–538. New York: Russell Sage Foundation.

Holzer, Harry J., and Keith R. Ihlanfeldt. 1996. Spatial factors and the employment of blacks at the firm level. *New England Economic Review* May/June:65–86.

Holzer, Harry J., and Keith R. Ihlanfeldt. 1998. "Customer Discrimination and Employment Outcomes for Minority Workers." *Quarterly Journal of Economics* 113(3):835–867.

Holzer, Harry J., Keith R. Ihlanfeldt, and David L. Sjoquist. 1994. Work, search, and travel among white and black youth. *Journal of Urban Economics* 35:320–345.

Holzer, Harry J., and Paul Offner. 2001. Trends in employment outcomes of young black men, 1979–2000. Paper prepared for Extending Opportunities Conference, Washington, DC.

Holzer, Harry, J., Steve Raphael, and Michael A. Stoll. 2002a. Can employers play a more positive role in prisoner re-entry? The Urban Institute Reentry Roundtable Discussion Paper.

————. 2002b. Perceived criminality, background checks, and the racial hiring practices of employers? Discussion Paper #1254–02, Institute for Research on Poverty, University of Wisconsin.

Holzer, Harry J., and Michael A. Stoll. 2001a. *Employers and welfare recipients: The effect of welfare reform in the workplace.* San Francisco: Public Policy Institute of California.

————. 2001b. *Meeting the demand: Hiring patterns of welfare recipients in four metropolitan areas.* Washington, DC: The Brookings Institution, Center on Urban and Metropolitan Policy.

Jargowsky, Paul A. 2003, *Stunning progress, hidden problems: The dramatic decline of concentrated poverty in the 1990s.* The Living Cities Census Series. Washington, DC: The Brookings Institution, Center on Urban and Metropolitan Policy.

Johnson, M. P., Helen F. Ladd, and Jens Ludwig. 2002. The benefits and costs of residential mobility programmes for the poor. *Housing Studies* 17(1):125–138.

Kasarda, John D. 1995. Industrial restructuring and the changing location of jobs. In *State of the Union: American in the 1990s, Volume One: Economic Trends,* ed. Reynolds Farley, 215–268. New York: Russell Sage Foundation.

Katz, Lawrence, Jeff Kling, and Jeffrey Liebman. 2001. Moving to opportunity in Boston: Early results of a randomized mobility experiment. *Quarterly Journal of Economics* 116(2):607–651.

Katz, Lawrence, and Kevin Murphy. 1992. Changes in relative wages, 1963–87: Supply and demand factors. *Quarterly Journal of Economics* 107(1):35–78.

Kemple, James J., and Joshua Haimson. 1994. *Florida's Project Independence: Program implementation, participation patterns, and first-year impacts.* New York: Manpower Demonstration Corporation.

Kirschenman, Joleen, and Kathryn Neckerman. 1991.We'd love to hire them but ... In *The urban underclass,* ed. Christopher Jencks and Paul Peterson, 203–234. Washington, DC: The Brookings Institution.

Ladd, Helen, F. 1994. Spatially targeted economic development strategies: Do they work? *Cityscape: A Journal of Policy Development and Research* 1(1):193–218.

LaLonde, Robert J. 1995. The promise of public sector-sponsored training programs. *Journal of Economic Perspectives* 9:149–168.

Levy, Frank, and Richard Murnane. 1992. Earnings levels and earnings inequality: A review of recent trends and proposed explanations. *Journal of Economic Literature* 30(3):1333–1371.

Levy, Frank, and Richard Murnane. 1996. *Teaching the new basic skills.* New York: The Free Press.

Lewis Mumford Center. 2001. *The new ethnic enclaves in America's suburbs.* Albany: State University of New York at Albany.

Manski, Charles F., and Irwin Garfinkel, eds. 1992. *Evaluating welfare and training programs.* Cambridge, MA: Harvard University Press.

Melendez, Edwin, and Bennett Harrison. 1998. Matching the disadvantaged to job opportunities: Structural explanations for the past successes of the center for employment training. *Economic Development Quarterly* 12:3–11.

Mills, Edwin. 2000. A thematic history of urban economic research. *Brookings-Wharton Papers on Urban Affairs* 1:1–52.

Moss, Philip, and Chris Tilly. 2001. *Stories employers tell.* New York: Russell Sage Foundation.

National Urban League. 2004. *New findings on recessions and their impacts on African-American unemployment and jobs.* National Urban League Institute for Opportunity and Equality, Washington, DC, April.

Northwest Center for Emerging Technologies. 1999. *Building a foundation for tomorrow: Skill standards for information technology.* Bellevue, WA: Northwest Center for Emerging Technologies.

O'Regan, Katherine M., and John M. Quigley. 1999. Spatial isolation of welfare recipients: what do we know? Program on Housing and Urban Policy Working Paper #W99–003.

Ong, Paul and Evelyn Blumenberg. 1998. Job access, commute and travel burden among welfare recipients. *Urban Studies* 35(1):77–93.

Osterman, Paul. 1995. Skill, training, and work organization in American establishments. *Industrial Relations* 34:125–146.

Raphael, Steven, and Michael A. Stoll. 2001. Can boosting minority car ownership rates narrow inter-racial employment gaps? *Brookings-Wharton Papers on Urban Affairs* 2:99–137.

———. 2002. *Modest progress: The narrowing spatial mismatch between blacks and jobs in the 1990s.* Washington, DC: The Brookings Institution, Center on Urban and Metropolitan Policy.

Rosen, Kenneth T., Grace J. Kim, and Avani A. Patel. 2003. *Shopping the city: Real estate finance and urban retail development.* Washington, DC: The Brookings Institution, Center on Urban and Metropolitan Policy.

Rosenbaum, James E., and Susan J. Popkin. 1991. Employment and earnings of low-income blacks who move to middle-class suburbs. In *The Urban Underclass*, ed. Christopher Jencks and Paul E. Peterson, 342–356. Washington, DC: The Brookings Institution.

Stoll, Michael A. 1999. Spatial job search, spatial mismatch, and the employment and wages of racial and ethnic groups in Los Angeles. *Journal of Urban Economics* 46:129–155.

———. 2000. Search, discrimination, and the travel to work in Los Angeles. In *Prismatic Metropolis: Race, Segregation and Dimensions of Inequality in Los Angeles*, ed. Lawrence D. Bobo, Melvin L. Oliver, James H. Johnson, Jr., and Abel Valenzuela, Jr., 417–452. New York: Russell Sage Foundation.

Stoll, Michael A., Harry J. Holzer, and Keith R. Ihlanfeldt. 2000. Within cities and suburbs: Racial residential concentration and the distribution of employment opportunities across sub-metropolitan areas. *Journal of Policy Analysis and Management* 19(2):207–231.

Stoll, Michael A., and Steven Raphael. 2000. Racial differences in spatial job search patterns: Exploring the causes and consequences. *Economic Geography* 76(3):201–223.

Stoll, Michael A., Steven Raphael, and Harry J. Holzer. 2004. Black job applicants and the hiring officer's race. *Industrial and Labor Relations Review* 57(2): 267–287.

Strawn, Julie. 1998. *Beyond job search or basic education: Rethinking the role of skills in welfare reform.* Washington, DC: Center for Law and Social Policy.

U.S. Census Bureau. 2005. Housing Vacancies and Homeownership, Annual Statistics: 2004. Washington, DC: U.S. Department of Commerce.

U.S. Department of Commerce. 1999. *The digital workforce: Building infotech skill at the speed of innovation.* Washington, DC: U.S. Department of Commerce.

———. 2000. *Digital economy 2000.* Washington, DC: U.S. Department of Commerce.

U.S. Department of Housing and Urban Development. 1997. The state of the cities. Washington, DC: U.S. Department of Housing and Urban Development.

U.S. Department of Labor. 1995. *What's working (and what's not): A summary of research in the economic impacts of employment training programs.* Washington, DC: U.S. Department of Labor.

———. 1996. *Involving employers in training: Best practices.* Washington, DC: U.S. Department of Labor.

Wachs, Martin, and Brian D. Taylor. 1998. Can transportation strategies help meet the welfare challenge? *Journal of the American Planning Association* 64:15–20.

Wilson, William J. 1987. *The truly disadvantaged: The inner city, the underclass, and public policy.* Chicago: University of Chicago Press.

Yinger, John. 1995. *Closed doors, opportunities lost: The continuing costs of housing discrimination.* New York: Russell Sage Foundation.

5 Employment Opportunities Beyond the 'Hood

African American and Hispanic Applicants in Atlanta, Los Angeles, New York, and Philadelphia

Michela M. Zonta

INTRODUCTION

While much of the community economic development field focuses on bringing jobs to disadvantaged minority neighborhoods, the reality is that the majority of residents find work outside their neighborhoods, and often the economic success of these neighborhoods depends largely on job openings beyond their boundaries. Unfortunately, equal access to the larger labor market is often affected by spatially related barriers, especially among minority communities. Urban labor markets have experienced substantial shifts during the past three decades, following the economic stagnation of the early 1970s and the subsequent restructuring of the national economy. While job growth has tended to be concentrated in those sectors that are both high- and low-technology based and draw upon a mix of skilled technicians as well as unskilled workers, manufacturing and other blue-collar industries have increasingly relocated out of central cities.[1] At the same time, racial discrimination in housing and mortgage markets and insufficient affordable housing in areas of job growth have continued to prevent many from moving with their traditional sources of employment.[2] The resulting jobs-housing imbalance has affected growing numbers of potentially productive African Americans and Hispanics who find themselves either jobless, facing longer commutes in comparison to white workers with similar characteristics, or locked in nonunionized, low-paying, and casual jobs.[3]

There is a consensus on the fact that the spatial jobs-housing imbalance does affect wages and employment rates among urban African Americans and to some degree among Hispanics. While most studies in this tradition have focused on wage levels and employment outcomes, only recently have scholars devoted more attention to the relationship between residential segregation and the job search process.[4] The job search of minority individuals residing in inner-city areas seems to be geographically more concentrated with respect to the efforts of comparable job seekers whose residential choices are not constrained. Specifically, search areas tend to be geographically restricted to areas immediately surrounding individuals' residences.

Job search studies have generally focused on the analysis of the supply side of labor rather than the demand side, partly because of the paucity of data on employers.[5] This is unfortunate because the proximity of firms to the residential location of potential job applicants of various racial/ethnic backgrounds deserves as much attention as individual job seekers' search behavior since firm location, among other firm characteristics, is likely to affect the flow and size of the pool of minority applicants, and ultimately the probability for them of being hired.[6] To be sure, it is hard to ascertain the causality of employer location with respect to the flow and size of applicants from different racial groups. In fact, employers might decide to locate in areas where the desired labor force is concentrated, thus reducing the probability of attracting potential applicants from other groups. None-theless, the relationship between firm location and applicant rates among residents of minority neighborhoods is worth exploring because establish-ments that are located at long distances from African American and His-panic concentrations would probably display higher applicant rates among those groups if the job search quality of such potential groups of applicants was not affected by spatially related barriers compared to white applicants with similar characteristics. Moreover, spatially related barriers affect Afri-can American and Hispanic applicant rates in different ways, as do different sociospatial contexts.

This chapter focuses on the recruitment of African American and His-panic job seekers by a sample of 1,069 firms filling low-skill job positions in the Los Angeles, Atlanta, New York, and Philadelphia metropolitan areas.[7] As in other parts of the nation, economic restructuring and demographic changes have had major impacts on the labor market structures of these four metropolitan areas. New York and Los Angeles exemplify the trends toward increasing economic and social polarization resulting from economic re-structuring. The post–Cold War decrease in defense investments has been largely responsible for the decline of the manufacturing sectors of Los An-geles and, to some degree, New York (Table 5.1).[8]

Manufacturing jobs have tended to decentralize, although in both regions the geography of industrial relocation has not resulted in a simple inner city–suburb bifurcation like in other classic monocentric metropolitan areas, but rather in the creation of economic nodes throughout the two jurisdictionally fragmented regions. At the same time, the sectors based on high-technology production and labor-intensive production as well as the business and fi-nancial service sector (FIRE)—particularly in the New York area, before September 11, 2001—have continued to expand, reinforcing the two re-gions' roles as major poles for the coordination of the flow of capital, production and trade at the international level.[9] On the other hand, Phila-delphia, which has historically been one of the largest industrial cities in the nation, has been hit even harder by economic restructuring. As in other Rust Belt cities, deindustrialization has resulted in the loss of jobs within the city's boundary and the relocation of the production of nondurable goods to the suburbs, mainly in the northeastern part of the city, as well as to the outer counties of the metropolitan area. In the central city, increasing numbers of

TABLE 5.1. Selected employment characteristics of study areas, 1971–2000

Year	Atlanta MSA	New York PMSA	Los Angeles PMSA	Philadelphia PMSA
Average Annual Job Growth Rates (Percentages)				
1971–1980	4.5	−0.9	2.4	0.7
1981–1990	4.3	0.9	1.4	1.5
1991–2000	3.6	0.5	−0.1	0.8
Manufacturing: Average Percentage of Total Jobs				
1971–1980	16.9	17.6	26.0	25.7
1981–1990	14.3	12.3	22.8	18.9
1991–2000	11.5	8.4	17.3	13.9
FIRE: Average Percentage of Total Jobs				
1971–1980	7.1	11.9	6.2	6.2
1981–1990	7.0	13.6	6.7	7.0
1991–2000	6.6	13.0	6.1	7.1
Wholesale/Trade: Average Percentage of Total Jobs				
1971–1980	27.6	19.7	22.7	21.5
1981–1990	27.7	18.6	23.1	22.8
1991–2000	26.6	17.4	22.2	22.1
Services: Average Percentage of Total Jobs				
1971–1980	19.6	23.8	21.2	NA
1981–1990	22.6	29.7	26.0	31.5
1991–2000	28.5	35.6	31.7	34.7

Source: Bureau of Labor Statistics

workers are employed in the service sector, especially in activities providing direct services to the city's population. The retail sector, in particular, attracts numerous job seekers, especially among recent immigrants.[10] In contrast, Atlanta has featured the highest job growth rates during the past two decades with respect to the other study areas. Much of the job growth in this region has occurred in the service sector. At the same time, the area has experienced a considerable geographic shift in the location of jobs, including low-skill jobs, to the northern part of the region. The movement of manufacturing jobs to this part of the area has affected employment rates among blacks residing in the southern suburbs of Atlanta.[11]

Economic restructuring has been accompanied by important demographic changes in the four metropolitan areas. As Table 5.2 shows, all four metropolitan areas have experienced population growth during the past two decades. Traditional ports of entry for immigrants, New York and Los Angeles have received increasing numbers of newcomers from Asia and Latin American countries, especially after the 1965 changes in immigration law. This is reflected in the racial/ethnic diversity of New York and Los Angeles. In 2000, 43 percent of the total population of Los Angeles was classified as Hispanic and nearly 13 percent was Asian/Pacific Islander. Similarly, New York is characterized by sizeable Hispanic and Asian/Pacific Islander populations, although these represent smaller proportions of the total population than in Los Angeles (23 percent and 10 percent). African American populations are far larger and more concentrated in Atlanta, New York, and

TABLE 5.2. Selected demographic characteristics of study areas, 1980–2000

	Metropolitan Area			
	Atlanta	Los Angeles	New York	Philadelphia
Population Growth (% Change)				
1980–1990	46	19	4	4
1990–2000	39	7	9	4
Total Population 2000	4,112,198	9,519,338	9,314,235	5,100,931
Racial/Ethnic Breakdown 2000				
%Black	29	10	25	21
%Hispanic	6	43	23	5
%NH White	59	31	40	70
%API	4	13	10	4
Dissimilarity of Blacks				
1980	0.77	0.81	0.77	0.79
1990	0.71	0.74	0.83	0.81
2000	0.65	0.67	0.82	0.72
Dissimilarity of Hispanics				
1980	0.31	0.57	0.69	0.63
1990	0.39	0.63	0.68	0.65
2000	0.51	0.63	0.66	0.60
Blacks in Predominantly Black Neighborhoods (%)	60	28	65	62
Hispanics in Predominantly Hispanic Neighborhoods (%)	4	69	44	22

Source: Census Bureau 1980, 1990, 2000

Philadelphia than in Los Angeles. As Table 5.2 shows, nearly 30 percent of Atlanta's population is black, whereas blacks account for 25 percent and 21 percent of the total population in New York and Philadelphia, compared with 10 percent in Los Angeles. In addition, while 28 percent of blacks in Los Angeles reside in predominantly black neighborhoods, such proportion is much larger in all other metropolitan areas, from 60 percent in Atlanta to 65 percent in New York.[12] In contrast, Hispanics are far more concentrated in Los Angeles than in any other metropolitan area. While almost 70 percent of Hispanics in Los Angeles reside in predominantly Hispanic neighborhoods, such proportion drops to 44 percent in New York. Both the size and concentration of Hispanics are relatively low in Philadelphia and Atlanta, whose populations have historically been characterized by a black-white dichotomy. Here the impact of recent arrivals from Asia and Latin America has been much smaller than in other areas, mainly because of a poor opportunity structure.

In general, growing numbers of newcomers have been associated with increasing levels of residential segregation among Asians and Hispanics, especially in traditional ports of entry. At the same time, African Americans have remained by far the most spatially isolated minority group, notwithstanding higher rates of black suburbanization—especially among an increasingly affluent black middle class—and decreasing levels of black residential segregation.[13] Table 5.2 shows that during the past two decades the residential segregation of African Americans, as measured by the dissimilarity index, has decreased in all metropolitan areas examined in this study with the exception of New York, where segregation levels have increased between 1980 and 2000.[14]

In spite of decreasing segregation levels, black residential segregation levels in Los Angeles, Philadelphia, and New York are still above the national average. In particular, while an average of about 65 percent of all African Americans residing in the nation's metropolitan areas would have to move to different neighborhoods in order to achieve a spatial distribution equivalent to that of whites, the percentage of African Americans who would have to move to achieve an even distribution reaches 72 percent in Philadelphia and 82 percent in New York. Very high levels of segregation in Philadelphia and New York are not surprising, since segregation usually tends to be higher in older metropolitan areas characterized by a sizeable black population and a long history of discriminatory housing practices.[15]

In both New York and Los Angeles, the core part of the metropolitan area has become increasingly Hispanic. While the Hispanic population of Los Angeles comprises predominantly individuals of Mexican descent, New York is characterized by large proportions of Puerto Ricans and immigrants from the Dominican Republic. In Los Angeles, the Mexican population has dramatically spread throughout the central and eastern parts of the region, whereas the size of the African American population has decreased during the past decades, partly due to the relocation of many African Americans to other areas. In Los Angeles, African Americans tend to be predominantly concentrated in an area southwest of downtown and north of Long Beach, stretching between Central Avenue—the historical area of black settlement— and the West Side. In contrast, the black population of Atlanta has experienced a considerable increase during the past two decades. In Atlanta, most blacks reside in the suburbs in the southern part of the region, while the suburbs in the northern side are predominantly white. Similarly, Philadelphia presents a dramatic spatial division of African Americans in the northwest and west, and whites in the eastern part of the metropolitan area.

Jobs and Potential Applicants: An Illustration

To illustrate the location of low-skill job openings with respect to the residential characteristics of African American and Hispanic potential labor pools, I performed a geographic information analysis (GIS) of data from the Survey on Human Resource Practices in the Metropolis. The survey was conducted in 1997 by Roger Waldinger at the University of California, Los Angeles, to study employment patterns and practices in New York, Philadelphia, Atlanta, and Los Angeles. The survey contains information on the size, hiring experiences, and other basic characteristics of each firm in a random sample of 1,069 establishments with noncollege position openings.[16] In addition, the survey provides specific information on the recruitment and hiring process as well as the characteristics of the person who filled the last position in each firm. All surveyed firms were geocoded, that is, each address was assigned longitude and latitude coordinates to represent the location of each establishment as a point on a computer-generated map.

Contextual data used to identify spatial concentrations of potential minority applicants come from Census 2000, Summary File 1. The population 18 to 64 years of age better approximates the labor force population and prevents the analysis from overrepresenting potential applicants concentrations due to the large presence of children among Hispanic immigrants. Further, to locate labor force concentrations without counting groups that are not likely to participate in the labor force, census tracts in which over 40 percent of the total population resides in group quarters—correctional facilities, hospitals, or dorms—are omitted from the analysis.[17] This is particularly important when dealing with populations for which incarceration rates are quite high.

The GIS analysis of the labor force distribution by race and ethnicity in the four metropolitan areas suggests that such patterns are very similar to those observed for the total population within each racial/ethnic group. Geographic concentration in groups of contiguous census tracts located in the central part of each metropolitan area seems to be an explicit characteristic of the residential patterns of African Americans in Los Angeles, Atlanta, and, to some degree, Philadelphia. New York, on the other hand, displays several African American clusters throughout the territory, with major concentrations in Harlem as well as in Bronx, Kings, and Queens counties (Figure 5.1). Furthermore, while Philadelphia and Atlanta feature a minor presence of predominantly Hispanic census tracts, Hispanics clearly

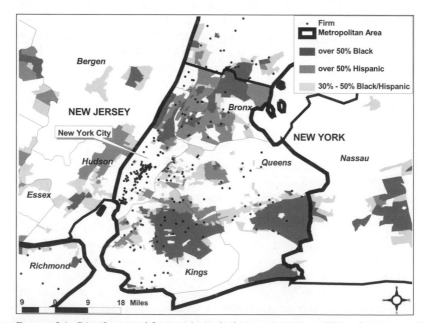

FIGURE 5.1. Distribution of firms and racial/ethnic composition of labor force, New York

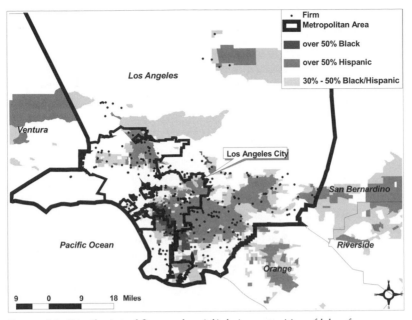

FIGURE 5.2. Distribution of firms and racial/ethnic composition of labor force, Los Angeles

constitute a substantial element in the sociospatial settings of New York and Los Angeles. In Los Angeles, besides the mega-barrio encompassing the central/eastern part of the county, Hispanic clusters can be found in the San Fernando Valley as well as in Long Beach and the northern part of the metropolitan area (Figure 5.2). In New York, the Hispanic labor force is predominantly concentrated in Bronx County as well as in smaller pockets throughout Manhattan, Queens, and Kings counties. In Los Angeles, New York, and Philadelphia, Hispanic clusters tend to be located in areas immediately adjacent to African American neighborhoods. Moreover, in the case of Los Angeles and New York, a number of large Hispanic clusters can also be found in neighboring counties.

A first look at the spatial distribution of surveyed firms reveals an even dispersion throughout the territory of the four metropolitan areas, with higher concentrations in Manhattan, downtown Los Angeles, downtown Philadelphia, and northern Atlanta. Several firms are located in predominantly African American or Hispanic census tracts or in very close proximity to them. In particular, 16 percent and 19 percent of firms in New York and Atlanta respectively are located in majority African American or Hispanic neighborhoods. The percentage of firms located in majority African American or Hispanic census tracts reaches nearly 40 percent in Los Angeles, whereas in Philadelphia only 8 percent of firms fall in such neighborhoods.

Table 5.3 shows the average distance of firms from potential pools of minority applicants. There is a striking difference in the distance from firms to majority white and minority neighborhoods.[18] While establishments are

TABLE 5.3. Average distance from firms to nearest neighborhoods of different racial/ethnic composition (miles)

Metropolitan Area	Neighborhood Racial/Ethnic Characteristics		
	Majority Black	Majority Hispanic	Majority Non-Hispanic White
Atlanta	6.3	14.4	0.6
Los Angeles	9.0	1.1	1.7
New York	2.1	2.2	0.3
Philadelphia	5.7	13.5	0.1
Total Firms	6	7	0.7

generally located at an average distance of less than 1 mile from predominantly white neighborhoods, the average distance is 6 miles from African American neighborhoods and 7 miles from Hispanic census tracts. There are, however, important differences among the four metropolitan areas based on the spatial and sociodemographic configurations of each region. The average distance to black and Hispanic neighborhoods is fairly short in New York and is virtually the same for both groups. Because of the scattered nature of the spatial distribution of African American and Hispanic neighborhoods in the New York metropolitan area and the presence of minority clusters at a short distance from the area's boundaries, even the most outlying establishments are relatively close to at least a few minority census tracts. In the case of New York, therefore, the distance of a firm to the nearest black or Hispanic majority tract does not necessarily reflect the distance to the nearest inner-city neighborhood. The distance to minority neighborhoods is longer whenever black or Hispanic enclaves are relatively small and tend to be geographically concentrated in a specific central sub-area. This is the case of African Americans in Los Angeles, where they represent a fairly small portion of the total population and tend to be concentrated southwest of downtown. Similarly, Hispanics represent a very small portion of the total population of Philadelphia and Atlanta and tend to be concentrated in a few specific neighborhoods. In contrast, whenever racial/ethnic groups represent large portions of the total population and cover much of the metropolitan area's territory, average distances from establishments to such enclaves tend to be shorter. This is the case of Los Angeles, where firms tend to be located at fairly short and similar distances from predominantly Hispanic and white neighborhoods.

Despite its easy computation and interpretation, the distance to the nearest predominantly African American or Hispanic neighborhood might fail to capture the increasing importance of the spatial relocation of some groups, especially among middle-class blacks, to traditionally nonblack or non-Hispanic areas in which they unlikely represent the majority of the population. Also, in areas characterized by dispersed small minority clusters, a firm might be very close to specific minority cluster while featuring an overall low accessibility to the African American or Hispanic labor force of the metropolitan area. A gravity model—measuring the aggregate accessibility of firms to the whole African American and Hispanic labor force dispersed throughout each metropolitan area—may help overcoming such limitations.[19]

The magnitude of the accessibility index varies depending on the size of the population as well as on how dispersed the population distribution is within each metropolitan area. An intermetropolitan comparison of the index reveals important differences that reflect variations in the size and geographic distribution of the pools of white and minority potential applicants, the concentration of firms, and the urban form of each metropolitan area. In general, the sample of firms in each metropolitan area displays the highest accessibility to the white labor force (Figure 5.3). Particularly high values of firms' accessibility to the white labor force in New York reflect a number of factors, including the high population density of the metropolitan area and the fact that many firms are located in the central business district, which is very close to affluent neighborhoods with large white populations (Figure 5.1). Similarly, the highest accessibility to Hispanic labor force in Los Angeles may be attributed to the large proportion of the area's labor force that is Hispanic (39 percent) and to the fact that most firms are located at a closer proximity to Hispanic neighborhoods than to white and black neighborhoods. The very low accessibility to black potential applicants in Los Angeles further depends on the small size of the black labor force in this region and its spatial concentration mainly in one cluster. Not surprisingly, Hispanics display the lowest accessibility in both Atlanta and Philadelphia, most likely due to the small size of the Hispanic labor force in these regions—6 percent and 7 percent respectively.

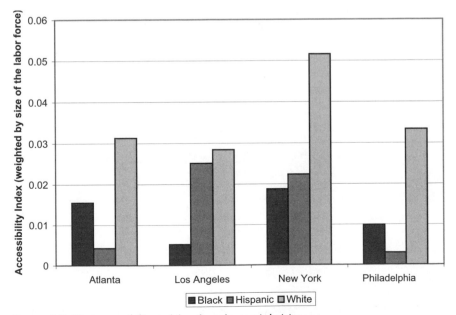

FIGURE 5.3. Firm accessibility to labor force by race/ethnicity

Firm Accessibility and Applicant Flows

How does spatial accessibility to the African American and Hispanic labor force affect firms' recruitment of minority applicants? Table 5.4 shows average African American and Hispanic applicant rates in each metropolitan area by varying degrees of firm accessibility to the African American and Hispanic labor force. The table also reports average percentages of black and Hispanic labor force in each metropolitan area. There is a clear difference in the proportion of applicants from either group depending on the degree of firm accessibility to pools of African American or Hispanic potential applicants. Firms characterized by a high accessibility to African American potential applicants receive an average of 22 percent of job applications from black job seekers compared to 15 percent in establishments with a low accessibility to African Americans. Similarly, firms featuring a high accessibility to the Hispanic labor force receive an average of 22 percent of job applications from Hispanic job seekers compared to 14 percent among firms with a low accessibility to Hispanics.

There are, however, important variations across the four study areas. A look at the average percentages of black and Hispanic applicants reported by firms reveals that while in some metropolitan areas minority applicant rates

TABLE 5.4. Mean black and hispanic applicant rates by accessibility of firms to minority labor force and metropolitan area

Metropolitan Area	Black Applicants (Percentage)			Percentage of Metropolitan Labor Force
	Total	Moderate/Low Accessibility to Black Labor Force[i]	High Accessibility to Black Labor Force[i]	Black Labor Force (%)
Total		15***	22***	
Atlanta	24	20*	29*	25
Los Angeles	8	7	10	8
New York	23	23	22	18
Philadelphia	18	14***	30***	15

Metropolitan Area	Hispanic Applicants (Percentage)			
	Total	Moderate/Low Accessibility to Hispanic Labor Force	High Accessibility to Hispanic Labor Force	Hispanic Labor Force (%)
Total		14***	22***	
Atlanta	4	5	3	7
Los Angeles	36	28***	47***	39
New York	18	12**	21**	20
Philadelphia	6	4**	11**	6

***$p<.001$; **$p<.01$; *$p<.05$
[i]Low and moderate accessibility correspond to bottom two quartiles, whereas high accessibility corresponds to top two quartiles of the accessibility index distribution.

are roughly in parity with the regional minority labor force, this is not the case for all areas. In particular, black applicant rates are greater at New York- and Philadelphia-based firms with respect to those regions' overall supply of African American workers. In contrast, the average percentage of Hispanic applicants at firms in Atlanta, Los Angeles, and New York is lower than those metropolitan areas' supply of Hispanic workers. Important differences also exist among metropolitan areas in terms of minority applicant rates by firm accessibility to minority workers. In particular, there is a significant difference in mean African American applicant rates in both Atlanta and Philadelphia, whereas there is virtually no difference in Los Angeles and New York.[20] Further, there are significant differences in mean Hispanic applicant rates by firm accessibility in Los Angeles, New York, and Philadelphia, although the magnitudes of such differences vary by metropolitan area. In Los Angeles, firms featuring a low accessibility to Hispanics receive an average of 28 percent of total applications from Hispanic job seekers compared to nearly 50 percent among establishments located at closer proximity to the Hispanic labor force. These findings suggest that specific sociospatial configurations and other characteristics might play an important role in enforcing or weakening the relationship between distance to African American or Hispanic potential applicants and application rates from either group.

The spatial distribution of firms receiving no applications from black and Hispanic job seekers and of those in which the majority of applicants are of African American and Hispanic origins reveals clear differences in the degrees of spatial dispersion of firms with respect to predominantly black and Hispanic neighborhoods.[21] In particular, firms with high proportions of black applicants tend to be geographically more concentrated in proximity of African American neighborhoods. This is particularly clear in Philadelphia, where blacks represent a large proportion of total applicants at firms located in traditional black neighborhoods. In Atlanta, on the other hand, firms with high proportions of black applicants tend to be located both within African American neighborhoods or in areas immediately adjacent to them, particularly in the northern part of the city where most of the job growth has taken place. In New York, several firms attracting large proportions of black applicants also tend to be located in predominantly African American neighborhoods. The relatively high spatial dispersion of black neighborhoods throughout the New York metropolitan area, however, is likely to weaken the relationship between firm accessibility to African Americans and black applicant rates. Such effect seems to be exacerbated by the presence of Manhattan, where many firms attract sizeable proportions of black applicants. In Los Angeles, very few firms feature considerable proportions of African Americans among their applicants, most likely due to the small size of the black population in the region. Such firms tend to be located outside of African American neighborhoods.

There are no major differences between firms located in black neighborhoods and those located in other areas in terms of structural characteristics of firms receiving sizeable proportions of African American applications.[22] Most

TABLE 5.5. Coefficients of models of black applicant rates

Variables	Logistic Regression Models			Tobit Regression Models[b]
	Black Applications	Hispanic Applications	Percentage of Black Applicants	Percentage of Hispanic Applicants
Accessibility to labor force[a]	.031**	.614***	.095***	.182***
Medium-sized firm	.027	.003	−.003	−.004
Large firm	.095	−.297	.014	−.099*
Transportation	.241	−.255	.032	−.145
Wholesale/retail	.422*	.060	.080*	−.051
FIRE	.260	−.887*	.091	−.231*
Services	.623***	−.169	.136***	−.108*
Other sector	−.097	−.327	−.006	−.091
White-collar job	.033	−.601***	−.047	−.231***
Close to public transportation	.064	.080	.034	.050
Recruits informally	−.148	.049	−.017	.043
Help-wanted signs/ads in newspaper	.763***	.479*	.058	.057
Recruits formally	.555*	.256	.076	.064
Racial diversity of firm's employees	2.775***	2.218***	.569***	.372***
Los Angeles	−.901***	1.135***	−.308***	.398***
New York	−.542	.580	−.248***	.128
Philadelphia	.239	.847***	−.070	.201**
Constant	−1.407***	−1.626***	−.110	−.251**
Observations	1,011	1,011	1,011	1,011
Uncensored observations			513	418

***$p<.001$; **$p<.01$; *$p<.05$
[a]Accessibility to black labor force for models on black applicants, and to Hispanic labor force for models on Hispanic applicants.
[b]Black applicants censored at $<=.02$; Hispanic applicants censored at $<=.016$.

firms are fairly large and feature blue-collar jobs predominantly in the service sectors of each metropolitan economy. Manhattan represents the only exception in that, not surprisingly, many local establishments receive applications for white-collar jobs in the financial and service sectors.

About half of the sampled establishments reported that they did not receive any applications from African Americans. Such firms are relatively more dispersed throughout the territory of each metropolitan area, with higher concentrations in the central business districts, although several can be found also within or at close proximity to African American neighborhoods. The latter tend to be small or medium-sized establishments and feature jobs in predominantly nontraditional black occupations. In Atlanta and Los Angeles, in particular, most of these firms are in the construction and transportation sectors, whereas in New York and Philadelphia many of these firms belong to the wholesale/retail and, to a lesser degree, the service sectors.

Firms attracting large proportions of Hispanic applicants show spatial patterns similar to those observed for firms with large numbers of African

American applicants. Specifically, such establishments tend to be concentrated in heavily Hispanic areas, especially in Los Angeles, where the highest concentration of this type of firms can be found both throughout the mega-barrio as well as in the San Fernando Valley. Such establishments are generally small and tend to be concentrated in the construction, wholesale, and service sectors. Further, Manhattan and downtown Los Angeles, as well as the Wilshire corridor in Los Angeles, display fairly large clusters of firms that reported not having received any Hispanic applications at the time of the survey. Nonetheless, these same areas also attract several Hispanic applications. In the case of downtown Los Angeles, several firms receive large number of Hispanic applications for blue-collar jobs in the wholesale/ retail and service sectors, requiring the operation of machines and minimal face-to-face contacts with clients.[23] This in not surprising, given the importance of the garment and furniture industries in this area as well as of low-paid services jobs catering to the central business district. In Manhattan, on the other hand, a number of establishments receive several Hispanic applications for clerical jobs in the service sector.

DETERMINANTS OF AFRICAN AMERICAN AND HISPANIC JOB APPLICATIONS

So far, the analysis has shown that, notwithstanding important variations across metropolitan areas, there seems to be a clear relationship between proximity to minority neighborhoods and the composition of job applicants in firms with entry-level positions. In particular, the analysis has shown that the location of establishments with respect to minority communities is related not only to whether firms receive any applications by minority job seekers but also to the proportions of minority applicants at each firm. In general, while firms attracting no minority applicants tend to be located at some distance from pools of potential African American and Hispanic workers, firms receiving most of their job applications from African American and Hispanic job seekers tend to be located within or in very close proximity to predominantly black or Hispanic neighborhoods. These findings suggest that a firm's location, among other characteristics, may affect its attractiveness in terms of flow and size of minority applicants. Specifically, firms located at close proximity to minority neighborhoods might attract many prospective applicants from those areas, whereas attractiveness tends to decay with distance from the overall minority population. Given these preliminary findings, it seems legitimate to explore (1) how much proximity matters in the propensity of a firm to attract minority applicants as well as in the size of the black and Hispanic applicant pools, and (2) how much these could be attributed to other spatially related factors. Further, do firm location and other spatially related factors affect African American and Hispanic application rates in comparable ways? Do regional differences matter?

The literature points to a number of spatially related costs that may affect the job search among African American and Hispanic jobs seekers by constraining their search to areas that are in close proximity to predominantly minority neighborhoods.[24] Often, African American and Hispanic job seekers residing in inner-city neighborhoods face significant transportation-related costs.[25] In automobile-dependent metropolitan areas like Los Angeles, for example, not having access to a car might impact the ability of certain groups, including low-income recent immigrants, to look for jobs outside of their neighborhoods.[26] Indeed, despite recent developments in the public transportation network of Los Angeles, many minority individuals still find themselves isolated in inner-city and immigrant neighborhoods that are poorly served by public transportation. Similarly, Atlanta's public transportation system serves mainly the downtown area and Fulton and DeKalb counties in the northern part of the metropolitan area, thus affecting the mobility of African Americans residing in the southern part of the city.[27] When relying upon public transportation, commuting times to distant potential job search areas are often very extended, thus representing a significant burden for minority job seekers. In addition, the long distance of many suburban establishments from bus stops might counteract the benefits of a job seeker's good access to public transportation.

Even when transportation costs are lower than in Los Angeles, as for many New York and Philadelphia residents, other types of spatially related costs might impact the job search of minority employment seekers. Information costs, for instance, are fairly common among inner-city residents, particularly among non–English-speaking immigrants.[28] Information on job vacancies through social networks and contacts represents one of the main mechanisms through which minority job seekers, especially among Hispanics, learn about job opportunities.[29] By relying on neighborhood-based networks of friends and relatives, however, many inner-city job seekers might have a poor knowledge of job opportunities beyond the restricted boundaries of their daily social activities. While this channel of information might be effective in providing information on local opportunities, it usually becomes less effective with increasing distance from one's neighborhood, by impacting the job search quality of many individuals.

Information on job opportunities depends also on the recruitment methods used by employers.[30] While many employers make use of informal methods of recruitment, like the use of social networks, others tend to use other methods that might help job seekers learn more about distant employment opportunities. For instance, intermediary agencies and various forms of advertisement generally provide the link to employment opportunities located beyond local settings and encompassing larger geographic areas. The literature suggests that African Americans have a higher propensity than other minority job seekers to rely upon formal methods. In such cases, formal methods might mitigate the impact of other spatially related barriers on African Americans' job search. Nonetheless, given the long history of racial discrimination in this country, the quality and geographic extent of the job search of minority seekers, especially among African Americans, might be influenced by their perception of racial discrimination in the job market and their fear of being rejected in particular racial settings.[31] Thus, in some instances, minority job seekers might deliberately avoid searching for employment in suburban areas characterized by large proportions of white residents or in firms catering mainly to a white clientele or in establishments featuring a predominantly white labor force.

Multivariate analysis shows that a close proximity to pools of potential black and Hispanic applicants increases the probability of firms to receive applications from the two groups, when holding firm characteristics and geographic location constant (See Appendix A for the model and statistical results). In particular, for each additional unit in the firm accessibility index to the black labor force, the odds of receiving black applications increase by nearly 50 percent. Similarly, for each additional unit in the firm accessibility index to the Hispanic labor force, the odds of receiving Hispanic applications nearly double. As expected, recruitment methods also make a difference in the degree to which firms attract black and Hispanic applicants. In particular, help-wanted signs and ads in newspapers double the odds of receiving black applications and increase those of receiving Hispanic applications by over 60 percent compared to firms featuring open recruitment methods. Furthermore, consistent with the literature, formal recruitment methods significantly encourage black job seekers to apply for advertised positions, holding other characteristics constant. The racial makeup of firms is strongly associated with the probability of receiving applications from both black and Hispanic job seekers.[32] Finally, geographic differences affect the odds of receiving any application from blacks and Hispanics. In Los Angeles, while the probability of attracting black applicants is lower than in other metropolitan areas, the opposite is true in the case of Hispanic applicants. Firms based in Los Angeles triple the odds of receiving Hispanic applications compared to Atlanta-based firms. Similarly, Philadelphia-based firms seem to attract Hispanic applicants more than in Atlanta.[33]

The analysis also explores the impact of firm accessibility on the percentage of applicants that are African American and Hispanic. The average percentage of African American and Hispanic applicants increases with increasing firm's spatial accessibility to the African American and Hispanic labor force respectively, although the impact of location seems to be stronger in the case of Hispanics. After controlling for other firm characteristics, each increase in the firm accessibility to black potential applicants is associated with nearly a 10 percent increase in the proportion of black applicants whereas in the case of Hispanics the net effect of firm accessibility is an 18 percent increase in the proportion of applicants. Firm size seems to have opposite effects for the two groups. Being a large firm increases a firm attractiveness with respect to African American job seekers, whereas it is associated with decreasing rates of Hispanic applicants.[34] This is consistent with previous findings, according to which while Hispanics tend to apply for jobs at medium-sized and small firms, African Americans generally feel more comfortable applying for jobs at large firms, which are usually perceived as more likely to comply with antidiscrimination laws than smaller establishments.[35]

Interestingly, while the firm's proximity to public transportation and recruitment methods do not seem to significantly affect the flow of black and

Hispanic applicants, the racial diversity of firm's employees plays a paramount role in the rates of black and Hispanic applicants. Specifically, each increase in racial diversity yields nearly a 57 percent increase in the proportion of African Americans among applicants, pointing to the importance of social factors in the job search among this group. Specifically, higher levels of racial heterogeneity, which in many cases might be associated with lower proportions of whites among employees as well as among a firm's clientele—hence with a lower probability for the firm to be located in job-rich suburbs—might attract more African American applicants because of minimal perceived racial prejudice in a job setting. Similarly, each increase in racial diversity is associated with a 37 percent increase in the proportion of Hispanic applicants, holding other characteristics constant.

Finally, regional differences seem to matter for both groups. Los Angeles–based firms, in particular, are associated with nearly a 40 percent increase in the proportion of Hispanic applicants and a 31 percent decrease in black applicants compared to Atlanta-based firms. New York–based firms are also associated with a decrease in black applicants, suggesting that different sociospatial configurations affect the relationship between geographic location of firms and the size and flow of minority applicants.

CONCLUSION

This chapter has examined how spatial barriers affect access to the larger urban labor market for residents of African American and Hispanic neighborhoods by examining the effects of proximity of firms with entry-level positions to minority neighborhoods on their probabilities of receiving applicants from the two groups and on the composition of such applicants. Given the limited economic base of most minority communities, employment outcomes for local residents depend on the ability to find work outside their immediate neighborhoods. There are, however, a number of barriers, such as the lack of appropriate skills and weak social networks. These problems are compounded by firms' locations with respect to pools of potential applicants. By analyzing the recruitment of African American and Hispanic job seekers by firms filling low-skill jobs, this study presents findings that are in general consistent with the spatial mismatch hypothesis. Firms that are closer to minority communities tend to both attract any African American and Hispanic applicants and receive relatively more African American and Hispanic applicants. Furthermore, the impact of location seems to be stronger in the case of Hispanics, suggesting that the job search area tends to be particularly restricted for Hispanics, many of whom are immigrants and tend not to have a strong familiarity with the larger labor market, while relying predominantly on informal and neighborhood-based networks of friends and relatives. Other firm characteristics—such as size, recruitment methods, and racial diversity—also affect the outcome, and at times the impacts on the two groups differ significantly. In particular, consistent with previous findings, larger firms seem to attract decreasing proportions of Hispanic applicants. Further, formal recruitment methods and racial diversity are associated with particularly high firm probabilities of receiving any applications from black job seekers, suggesting that the perception of racial discrimination in the labor market might still affect the job search practices of African Americans, despite the enforcement of antidiscrimination laws. Contrary to what one might expect, establishments' proximity to public transportation does not seem to significantly affect the flow of African American and Hispanic applicants to firms. Such finding may suggest that other factors should be taken into consideration in an analysis of this kind, namely the accessibility of public transportation in minority neighborhoods that could link potential applicants to establishments. The lack of such information represents a limitation for this study, suggesting that more attention should be paid in future analyses at transportation networks in minority neighborhoods and their heterogeneity across different metropolitan contexts in order to understand better the opportunities and dynamics occurring at both ends of the job search trip. The study finds regional differences for both African Americans and Hispanics, implying that urban labor markets do not operate in a uniform way and that it is important to pay attention to such differences when testing the spatial mismatch hypothesis.

The findings of this study have important implications for community economic development. In particular, given the consistent impact of proximity on the flows of minority job applicants across different labor markets and ultimately on their probability of being hired, it is important to lower the spatial barriers to employment opportunities for residents of minority neighborhoods both through traditional community economic development tools and by exploring alternative approaches focusing on regional labor markets and their accessibility by different racial/ethnic populations. In particular, community economic efforts ought to focus more on linking potential minority applicants to employment opportunities that are beyond the reach of minority neighborhoods due not only to poor transportation linkages but also other factors that may be often overlooked, such as the recruitment methods of employers and information about job openings. Information networks, especially among segments of the labor force consisting of large proportions of recent immigrants, ought to be strengthened in order for potential applicants to learn more about job opportunities that are beyond the reach of informal and neighborhood-based social networks. Such efforts imply a thorough awareness of job opportunities at the regional level as well as of the spatial barriers that affect each minority group in a distinct way.

APPENDIX A—REGRESSION MODEL AND RESULTS

Both a logistic regression and tobit regression are used to explore whether firms' proximity to African American and Hispanic labor force affects job applications from the two groups after controlling for other spatially related job search costs and selected firm characteristics. In the logistic regression models, the outcome is a dichotomous variable coded 1 for one or more applications from minority job seekers—black applicants in the model for blacks and Hispanic applicants in the model for Hispanics—and 0 for no minority applications. In contrast, the dependent variable in the tobit regression models is the proportion of African Americans or Hispanics among each firm's applicants. The independent variables for all regression models include (1) the normalized accessibility index, which is an indicator of firm location with respect to African American and Hispanic potential applicants; (2) firm proximity to public transportation, coded 1 for firms located up to 3 minutes away from a public transit stop, and 0 for those located farther away; (3) a series of dummy variables indicating the recruitment method (formal methods, help-wanted signs and ads in newspapers, informal methods, and walk-ins); (4) a racial diversity index of firm employees; (5) firm characteristics, including type of industry, white-collar jobs, and firm size; and (6) dummy variables for each metropolitan area to account for regional variations. The omitted categories are small, for firm size; construction, for type of industry; blue-collar jobs; more than 3 minutes away from public transportation; walk-ins; and the Atlanta metropolitan area. The table contains the results of the logistic and tobit regressions performed for both black and Hispanic applicants.

NOTES

1. I would like to thank Roger Waldinger and Nelson Lim for providing access to the data set used for this study and for their helpful comments and suggestions.

2. See Kasarda (1985), Wilson (1980; 1987).

3. For comprehensive reviews of the spatial mismatch literature see Holzer (1991), Kain (1992), Ihlanfeldt and Sjoquist (1998).

4. See Stoll and Raphael (2000), Leonard (1987), Stoll (2000).

5. One exception is represented by the recently released volumes of the Multi-City Study of Urban Inequality.

6. See also Holzer and Ihlanfeldt (1996), Holzer and Reaser (2000), Stoll, Holzer, and Ihlanfeldt (2000).

7. The study employs the Census Bureau's definition of metropolitan areas: the Metropolitan Statistical Area of Atlanta and the Primary Metropolitan Statistical Areas of Los Angeles, New York, and Philadelphia. While Los Angeles PMSA coincides with the county, the other metropolitan areas consist of multiple counties. New York PMSA and Philadelphia consist of eight and nine counties respectively, whereas Atlanta MSA encompasses twenty counties. The following counties constitute New York PMSA: New York, Putnam, Westchester, Rockland, Bronx, Queens, Kings, and Richmond. Atlanta MSA includes the following counties: Pickens, Bartow, Cherokee, Forsyth, Fulton, Gwinnett, Barrow, Paulding, Cobb, DeKalb, Walton, Carroll, Douglas, Rockdale, Newthon, Clayton, Henry, Fayette, Coweta, and Spalding. Philadelphia PMSA encompasses the following counties: Philadelphia, Bucks, Montgomery, Chester, and Delaware in the state of Pennsylvania, and Burlington, Camden, Gloucester, and Salem in the state of New Jersey.

8. See Abu-Lughod (1999), Scott and Soja (1996), Soja (2000).

9. Ong, Bonacich, and Cheng (1994), Abu-Lughod (1999), Sassen (1991).

10. See Goode and Schneider (1994).

11. See Hartshorn and Ihlanfeldt (2000), Stoll, Holzer, and Ihlanfeldt (2000), Moss and Tilly (2001).

12. Predominantly black neighborhoods are defined as the census tracts in which blacks account for 50 percent or more of the tract population. Similarly, predominantly Hispanic neighborhoods are defined as the census tracts in which Hispanics account for 50 percent or more of the tract population.

13. See Massey and Denton (1989; 1993), Denton and Massey (1988; 1991), Farley (1997), Frey and Farley (1996), Farley and Frey (1994).

14. The most commonly used measure of segregation is the index of dissimilarity D, popularized by Duncan and Duncan in the 1950s. This index is commonly used to investigate the degree of evenness among particular groups, that is the differential distribution of minority and majority members across parcels within an urban area. Specifically, the index measures the proportion of the minority or majority population who would have to be redistributed so that each parcel would have exactly the same composition as the city as a whole (Duncan and Duncan, 1955).

15. See Massey and Denton (1989; 1993), Denton and Massey (1988; 1991), Farley (1997), Frey and Farley (1996).

16. A total of 230 establishments were surveyed in Atlanta, 314 in Los Angeles, 310 in New York, and 215 in Philadelphia.

17. See Massey and Denton (1987).

18. I calculated the Euclidean distance of each establishment from the centroid of the nearest majority African American or Hispanic census tract. Given the observed patterns of concentration of African American and Hispanic groups in clusters of contiguous census tracts in the four metropolitan areas, this measure is likely to represent a fairly good approximation of the distance of firms to African American and Hispanic enclaves. To capture the pockets of black and Hispanic labor force that are beyond the boundaries of each metropolitan area, the calculations take into account those tracts located within a 30-mile distance from such boundaries. Indeed, a number of firms are located very close to the geographic boundaries of their respective metropolitan area. In some cases, such firms are located far from the inner-city minority labor force, but at close proximity to minority clusters located in neighboring counties. These firms might not receive many applications from job seekers residing in the core of the metropolitan area but rather attract potential applicants from labor force clusters located beyond metropolitan administrative boundaries.

19. I calculated the aggregate accessibility index that, in spite of its complexity in terms of computation and interpretation, offers some advantages with respect to the Euclidean distance. By taking into account the entire labor force across racial/ethnic groups, the index is not affected by the omission of census tracts whose minority population has been growing but has not reached a majority yet. The number of people per mile represents the unit of the index and the closer the people of each metropolitan area are, in aggregate, to a firm, the greater will be the value of the index. See Plane and Rogerson (1994) for a discussion of the index. The accessibility index is computed as follows:

$$V_i = \sum_{i=1}^{r} (P_i/d_{ij})$$

Where V_j is the accessibility index value at any firm j, P_i is the population in the labor force of every census tract i in each metropolitan area, and d_{ij} is the distance from the centroid of each census tract of the metropolitan area to the firm.

20. Interestingly, there is an opposite relationship in New York, although the difference in means is not significant.

21. Maps not shown but available from the author.

22. Data are not shown but are available from the author.

23. In general, establishments based in the central business district with noncollege positions receiving large proportions of black and Hispanic applications seem to be far fewer than what one might expect given the proximity of these areas to large pools of potential minority applicants. There are, however, some exceptions. For example, the average percentage of Hispanic applicants at establishments located in downtown Los Angeles is 44 percent, compared to 30 percent among whites, and 4 percent among blacks. In the central business districts of other metropolitan areas, the percentages of black applicants are much higher than in Los Angeles, although they are generally lower than those of white applicants.

24. See Marsden and Gorman (2001), Holzer and Ihlanfeldt (1996), Holzer and Reaser (2000).

25. See Taylor and Ong (1995) for a discussion of the "transportation mismatch."

26. See Stoll (1999).

27. See Hartshorn and Ihlanfeldt (2000).

28. See Ihlanfeldt (1998), Holzer (1987), Ihlanfeldt and Sjoquist (1990).

29. See Marsden and Gorman (2001), Moss and Tilly (2000).

30. See Moss and Tilly (2000).

31. See Stoll (1999; 2000).

32. While in the case of Hispanics, each additional unit of the diversity index increases the odds of receiving applications nine times, the odds increase 16 times in the case of black applicants, pointing to the high importance of racial diversity in the firm for both groups.

33. The logistic regression models also show that the type of industry makes a difference in the degree to which establishments attract black and Hispanic applicants. Wholesale/retail and service firms tend to be associated with significantly higher probabilities of attracting any black applicants. In contrast, the model for Hispanic applicants shows that the coefficient associated with establishments in the FIRE sector is negative and significant, revealing that Hispanics tend not to apply for jobs at such firms, holding accessibility and other characteristics constant. Similarly, white-collar jobs seem not to attract Hispanic applicants.

34. The coefficient for blacks, however, is not significant.

35. Findings also suggest that while white-collar jobs are associated with significantly decreasing Hispanic applicant rates, type of industry seems to be associated with opposite effects for the two groups. Specifically, compared to the construction sector, service sectors are associated with significantly decreasing applicant rates among Hispanics, whereas the opposite is true for African Americans.

REFERENCES

Abu-Lughod, Janet L. 1999. *New York, Chicago, Los Angeles: America's Global Cities*. Minneapolis: University of Minnesota Press.

Denton, Nancy A., and Douglas S. Massey. 1991. Patterns of neighborhood transition in a multiethnic world: U.S. metropolitan areas 1970–1980. *Demography* 28(1):41–63.

———. 1998. Residential segregation of blacks, Hispanics, and Asians by socioeconomic status and generation. *Social Science Quarterly* 69(4):797–817.

Duncan, Otis Dudley, and Beverly Duncan. 1955. A methodological analysis of segregation indexes. *American Sociological Review* 20:210–217.

Farley, Reynolds. 1997. Racial trends and differences in the United States 30 years after the Civil Rights decade. *Social Science Research* 26:235–262.

Farley, Reynolds, and William H. Frey. 1994. Changes in the segregation of whites from blacks during the 1980s: Small steps toward a more integrated society. *American Sociological Review* 59:23–45.

Frey, William H., and Reynolds Farley. 1996. Latino, Asian, and Black segregation in U.S. metropolitan areas: Are multiethnic metros different? *Demography* 33(1):35–50.

Goode, Judith, and Jo Anne Schneider. 1994. *Reshaping Ethnic and Racial Relations in Philadelphia: Immigrants in a Divided City.* Philadelphia: Temple University Press.

Harthshorn, Truman A., and Keith R. Ihlanfeldt. 2000. Growth and change in metropolitan Atlanta. In *The Atlanta Paradox,* ed. David L. Sjoquist, 15–41. New York: Russell Sage Foundation.

Holzer, Harry. 1991. The spatial mismatch hypothesis: What has the evidence shown? *Urban Studies* 28:105–122.

Holzer, Harry J., and Jess Reaser. 2000. Black applicants, black employees, and urban labor market policy. *Journal of Urban Economics* 48:365–387.

Holzer, Harry J., and Keith R. Ihlanfeldt. 1996. Spatial factors and the employment of blacks at the firm level. *New England Economic Review* May/June:66–86.

Hum, Tarry, and Michael Zonta. 2000. Residential Patterns of Asian Pacific Americans. In *The State of Asian Pacific America: Transforming Race Relations,* ed. Paul M. Ong, 191–242. Los Angeles: LEAP, Asian Pacific American Public Policy Institute and UCLA Asian American Studies Center.

Ihlanfeldt, Keith R., and David L. Sjoquist. 1990. Job accessibility and racial differences in youth employment rates. *American Economic Review* 80:267–276.

———. 1998. The spatial mismatch hypothesis: A review of recent studies and their implication for welfare reform. *Housing Policy Debate* 9:849–892.

Kain, John F. 1992. The spatial mismatch hypothesis: Three decades later. *Housing Policy Debate* 3:371–460.

Kasarda, John D. 1985. Urban change and minority opportunities. In *The New Urban Reality,* ed. P. Peterson, 33–67. Washington, DC: Brookings Institution Press.

Leonard, Jonathan S. 1987. The interaction of residential segregation and employment discrimination. *Journal of Urban Economics* 21:323–346.

Marsden, Peter V., and Elizabeth H. Gorman. 2001. Social networks, job changes, and recruitment. In *Sourcebook of Labor Markets: Evolving Structures and Processes,* ed. Ivar Berg and Arne L. Kalleberg, 467–502. New York: Kluwer Academic/Plenum.

Massey, Douglas S., and Nancy A. Denton. 1993. *American Apartheid: Segregation and the Making of the Underclass.* Cambridge: Harvard University Press.

———. 1989. Hypersegregation in U.S. metropolitan areas: Black and Hispanic segregation along five dimensions. *Demography* 26(3):373–391.

———. 1987. Trends in the residential segregation of blacks, Hispanics, and Asians: 1970–1980. *American Sociological Review* 52:802–825.

Moss, Philip, and Charles Tilly. 2001. *Stories Employers Tell: Race, Skill, and Hiring in America.* New York: Russell Sage Foundation.

Ong, Paul, Edna Bonacich, and Lucie Cheng. 1994. *The New Asian Immigration in Los Angeles and Global Restructuring.* Philadelphia: Temple University Press.

Ong, Paul, and Michela Zonta. 2001. Trends in earning inequity. In *The State of California Labor*, eds. Paul M. Ong and Jim Lincoln, 39–60. Los Angeles and Berkeley: University of California, Institute of Industrial Relations.

Plane, David A., and Peter A. Rogerson. 1994. *The Geographical Analysis of Population: With Applications to Planning and Business*. New York: J. Wiley.

Sassen, Saskia. 1991. *The Global City: New York, London, Tokyo*. Princeton: Princeton University Press.

Scott, Allen J., and Edward W. Soja, eds. 1996. *The City: Los Angeles and Urban Theory at the End of the Twentieth Century*. Berkeley and Los Angeles: University of California Press.

Soja, Edward W. 2000. *Postmetropolis: Critical Studies of Cities and Regions*. Malden, MA: Blackwell.

Stoll, Michael A. 2000. Search, discrimination, and the travel to work. In *Prismatic Metropolis: Inequality in Los Angeles*, ed. D. Bobo et al., 417–452. New York: Russell Sage Foundation.

———. 1999. Spatial mismatch, discrimination and male youth employment in the Washington, DC Area. *Journal of Policy Analysis and Management* 18:77–98.

Stoll, Michael A., and Steven Raphael. 2000. Racial differerences in spatial job search patterns: Exploring the causes and consequences. *Economic Geography* 76(3):201–223.

Stoll, Michael A., Harry Holzer, and Keith R. Ihlanfeldt. 2000. Within cities and suburbs: Racial residential concentration and the spatial distribution of employment opportunities across sub-metropolitan areas. *Journal of Policy Analysis and Management* 19(2):207–231.

Taylor, Brian D., and Paul M. Ong. 1995. Spatial mismatch or automobile mismatch? An examination of race, residence and commuting times in U.S. metropolitan areas. *Urban Studies* 32:1453–1473.

Wilson, William Julius. 1980. *The Declining Significance of Race: Blacks and Changing American Institutions*. 2nd ed. Chicago: University of Chicago Press.

———. 1987. The truly disadvantaged: The inner city, the underclass, and public policy. Chicago: University of Chicago Press.

Zonta, Michela. 2005. Housing policies and the concentration of poverty in urban America. Review Essay. *Social Service Review* 79(1):181–185.

6 Economic Development in Latino Communities

Incorporating Marginal and Immigrant Workers

ABEL VALENZUELA JR.

INTRODUCTION

Immigrant and contingent workers from Mexico, Central America and elsewhere have taken on increased labor market significance in the United States for several reasons. First, they continue to represent a significant proportion of the population and in recent years have grown in size—Latinos[1] are disproportionately represented in their ranks. Second, the concentration of Latinos and other racial minority groups in segregated and poor communities makes them especially vulnerable to larger macro changes and economic restructuring, both of which impact their employment and wage outcomes. Finally, continued increases in the number of low-skilled Latino immigrants, coupled with diminished labor market mobility opportunities and a host of human capital and other barriers, relegate a significant proportion of them to the ranks of the working poor. Combined, all of these factors contribute to higher rates of poverty among Latinos and make them an increasing share of the total poor. Economic development is a viable tool to ameliorate working poverty among Latinos, but only if mainstream economic development strategies are reconsidered to account for the growing demographic that is immigrant and that works on the margins in contingent jobs.

In this chapter, I argue that economic development in Latino communities needs to play a more central role in addressing marginal workers (the working poor and contingent workers) and immigrant workers—a large segment of the Latino working community. To make my case, I first discuss the growing pattern of Latino poverty and the working poor, including part-time, unemployed, and contingent workers. I then briefly discuss the prevailing models of economic development, paying particular attention to entrepreneurialism—perhaps the one model in the economic development literature that attempts to acknowledge, albeit peripherally, the importance of work as an economic development strategy. I discuss how contemporary definitions and interpretations of entrepreneurship are elitist and overly focused on firm or small business development. As a result, economic development frameworks that rely on entrepreneurship models as their primary strategy for intervention fail to adequately address a large portion of the marginal and immigrant labor pool. I close by discussing strategies that incorporate immigrant, working poor, and contingent workers not only in entrepreneurship models but also in larger economic and community development strategies.

THE LABOR-MARKET FOUNDATION OF LATINO POVERTY

Latino poverty is inextricably tied to the labor market. In the year 2000, when the unemployment rate fell to 4.0 percent—its lowest level in more than three decades—the overall poverty rate also fell to its lowest level since 1979. At this time, poverty rates for Latinos were also at all-time lows. Unfortunately, 2000 was the high-water mark for the longest economic expansion in the United States; since then, the economy has gone through a recession and a "jobless recovery." Even in 2000, when poverty rates had fallen for most Americans, troubling trends remained. Although Latino poverty declined during the 1990s' boom, its rate remained comparatively high (21.2 percent) and well above the white poverty rate of 7.5 percent. Well over seven million Latinos lived in poverty in the United States. Equally troubling was the fact that over one-third of Latina female-headed households fell into this category. The poverty rates of families headed by married couples are highest among Latinos, suggesting strong cultural ties to marriage and two low-income earners. A significant number of Latinos are found in metropolitan areas where central cities have become the largest repository of poor people. According to a recent study of the working poor in Los Angeles (More 2000), one in four workers in the county is poor.[2] The report counts over one million Los Angeles residents as working poor (among them janitors, maids, teaching assistants, seamstresses, actors, and parking lot attendants) and decries the fact that while overall employment in Los Angeles increased by only 2 percent during the 1990s, the ranks of the working poor swelled by 34 percent. According to the report, the working poor in Los Angeles are increasingly middle-aged, full-time workers who live in two-adult households with children. They are also overwhelmingly immigrant and Latino.

Three frameworks help us understand Latino poverty in the United States. They are the urban underclass, the immigration of low-skilled workers, and the theory of labor market disadvantage and economic restructuring. The urban underclass model, drawn primarily from Wilson's (1987) theory of understanding black urban poverty, is probably the most widely used framework for explaining Latino poverty as well. Wilson's model proposes a distinction between those who are poor and live in mixed-class (i.e., nonpoverty) neighborhoods and the poor who live in neighborhoods with high concentrations of poor families. The neighborhood effects of concentrated poverty tend to perpetuate the social disadvantage of inner-city residents and feed their pathological behaviors (i.e., welfare dependency, single-headed households, violent crime, and gang- associated behavior). Those who have attempted to assess the applicability of the underclass hypothesis to Latinos focus on five important characteristics: (1) the dislocation of local urban economies, (2) the concentration of poverty and residential segregation, (3) the changing class structure and migration patterns, (4) the stability of the family and other neighborhood institutions, and (5) welfare dependency.

Most of the literature (Moore and Pinderhughes 1993) rejects the proposition that the underclass is a theory useful to understanding Mexican, or for that matter, Latino, poverty. While evidence of all five of these characteristics exist for Latinos, the model falls short as an explanatory framework for two primary reasons. First, residential segregation patterns for Latinos are not as severe as they are for African Americans, and as a result, the harsh concentration thesis that Wilson uses convincingly to explain pathological behaviors and social dislocations among the black poor loses its strength when applied to Latinos. Second, the instability of family and other neighborhood institutions is also less severe for Latinos than it is for African Americans, primarily because of the massive immigration of Latinos during the past three decades, which has replenished communities and in essence served as a buffer for impoverished communities. Immigrants bring with them strong culturally based family values; ties to the church; a strong work ethic; and a high tolerance for abuse, discrimination, and poor work conditions. The result is that despite high rates of exploitation, Latino immigrants will work in jobs that many will not. Even though poverty clearly exists in Latino communities throughout the United States, and is in many instances concentrated in a geographic area or *barrio*, the barrio is rarely afflicted by the dire blight or economic inactivity found in impoverished black ghettos. For example, *bodegas*, street vendors, day laborers, small ethnic businesses, and other forms of economic activity clearly take place in poor Latino communities.

The idea that immigration is an explanatory thesis for understanding Latino poverty is similarly inadequate. The framework is simple, and revolves around two possible explanations: the quality of recent cohorts argument and the effects of immigration on the labor market. The first explanation argues that recent (post-1965) immigrants to the United States are less skilled than earlier migrants, resulting in poor labor-market outcomes. The second explanation involves segmented job competition (Ong and Valenzuela 1995) and argues that as close substitutes, Latino immigrants and low-skilled natives compete for jobs, which leads to lower wages, higher unemployment, and increased poverty.

The immigration thesis, like the underclass thesis, cannot adequately explain Latino poverty. The evidence that today's immigrants are less skilled than earlier waves is mixed and often relies on immigrant characteristics rather than on the evolution of employers' demands in a changing U.S. economy—one that increasingly relies on low-skilled workers. As a result of this oversight, demand analyses go largely ignored, when, clearly, bifurcated labor markets depend on and demand workers who will undertake jobs requiring few skills and consisting of dirty or difficult tasks. And again, as described in the underclass hypothesis, immigrants are rejuvenating ethnic neighborhoods through consumer spending, small business start-ups, alternative income-generating activities, and other economic activities. Finally, the debate on job competition is mixed and arguably leans toward little or no effect on native employment (see Ong and Valenzuela 1995 for a review of this literature).

The last model, labor market disadvantage and economic restructuring, offers a more convincing explanation. In this model, poor labor-market outcomes among Latinos are attributed to seven factors or characteristics that immigrants bring with them or that are prevalent among native-born Latinos. They are (1) lower educational attainment and youthfulness, (2) a lack of English proficiency, (3) being unauthorized or illegal, (4) their country of origin, (5) tenure in the United States, (6) their concentration (segregation) in low-wage firms, industries, and occupations, and (7) their race (phenotype) and gender background (Valenzuela and Gonzalez 2000). The research shows that these factors adversely affect wages and joblessness for Latinos. Higher rates of unemployment for Latinos are of special concern because researchers have found that differences in unemployment are not primarily explained by personal characteristics or education. Rather, Latinos have a higher probability of experiencing one or more spells of unemployment but, interestingly, have a lower duration of unemployment. That is, job turnover is high and rapid, as Latinos and immigrants cycle in and out of low-skill jobs. This latter fact is the result of Latinos having a lower reservation wage—a greater disposition to accept lower-paying work after losing a job. There is also a higher proportion of involuntary part-time work among Latinos, indicating that Latinos prefer to stay in less desirable jobs rather than face unemployment.

Economic restructuring and other macro changes in labor markets are disproportionately affecting Latinos, often by relegating them to unsteady jobs with low pay. The transformations brought about by economic restructuring—on industrial production, the demand for labor, and the spatial distribution of resources—greatly affect local labor markets and are particularly harmful to Latinos and immigrants. Race, gender, and nativity discrimination in employment and housing also lead to fewer employment opportunities and higher unemployment. Economic restructuring also affects the employment opportunities of Latinos through three well-documented processes. First, industrial change could induce a skill mismatch between the (higher) skill requirements of new jobs and the existing (lower) skills of workers. Usually, this change in skill requirements involves a relocation of jobs from the inner city to the surrounding suburban areas, which also disproportionately affects the employment opportunities of Latinos. Second, the expansion of service jobs also affects Latinos through increases in low-wage and low-skill jobs in this sector. Workers in the service sector have less stable jobs and restricted employment opportunities. Third, industrial restructuring and the decline of specific industries have led to realignments in ethnic job queues. Industries on the decline use immigrant labor and small ethnic entrepreneurs to lower production costs, resulting in ethnic succession in employment. The use of this labor supply enhances labor flexibility, which relies on part-time and temporary workers or what are known as contingent workers.

An integral part of economic restructuring is a secular expansion of informal employment and growth in the use of contingent workers. Informal work—variously referred to as the "underground" sector, "hidden" work, or the "shadow" economy (see Williams and Windebank 1998)—is paid work that takes place beyond the realm of formal employment. It involves the paid production and sale of goods and services that are unregistered by, or hidden from, the state for tax, social security, and/or labor law purposes, but which are legal in all other respects (Williams and Windebank 2000; Feige 1990; Portes 1994; Thomas 1992). Therefore, paid informal work includes all legitimate activities where payments received by individuals are not declared to the authorities, usually through cash.

Micro-entrepreneurs are key components of the informal economy. Because of difficulties in finding meaningful paid employment as well as a lack of resources, many Latinos turn to self-employment in the informal economy. A typical firm or individual in the informal economy requires few if any resources; street venders and laborers selling fruit or themselves require little if any capital. In addition, the skill requirements are marginal, certainly unknown to potential employers, and the knowledge base of these two enterprises need not be sophisticated to understand the day-to-day mechanics. In essence, anyone with the right motive, character, and gumption can be a day laborer or fruit seller. Lack of resources and labor force disadvantage are key to self-employment in the general economy, and the informal economy is no different. The corollary, of course, is that those with resources normally avoid the informal economy, since their resources permit entry into the mainstream economy (Light and Rosenstein 1995).

Among Latinos, the undocumented are disproportionately more likely to participate in the informal economy, either through employment or self-employment. Unauthorized immigrants have little choice but to engage in informal employment as a means of economic survival. As a result, the most visible forms of informal economic activities are replete with immigrant participants, ostensibly immigrants who lack proper documents or have false documents. A recent analysis of the 2000 census estimates that about 8.5 million unauthorized immigrants resided in the United States on April 1, 2000. Assuming that the distribution of unauthorized immigrants has not significantly changed since 1996, approximately 3.4 million unauthorized immigrants reside in California. Heer and Passel (1987) and Marcelli (1999) estimate that Los Angeles County is home to the largest number of unauthorized immigrants in the nation. Many of these immigrants undoubtedly work in the informal sector (see also Lopez-Garza 2003).

The growth and visibility of the informal economy occurred simultaneously with labor flexibility—the change from predominantly secure employment (full-time, for an indefinite period, with a single employer) to insecure (self-employed, part-time, temporary, subcontract) work. Early work on this subject by Portes and Benton (1984) and Portes and Sassen-Koob (1986) shows that from the end of World War II until 1980, Latin America underwent a rapid and sustained process of industrial development that also included informal and self-employed work. Tilly (1996:13) also clearly documents the growth of part-timers in the workforce, stating that "since the 1950s, the proportion of part-time workers has grown gradually, climbing from 13 percent in 1957 to 19 percent in 1993." Finally, employers, in their attempts to reduce costs, have increased their use of employment intermediaries—such as temporary help services and contract companies— and are relying more on alternative staffing arrangements such as on-call workers and independent contractors (Polivka 1996; Henson 1996).

In response to these changes, be they perceived[3] or real, a new category of workers known as contingents emerged. First coined in 1985,[4] the term *contingent work* described a management technique of employing workers only when there was an immediate and direct demand for their services— such as during a temporary layoff or a spurt in demand for a particular product. Since its initial use, the term has been applied to a wide range of employment practices, including part-time work, temporary help service employment, employee leasing, self-employment, contracting out, employment in the business services sector, and home-based work. It is also often used to describe any nontraditional work arrangement that deviates from the norm of a full-time wage and salary job.

People participate in contingent work for a variety of reasons. Some workers prefer a flexible schedule as a result of school, family, or other obligations and are willing to forego steady work at a higher wage for the flexibility that contingent work affords them. Others partake in the contingent market to earn additional income, supplementing pay from their full- or part-time employment elsewhere. Still others are unable to find a steady job and hope that their work in this market will eventually lead to permanent employment.

Immigrant and Latino workers participate in the contingent market for all these reasons but also share at least two factors that should be weighted more heavily. They participate because they seek an alternative to the formal noncontingent labor market and because they have no other employment options. The first statement claims that immigrants participate in the flexible labor market because they have adapted to the lower incomes generated from their "regular" jobs' low pay. Contingent work is at the very least a supplement, if not an alternative, to participation in a low-skill, low-pay job in the formal, albeit secondary, sector of the economy. Sassen-Koob (1987) argues that immigrants constitute the main workforce for firms that operate by informal labor subcontracting or produce goods and services directed at the affluent or high-income sectors of the population (e.g., domestic help, gardening, cleaning services). According to this view, immigrants are the primary labor force for the numerous low-wage jobs that the new economy has created, especially in such industries as apparel, electronics, and footwear. Immigrants have little choice but to participate in flexible labor market opportunities if they are to subsist with meager low-wage jobs in the formal economy.

No single factor in isolation from others can adequately explain Latino poverty. Rather, it is a combination of labor market dynamics that contributes to Latinos' disadvantage and above-average poverty rates. In addition, low human capital investments and immigrant characteristics (i.e., fluency, legalization) seem to also mediate to some degree their labor market prospects. Obviously, macroeconomic trends since the mid-1970s, which have led to higher poverty rates, have affected Latinos and other population groups. But labor market disadvantage, as reflected by lower wages and higher unemployment, seems to be a better explanation of Latinos' higher poverty rates. Coupled with a changing economy that favors services and other forms of marginal work—such as contingent employment, jobs with nonstandard relations, and informality—the result is that many Latinos who do work do so for poor pay.

LATINO ECONOMIC DEVELOPMENT: ALTERNATIVE ENTREPRENEURS?

The term *economic development* has slightly different meanings depending on its use and user. Often, adding *community* to the term gives the overall meaning of the phrase a more localized or spatial component that is important, especially if we are to pay attention to communities in a geographic or spatial context. In my use of the term, I draw from Melendez and Stoll (2000), but I place a greater emphasis on workers. I refer to community economic development for Latinos as a process whereby community institutions—be they government, churches, businesses, or local groups—work together to increase employment opportunities and wages for marginal workers. Increasing work-based opportunities requires different strategies and relationships to stimulate social and economic development. Given the role of information and social networks, a spatially-based focus would also have to play a significant process in improving employment outcomes. More broadly speaking (i.e., beyond a strictly work emphasis) economic development often includes housing development, small business incentives, improvement of public goods (i.e., city services and transportation), and augmentation of educational resources (i.e., after school programs).

A review of the literature on economic development identifies four broad categories or strategies for development intervention: entrepreneurial-based, place-based, community-based, and special interest–based. These categories are useful for discussion purposes, but they are by no means mutually exclusive; rarely is one economic development practiced singularly. A community development corporation, for example, with local residents as part of its board of directors, will often (but not always) focus on several development strategies aimed at a specific racial or ethnic group or some other community constituent. Their activities might range from developing day care centers to building and managing housing units. To think of economic development strategies as distinct or separate, particularly in ameliorating poverty and other poor social conditions, is folly—economic development strategies are quite often practiced with and in concert with different entities and actors, whether they be place-based, community-based, or special interest-based.

The exact origins of economic development are not clear. Several important processes, such as urbanization, the industrial revolution, the advent of public housing at the turn of the twentieth century, the City Beautiful Movement, and the rise of the city as the center for corporate, cultural, and economic activity have all contributed to the shaping of what we today know as economic development. But it is difficult to pinpoint precisely when, by whom, and how economic development began. We do know, however, that labor organizing during the 1930s shaped some of the initial thinking about community organizing and helped mold what eventually became economic development. Unions in the 1930s were particularly focused on increasing their membership, which made "factory towns" a prime target for mobilization and union drives. Organizers and workers were responding, of course, to the poor working and pay conditions in these towns, which in turn resulted in poor living conditions. The lack of a federal safety net and inaction by local officials (elected and otherwise) to the plight of the urban working poor galvanized workers. Labor organizers capitalized on the state's inaction and promised better wages, work conditions, health benefits, and other workplace issues that affected quality of life. The organizers worked closely with local leaders, churches, and others to mobilize communities into viable forces that would challenge factory rule and prompt stronger government intervention. As a result, a new generation of labor and community organizers evolved, setting in place one of the earliest examples of community economic development.

Not lost in this important historical artifact is the main point of this chapter—that a Latino economic development framework should focus on labor and the working poor. Union drives, especially in immigrant-rich urban centers, have become more important to the labor movement. Some of the most recent and important labor victories have come as a result of Latino immigrants who mobilized churches, schools, students, elected officials, community leaders, and others in campaigns for fair or living wages (Waldinger et al. 1997). Traditional union drives, however, only partially resolve overall labor market inequalities, and only for a certain segment of the working population—those who belong to unions or are targeted by unions for organizing. Left behind are nontraditional or contingent workers, many of whom work on a temporary basis for different or daily employers, under secretive or "invisible" contexts (e.g., domestics inside someone's home), and are impoverished.

The historical and contemporary relationship that labor and economic development share is clear. And to be sure, economic development strategies have always advocated for increased employment opportunities, small and large business development, and a host of other "business-related" activities. When combined, these activities would nurture the development of local or community economies to combat poverty. To say that economic development was not concerned about jobs or is currently ambivalent about them is patently false. I can, however, state with confidence that local economic development is less concerned with and in many instances ignores an increasingly large and important segment of the work force: the working poor and especially contingent workers, who are increasingly comprised of immigrants, Latinos, and other minorities. The entrepreneurship model is one economic development strategy that addresses, if at least peripherally, the labor market issues that I describe in this chapter.

The entrepreneurship model in economic development is far-reaching and as a result varied in its definition, implementation, and impact. In quick summary, the entrepreneurship model places emphasis on strategies that provide mechanisms linking expanding industries and businesses to the job and business readiness of ethnic and racial minorities. The idea is that small businesses have clear and important roles in neighborhoods and shouldn't be dismissed in any larger economic development strategy. One shouldn't, however, confuse their role in generating meaningful employment opportunities and better wages. Nontraditional forms of entrepreneurialism may provide an alternative framework of how economic development might better incorporate marginal workers into its strategies.

Entrepreneuralism and Marginal Workers

Students of entrepreneurship are concerned with defining and understanding different and relational terms that describe, differentiate, and give agency to economic activity outside of the general wage economy. Among those few academic disciplines (e.g., economics, sociology, urban planning, business schools) that study entrepreneurship, definitions vary. Mainstream economists are perhaps the most conservative, arguing that only medium and large-sized firms constitute entrepreneurs, and that only innovators or the elite entrepreneurs belong to this class (Wilken 1979; Kilby 1971). Archer (1991) provides a tiered definition with the top representing an "industrial/merchant elite" that comprises 21 percent of all self-employed. This elite is followed by two other categories: the general merchants and proprietors (51 percent of all self-employed) and the lower-level petty merchants and proprietors (28 percent). Because of the varied definitions, the size, location, and impact of the entrepreneurial market remains unresolved. The most general definition of entrepreneurship is "performance of services that are required but not available in the market." Light and Rosenstein (1995) challenge many of these narrow and conceptually problematic definitions by bringing into the fray the self-employed that would include nontraditional types of entrepreneurs (i.e., domestic workers, street vendors, flea market sellers, and day laborers). They argue that definitions of entrepreneurship are elitist with a preponderance of attention focusing on small and medium-sized businesses, innovation, firm location, and physical presence, and a host of other traditional notions of entrepreneur and immigrant business.

Recent work by immigration scholars and others (Hondagneu-Sotelo 2001; Romero 1992; Valenzuela 1998; Valenzuela 2001) challenges the narrow definition of entrepreneurship by bringing agency to alternative immigrant self-employment. While on the surface (e.g., day laborers and street vendors) alternative immigrant business ventures may seem unstructured, chaotic, and desperate, they may actually be more organized than previously thought. Much of the literature on Latino immigrant labor has either labeled this market as informal or underground economy or has dismissed it as a pseudo-economy comprised of the poorest and most unqualified recently arrived illegal immigrants (Waldinger 1996). But this explanation leaves unanswered the question of why some groups are so much better at, or at least more prone to participate in, informal entrepreneurship. If all that is required for informal entrepreneurship is the absence of any other skills or credentials, there shouldn't be much variation in the fortunes of those who participate in it. Understanding unequal participation in entrepreneurial activities might begin to solve this puzzle.

Unequal participation in entrepreneurship is a type of simple disadvantage theory (Aurand 1983). This theory asserts that disadvantage (unemployment, business cycles) in the general labor market encourages self-employment, regardless of the resources of those disadvantaged. That is, high unemployment or underemployment leads people to seek alternative income-generating tasks, and entrepreneurialism is often the alternative of choice. General disadvantage, however, does not impact all employees equally. Light and Rosenstein (1995) draw a distinction between general disadvantage, resource disadvantage, and labor market disadvantage. The first two types of disadvantage occur when as a result of some current or past experience—such as slavery—their members enter the labor market with fewer resources than other groups. This lack of resources could manifest itself in lower levels of human capital, poor work ethic, poor nutrition and health, few networks or contacts, and low self-confidence (Light and Rosenstein 1995). Labor market disadvantage, by contrast, arises when groups receive below-expected returns on their human capital for reasons unrelated to productivity (e.g., racial and gender discrimination).

Theories of disadvantage provide a nice bridge for understanding self-employment or marginal work as a mobility ladder or as a survivalist strategy. It is also within this context that the informal economy—at least in how it pertains to entrepreneuralism—is usually discussed in North America. This body of literature asks whether certain ethnic groups pursue entrepreneurship as a better alternative (higher income returns on human capital or better lifestyle) to wages or salaries in the general labor market. Or do immigrants use self-employment as a survivalist strategy—as an alternative to unemployment and underemployment (Jones 1988)? Light and Rosenstein (1995) divide survivalist entrepreneurs into two types: value entrepreneurs and disadvantaged entrepreneurs. Value entrepreneurs choose self-employment rather than low-wage jobs for a number of different reasons, many having to do with (as the name suggests) their values. For example, Bates (1987) argues that women comprise a large number of value entrepreneurs because many of them are attracted to the benefits of self-employment, such as the ability to juggle home and work more flexibly. Others prefer the entrepreneur's independence, social status, lifestyle, or self-concept (Light and Rosenstein 1995; Valenzuela 2001). Gold (1992) documents that some of the attraction of entrepreneurship for Vietnamese workers is its "ability to provide them with a level of independence, prestige, and flexibility unavailable under other conditions of employment." Value entrepreneurs, in other words, select self-employment for many nonmonetary reasons.

On the other hand, disadvantaged (survivalist) entrepreneurs primarily undertake self-employment because as a result of labor market disadvantage they earn higher returns on their human capital in self-employment than in wage and salary employment (Light 1979; Min 1988: Chapter 4 in this volume). As a result of labor force disadvantage—be it physical disability, ethnoracial discrimination, unrecognized educational credentials, exclusion from referral networks, undocumented status, little to no work experience, or any other unfair labor market attribute, disadvantaged entrepreneurs earn more in self-employment than in regular wage work.

Immigrants with low levels of human and other capital (social, cultural, financial), if confronted with a difficult and competitive labor market, may very well opt for survivalist entrepreneurship. It is an option, perhaps not viable in the sense that one escapes destitution, but an option that affords one a modicum of survival. In Los Angeles, we see this quite frequently in the informal and fringe commodity market, where street vendors, day laborers, domestics, food shacks/carts, and bodegas abound. At the very least, survivalist entrepreneurs produce goods and services that enhance themselves and their community's wealth—the alternative being unemployment and deeper impoverishment (Light and Rosenstein 1995).

Similarly, contingent workers, given the option to toil under extreme hardship in the general-wage economy under conditions of minimum wage, repetitive and arduous tasks, constant supervision, and few options for mobility, may prefer day labor or domestic work for reasons of value. Both of these markets provide flexibility, wages that tend to be higher than the minimum rate, a diversity of jobs and tasks, opportunities for mobility, and the extremely empowering and underrated feeling of turning down a job or negotiating for a fair wage.

Understanding how immigrant and marginal workers fit within the broader entrepreneurial rubric allows us to critically assess their participation or lack thereof. Equally important, it makes us rethink and redefine mainstream entrepreneur programs, so they can better incorporate immigrant and marginal workers.

Economic Development for Marginal Workers

Below, I identify three key areas that economic development strategies should consider if they are to improve employment and wage and income prospects for marginal workers. The first is a place-based strategy that emphasizes the role of community institutions, ethnic networks, businesses, churches, and civic organizations. Second, we need to consider traditional and nontraditional employment and training programs to reach the most vulnerable of the working poor. Finally, I advocate a mixture of traditional, worker-focused strategies that increase employment prospects and improves wages for marginal workers.

Organizing Labor in Immigrant Communities

Like Melendez (1998), I argue that a "community"-based strategy for promoting economic development in impoverished communities involves the identification of community assets, strengthening their capacity, and strengthening the links between different organizations and individuals and the mainstream economy. I depart from Melendez by placing less emphasis on a transition to the mainstream economy, primarily because for a significant amount of marginal workers such a transition may not be realized, particularly if they lack legal documents. Clearly, transitioning from unstable to stable employment, from part- to full-time work, from low-skill to higher-skill jobs, and from poor- to well-paying occupations is the optimal objective in economic development for poor workers. But there remain a significant number of workers whose transition to stable and better paying jobs may never be realized. For these workers we need to "think outside of the box."

So in addition to mobilizing the key organizations and actors, including the small business sector—those who link residents to employment, housing developers, and other key institutions—we need to create or identify programs that improve prospects for marginal workers, even if it means that their status as marginal workers remains while their employment and wage prospects improve. That is, some men and women may very well remain in the day labor or domestic market, never fully transitioning to permanent and better-paid employment. Domestics, perhaps due to their limited human capital acquisition, the flexibility realized in having a route or series of homes to clean, or having little or no experience in another trade, may very well remain domestics. The same can be said about day laborers. Under certain conditions, both of these employment examples can be decent, dignified, and wage-worthy jobs. The key is to nurture those programs that already exist, to create others that don't, and to harness social and network ties that aid poor people in coping with daily problems and allow them to survive harsh economic times.

Early in this chapter, I recalled the early importance of the labor movement in community and economic development. I believe that then as now, economic development should revolve around organizing labor in communities. The primary difference between now and then, aside from the fact that communities to be organized today are Latino, is that the organizing needn't be in the traditional union model but rather in a context that channels together many of the unique survival and economic activities already taking place in Latino communities.

For example, when the Los Angeles Metropolitan Transportation Authority went on strike two years ago, and deprived most of the L.A. region of bus service, informal entrepreneurs met much of the travel demand for people who otherwise would have been stranded. *Camionetas*, or minivans, served as makeshift "gypsy" taxis and ferried low-income residents throughout Los Angeles. The *camionetas* have existed for some time, but the MTA strike saw them expand—serving areas like the western Wilshire corridor, previously only served by buses—and become more visible to the non-Latino population. Their exposure has grown as the media has become increasingly interested in topics like transnational transportation, smuggling, and unregulated informal industries. For economic development strategists, harnessing (either through regulation or some other, more creative way) this alternative and very entrepreneurial activity to meet the needs of low-income residents and workers is an avenue that offers considerable promise.

The *camionetas* arose in the absence of good public transportation, but informal entrepreneurship can also arise in cases where formal services are present but too expensive. Day care is an excellent example. The high cost of regulated day care centers has made them inefficient, and thus scarce, in poor communities, and low-income families and single women almost never use them. Nevertheless, thousands of marginal workers, most with families and children, go to work every day and leave their children under some sort of supervision. How? In immigrant and low-income communities, the answer is nonparental informal childcare. Makeshift centers, extended-family sitters, and other arrangements care for literally thousands of children belonging to immigrant and marginal workers. Advocating for easier licensing, reevaluating requirements for "safe" centers, and alternative or cooperative ownership arrangements could lead to not only improved and accessible day care but also the development of an industry that already exists but is not formalized.

Finally, creative worker "unions"—centers where marginal workers such as domestics and day laborers participate in their employment exchange—already exist but often suffer from few resources, low membership, and inconsistent employment opportunities for their members. For example, about a dozen day labor centers exist throughout Los Angeles and Orange County. Besides offering shelter and a safe place to exchange labor for wages, some also provide wage claim resources and tool exchange programs; ESL, citizenship, and other "adult education" training; and information on free health services. Despite these important amenities, the workers' primary concerns usually turn back to their lack of consistent or semiconsistent employment. Thinking creatively about how demand for their services might be increased or regularized (i.e., a day labor temporary agency) would not only go a long way toward providing laborers with stable income but also empower them through some of the services already being offered at these sites.

Similarly, domestic worker programs are organizing creatively to empower themselves by strategizing on alternative compensation formulas, increasing demand, and regularizing employer treatments, expectations, and overtime pay. Their entrepreneurial creativity has clearly enabled a small but growing group of domestic workers to develop economically. These are just a few examples of how the working poor and others who live in immigrant concentrated neighborhoods in Los Angeles and elsewhere have developed organizations, social networks, and alternative forms of entrepreneurialism to cope with daily problems, difficult economic times, and marginal employment.

Employment and Training for Marginal Workers

It is difficult for traditional workforce development or employment and training programs to succeed because of constant and significant structural changes in the U.S. economy, which in turn have also restructured local labor markets and the workplace. Other factors, some of which were discussed earlier, similarly make success in employment and training difficult. For example, Latinos experience more frequent job displacement, lower unionization rates, increases in part-time and contingent work, and a higher degree of segregation in low-skill, low-pay, and difficult-to-transfer occupations. As a result, effective employment programs need to involve collaborations or networks of several community organizations that focus on adult education and placement.

According to Melendez (1998), cities that have the most successful employment and training programs have developed umbrella organizations that bring together not only community groups but also state and local agencies, employers, community colleges, and others involved in vocational skills training for disadvantaged populations. As an example, Melendez refers to the Center for Employment and Training (CET) as a best practice for producing long-term earnings and employment gains for minority workers. The CET model integrates vocational and basic skills education, including ESL training. All occupational skills programs through CET are developed in cooperation with employers. Other employment and training examples (Quality Employment through Skills Training) include connecting residents in targeted areas to regional employment opportunities in growing businesses and industries. The key here is the implementation of an employment development plan for each participant. Trainees attend a weekly counseling meeting organized by occupational groups or "case workers" and receive a host of complementary support services. The program ensures that trainees have access to social services—such as individual and joint counseling, educational financial assistance, and other services. There is a strong emphasis on mediating relations with employers and facilitating trainees' access to jobs.

Both of these alternative employment and training programs were designed to respond to different workers and distinct segments of the labor market. The former focuses on more-difficult-to-serve workers (high school dropouts, young mothers receiving public assistance, dislocated workers, former criminal offenders, and others) and aims at entry-level positions in growing industries, while the latter places participants in jobs that require more specialized education and skills. The point is that specialized training programs with a clearly defined market niche and worker in mind can be developed. Creative employment and training programs for informal and contingent workers might, for example, consider the construction trades, home care providers, garment industry, or other jobs that already rely on contingent labor. Central to this strategy is that while skills enhancement is necessary, without systematic connections to employers, it becomes very difficult to promote employment of disadvantaged workers (Melendez 1998).

Traditional Economic Development and Other Mainstream Strategies

The final component for developing viable economic opportunities for marginal Latino workers involves supporting and working closely with traditional and nontraditional labor-based strategies such as union membership drives, actively supporting strikes, participating in campaigns for living wage ordinances, mobilizing on popular and unpopular legislative initiatives that benefit immigrant workers, exposing illegal or unduly harsh working conditions, and supporting federal programs such as the Earned Income Tax Credit, which primarily benefits the working poor.

Living wage ordinances are critical to local economic development in cities that often provide large infrastructure and other employment opportunities. These ordinances should be accompanied by efforts to increase the employment prospects of local residents in city jobs, especially if living wage legislation is passed and implemented. The potential for local government work to impact the immigrant and working poor in the Los Angeles regional economy should not be underestimated, considering that Los Angeles County alone has 88 different municipalities. When coupled with the 4 other regional counties (Ventura, San Bernardino, Riverside, and Orange), the opportunity to impact wages and employment opportunities through living wage ordinances in the region is potentially large.

Immigrants without documents are a particularly vulnerable population and work force. Their numbers in California far exceed those in any other state, and Los Angeles has the largest concentration of unauthorized immigrants of any metropolitan area. The lack of legal documents, including driver's licenses, makes these workers vulnerable to exploitation and other workplace abuses, and—in areas with poor public transit—can make simply getting to work an ordeal. Supporting efforts to normalize the status of these workers is important. The executive body of the AFL-CIO, organized labor's governing body, recently called for a general amnesty program that would legalize several million people already residing in this county—most of whom are from Mexico and Central America. For the unions, the campaigns for normalization are strategic; for Latinos and other immigrant workers they offer the potential to greatly swell labor's ranks. Labor leaders correctly assume that these workers would be more likely to join unions and organize if their status became regularized; legal workers cannot be threatened with deportation and other immigration sanctions and are thus in a better position to organize once they have the protections afforded to legal residents.

Political power is important to more effective and efficient economic development. Political power can channel government resources and other opportunities to disadvantaged communities and marginal workers. Not lost to immigrants and other ethnic and racial groups, workers are increasingly participating in nonlinear modes of political participation, such as union drives, public protests, precinct walking, and hometown associations. Supporting other political activities besides voting registration drives and getting out the vote, while clearly important, increases opportunities for multitiered approaches to economic development, such as supporting a day laborer's or domestic worker's bill of rights.

Finally, supporting traditional development strategies from place-based to community development corporations need to, at the very least, remain intact or expanded. No singular strategy, other than massive economic redistribution, which is unlikely, will adequately develop economic opportunities for Latinos in poverty. A multitiered or holistic approach, with a particular emphasis on marginal workers, will lead to more equal labor market opportunities.

CONCLUSION

Latinos in Los Angeles and elsewhere in the United States are resilient and also creative. They have worked hard to develop different strategies and resources to cope with labor market inequality. Immigrants in these same communities have similarly developed important neighborhood-based networks that provide family support, jobs, child care, food, and other important resources necessary for sustenance. Small businesses provide important consumer goods, services, and often credit to the creditless. Community development strategies, often the staple of economic development in inner cities, along with service providing agencies and other nonprofit organizations, attract extramural resources (government and private) to the area and provide an important institutional base for the community. Clearly, these institutions and processes serve an invaluable role in connecting residents to services, providing affordable homes, food, jobs, and opportunities outside their neighborhoods. These forms of local economic development need to continue if Latinos are to continue making progress, however incremental it may be, on different socioeconomic indictors.

The hard-to-employ marginal worker, however, needs to have a more central place in the practice of economic development. Traditional economic development strategies should attempt to incorporate difficult-to-serve workers while also supporting and advocating for creative or alternative forms of entrepreneurship and development strategies. To do otherwise would be neglectful of a sizable and growing component of the Latino population. To include them would be mindful of current neighborhood economic activities, demographic patterns, and social processes in Latino communities.

NOTES

1. Throughout this chapter, I use the term *Latino* to refer to people primarily from Mexico, Central American, Puerto Rico, and Cuba but also to those from the rest of Latin America. As a result, I treat these four groups and the rest of Latin America as one homogeneous group despite their different cultural, national, economic, and political roots. These differences likely result in varied labor market and other outcomes in the United States—though I'm not convinced the effects would be large if focused on low skilled workers. Ultimately, the treatment of these peoples as one is

because I do believe that economic development strategies should focus on the unique circumstances of immigration, low skill, and marginality, and a large proportion of the people who fit these qualifications happen to be of Latin American origin.

2. Defined as qualifying for government assistance.

3. Even though the majority of studies have found no change in workers' overall job tenure, reports of corporate downsizing, production streamlining, and increasing use of temporary workers have caused many to question employers' commitment to long-term, stable employment relationships (Polivka 1996).

4. *Contingent work* was first used by Audrey Freedman in testimony before the Employment and Housing Subcommittee of the Committee on Government Operations, House of Representatives, Congress of the United States.

References

Archer, M. 1991. Self-employment and occupational structure in an industrialising city: Detroit, 1880. *Social Forces* 69:785–809.

Aurand, H. W. 1983. Self-employment, last resort of the unemployed. *International Social Science Review* 58:7–11.

Bates, T. 1987. Self-employed minorities: Traits and trends. *Social Science Quarterly* 68:539–551.

Feige, E.L. 1990. Defining and estimating underground and informal economies. *World Development* 18(7):989–1002.

Gold, Steven. 1992. *Refugee Communities*. Newbury Park, CA: Sage.

Heer, David. M., and Jeffrey S. Passel. (1987 Comparison of two methods for computing the number of undocumented Mexican adults in Los Angeles County. *International Migration Review* 21(4):1446–1473.

Hondagneu-Sotelo, Pierrette. 2001. *Domestica: Immigrant Workers Cleaning and Caring in the Shadows of Affluence*. Berkeley: University of California Press.

Jones, Y.V. 1988. Street peddlers as entrepreneurs: Economic adaptation to an urban area. *Urban Anthropology* 17:143–170.

Henson, Kevin D. 1996. *Just a Temp*. Philadelphia: Temple University Press.

Kilby, P. 1971. Hunting the Heffalump. In *Entrepreneurship and Economic Development*, ed. P. Kilby. New York: Free Press.

Light, I. 1979. Disadvantaged minorities in self-employment. *International Journal of Comparative Sociology* 20:31–45.

Light, Ivan, and Carolyn Rosenstein. 1995. *Race, Ethnicity, and Entrepreneurship in Urban America*. Hawthorne, New York: Aldine de Gruyter.

Lopez-Garza, Marta. 2003. *Asian and Latino Immigrants in a Restructuring Economy: The Metamorphosis of Los Angeles*. Palo Alto: Stanford University Press.

Marcelli, Enrico A. 1999. Undocumented Latino immigrant workers: The Los Angeles experience. In *Illegal Immigration in America*, ed. David W. Haines and Karen E. Rosenblum, 193–231. Westport, CT: Greenwood Press.

Melendez, Edwin. 1998. The economic development of El Barrio. In *Borderless Borders: U.S. Latinos, Latin Americans, and the Paradox of Interdependence*, ed. Frank Bonilla, Edwin Melendez, Rebecca Morales, and Maria de los Angeles Torres, 195–227. Philadelphia: Temple University Press.

Melendez, Edwin, and Michael A. Stoll. 2000. Community economic development and the Latino experience. In *The Collaborative City: Opportunities and Struggles for Blacks and Latinos in U.S. Cities*, ed. J. J. Betancourt and D. Gills, 215–228. New York: Garland Press.

Min, P. G. 1988. *Ethnic Business Enterprise: Korean Small Business in Atlanta.* New York: Center for Migration Studies.

Moore, Joan, and Raquel Pinderhughes, eds. 1993. *In the Barrios: Latinos and the Underclass Debate.* New York: Russell Sage Foundation.

More, Paul, Patrice Wagonhurst, Jessica Goodheart, David Runsten, Enrico Marcelli, Pascale Joassart-Marcelli, and John Medearis. 2000. The Other Los Angeles: The working poor in the city of the 21st century. Los Angeles: Los Angeles Alliance for a New Economy.

Ong, Paul, and Abel Valenzuela Jr. 1995. The labor market: Immigrant effects and racial disparities. In *Ethnic Los Angeles,* ed. Roger Waldinger and Mehdi Bozorgmehr, 165–191. New York: Russell Sage Foundation.

Polivka, Anne. 1996. Contingent and alternative work arrangements, defined. *Monthly Labor Review* (October):3–9.

Portes, Alejandro. 1994. The informal economy and its paradoxes. *The Handbook of Economic Sociology,* ed. Neal J. Smelser and R. Swedberg, 426–452. Princeton: Princeton University Press.

Portes, Alejandro, and Lauren L. Benton. 1984. Industrial development and labor absorption: A reinterpretation. *Population and Development Review* 10:589–611.

Portes, Alejandro, and Saskia Sassen-Koob. 1986. Making it underground: Comparative material on the urban informal sector in Western market economies. *American Journal of Sociology* 93:30–61.

Romero, Mary. 1992. *Maid in the U.S.A.* New York: Routledge.

Sassen-Koob, Saskia. 1987. Growth and informalization at the core: A preliminary report on New York City. In *The Capitalist City: Global Restructuring and Community Politics,* ed. Michael P. Smith and Joe R. Feagin, 138–154.

Thomas, J. J. 1992. *Informal Economic Activity.* New York: Harvester Wheatsheaf, Hemel Hempstead.

Tilly, Chris. 1996. *Half a Job: Bad and Good Part-time Jobs in a Changing Labor Market.* Philadelphia: Temple University Press.

Valenzuela, A. 2001. Day Labourers as Entrepreneurs? *Journal of Ethnic and Migration Studies* 27(2):335–352.

Valenzuela, Abel Jr., and E. Gonzalez. 2000. Latino earnings inequality: Immigrant and native-born differences. In *Prismatic Metropolis: Inequality in Los Angeles,* ed. Lawrence Bobo, James Johnson Jr., Melvin Oliver, and Abel Valenzuela Jr., 75–89. New York: Russell Sage Foundation.

Waldinger, R. 1996. Ethnicity and opportunity in the plural city. In *Ethnic Los Angeles,* ed. R. Waldinger, and M. Bozorgmehr. New York: Russell Sage Foundation.

Waldinger, R., C. Erickson, R. Milkman, D.J. B. Mitchel, A. Valenzuela Jr., K. Wong, and M. Zeitlin. 1997. The Justice for Janitors Campaign in Los Angeles. Chapter 6 in *Organizing to Win,* ed. Gate Bronfenbrenner, Sheldon Friedman, Richard Hurd, Rudy Oswald, and Ronald L. Seeber, 142–167. Ithaca, NY: Cornell University Press.

Wilken, J. 1979. *Entrepeneurship: A Comparative and Historical Study.* Norwood, NJ: Ablex.

Wilson, William Julius. 1987. *The Truly Disadvantaged.* Chicago: University of Chicago Press.

Williams, Colin, and Jan Windebank. 1998. *Informal Employment in the Advanced Economies: Implications for Work and Welfare.* New York: Routledge.

———. 2000. Paid informal work in deprived neighborhoods. *Cities* 17(4): 285–291.

III Business Development

THE FIRST TWO sections have documented the nature and magnitude of the poor employment outcomes for many residents of minority communities and offered a set of recommendations to overcome multiple barriers. Clearly, there is a need to bridge the geographic divide between place of residency and the "outlying" jobs. Increasing access to opportunities throughout the region, however, is just one approach. The alternative is to bring jobs into the neighborhood by bringing in businesses. The traditional approach has been to attract mainstream firms through tax credits, subsidies, and the provision of infrastructure. Unfortunately, these carrots either have been ineffective in stimulating new economic activities or have proven to be very expensive relative to the outcomes. Moreover, attracting businesses to minority neighborhoods may not necessarily lead to employment of local residents.

What the dominant approach to business development ignores is the current and potential role of minority-owned businesses. Little is known about the potentials of these businesses for improving economic conditions in these neighborhoods and for their residents. The three chapters in this section help fill this gap by presenting three examples of minority-based entrepreneurship and their roles in generating jobs, as well as their limitations. The chapters also examine the potentials, challenges, and inherent limitations of minority businesses and discuss policies and strategies to foster business growth and job creation within minority neighborhoods.

There are many good reasons for explicitly incorporating and promoting minority-owned businesses within community economic development. This is demonstrated in Thomas Boston's chapter on black businesses. These businesses are more likely to employ black workers, including those living in low-income neighborhoods. While these businesses tend to be smaller than average, the more established and larger black-owned firms generate "good" jobs. Moreover, Boston's case study of Atlanta shows that these firms can play an important in role revitalizing economically distressed neighborhoods. The good news is that the number of black businesses has expanded rapidly over the last couple of decades. Nonetheless, blacks are still dramatically underrepresented among all business owners, and community economic development (CED) should play a role in expanding opportunities for minority entrepreneurship.

However, there are limitations to minority-owned businesses, and this is the subject of Tarry Hum's chapter on the ethnic enclave economies. Her case study of Asian businesses in New York shows enormous variation in size, sales, and potential. Enclave economies have often been idealized for their ability to support and sustain ethnic networks, but frequently they offer only part-time employment without benefits or dead-end, low-wage jobs. Lacking economic and human capital, many enclave businesses have to draw from personal savings, borrow from family members, and rely on family labor. Examining New York's Asian enclaves, Hum finds that external factors, such as rising rents or sudden disasters like September 11, 2001, can completely paralyze ethnic businesses and lead to their demise. She argues that harnessing ethnic entrepreneurial energy to promote viable economic development requires targeted policy efforts to link enclave businesses with public- and private-sector assistance.

Some of the same potentials and limitations identified by Boston and Hum can be seen in CED efforts in American Indian communities. Gaming represents a controversial strategy to develop jobs and generate income within the compounds of Indian reservations. Ted Jojola and Paul Ong's chapter delves thoroughly into the issue of gaming, finding that despite positive outcomes in job generation, gaming does not represent a panacea for addressing poverty. There is no doubt that gaming has improved the socioeconomic status of tribes that have built casinos on the reservations. At the same time, the evidence shows that gaming has failed to eliminate disparities among individuals living on reservations and has opened a deep gap between gaming and nongaming tribes.

7 The Role of Black-Owned Businesses in Black Community Development

Thomas D. Boston

Introduction

Over the last three decades, central cities have been burdened by high rates of unemployment, significant population losses, and concentrated poverty. The economic expansion of the 1990s moderated this burden to some extent, reducing by 24 percent (to 2.5 million) the number of people living in neighborhoods where the poverty rate was 40 percent or more (Jargowsky 2003). Still, by the turn of the new millennium 67 cities had poverty rates of 20 percent or higher (U.S. Department of Housing and Urban Development 2000). Central-city unemployment and poverty are concentrated heavily in the low-income Black inner-city communities. These neighborhoods have been abandoned by businesses once located in and around the central business district and have been largely sidestepped by investors, who have favored developing businesses in more suburban locations. The lack of jobs within these neighborhoods combined with the dispersal of cities away from the urban core has created an employment barrier in the form of a spatial mismatch. (See Chapters 4 and 5.)

The most extreme manifestations of economic distress and neglect are found in the large, densely populated public housing projects within central cities. A recent study of a distressed public housing project found that in 1995 only 18 percent of household heads 16 to 62 years of age were employed, 49 percent depended upon welfare as their primary source of income, 98 percent of households were Black, and 87 percent were headed by single women (Boston 2005a). The presence of these projects has an adverse impact on the surrounding communities, leading to the development of what is known as "underclass" neighborhoods (Wilson 1996). These communities lack many of the attributes and capacities that typically are necessary for economic development. In addition to economic capital, these neighborhoods also lack social capital. Civic organizations and social, religious, and political groups are usually too weak to protect the quality of schools, demand infrastructure improvements, and regulate zoning patterns for commercial and residential development. The poor housing conditions of these communities are compounded by extreme social and human circumstances. Most residents live in constant fear of gunfire, drug traffickers, and other crime.

Communities like these, as well as other low-income Black neighborhoods, desperately need economic development. But there remains a good deal of debate about the most appropriate strategy (Ferguson and Dickens 1999; Boston and Ross 1997). Participants in these debates usually argue over whether the development principles are sufficiently holistic and about the role the public and private sectors should play in redevelopment. The debates also include issues such as affordable housing, gentrification, and the relative merits of mixed-income development. An issue rarely considered, however, is the role that Black-owned businesses can play in the revitalization of Black communities.[1] Black-owned businesses are often dismissed because they are only a small part of the whole economy. In 1997, these firms comprised only 4 percent of all firms and generated 0.4 percent of all sales.[2] Even among a more restrictive universe of minority-owned businesses, Black-owned businesses comprised only 27 percent of firms and generated 12 percent of sales. The aggregate statistics, however, obscure some important characteristics of Black-owned businesses, which are described in detail later in this chapter. First, Black business owners have an affinity for the residents of distressed Black communities and are committed to community development. Second, Black-owned businesses are becoming increasingly important as generators of jobs for Black workers. This has resulted from the rapid growth of these businesses and their tendency to employ Black workers. Third, a significant portion of the workforce in Black-owned firms is drawn from low-income inner-city neighborhoods; indeed, some of the most successful Black businesses are located in low-income neighborhoods. Fourth, the quality of the average job for Black workers in Black-owned businesses is superior to that for Black workers in firms owned by Whites. Finally, revitalization offers numerous opportunities to promote the growth of Black-owned businesses. Ignoring the potential contributions of Black-owned business, therefore, would be an unfortunate oversight.

In the remaining sections of this chapter, I explore these themes in more detail and also draw upon the results of a case study of low-income neighborhood revitalization in Atlanta. The chapter draws on national data and information and data and information for the Atlanta region. The next section documents the employment-generating capacity of Black-owned businesses. While Blacks are substantially underrepresented among business owners, they are nonetheless a sizeable and growing source of employment for Blacks. The middle section of the chapter examines the role of these businesses in low-income Black neighborhoods. The evidence shows that Black owners want to help these neighborhoods and contribute to the employment base in these communities. Given Black-owned businesses' potential and willingness, it is good policy to incorporate Black-owned business in efforts to revitalize the most distressed neighborhoods, those with public housing projects. The final section presents a case study of how this can be done by examining an effort in Atlanta through the U.S. Department of Housing and Urban Development's (HUD's) HOPE VI program. The chapter concludes with some recommendations about the role of Black-owned businesses in Black community development.

BLACK-OWNED BUSINESSES AS EMPLOYERS

Black entrepreneurs are motivated by much the same economic drive that motivates other entrepreneurs. Clearly, seeking profits is a fundamental factor, but it is not the only one. In a recent national survey of 350 CEOs of the fastest growing Black-owned companies in the country, Black CEOs were asked to identify the factors that had the greatest influence on their decision to start their business (Boston 2003). Of the Black CEOs, an overwhelming majority (80 percent) responded that the most important reason for starting their own business was the desire to exercise more control over their destiny. The second most important reason, cited by 75 percent of Black CEOs, was the desire to use their management experience and education.

In pursuing business opportunities, Black-owned businesses have a positive effect on Black employment. This can be seen in an analysis of business EEO-1 reporting data for Atlanta covering the years 1996 through 1998. By law, these data are collected on all firms that register to provide goods and services to the City of Atlanta. These firms are not necessarily representative of all firms because many firms are too small to seek government contracts, operate in industries that are not appropriate for government contracts, or are uninterested in pursuing government contracts. It is likely that the businesses in the EEO-1 data set are more successful and larger than non-contracting firms. Despite this data limitation, the data does provide insights into hiring practices by the race of the owner. Of the 1,381 firms in the sample, 802 (58 percent) were owned by Blacks, and 437 (32) percent were owned by Whites. In total, these firms employed 23,298 workers: 11,146 White, 10,670 Black, and 1,482 other minority or racial groups. Racial employment patterns differed significantly in Black-owned and White-owned firms. Over three-quarters (76 percent) of all employees in Black-owned firms were Black, while 16 percent were White. By contrast, Blacks comprise 29 percent of the employees in firms owned by Whites. These co-race hiring practices have continued in recent years. My estimate, based on data for the third quarter of 2003, is that Black workers comprise almost two-thirds (64 percent) of the workforce in Black-owned firms (see Boston 2003). The data clearly show that the racial employment patterns of businesses vary significantly by the race of the owner. Whites are more likely to be employed by Whites, and Blacks are much more likely to be employed in greater percentages in Black-owned firms.

The most recent census of Black-owned businesses indicates that employment in these businesses is growing rapidly and therefore is becoming an increasingly important generator of jobs. In 1997 (the most recent year for which census data on minority businesses are available) the total employment capacity of Black-owned firms was 718,341 workers. Fifteen years earlier, in 1982, Black-owned businesses employed just 165,765 workers (see Table 7.1.) Over this 15-year period the annual employment growth in the economy was 1.76 percent, while the employment growth in Black-owned businesses was 9.77 percent annually.

TABLE 7.1. Total civilian employment and employment in Black-owned firms

Employment Category	1982	1997	Annual Growth	2010 Projection
Total U.S. civilian employment	99,526,000	129,588,000	1.76%	151,412,160
Total U.S. Black civilian employment	9,189,000	13,969,000	2.79%	18,036,900
Total workers employed in Black-owned firms	165,765	718,341	9.77%	2,421,927
Number of Blacks employed by Black-owned firms (estimate)	106,089	459,738		1,550,033
Estimated percentage of Black workers in Black businesses	1.2%	3.3%		8.6%

Source: Fullerton and Toossi (2001).

Because of the strong tendency for co-race hiring by Black-owned businesses, they provide an increasing source of employment for Black workers. The most appropriate yardstick for comparing the employment contribution of Black-owned businesses is the total Black employed workforce. There is no single source of data for this yardstick, but extrapolating from existing information provides reasonable estimates (see Table 7.1). Total civilian employment and Black employment are derived from employment tables of the Council of Economic Advisors, Economic Report of the President, 2004. Total employment in Black businesses is derived from the U.S. Department of Commerce's *Survey of Minority-Owned Business Enterprises* (*SMOBE*) for 1982 and 1997. The estimated share of the jobs in Black businesses held by Black workers comes from the ING Gazelle Index, which is based on a national survey of 350 Black CEOs (Boston 2003). These CEOs indicated that 64 percent of their workforce is Black. Applying this factor to the *SMOBE* data, I estimate that Black-owned businesses provided jobs for over 3 percent of all employed Black workers in 1997, up from about 1 percent in 1982. While the 3 percent figure in 1997 was only a small fraction of all Black employment, the increase between 1982 to 1997 is very promising.

If the observed trend in the recent past continues into the future, then Black-owned businesses will become an even more important source of Black employment. Employment projections to the year 2010 are based on Fullerton and Toossi (2001), which estimated the total civilian labor force in 2010 at 157,721,000 and Black civilian labor force at 20,041,000. To get the total number of employed workers we adjusted these figures downward by the 2010 projected unemployment rates of 4 percent and 8 percent respectively for all employees and Black employees. Estimates of the 2010 total employment in Black-owned businesses and Black employment in Black businesses are based on projecting the 1982 to 1997 employment growth trend of 9.77 percent to the year 2010. If this annual growth in employment in Black-owned businesses continues, I project that 8.6 percent of all Black workers will be employed by Black-owned businesses (see Table 7.1).[3]

The jobs generated by Black-owned businesses are diverse and include what are considered "good jobs." The 1997 *smobe* data show that average pay per employee in Black-owned business was only 70 percent of the average pay per employee for all firms. While this is cause for concern, it is also important to recognize that not all Black-owned firms are low-wage firms. This can be seen in the data on Black employees in firms submitting eeo-1 reports to Atlanta, which was described earlier. The 798 Black-owned firms employed a total of 8,107 Black workers. The sample also included 436 White-owned firms that employed a total of 3,270 Black workers. Of the 8,107 Black workers employed by Black-owned firms, 1,598 (about 20 percent) are employed by Black-owned firms that operate in the business service industry, and about 14 percent are employed by firms operating in engineering and management service industries. By contrast, only 9 percent of the 3,270 Black workers employed by White owners are in firms that operate in business services, and just 2 percent are in firms in engineering and management services. Firms operating in the business service industry and management and engineering industries require higher levels of education and skills and provide greater pay and more stable career ladders. Of all Black workers in Black-owned firms, about 14 percent work in the general building construction industry while 17 percent of Black workers in White-owned businesses are employed in this industry. The general building construction industry, however, does not require high levels of education; the pay is lower, and jobs are less stable.

The racial employment pattern by industry is important because firms operating in business service and engineering and management service industries generally provide superior employment opportunities in comparison to firms operating in general building construction. While firms in the former industries require more professional or skilled labor, general construction contracting firms have numerous jobs that require only low-skill labor. Drawing a parallel from labor market segmentation literature, firms in the first two industries and other high-skilled industries are considered to be in the primary sector. By contrast, general construction contracting and other firms requiring low-skilled or general labor are considered to be in the secondary sector. Blacks employed by Black-owned businesses have a greater likelihood of being employed in the primary sector in comparison to Blacks employed by White-owned firms. This pattern is consistent with the statement that the quality of employment for Blacks is better in Black-owned businesses than it is for Blacks employed in businesses owned by Whites. However, this pattern applies only to those participating in government contracting. While it is unknown whether this applies to all firms, the findings demonstrate that Black-owned firms have a real potential to generate "good jobs" for Black workers.

Black-Owned Businesses and Low-Income Black Neighborhoods

Business owners are commonly perceived as individuals who are driven by market forces and naked self-interest. While this is true to some degree—one rarely succeeds in business by ignoring the market's demands—many successful business owners also develop passions for supporting the arts, education, environmental preservation, or other philanthropic causes. The most publicly known examples are philanthropic billionaires such as Bill Gates in Seattle, Eli Board in Los Angeles, George Soros in New York, and Ted Turner in Atlanta (Business Week 2002; Whelan 2004). However, civic-minded business leaders are not limited to the super-rich. While business owners frequently become major benefactors to nonprofit organizations, White business owners seldom express a passion for revitalizing low-income inner-city neighborhoods. By contrast, Black business owners commonly profess a strong commitment to community development. In the survey of 350 Black CEOs cited earlier, 71 percent stated a desire to serve their community as a factor for starting their business, making it the third most important reason. Only 19 percent of Black CEOs said serving their community was a minor influence, and just 6 percent said it had no influence on their decision (Boston 2003).

A similar result was found by a 1995 survey of Black businesses located in the Atlanta Metropolitan area. The owners were asked if they felt that "Black entrepreneurs [had] a special responsibility to aid in improving Black communities." Of the 222 respondents, 82 percent either strongly agreed or agreed with the statement, while 11 percent were neutral and only 2 percent disagreed or strongly disagreed (see Table 7.2). Nor was this a function of where the businesses were located; responses did not differ significantly between those businesses operating within the City of Atlanta and those located outside the city but within the 18-county metropolitan area.

Not only are Black entrepreneurs personally committed to helping black communities, they create jobs for blacks in low-income inner-city commu-

Table 7.2. Survey results on whether Black business owners feel a special responsibility to assist in the improvement of Black communities

	Atlanta City Limits (Percentage of Total)	Other Metro Locations (Percentage of Total)	Table Total (Percentage of Total)
Strongly agree	46.7%	46.0%	46.3%
Agree	36.7%	35.3%	35.9%
Neither agree nor disagree	11.7%	9.8%	10.6%
Disagree	1.1%	1.5%	1.3%
Strongly disagree	0.5%	—	0.2%
Not applicable	1.2%	5.1%	3.4%
Missing value	2.1%	2.4%	2.2%
Total	100%	100%	100%

Source: 1995 survey conducted by the author; see also Boston 1999: chapter 3.

nities. Bates (1993:77) has observed that "Black employers tend to utilize a work force consisting largely of minority workers, and this is true whether they are located in inner-city ghettos, central business districts, or outlying suburban areas." White-owned businesses behave quite differently. Among small-business employers located in nonminority areas of the applicable 28 cities, 63 percent of the White firms (versus 3 percent of the Black firms) had no minority employees at all. More surprisingly, even when located within minority communities, most White-owned firms employ predominately nonminority workforces, and many employ no minority workers whatsoever. In sum, the evidence clearly suggests that the race of owners is a major determinant of Black workers' access to jobs regardless of location. For Blacks in low-income communities, the presence of Black-owned businesses is a critical factor in determining employment opportunity.

Moreover, Black-owned firms tend to hire inner-city workers regardless of the firms' location within the region. A 1995 survey of 223 Black-owned firms in Atlanta showed that one-fifth of the employees in Black-owned firms lived in low-income inner-city neighborhoods. The survey also showed that Black-owned firms in the City of Atlanta hired 25 percent of their workforce from low-income neighborhoods, while Black-owned firms located outside Atlanta but within its 18 county Metropolitan area hired 19 percent of their workforce from low-income inner-city neighborhoods (Boston 1999:56).

While black entrepreneurs have a commitment to serving their community, it is not necessarily at the expense of good business practice. A study by Boston and Ross (1997:347–348) found that some of the most successful Black-owned businesses are located in low-income neighborhoods. An analysis of data from the early 1990s for 722 Black-owned firms located within the Atlanta metropolitan area showed that over a quarter were located in zip code areas where the median family income was below twenty-five thousand dollars. The data also revealed that the most successful Black-owned businesses, as measured by gross revenue, were located in the lowest-income zip codes (see Table 7.3.) Unfortunately, we do not have data

TABLE 7.3. Employment characteristics of Black-owned businesses by income characteristics of the zip codes where they are located

Income Class of Zip Code Based on 1990 Census	Number of Firms	Mean Revenue of Businesses in Income Class	Mean Employment per Firm	Black Employment as a Percentage of Rotal Employment
$0 to $14,999	20	$2,089,239	11.7	81.8%
$15,000 to $24,999	161	$707,021	11.3	76.7%
$25,000 to $39,999	255	$263,719	6.6	73.1%
$40,000 to $59,000	182	$723,485	7.3	74.6%
$60,000 and greater	62	$576,181	8.1	77.1%
Total	722	$606,208	8.9	77.1%

Source: Boston and Ross 1997.

on profits, largely because that information is both difficult to measure and proprietary. Nonetheless, size and profits tend to be correlated, thus the available measure based on revenue is useful. The mean revenue of businesses in zip codes where income was fifteen thousand dollars or less was $2,089,239. The median revenue of firms in such zip codes was also higher than that of firms in other locations. Mean revenue is second largest for Black-owned firms located in zip codes where family income varied between fifteen thousand dollars and twenty-five thousand dollars.

NEIGHBORHOOD REVITALIZATION, BLACK-OWNED BUSINESSES, AND HOPE VI

Revitalization requires the hiring of professional consultants to create a master plan for the design and development of the community. It also requires architects and contractors to do the actual housing construction or renovation, the construction of recreational and community facilities, and the creation of sidewalks and open spaces. In addition, building affordable housing—a centerpiece of most redevelopment projects—typically involves public/private partnerships, which in turn create financing and bonding opportunities. New rental properties create property management, building maintenance, and janitorial opportunities. Along with these services, landscaping and lawn care services are also required. Businesses that specialize in supplying construction materials, office supplies, and other equipment are also needed. Business opportunities also come in the form of the human and supportive services that are typically provided to revitalize low-income neighborhoods. These services include workforce readiness programs, early childhood educational programs, and childcare services. Finally, residents of revitalized communities usually demand new retail and commercial establishments. In short, redeveloping low-income Black neighborhoods can create numerous business opportunities, and these businesses in turn have the potential of generating employment for local residents (Boston 2005b).

While any business or entrepreneur can take advantage of the opportunities generated by neighborhood revitalization, the employment practices of Black business owners make Black-owned businesses especially attractive options. To illustrate this point, we next examine the revitalization that is currently transforming Atlanta's low-income public housing projects into mixed-income communities, through use of the government's HOPE VI Program.

In October 1992, Congress established the Urban Revitalization Demonstration Program, commonly known as HOPE VI. The objectives of this program are to (1) improve the living environments of residents of severely distressed public housing through the demolition, rehabilitation, reconfiguration, or replacement of obsolete units; (2) revitalize sites where public housing is located and improve the surrounding neighborhoods; (3) decrease the concentration of poverty; and (4) build economically sustainable communities. Between fiscal years 1993 and 2001, HUD awarded approximately $4.5 billion in HOPE VI grants to 98 public housing authorities for the revitalization of 165 sites (U.S. General Accounting Office [GAO] 2003:2–4).

One of the features of the HOPE VI Program in Atlanta is the large number of involved Black-owned businesses. As the introduction to this chapter stated, the most disadvantaged Black neighborhoods are those with large public-housing projects; consequently, the HOPE VI projects provide a severe test of the outcome of incorporating Black-owned businesses.

The problems in public housing operated by the Atlanta Housing Authority (AHA) are primary examples of what HOPE VI is designed to address. Densely populated public housing projects in Atlanta were once characterized by squalid living conditions, concentrated poverty, and high crime rates. One of AHA's worst properties was East Lake Meadows, the public housing project whose recurring violence earned it the nickname "Little Vietnam." AHA built East Lake Meadows in 1970. The 650-unit complex was located 4.5 miles east of the Atlanta Central Business District. By June 1992, the living conditions at East Lake Meadows were so squalid that over a quarter of its 650 units were vacant. In December 1995, there were only 387 families (1,397 persons) living in East Lake Meadows. Almost 60 percent of these families were dependent on welfare as a primary source of income, and only 13 percent of household heads ages 16 to 62 were employed. In 1995, the median household income of assisted families was just $4,536—less than one-half the income defining the 1995 poverty line for a family of three. The poverty rate in this public housing development was over 90 percent. The low labor-force participation and high welfare dependency among adults created a situation where only 16 percent of total household income was generated in the labor market. The remainder came from welfare, social and supplemental security, and other nonlabor market earnings (Boston 2005a). The socioeconomic status of these families was made worse by the deteriorated environment in which they lived.

The problems, however, were not limited to just one housing project. A 1994 Inspector General's Audit Report of AHA's housing properties found that 88 percent of the housing facilities did not meet minimum standards. In one of its own internal reports, AHA noted that rapes, burglaries, homicides, assaults, and drug-related arrests were "normal occurrences in most of the developments." Residents feared sitting on their porches, sleeping in their beds, and hanging clothes on the line (U.S. Department of HUD 1994).

HOPE VI offered a possible means of addressing the deep-seated problems in AHA projects. AHA is currently involved in one of the nation's most ambitious attempts to revitalize distressed public housing projects and turn them into mixed-income communities. To date, AHA has revitalized seven projects and created nine new mixed-income communities in their place. These new communities contain 3,404 units of mixed-income apartments that rely on mixed-financed public, private, and nonprofit funds. On average, just over 40 percent of the units are reserved for public housing eligible residents, 23 percent are rent-subsidized units, and 36 percent are leased at market rates. AHA is currently revitalizing three more conventional public housing projects, which will construct an additional 2,433 mixed-income rental units. Today these projects have been transformed into communities that are among the most attractive rental properties in the city.[4]

The revitalization of East Lake Meadows began in 1997 and was completed in 2000. In 2001, among the original residents who lived in East Lake Meadows and now live in the Villages of East Lake, the social and economic conditions were as follows: 48 percent were employed, the median household income was $7,322, income derived from labor market earnings comprised 52 percent of all income, 68 percent of the residents lived below the poverty line, and only 3 percent were dependent on welfare. The drastic decline in welfare dependency resulted from both welfare reform and the economic boom of the late 1990s. Similar improvements also occurred among other AHA HOPE VI projects (Boston 2005a). (See Chapter 2 for similar results in other geographic areas.) Obviously the economic and social status of residents still demands a great deal of improvement, but conditions have nevertheless improved drastically over a decade. For example, the number of violent crimes in the neighborhood decreased from 441 in 1992 to just 33 ten years later.

The new mixed-income community reserves 50 percent of the rental units for public housing eligible residents, and 50 percent are rented at market rates. The public housing units float, meaning that they are interspersed throughout, and the units rented by public housing assisted residents are not distinguishable from those rented by market-rate tenants. The revitalized community has a new high-performing charter school, an early learning center, a public golf course, a youth golf academy, a new YMCA, new retail developed and anchored around Publix Grocery, and a private golf course that is now home to the PGA Tour Championship.

AHA's neighborhood revitalization has generated enormous business opportunities. The total value of contracts awarded by AHA between 1998 and 2001 for the procurement of goods and services was $225.9 million. Most of these expenditures were related to the revitalization of its properties. New construction had the largest value of awards ($106.1 million or 47 percent). General services received $45.3 million or 20 percent, while substantial rehabilitation received $32.0 million or (14 percent) and professional services received $18.2 million (8.1 percent). These contracts have stimulated other economic activities. About $184 million of HOPE VI and other public housing development grants have been leveraged to generate $723 million of additional investment, mainly in the private sector. Table 7.4 provides information on the total amount of development spending that occurred in 6 public housing neighborhoods that have been revitalized.

Black businesses have tapped into many of these opportunities. Of the total value of awards by AHA, 53 percent were awarded to minority businesses, with $97.3 million, or 43 percent, going to Black business owners.[5] The latter is a remarkable accomplishment given that in 1997, Black-owned businesses comprised only 11 percent of all firms in the Atlanta metropolitan area and generated only 1 percent of all revenues.[6] The largest share of contracts awarded to Black businesses was in new construction ($71.3 million) and services ($16.7 million).[7] Interestingly, AHA achieved these

TABLE 7.4. HOPE VI grants and leveraged expenditures
for each community

Original Development	HOPE VI Grant ($M)	Total Leveraged Spending ($M)
Techwood/Clark Howell	43.0	153.0
East Lake Meadows	33.0	128.0
John Eagan Homes	21.0	140.0
John Hope Homes	17.0	150.0
Harris Homes	35.0	85.0
Capitol Homes	35.0	251.0
Totals	184.0	907.0

levels of Black participation through voluntary policies based on race- and gender-neutral measures, not through racial mandates. While most of the jobs generated by the Black-owned businesses were not in the professional category, they are appropriate for the skill levels of many of the residents. Equally important, HOPE VI supported efforts to stimulate entrepreneurship among the residents by funding "community programs designed to provide residents with the tools needed to launch their own businesses and become self-sufficient" (U.S. GAO 1998). The Black-owned firms that participated in the revitalization projects were, then, very much a major component in the turnaround.

While the evidence is clear about the incorporation of Black-owned businesses into the economic development strategy, less is known about the employment outcomes for residents. Of course, there is the overall improvement discussed earlier, but it is difficult to discern the direct contributions of Black businesses because, unfortunately, there are no solid data at this time about hiring patterns. What is likely is that the Black firms that contracted with AHA are either a part of the EEO-1 firms described earlier or are very similar to those firms in terms of hiring practices. It is, then, reasonable to assume that many of the jobs generated by Black-owned businesses in the revitalization efforts went to Black workers, including those who reside in the revitalized neighborhoods. There are two problems with this from a policy perspective. The first is that the assertion is a conjecture, although a very plausible one. What is needed to guide future efforts is a reasonably precise estimate of the magnitude of the direct and indirect impacts of Black-owned businesses on local employment. The second problem with the current strategy is that it implicitly depends on preexisting mechanisms (the hiring practices and patterns of Black-owned businesses) to produce desirable employment outcomes for Blacks. What may be better is to identify those mechanisms, make them an explicit part of the revitalization, and find ways to strengthen them.

HOPE VI in Atlanta is not a panacea for economic distressed neighborhoods but a useful model that points in the right direction in terms of incorporating Black-owned businesses into neighborhood revitalization. Despite the improvements in employment, many of the residents still are poor. Nevertheless, the efforts demonstrate that Black businesses can tap and be tapped to promote revitalization. Moreover, by doing so, this strategy has the potential to contribute to the growth of Black-owned businesses, which in turn can generate greater demand for Black workers. Over a longer time horizon, these efforts should be seen as building a useful foundation for future economic improvement in these neighborhoods, and that will require attracting new investments and upgrading the skills of local residents.

CONCLUDING REMARKS

Despite being underrepresented in the total economy, Black-owned businesses have the potential to benefit Black workers nationally and within local communities. If the projection for employment growth is realized, it may have significant policy implications for reducing the disparity between Black and White unemployment rates. The Black unemployment rate has consistently been about twice the rate of White unemployment.[8] From January 2004 to October 2004, the unemployment rate of Blacks was 10.4 percent, compared 4.9 percent for whites. This racial disparity has been resistant to government policies to reduce unemployment through economic growth stimulated by demand stimulus. Such policies rely on the benefits to trickle down, but they do nothing to alter the underlying social and economic structure and dynamic that determines how benefits are distributed by race. The result is that racial disparities remain intact. Such disparities do not change even in response to government supply-side policies that have been aimed at improving the workforce readiness of Blacks. This is due in part to the fact that discriminatory practices persist and may have increased with the retreat from affirmative action. The growth of Black-owned businesses has the potential to alter the labor-market dynamics that currently disadvantage Black workers. Because Black-owned businesses hire disproportionately more Black workers, a substantial growth in this demand can permanently reduce the ratio of Black to White unemployment. What remains problematic is whether the projected growth of Black-owned businesses will materialize. For this to happen, there is a need for public policy that supports and promotes this growth.

Black-owned businesses have the potential for generating jobs in low-income neighborhoods. Atlanta's projects under HUD's HOPE VI provide a model of how to incorporate Black-owned businesses in revitalization efforts. AHA's strategic vision focused not just on providing new housing but also on improving the human development of families. To achieve its goal, AHA retained private development partners who shared its vision and commitment. The Atlanta experience illustrates that Black-owned businesses can be part of community economic development. However, the HOPE VI projects have concentrated on the reconstruction of these neighborhoods. What is needed is sustainable economic growth, and that requires an expanded role for Black entrepreneurs, along with programs to enhance the marketable skills of local residents.

The evidence presented in this chapter shows that Black-owned businesses can indeed be a critical component of economic development in disadvantaged neighborhoods. Most community development strategies are focused on encouraging businesses to relocate to low-income communities. The logic behind this strategy is that new businesses will bring new jobs, and new jobs for local residents—particularly new jobs that pay livable wages—are central to inner-city revitalization. But while business development is a necessary component of the revitalization of low-income communities, it is not necessarily the case that attracting businesses to a poor community will lead to the employment of local residents. This is true for a number of strategies discussed by Michael Stoll in Chapter 4, including enterprise zones and tax incentives. For example, Sawicki and Moody (1997:78) point out that jobs created by businesses located in enterprise zones do not usually go to residents of those zones. They note that physical proximity to jobs is not as important as social and economic networks; who and what you know is often more important than where you are. Tax incentives have also proven to be largely ineffective in generating jobs for residents of low-income neighborhoods (Spencer and Ong 2004). The situation is different, however, for Black-owned businesses. As documented in this chapter, these businesses do generate employment opportunities for local residents. Unfortunately, very few of the strategies that have been proposed for redeveloping or re-vitalizing Black inner-city communities have emphasized the importance of including Black-owned businesses. Moreover, Black-owned businesses have the capacity to be involved in all aspects of rebuilding Black communities, including the design and construction, securing financing, and providing maintenance and supportive services.

Black-owned businesses are not a panacea for the myriad of problems facing economically distressed Black neighborhoods; nonetheless, we have seen in this chapter that the overwhelming majority of Black business owners share a strong commitment to community development. Given that they are also an increasingly important source of jobs for Black workers, it seems almost natural, even if not yet widely accepted, that these businesses must become a crucial element in Black community development. What is needed are policies and practices that give an explicitly greater role for Black-owned businesses in efforts to economically revitalize Black com-munities. While this chapter provides some insights that can help guide the development of these policies and practices, more detailed research is needed to both understand how Black-owned businesses currently operate and how they can become more effective as a community economic development tool.

NOTES

1. One notable exception was the strategy of "Black Capitalism" introduced during the Nixon administration as a means of quieting African American protests and rebellions. Although this was the intended objective, the initiative ultimately led to the creation of the Small Business Administration 8(a) Program, which opened new avenues for minority businesses in government contracting. Shortly after the federal government's initiative, Mayor Maynard Jackson of Atlanta introduced the nation's first local minority business affirmative action plan. His actions are widely viewed as having led to the emergence of a new generation of African American

businesses nationally. Similar set-aside contracting programs were adopted by other cities, as well as by many states, and were used as a vehicle for African American entrepreneurs to gain access to markets in nontraditional and fast growing industries. So a policy that was introduced with dubious motives ultimately created new business and employment opportunities for African Americans.

2. Statistics are from "1997 Economic Census Minority- and Women-Owned Businesses," downloaded from the U.S. Bureau of Census web site, http://www.census.gov/epcd/mwb97/us/us.html, November 21, 2004.

3. While this projected increase will not solve the massive labor-market problems facing Blacks, the newly created jobs can nonetheless be important at the margin. Creating employment equivalent to 4 percent of the Black labor force could help attenuate the unemployment gap between whites and blacks, which was about 6 percent in 2004 (4.8 percent versus 10.4 percent).

4. HOPE VI also has some limitations, particularly for the residents who were dislocated. See National Housing Law Project (2002).

5. Businesses owned by Asian and Pacific Islanders received $6.3 million or 2.8 percent. Businesses owned by Native Americans and Hispanics received 0.1 percent and 0.8 percent, respectively.

6. Statistics are from "1997 Economic Census Minority- and Women-Owned Businesses, Atlanta, GA MSA," downloaded from the U.S. Bureau of Census web site, http://www.census.gov/epcd/mwb97/metro/M0520.html, November 21, 2004.

7. In comparison, the largest share of contracts awarded to White-owned businesses was in Services ($28.4 million or 62.6 percent); New Construction ($27.9 million or 26.3 percent) followed.

8. Based on unemployment rates from 1972 to 2004 as reported by the U.S. Bureau of Labor Statistics web site, http://data.bls.gov/servlet/SurveyOutputServlet, downloaded November 21, 2004.

References

Bates, Timothy. 1993. *Banking on Black Business: The Potential of Emerging Firms for Revitalizing Urban Economies* Washington, DC: Joint Center for Political and Economic Studies.

Boston, Thomas D. 1999. *Affirmative Action and Black Entrepreneurship*. New York: Routledge.

Boston, Thomas D. 2003. *The ING Gazelle Index*, Third Quarter, 2003. www.inggazelleincdex.com.

Boston, Thomas D. 2005a. "The Effects of Revitalization on Public Housing Residents: A Case Study of the Atlanta Housing Authority." *Journal of the American Planning Association* 71(4):393–407.

Boston, Thomas D. 2005b. "Environment Matters: The Effect of Mixed-Income Revitalization on the Socioeconomic Status of Public Housing Residents," 1–96. Working paper 1, School of Economics, Georgia Institute of Technology. http://www.econ.gatech.edu/people/faculty/boston.htm.

Boston, Thomas D., and Catherine L. Ross, eds. 1997. *The Inner City: Urban Poverty and Economic Development in the Next Century*. New Brunswick: Transaction Publishers.

Business Week. 2002. The new face of philanthropy, 1–4. Business Week on-line. December 2, 2002. http://www.businessweek.com/print/magazine/content/02.48/b381000.

Ferguson, Ronald, and William Dickens. 1999. *Urban Problems and Community Development.* Washington, DC: Brookings Institution Press.

Fullerton, Howard Jr., and Mitra Toossi. 2001. Labor force projections to 2010. *Monthly Labor Review* 124(11):21–38.

Jargowsky, Paul. 2003. Stunning progress, hidden problems: The dramatic decline of concentrated poverty in the 1990s. Washington, DC: The Brookings Institution.

National Housing Law Project. 2002. False HOPE: A critical assessment of the HOPE VI Public housing redevelopment program. The National Housing Law Project, Poverty & Race Research Action Council, Sherwood Research Associates, and ENPHRONT (Everywhere and Now Public Housing Residents Organizing Nationally Together): 1–41. Washington, DC.

Spencer, James, and Paul Ong. 2004. An analysis of the Los Angeles revitalization zone: Are place-based investment strategies effective? *Economic Development Quarterly* 18:368–383.

Sawicki, David, and Mitch Moody. 1997. Deja vu all over again: Porter's model of inner city redevelopment. In *The Inner City: Urban Poverty and Economic Development in the Next Century,* eds. Thomas D. Boston and Catherine L. Ross, 75–94. New Brunswick: Transaction Publishers.

U.S. General Accounting Office. 1998. *HOPE VI, Progress and Problems in Revitalizing Distressed Public Housing.* GAO-98-187. Washington, DC: U.S. General Accounting Office.

U.S. Department of Housing and Urban Development, Office of Audit, Region IV. 1994. "Audit Report: Housing Authority of the City of Atlanta Public Housing Management Operations. March 11, 1994.

U.S. Department of Housing and Urban Development. 2000. *The State of the Cities 2000: Megaforces Shaping the Future of the Nation's Cities.* Washington, DC: U.S. Dept of Housing and Urban Development.

Whelan, David. 2004. America's richest charity and the Forbes 400. *Forbes.* http://www.forbes.com/personalfinance/philanthropy/2004/09/23/cz_dw_0923philan_rl04.html.

Wilson, William J. 1996. *When Work Disappears: The World of the New Urban Poor.* New York: Alfred A. Knopf.

New York City's Asian
Immigrant Economies
*Community Development Needs
and Challenges*

TARRY HUM

THE INCORPORATION EXPERIENCES and outcomes of Asian immigrants in the urban economy are a study in contrasts, and these contrasts
are reflected in the socioeconomic disparities within the Asian immigrant
population. The economic success that is exemplified by high rates of Asian
immigrant self-employment is counterbalanced by the persistence of working poverty and labor exploitation in garment and restaurant sweatshops.
Problematic though they may be, Asian immigrant economies are now integral to the economic landscape of many gateway cities, including Los
Angeles, Chicago, and New York. Small immigrant-owned businesses have
helped revitalize numerous local neighborhoods, transforming some into
ethnic enclaves that serve as sites for new immigrant settlement and concentrated labor and housing markets.

The seminal work on immigrant incorporation by Alejandro Portes and his
colleagues developed the idea of a "context of reception" to describe the
mechanisms that facilitate the economic incorporation of new immigrants
(Portes and Bach 1985; Portes and Rumbaut 1990 Portes and Zhou 1992).
Immigration is a social process based largely on informal ethnic networks that
promote a particular set of conditions for socioeconomic integration in the
host country through the formation of occupational niches and immigrant
enclaves (Portes and Bach 1985; Portes and Rumbaut 1990; Tilly 1990;
Waldinger 1996). Economic outcomes are not solely a result of individual
skills or ambitions but are determined by the social context in which immigrants are received (Portes and Bach 1985). A critical component of this
context of reception is the establishment of an ethnic community, especially
one with a large co-ethnic entrepreneurial base. The formation of enclaves—
defined as "spatially clustered networks of businesses owned by members of
the same minority"—promotes an alternative strategy for economic incorporation resulting in gains that are not typically accrued through immigrant employment in the general labor market (Portes 1995:27).

A policy consequence of emphasizing the voluntary nature of spatial
clustering and social isolation and the centrality of ethnic resources in
creating economic opportunities is that Asians and their enclave neighborhoods are viewed as "exceptional" due to the mediating effects of immigrant
entrepreneurship and co-ethnic relations built on reciprocity and trust

(Zhou 1992, Teitz 1989). Other researchers argue that immigrant economies do not create improved employment and mobility opportunities but
rather buffer unemployment and underemployment as well as the impacts of
working poverty (Ong 1984). The social isolation of immigrant enclaves
enables ethnic institutions to dominate community politics and business
development (Kwong 1996). Rather than bounded ethnic solidarity, class
divisions in enclave communities are evident in the degree of labor exploitation found in many co-ethnic workplaces (Kwong 1996, Ong et al.
1999). Moreover, the limitations of niche formation and concentration in
marginal sectors in a postindustrial urban economy are becoming apparent
in economic enclaves such as Manhattan's Chinatown (Wang 2000a). Increasingly, community and business leaders need to address the decline of
mature sectors—namely, the garment industry—and the subsequent displacement of immigrant workers with little or no English language proficiency and limited transferable skills.

Much economic development research on communities of color focuses on
African American poverty. While this is certainly a critical research and policy
area, the shifting demographics of American cities suggest that the contributions and challenges facing immigrant economies should also be an integral part of understanding the urban political economy. This chapter is a
study of Asian immigrant economies in New York City. Despite their notable
presence, there is no comprehensive study of Asian- or immigrant-owned
small businesses in New York City. New York City is an instructive case study
for several reasons. First, it has the largest concentration of Asian Pacific
American (APA) owned firms in the nation.[1] Second, immigrant economic
activity in New York City is extensive and varied, as evidenced by the multiple
and ethnically distinct nodes in Manhattan, Brooklyn, and Queens. Third, the
aftermath of September 11 makes even more transparent some enduring
problems endemic to immigrant economies, and lastly, numerous studies
show that relative to Asian immigrants in other gateway cities (such as Los
Angeles), Asian immigrants in New York have less human capital and tend to
be concentrated in ethnic enclaves where employment is typically poorly paid,
low skilled, and largely without benefits (Zhou 1998; Ettlinger and Kwon
1994). Hence, the issues of community economic development are especially
relevant to sustaining the livelihood of New York City's Asian neighborhoods
and present critical strategies for countering working poverty.

The downturn in New York City's economy was deepened by the tragic
events of September 11, 2001. In the immediate aftermath of the terrorist
attacks, several major corporations moved their office spaces out of Lower
Manhattan; others downsized their workforces, and the ripple effects were
widespread and deep (Bagli 2002; Parrot 2001). Nearly three years later,
researchers and policy makers are still taking stock of the long-term repercussions and possible lessons. One lesson quick to emerge is the danger of
New York's heavy dependence on the financial sector (Center for an Urban
Future 2003; Dolfman and Wasser 2004). Advocates have called for a shift
away from corporate welfare and tax-cutting strategies and a movement
toward support of small business. Small business, these advocates argue, has

a record of consistent performance in economic revitalization and job creation.[2] A recent mayoral executive order, perhaps in response to these sentiments, changed the name of the Department of Business Services to the Department of *Small* Business Services.

As is the case in several metropolitan areas, Asian-owned businesses comprise a sizable and growing segment of New York businesses.[3] The latest economic census (of 1997) indicates that close to 97,000 firms, or 15 percent of New York City businesses, are owned by Asian Pacific Americans (APAs). By the late 1990s, APAs owned nearly half (45 percent) of all New York's minority businesses. Paralleling the residential concentration of Asian New Yorkers, nearly all APA firms are located in Queens, Manhattan, or Brooklyn. While Manhattan Chinatown figures dominantly in the study of Asian businesses and neighborhood economies, Queens is also a dynamic economic center. In fact, approximately two-fifths of APA firms are located in the borough of Queens; by 1997, they accounted for a full quarter of all Queens firms.[4]

Immigrant businesses are a growing part of urban economies, and their contribution to the revitalization of local neighborhoods is frequently touted. Revitalization, however, is not the sole defining characteristic of immigrant entrepreneurialism; working poverty and concentration in marginal industry sectors are also prominent features of immigrant economies. Although the aftermath of September 11 highlighted hardships for Manhattan's Chinatown, which is located only a few blocks away from Ground Zero, academic and community leaders had sounded the alarm on the state of immigrant economies well before (Ong et al. 1999; Ong and Umemoto 1994; Wang 2000a; Urban Institute 2000). Pointing to the decline of those industries that anchor immigrant economies, the lack of public investment, and the patterns of persistent worker exploitation, community leaders sought to refocus public discussion on the outstanding needs and deepening economic crisis in the Asian immigrant "success" story.

This chapter seeks to seize this moment when urban policy makers view immigrant small businesses as vital economic engines to profile both the significant contributions and notable dilemmas. Despite the limited amount of official data on immigrant small businesses, a synthesis of those resources available provide an informational baseline. The recent public attention on immigrant small businesses presents an opportunity to define strategies and resources that will promote high road linkages to the regional economy, rather than low-road competitiveness based on price (Pastor et al. 2000). In this ongoing process of reimagining New York City's future as a global capital, it is incumbent that we engage in a rebuilding process whose outcomes will lift all New Yorkers.

NEW YORK CITY'S ASIAN IMMIGRANT ECONOMIES

New York's rapidly growing immigrant population represents another underutilized asset that could prove critical to New York's economic growth in the decade ahead. (Center for an Urban Future 2003:5)

In 1997, there were a total of 101,822 APA firms in the New York Primary Metropolitan Statistical Area (PMSA), with the overwhelming majority (95 percent) located in one of the five counties or boroughs that make up New York City. Between 1987 and 1997, the number of APA firms increased threefold—far exceeding the 92 percent increase in the total number of firms in New York City during the same period (Table 8.1). Reflecting the diverse ethnic composition of APA New Yorkers, the three largest groups of firm owners are Chinese (45 percent), Asian Indian (20 percent), and Korean (17 percent). There are notable interethnic differences in firm characteristics ranging from the average firm sales and receipts, the share of firms with paid employees, the firm size, and employee earnings (Table 8.2).[5]

The overwhelming majority of New York businesses are small; only one in four (26 percent) employ paid workers. Korean firms are an exception, however, as 45 percent have paid employees. While the overall share of APA firms with paid employees is comparable to that of city businesses in general, APA firms are significantly smaller, with an average of 5 compared to 17 paid employees. As noted, Korean firms are most likely to be employers, but their average firm size of 4 paid employees is slightly smaller than the average number of paid employees for APA employers.

Variations in sales and receipts further differentiate APA firms. Relative to New York firms, the size of sales and receipts for APA firms is quite modest. In comparison to an average sales and receipts figure that exceeds a million dollars for New York—area businesses, the average for APA firms is a mere $250,460. A striking exception is Japanese firms (with paid employees), whose average sales and receipts total over 2 million dollars, but these firms represent only 8 percent of area APA firms. While Korean firms are most likely to be employers, their average annual sales and receipts are $432,000 in comparison.

Among APA firms with paid employees, the average 1997 wage was $25,000—a little over one-half the average wage of $45,000 for private-sector employees in New York area firms at large. Again, an exception is paid employees in Japanese-owned firms, whose average earnings are nearly $63,000, but these employers are a tiny fraction (3 percent) of APA firms with paid employees. Among the top three Asian entrepreneurial groups, paid employees in firms owned by Chinese and Koreans earned an average of $19,000 compared to the $30,000 average earned by those employed in South Asian firms.

The industrial mix for APA firms is different from that of New York firms at large. While concentration in a few key industries is common, APA firms cluster in distinct niches. The dominant industry in the New York metropolitan area is the service sector, which accounts for 44 percent of all firms (Table 8.3). The second largest industry is finance, insurance, and real estate (FIRE), representing 13 percent of New York firms, closely followed by retail trade at 12 percent. These three industry sectors represent more than two-thirds of all New York metropolitan area firms. The profile of APA firms, however, looks quite different. While the service industry is also the largest sector for APA businesses, its level of concentration at 33 percent is

TABLE 8.1. 1987–1997 Growth trends in NYC firms

	1987					1997					1987–1997 Growth Trends		
	Total Firms	Minority Firms	% Minority (Total)	APA Firms	% APA (Minority)	Total Firms	Minority Firms	% Minority (Total)	APA Firms	% APA (Minority)	All Firms	Minority Firms	APA Firms
New York City	339,618	71,763	21%	26,870	37%	651,582	217,242	33%	96,952	45%	92%	203%	261%
Queens	83,017	25,865	31%	12,201	47%	159,668	74,300	47%	39,345	53%	92%	187%	222%
Manhattan	144,679	16,656	12%	6,735	40%	262,825	56,787	22%	29,375	52%	82%	241%	336%
Brooklyn	72,012	17,929	25%	5,051	28%	148,471	54,704	37%	21,356	39%	106%	205%	323%
Bronx	23,508	9,577	41%	1,880	20%	55,309	25,982	47%	4,293	17%	135%	171%	128%
Staten Island	16,402	1,736	11%	1,003	58%	25,309	5,469	22%	2,583	47%	54%	215%	158%

Source: 1987 and 1997 Survey of Minority-Owned Business Enterprises Data, Economic Census, US Census Bureau.

TABLE 8.2. Asian pacific american owned firms by ethnic group

	Number of Firms	% API Firms	Average Sales/Receipts	Firms with Paid Employees				
				Number of Firms	% Firms w/Employees	Average Sales/Receipts	Average No. Employees	Average Payroll
Total New York PMSA	784,876	—	$1,203,891	207,665	26%	$4,413,506	17	$45,390
Asian and Pacific American	101,814	100%	$250,460	26,168	26%	$881,500	5	$24,906
Chinese	45,455	45%	$240,956	9,900	22%	$1,008,490	6	$18,813
Asian Indian	20,527	20%	$317,786	5,423	26%	$1,115,006	5	$30,414
Korean	17,219	17%	$218,088	7,685	45%	$432,102	4	$19,068
Japanese	4,886	5%	$449,632	867	18%	$2,421,775	10	$62,866
Filipino	3,472	3%	$218,759	745	21%	$936,133	11	$31,098
Vietnamese	1,255	1%	$36,934	122	10%	$189,131	3	$13,759
Other Asian	9,000	8%	$128,313	1,425	16%	$529,443	3	$22,698

Source: 1997 Survey of Minority-Owned Business Enterprises Data, Economic Census, US Census Bureau.

Table 8.3. 1997 Industry Composition for New York, NY PMSA[a]

	Total Firms	Dist.	Minority Firms	Dist.	% Minority Firms of Total Firms	APA Firms	Dist.	% APA Firms of Minority Firms	% APA Firms of Total Firms
TOTAL INDUSTRIES	785,894	100%	258,928	100%	33%	101,822	100%	39%	13%
Services	347,145	44%	100,791	39%	29%	33,238	33%	33%	10%
Finance, insurance, and real estate	101,048	13%	11,467	4%	11%	5,584	5%	49%	6%
Retail Trade	91,010	12%	37,561	15%	41%	18,892	19%	50%	21%
Transportation, comm. & utilities	53,502	7%	33,500	13%	63%	11,653	11%	35%	22%
Construction	43,751	6%	12,799	5%	29%	3,449	3%	27%	8%
Wholesale Trade	35,058	4%	8,178	3%	23%	5,669	6%	69%	16%
Manufacturing	20,872	3%	4,596	2%	22%	2,337	2%	51%	11%
Agricultural services	4,700	1%	704	0.3%	15%	60	0.1%	9%	1%
Industries Not Classified	88,808	11%	49,332	19%	56%	20,940	21%	42%	24%

[a]New York, NY PMSA includes five counties that comprise NYC; Manhattan, Queens, Brooklyn, Bronx, and Staten Island, as well as the northern suburban counties of Westchester, Rockland, and Putnam.

Source: 1997 Survey of Minority-Owned Business Enterprises Data, Economic Census, US Census Bureau.

notably less than for New York area firms at large. Moreover, FIRE-related enterprises are a mere 5 percent of APA firms. It is retail trade, not FIRE, that follows services as the second most common industry sector, while firms in the transportation, communications, and utilities sector make up 11 percent of all APA businesses in the New York metropolitan area.

In the five years between the 1992 and 1997 economic censuses, the total number of APA firms doubled, and growth was especially notable for firms in the trade sectors (retail and wholesale) and the transportation, communication, and utilities sector. The prominence of transportation, communications, and utilities is somewhat surprising, but it is a sector common not just to APAs but to many minority-owned businesses in New York City. In fact, 63 percent of the New York metropolitan area's 53,502 firms in this sector are owned by minorities.[6] Few of the APA firms (7 percent) in this sector have paid employees, probably because many of them are owner-operators of taxicabs (Schaller 2004). A final observation on the industrial composition of APA firms in the New York metropolitan area is that 21 percent are categorized as "industries not classified"—meaning that the Census Bureau does not know what one in five APA firms do. Needless to say, this underscores the need for further study.[7]

APA firms are concentrated in Manhattan and Queens, with Brooklyn emerging as a third economic center. This pattern accords with findings of the Center for an Urban Future, which noted that "Although Manhattan remains by far the densest center for new business in the city, the most dramatic growth in recent years has been in the other boroughs" (2003:32). From 1987 to 1997, the growth of APA firms consolidated around the core boroughs of Manhattan, Queens, and Brooklyn; by 1997 only 7 percent of New York City's APA firms were located outside these boroughs. The densest concentration of APA firms is in the borough of Queens, but more than half of APA firms with paid employees are located in Manhattan, suggesting that Manhattan remains the center of the Asian immigrant labor market. While the increase in APA enterprises was especially dramatic in Brooklyn, the significantly lower average 1997 earnings for paid employees may indicate that marginal employment conditions are prevalent in Brooklyn firms.

Given the small scale of the immigrant economy, the self-employed are one of its key components. To examine the propensity for self-employment, Table 8.4 provides data for the three largest Asian immigrant groups—Chinese, Asian Indian, and Korean. Despite the common view that there are extraordinarily high self-employment rates among immigrant Asians, Asian immigrants are actually only slightly more likely than other groups to work for themselves; 11 percent of foreign-born Asians are self-employed compared to 9 percent of all New Yorkers. Korean immigrants, however, are exceptional, as nearly one in four is self-employed. Almost 40 percent of self-employed New Yorkers are female. While this gender ratio is applicable for self-employed immigrant Chinese and Koreans, a gender gap is significant for immigrant Asian Indians; only 16 percent of their self-employed are women.

TABLE 8.4. Self-Employed new yorkers by nativity and ethnic groups

	New Yorkers	FB New Yorkers	FB Asians	FB Chinese	FB Koreans	FB Asian Indian
Total Labor Force	4,439,597	1,936,426	422,457	191,666	50,324	87,227
Self-Employment						
Rate	9%	10%	11%	9%	21%	11%
Female	38%	36%	32%	37%	38%	16%
Average Age	45 years	44 years	44 years	45 years	46 years	42 years
Educational Attainment						
Did not complete High School	21%	32%	28%	42%	15%	28%
High School Graduate	19%	23%	22%	18%	26%	25%
Some College	20%	19%	16%	12%	21%	12%
College and more	40%	25%	34%	27%	39%	36%
Does not speak English	13%	26%	34%	49%	52%	7%
Top Six Industry Categories	Construction	Construction	Taxi and Limosine Services	Restaurants	Dry cleaning/ Laundry	Taxi and limousine service
	Independent artists	Taxi and limousine service	Construction	Construction	Grocery stores	Construction
	Taxi and limousine service	Child day care services	Restaurants	Dry cleaning/ Laundry	Nail salons	Restaurants
	Child day care services	Private households	Dry Cleaning	Cut and sew apparel	Construction	Grocery stores
	Restaurants	Restaurants	Grocery Stores	Taxi and limousine service	Taxi and limousine service	Child day care services
	Legal services	Grocery stores	Nail Salons	NS Retail trade	Restaurants	NS Whlse trade

	33%	41%	43%	40%	52%	54%
% of All Industry Categories						
Top Six Occupational Categories	Taxi Drivers and Chauffeurs	Taxi Drivers and Chauffeurs	Taxi Drivers & Chauffeurs	Managers-Retail Salespers.	Managers-Retail Salesper.	Taxi Drivers and Chauffeurs
	Child Care Workers	Child Care Workers	Managers-Retail Salespers.	Retail Salespersons	Misc. Personal Appearance Workers	Managers-Retail Salesper.
	Managers-Retail Salespers.	Managers-Retail Salespers.	Retail Salespersons	Chief Executives	Cashiers	Retail Salespersons
	Lawyers	Maids and Housekeeping Cleaners	Chief Executives	Taxi Drivers and Chauffeurs	Managers of Production and Operations	Child Care Workers
	Designers	Retail Salespersons	Cashiers	Cashiers	Laundry & Dry-Cleaning Workers	Physicians and Surgeons
	Maids and Housekeeping Cleaners	Driver/Sales Workers & Truck Drivers	Child Care Workers	Tailors, Dressmakers, and Sewers	Taxi Drivers and Chauffeurs	Driver/Sales Workers & Truck Drivers
% of All Occupational Categories	25%	33%	32%	25%	43%	48%
Average 1999 Total Earnings	$42,258	$29,214	$28,235	$23,597	$30,595	$30,426

Source: 2000 Publis Use Microdata Samples (5%). US Census Bureau.

In *Race, Self-Employment, and Upward Mobility: An Illusive American Dream,* Timothy Bates (1998b) argues that human and financial capital are the key ingredients for successful business ownership. Self-employed New Yorkers have significant amounts of human capital; 40 percent hold at least a college degree. The share of college graduates drops notably for self-employed immigrant New Yorkers, although self-employed Asians are well represented at both ends of the educational spectrum. Among immigrant Chinese entrepreneurs, for example, educational attainment is highly bi-furcated: while 27 percent are college graduates, 40 percent have not even completed high school.[8] In contrast, the educational attainment levels for immigrant Korean and Asian Indian self-employed workers are consistent with the human capital profile of self-employed New Yorkers.

The industry and occupational categories coupled with the average 1999 earnings show a concentration in narrow economic niches with fairly modest returns. In addition to listing the most common industry and occupational types, Table 8.4 notes the share these top 6 categories represent among the self-employed as a measure of relative industry and occupational con-centration. The top six industry categories for self-employed New Yorkers represents a mix of service industries reflected in varied occupational types which include designers and lawyers, as well as taxi drivers and child care workers. These industries and occupations, however, represent only a third or fewer of all self-employed New Yorkers. The concentration in a handful of industries is significantly higher for immigrant self-employed, especially Koreans and Asian Indians; more than 50 percent of the self-employed are located in only six industries. The list of industry and occupational categories for self-employed immigrant Asians accentuates ethnic niches in immigrant-dominated industries such as restaurants, dry cleaning and laundry services, taxi and limousine services, nail salons, construction, and grocery stores. A final observation is that the average 1999 total earnings for self-employed New Yorkers is quite modest, with earnings for immigrant self-employed notably lower than the overall average—particularly for Chinese im-migrants.

Official data sources provide a general profile of the self-employed and their enterprises, but much remains to be learned about the characteristics of immigrant-owned businesses. For example, we do not have a sense of the geography of immigrant small businesses beyond the county level. While studies describe immigrant businesses as "economic engines" of neighbor-hood revitalization, we lack the data to map their locational patterns and see whether and how they are spatially clustered. Additionally, industry cate-gories are broad and don't provide information about specific ethnic niches—further limiting our ability to correlate ethnic and spatial patterns with industry niches. Finally, while there is much anecdotal evidence on the presence of a large Asian informal economy, there is no coordinated research effort to measure the size, scope, and practices of informal immigrant small businesses.

The research that has been done, including the extensive work of Peter Kwong and Ken Guest on the growing undocumented Fukienese population in Manhattan Chinatown and Brooklyn's Sunset Park, indicates that the informal labor market is regulated, in part, by employment agencies that disburse immigrant workers throughout the country (Kwong 1997; Guest 2003). The network of employment agencies that provides cheap labor to immigrant niche businesses (such as restaurants, greengrocers, and dry cleaners) was recently uncovered in an investigation by Elliot Spitzer, the New York State Attorney General. As part of his effort to penalize businesses that pay their employees less than the state minimum wage of $5.15, Spitzer and his staff uncovered numerous employment agencies that supply businesses with immigrant workers. The workers are recruited largely through advertisements in ethnic newspapers, or by word of mouth (Greenhouse 2004). The New York State Attorney General also claimed that some of these employment agencies discriminated based on nationality, age, and sex and that some charged exorbitant fees for their services.[9] Of the 9 employment agencies that Spitzer took action against, all but one is located in an immigrant neighborhood in Queens (Lombardi 2004).

The informal Asian immigrant economy takes many forms. Of these, street vendors are perhaps the most visible. Street vendors are a ubiquitous feature of many immigrant neighborhoods throughout New York City including Manhattan Chinatown, Jackson Heights, and Sunset Park (Lin 1998; Berger 2003; Russ 2002). These marginal enterprises typically entail immigrants selling a range of products on the streets with, at times, little more than a cardboard box to sit on.[10] The vendors are often the targets of complaints about unfair competition, health and sanitation conditions, pedestrian safety and street overcrowding, but street vending remains a timeless feature of immigrant neighborhoods (Ponce de León 2003; Lin 1998). Like street vendors, Chinese and Asian Indian day laborers are another highly visible aspect of the informal Asian economy. The growing number of Asian day laborers has been well documented; photojournalist Michael Kamber did a comprehensive essay on Sikh day laborers in Richmond Hill, Queens,[11] and City Councilor John Liu of Flushing, Queens, recently commented on the many Asian immigrant day laborers who descend on particular street corners in Flushing's downtown in search of work (Virasami and Rayman 2004b).

Day labor is characterized by transience and anonymity, and this—along with its illegality—prevents most people from being aware of it, even though much of its work takes place in plain sight. The work, being unregulated, often does not pay well and can frequently be dangerous. The tragic death of a Chinese day laborer on a construction site in Elmhurst, Queens, underscores the hazards faced by many day laborers. The contractor, also a Chinese immigrant, had failed to provide the proper structural support necessary for excavation work, and a concrete wall collapsed as a result, crushing the worker. The worker's name, Jian Quo Shen, was not known until several days later, when friends concerned about his absence contacted the police.[12] Shen's death marks the fourteenth time in the last five years that an immigrant day laborer has died at a work site due to unsafe work conditions (Virasami and Rayman 2004a).

THE LIMITS OF THE IMMIGRANT ECONOMY

Compared to other large cities, too few immigrant-owned businesses in the city grow beyond the mom and pop stage. (Center for an Urban Future 2003:29)

Immigrant-owned businesses are lauded for revitalizing urban economies (von Hoffman 2003; Portes and Zhou 1992; Marcuse 1997; Teitz 1989). These small businesses stemmed urban decline in many local neighborhoods by revitalizing vacant storefronts, providing vital products and services, and contributing to the cultural milieu of a cosmopolitan city. But while immigrant businesses have enlivened the economies of numerous local neighborhoods, they also pose important challenges for community economic development. One of the biggest problems in immigrant neighborhoods is not joblessness but underemployment, usually driven by low wages, lack of benefits, and part-time or intermittent work (Ong and Miller 2002). A recent community survey conducted by the Asian American Legal Defense and Education Fund found that low wages, sweatshop conditions, and dwindling job opportunities—particularly in the garment industry—were top concerns of Asian immigrants in Manhattan Chinatown, Sunset Park, and Elmhurst (Hum 2004).

While official data provide an aggregate profile of APA firms, there is little data on the operations of small immigrant businesses. A recent business survey conducted in Brooklyn's Sunset Park—New York's third largest Asian concentration—offers some important insights on the nature of immigrant economies.[13] Almost all the Asian firms surveyed in Sunset Park were owned or managed by an immigrant, and nearly a third by an immigrant who had emigrated in the past decade. The overwhelming majority of Sunset Park businesses are small firms with five or fewer employees. The neighborhood's Asian immigrant economy is anchored by numerous storefront businesses, restaurants and groceries, garment factories and related shops. Virtually all of the surveyed firms hired co-ethnic workers and typically drew from the local labor market as a majority of both firm owners/managers and workers are Sunset Park residents.

The survey found that Sunset Park's local labor market generates largely part-time employment that pays slightly above the minimum wage and typically does not provide health insurance, which suggests that working poverty is a prominent result of the neighborhood's economy. Firm operations are highly dependent on informal ethnic networks and resources. Common strategies to raise capital are personal savings and borrowing from family members. Firms seldom reach out to business organizations or institutions since the most common sources of business support are newspapers, friends or relatives, and word of mouth.

Drawn by its extensive consumer market businesses locate in Sunset Park for its potential for business growth and relatively affordable rents. However, these small businesses, which provide goods and services largely to an immigrant consumer base, are also highly reliant on informal sources of start-up capital and business information. They engage in informal hiring strategies such as referrals and recommendations from friends or family, and they seek workers who have prior work experience and therefore require little orientation and training to the world of work. And although affordable rents remain an advantage of Sunset Park, rents are increasing, which exacerbates an economic environment that is already hypercompetitive. These are common issues that face immigrant economies. These concerns require policy attention and resources in order to ensure the development of a local neighborhood economy that provides an economic livelihood based on stable employment, livable wages, and mobility opportunities.

Asian immigrant workers are differentiated by ethnic- and gender-specific occupations. The data summarized in Table 8.5 confirms the high level of immigrant concentration in a handful of occupations and industries. In spite of the continuing decline of the U.S. garment industry, nearly one-quarter of immigrant Chinese women work as sewing machine operators. Chinese men are similarly concentrated in jobs as cooks or waiters.

Korean and Asian Indian immigrants are not concentrated as acutely as immigrant Chinese workers, but they are nevertheless defined by certain occupations. For example, comparable to their self-employed counterparts, many Asian Indian male workers are taxi drivers. Nearly one in ten immigrant Asian Indian female workers is a cashier, and employment in health related occupations—such as home health aides or registered nurses—is also an important niche for Asian Indian women. For female Koreans, retail positions are among the top occupational categories, and the largest niche is personal appearance workers. Immigrant Korean men are similarly concentrated in retail positions, however in contrast to immigrant Asian women, their top occupational category is a supervisory position.

Table 8.5 includes the median 1999 wages for immigrant workers by ethnicity and gender. Relative to other gender and Asian ethnic groups, Korean and Asian Indian men have the highest median wage, at approximately $22,000. But the uniformity in the low wages of immigrant Asian workers is alarming, especially since the cost of living in New York City is among the highest in the United States.

By synthesizing various official data resources and the neighborhood business survey, we can get a rough picture of New York's Asian immigrant economies. The picture that emerges is one of a sizable business sector defined by distinct ethnic niches with modest returns to employment and low levels of human capital. The underrepresentation of immigrant businesses in high value and high growth sectors was also noted in a recent survey of Los Angeles–based minority-owned businesses conducted by the Community Development Technologies Center.[14] Asian immigrant firms are often embedded in a high level of ethnic-based interindustry integration. Asian businesses generate backward (as suppliers of production inputs), forward (as distributors of finished products/outputs), and consumption linkages (Lin 1998). For example, ethnic food manufacturers supply ethnic supermarkets that are patronized by co-ethnic immigrants (also employed in ethnic businesses), whose consumer dollars are then recirculated in the ethnic economy. This vertical integration of immigrant-owned businesses contributes to a

TABLE 8.5. Foreign born workers in private sector firms

	Chinese		Asian Indian		Korean	
	Women	Men	Women	Men	Women	Men
Total	73,933	77,815	23,518	39,083	17,856	15,895
Top Six Industries	Cut and Sew Apparel (28%) Restaurants and Food Ser. (7%) Banking (4%) Securities, Financial Inv. (3%) Manufacturing NS Ind. (3%) Hospitals (3%)	Restaurants and Food Ser. (27%) Cut and Sew Apparel (8%) Construction (5%) Securities, Financial Inv. (4%) Banking (3%) Grocery Stores (2%)	Hospitals (7%) Banking (6%) Cut and Sew Apparel (6%) Restaurants and Food Ser. (5%) Nursing Care Facilities (4%) Grocery Stores (3%)	Taxi and Limo Serv. (8%) Restaurants and Food Ser. (10%) Construction (7%) Hospitals (7%) Grocery Stores (3%) Securities, Financial Inv. (3%)	Nail Salons and Pers. Care (13%) Restaurants and Food Ser. (7%) Grocery Stores (6%) Cut and Sew Apparel (5%) Banking (4%) Securities, Financial Inv. (4%)	Grocery Stores (9%) Restaurants and Food Ser. (8%) Dry Cleaning and Laundry Ser. (5%) Construction (5%) Securities, Financial Inv. (3%) Banking (3%)
Industry Concentration[a]	48%	49%	31%	35%	39%	33%
Top Five Occupations	Sewing Machine Oper. (24%) Cashiers (4%)	Cooks (16%) Waiters (5%)	Cashiers (9%) Nursing, Home Health Aides (6%)	Taxi Drivers and Chauffeurs (7%) Supervisor/Mger Retail Sales (5%)	Misc. Personal Appearance Workers (14%) Cashiers (9%)	Supervisor/Mger Retail Sales (9%) Cashiers (6%)

	Accountants and Auditors (4%) Nursing, Home Health Aides (3%) Production Workers (3%) Retail Salespersons (3%) Secretaries and Admin. Assts. (3%)	Driver/Sales Workers (4%) Production Workers (3%) Cashiers (3%) Retail Salespersons (3%)	Registered Nurses (4%) Sewing Machine Operators (4%) Retail Salespersons (4%) Accountants and Auditors (3%)	Cashiers (4%) Retail Salespersons (3%) Security/Guards (3%) Waiters (3%)	Designers (5%) Waiters (4%) Retail Salespersons (4%) Supervisor/Mger Retail Sales (3%)	Retail Salespersons (4%) Cooks (3%) Sales, Wholesale/Mfg (3%) Accountants (3%)
Occupation Concentration[b]	41%	34%	30%	25%	39%	31%
English Language Ability not well or at all	50%	51%	7%	7%	40%	42%
Education						
Less than High School	42%	43%	21%	21%	11%	11%
High School Graduate	20%	19%	23%	22%	23%	22%
Some College	13%	14%	20%	17%	21%	24%
College Graduate	17%	15%	23%	22%	30%	29%
Graduate or Professional Degree	7%	9%	12%	18%	14%	13%
Median 1999 Wages	$10,000	$14,400	$15,400	$22,000	$15,000	$21,860

Source: 2000 Public use Microdata Samples (5%), US Census Bureau.
[a]Industry concentration is defined as the percentage of the top six industries as a share of all industries.
[b]Occupational concentration is defined as the percentage of the top six occupations as a share of all occupations.

perception of self-sufficient and insular ethnic economies (Teitz 1989). This perception is misleading. Immigrant businesses are not isolated from general market conditions, and dense ethnic linkages may close off access to opportunities in the mainstream. As Yu Zhou notes in her 1998 study of ethnic economies in New York City and Los Angeles, "Dependency on ethnic networks . . . can also lead to over concentration in certain sectors, making these super-competitive and exploitative" (p. 545).

Limited business networks and sources of business information pose significant barriers to the immigrant self-employed. The lack of English language ability contributes to "closed business and civic networks" in already limited ethnic and geographic markets (Community Development Technologies Center 2001), particularly for the Chinese immigrant self-employed, who are more likely to be hindered by human capital deficiencies. The survey of immigrant businesses in Brooklyn's Sunset Park found the most common resources for business information and support are from ethnic media or social relations (Hum 2002). Membership in a business or trade association or a similar institution is rare, suggesting that immigrant firms are not well organized or formalized into groups that can advocate for collective interests.

Business development is an essential cornerstone for economic vitality, and it is perhaps even more important for Asian immigrants, since their employment is overwhelmingly centered in ethnic-owned firms. Because Asian firms are concentrated in residential enclave neighborhoods, economic development and community development are intricately linked in APA communities (Ong et al. 1999). This is certainly the case for Manhattan Chinatown and for satellite neighborhoods like Brooklyn's Sunset Park. This relationship is also confirmed by the Queens County Overall Economic Development Corporation (QCOEDC), which defines "economic engine" neighborhoods as those with "substantial economic activity, especially manufacturing and retail trade, as well as multiple transportation modes," and defines "retail hub" neighborhoods as those with "significant retail shopping hubs and/or development potential" (2002, p. 47). The QCOEDC's economic engine neighborhoods include concentrated Asian enclaves like Flushing, Jackson Heights, and Elmhurst, and its retail hubs include Richmond Hill and Sunnyside, which have substantial and growing Asian populations.

While economic activity is a prominent attribute of Asian immigrant neighborhoods, so too is poverty. A quick scan of poverty rates by neighborhood shows that it is these same economic and retail hub neighborhoods that also have high rates of Asian poverty. One-third of the Asian residents in Manhattan Chinatown and Sunset Park live below the poverty level—greatly exceeding the citywide poverty rate of 20 percent. Queens's economic neighborhoods also experience relatively high rates of Asian poverty—24 percent in Flushing, 22 percent in Sunnyside, and 19 percent in Jackson Heights. By contrast, the poverty rate for Asians residing in Queens' suburban-like neighborhoods, such as Bayside, is notably lower, at 10 percent. Typical of immigrant ethnic economies, business prosperity and residential poverty are often found in the same spatial settings or enclaves.

Hence, strategies for community economic development need to be comprehensive and must promote not just business viability but also labor standards that ensure living wages, health benefits, and safe work environments.

The tragic events of September 11 exposed the vulnerabilities of an immigrant economy based largely on tourism and the declining manufacturing sector. After the terrorist attacks, the Asian American Federation of New York (AAFNY) set out to quantify September 11's impacts on Chinatown's economy. The resulting reports show that Chinatown's key industries—in garment, restaurant, retail, and tourism—were hardest hit and lost millions of dollars in revenue with continuing impacts a year after the tragic events. Chinatown workers accounted for almost 10 percent of the 83,100 New Yorkers who lost their jobs in the aftermath of September 11 (Lee 2002), and nearly three quarters of Chinatown's workers (approximately 25,000) were temporarily dislocated in the weeks immediately following the World Trade Center attacks; nearly one-quarter (8,000) remained unemployed 3 months later. AAFNY found that even a year after September 11, one-third of restaurant workers worked reduced hours, and approximately 65 garment shops had permanently shut their operations.

It is estimated that 3,500 garment workers were displaced as a result of the September 11 impacts on New York's garment industry (Chin 2003). Given that immigrant Chinese women rely heavily on this industry for entry-level employment, the magnitude and consequences of this dislocation are significant. The decline of the Chinatown's garment industry and the consequential rise in underemployment and unemployment have ripple effects in surrounding immigrant neighborhoods, since Chinatown garment workers are frequently residents of Brooklyn or Queens. Based on interviews with 61 garment workers approximately a year after the September 11 attack, Hunter College Professor Margaret Chin (2003) determined that many had difficulty obtaining financial assistance from the myriad array of relief funds.

Chin (2003) also discussed the limitations that immigrant workers' social networks placed on their job search efforts. Because few immigrants knew anyone who was not a garment or restaurant worker, many had difficulty finding work outside these troubled sectors. The insular and dense social ties that define many immigrant communities are not useful for finding employment outside the immigrant economy. Chin (2003) describes how her interviewees and their family members had "little connection to jobs or people outside of the enclaves" (p. 52). This finding underscores an impending crisis in the Chinese immigrant economy; the shrinkage of traditional manufacturing production centers in Manhattan's midtown Garment Center and Chinatown leaves the economy deeply vulnerable (Berger 2004). At a June 25, 2004, workshop on "A New Chinatown," the leaders of three traditional organizations—the Consolidated Chinese Benevolent Association (CCBA), the Flushing Chinese Business Association, and the Brooklyn Chinese American Association—discussed the inevitable demise of the city's garment industry and agreed with the CCBA's prediction that the garment industry will cease to be a viable anchor for Chinatown's immigrant economy within the next ten years.[15] Sustaining the economic livelihood of Asian immigrant communities will require new strategies for job creation and workforce development, especially for workers with limited English language proficiency.

AAFNY's economic analysis of Chinatown made two key observations about the nature of immigrant small businesses. The first was vulnerability to external shocks. Most of Chinatown's 3,855 businesses operate on thin profit margins that magnify the impact of short-term losses. The second observation related to the informality of immigrant firms. The majority are cash based, making it difficult for owners to produce documentation of a credit history or business operations. This inability to produce documentation is a barrier to qualifying and securing bank loans. Collateral requirements and language barriers also pose challenges to small business owners in their efforts to secure Small Business Administration (SBA) loans. As AAFNY noted,

> Beyond the direct impact of infrastructure bottlenecks on Chinatown's businesses, distinctive characteristics of Chinatown's economy have heightened barriers to recovery and must be addressed in restoring the community's economic vitality. (2002, p. 20)

As a result of the requirements of many September 11 assistance programs, only a small number of eligible Chinatown businesses even requested assistance, and among those that did, many received relatively smaller grants and loans than other businesses. Despite massive losses and extensive outreach, less than 10 percent of Chinatown businesses (353 out of 3,855) received SBA loans totaling $21 million. About 61 percent of these businesses received loans for less than $50,000, compared to a citywide average of $80,000. While many more businesses were assisted by Empire State Economic Development Corporation grants, the average grant of $9,700 for Chinatown businesses was significantly less than the average grants of $15,738 to $21,983 for businesses in lower Manhattan. The AAFNY report noted that the assistance was not enough to make up for the losses endured by Chinatown businesses—for example, the Chinatown garment industry lost $490 million, but Chinatown received only $60 million in compensatory aid.

Despite the growing significance of New York City immigrant small businesses, a recent panel focusing on them highlighted the absence of a "macro" perspective on the numerous "immigrant marketplaces" that are transforming the city's economic streetscape.[16] A "macro" view of Asian immigrant small businesses highlights several additional challenges such as employment practices, real estate costs, and limited informal networks. While many immigrant businesses are mom-and-pop operations, the share of firms that employ paid workers increased from 17 percent of APA firms in 1987 to slightly more than 1 in 4 by 1997 (Table 8.6). Moreover, the number of employees has also increased from an average of 3 in 1987 to 5 in 1997. While employment in Asian small businesses is a key labor market incorporation strategy for immigrants, the nature of these small businesses point to limited avenues for skill acquisition and mobility, lack of health insurance, prevalence of part-time work, and concentration in ethnic niches. Worker advocacy groups continually struggle for basic labor rights for

TABLE 8.6. Firms owned by Asian Pacific Americans in New York City 1987–1997

	1987					1997				
	Total Firms	Number of Firms with Employees	Percentage of Firms with Employees	Number of Employees	Average Number or Employees	Total Firms	Number of Firms with Employees	Percentage of Firms with Employees	Number of Employees	Average Number of Employees
Queens	12,201	1,568	13%	3,499	2.2	39,345	5,553	14%	30,984	5.6
Manhattan	6,735	1,669	25%	6,094	3.7	29,375	13,596	46%	73,645	5.4
Brooklyn	5,051	676	13%	1,874	2.8	21,356	4,149	19%	9,837	2.4
Bronx	1,880	339	18%	798	2.4	4,293	1,386	32%	7,948	5.7
Staten Island	1,003	232	23%	407	1.8	2,583	363	14%	2,857	7.9
Total NYC	26,870	4,484	17%	12,672	3	96,952	25,047	26%	125,271	5

Source: 1987 and 1997 Survey of Minority—Owned Business Enterprises Data, Economic Census, US Census Bureau.

immigrant workers such as payment of wages, overtime pay, minimum wage, an eight-hour workday, and health benefits.

Although poor working conditions are pervasive, the insularity of immigrant economies has kept exploitative conditions largely out of the public eye, with the exception of the occasional media exposé on sweatshops.[17] The reliance on non–co-ethnic immigrant workers has also helped give some attention to the substandard employment conditions common in immigrant economies. Increasingly, for example, Asian immigrant employers rely on Latinos as a source of low-wage labor; some prime examples are New York's Korean greengrocers and their largely Mexican workforce (Kim 1999). As Kim argues, "Latino employment in Korean-owned businesses keeps the ethnic economy viable by providing for much needed low-cost labor," (p. 599). In a much-publicized case, Mexican workers, successfully organized by the garment workers' union, UNITE, forced Korean greengrocers to sign a code of conduct negotiated by the New York State Attorney General (Greenhouse 2002). Far from significant concessions for labor improvements, the code of conduct essentially reestablishes the floor on employment standards by enforcing the minimum wage, overtime pay, a 40-hour work-week, and an unpaid day of rest per week.[18]

The rising cost of operating a business, due in part to escalating rents in many New York neighborhoods, poses serious challenges to the immigrant economy. The preliminary findings of a survey of immigrant-owned businesses in Queens found that the most pressing problem facing immigrant entrepreneurs is the cost of space (Queens County Overall Economic Development Corporation 2004). Similarly, a survey of small businesses in Sunset Park found that while neighborhood location was initially an attraction—due to an extensive consumer market, the potential for business growth, and relatively affordable rents—a key concern now is the continuing rise in rental costs (Hum 2002). One widespread solution to this problem is to lease subdivided storefront space to businesses that occupy little more than a stall, creating a retail layout similar to swap meets in Los Angeles. Escalating real estate costs have also been documented as a factor in the displacement of manufacturing in traditional production centers, such as the Midtown Garment Center and Manhattan Chinatown.[19] Gentrification pressures from neighboring areas like Soho and Tribeca continually threaten the residency of longtime Chinese residents and the small businesses that make up Chinatown's local economy. Gentrification pressures similarly shape the future of outer borough neighborhoods such as Sunset Park that must contend with spillover development pressures from neighboring affluent Park Slope and Bay Ridge.

POLICY AND PROGRAMS TO IMPROVE IMMIGRANT ECONOMIES

In his important work on the competitive advantages of the inner city, Michael Porter argues that a social model of community development has hindered the economic development of inner-city neighborhoods (Porter

1995, 1997). The experience of immigrant economies, however, underscores the limitations of a market-driven model of economic development and lends support to a continued and expanded public role in addressing working poverty and urban inequality. The dominant perceptions of immigrant self-sufficiency, insularity, and enclave prosperity further contribute to a void in public policy considerations of immigrant community development contributions as well as outstanding dilemmas and needs (Ong et al. 1999). This observation that the issues and barriers facing immigrant businesses are absent from the public policy radar screen is reiterated in the Center for an Urban Future report statement, "right now there isn't even an appreciation of the significant obstacles that immigrant businesses face by the city's economic development officials" (2003, 28). This chapter discusses several key policy areas that must be part of a comprehensive strategy to improve conditions in immigrant economies: small business assistance, community and workforce development, and worker centers.

ASSISTING IMMIGRANT BUSINESSES

There are two ways that improved government intervention can assist immigrant small businesses. One is to foster an "enabling environment" that encourages immigrant entrepreneurs to form business networks and institutions, employ broader market penetration strategies, integrate technology, and adhere to labor standards. The second strategy is to develop culturally competent strategies to inform and engage immigrant entrepreneurs in the myriad business assistance and regulatory agencies such as the SBA, New York City's Department of Small Business Services, and the many institutions that promote business and economic development. The objective is not to create new programs but to improve immigrant connections, outreach, and access to existing resources.

An "enabling" environment would address the barriers faced by entrepreneurial immigrants in establishing and sustaining their small businesses. While immigrant businesses rely on bonding capital, that is, strong social ties based on intraethnic relationships as evidenced by the reliance on friends and family as sources of capital and information, economic development beyond narrow ethnic niches requires bridging capital, which is based on weak social ties to mainstream institutions and individuals (Pastor et al. 2000). Citibank Vice President and Senior Business Development Officer Ali Hirji has noted that a key component of an enabling environment is an improved connection between banking institutions and immigrant communities which would "do a better job in the context of leveraging the current opportunities that exist."[20]

In addition to improving their access to business resources, immigrant small business owners need to establish competency in basic practices like recordkeeping and establishing a credit history. Without these basic skills, it is impossible to break out of traditional immigrant niches. Moreover, because low-skilled immigrants, particularly those with limited English language skills, depend heavily on ethnic economies for employment, it will be very important to help immigrant-owned firms to move into more-profitable economic sectors.

An enabling environment should include an intermediary organization that delivers resources to individual firms about competitive strategies other than wage cutting, such as innovative production techniques and organization (Appelbaum, Bernhardt, and Murnane 2003). A central point of agreement for the "Restarting New York City's Economic Engine" panelists was the importance of formalizing networks among entrepreneurial immigrant groups and mainstream institutions. The formation of an intermediary organization such as a chamber of commerce or business roundtable to facilitate network building was proposed. As Tatiana Wah (2003) noted in her study of Afro-Caribbean immigrant businesses,

> Socialization—for example, through participation in merchant associations and chambers of commerce—will grow their networks and markets, increase their learning of business skills and the need to gain political influence, and capitalize on collective ethnic and non-ethnic resources. (p. 24)

Intermediary organizations are critical to forming and sustaining linkages to mainstream regional economic, political, and social institutions. According to researchers, intermediary institutions demonstrate how "interfirm cooperation can set industry standards and disseminate best practices; how training consortia can reduce training costs for individual employers and encourage cross-firm mobility; and how multi-employer bargaining and high local union density can establish strong job quality and productivity norms" (Appelbaum, Bernhardt, and Murnane 2003:25).

By establishing intermediary organizations that provide resources and formalize networks, the enabling environment promotes a "high road" strategy for immigrant small businesses. Whereas ethnic networks and social capital provide important resources for business start-up, integration into mainstream business networks and economy is essential for success. In summary, immigrant groups may have high rates of business ownership, but the long-term viability of immigrant economies requires the technical capacity and the bridging social capital to establish the "necessary connections with wider business markets" that can "create a consistent flow of wealth and employment by exploiting new market niches" (Gittell and Thompson 1999:511).

Integral to an entrepreneurial support system are "culturally competent" financial institutions, business assistance programs, and government regulatory agencies. In addition to providing multilingual services and materials and appropriate outreach strategies and venues, culturally competent institutions need to understand the institutional landscape of immigrant communities. As Joyce Moy, Director of LaGuardia Community College's Small Business Outreach Center, commented, "You can't sit there and expect these people who are struggling for their survival to walk into your office in downtown Manhattan for help—you have to get into the communities. It's really as simple as that."[21] A culturally competent business environment recognizes that the long-term prospects of immigrant economies depend on cultivating an "export orientation" that extends beyond typical enclave concentrations in food products, restaurants, and garment manufacturing. Economic development in immigrant economies needs to cultivate entrepreneurs that can "successfully engage in the kinds of work required to identify and capture new market opportunities" (Lichtenstein and Lyons 2001:5).

Conventional business assistance programs should be supplemented by resources that promote technical skills to adapt to changing market conditions and build networks to regional growth industries and institutions. A potential model for an enriched community focused entrepreneurial development program is the Microenterprise Fund for Innovation, Effectiveness, Learning and Dissemination (FIELD), which is run by the Apsen Institute. FIELD includes a mentoring program that partners microbusinesses with established businesses to help develop capacity to access market opportunities.[22]

TOURISM AND BUSINESS IMPROVEMENT DISTRICTS — NEW DIRECTIONS FOR COMMUNITY DEVELOPMENT?

The crisis of September 11 created a rare opportunity to reenvision Chinatown's development and its relationship to the regional economy. In important ways, this planning process will likely inform community development approaches in New York's other immigrant neighborhoods. To commence the comprehensive planning process, Asian Americans for Equality (AAFE) launched the Rebuild Chinatown Initiative (RCI) by hiring a consultant firm to conduct surveys and focus group discussions and then sponsored a conference in November 2002 to announce the findings. Panelist Kathryn Wylde, the president and CEO of the New York City Partnership and Chamber of Commerce, advised the conference participants to think "outside the box" rather than reflexively focus on bringing tourism back to Chinatown. One of the lessons of September 11, after all, was the fragility of a neighborhood economy based on tourism. Wylde advised the community to plan more broadly and creatively.[23]

A few months ago, AAFE released its comprehensive RCI plan, which represents the unofficial "unified community perspective" that will inform and guide Chinatown's involvement in discussions of rebuilding Lower Manhattan. Despite Wylde's advice, the vision put forth centers on revitalizing the tourist economy by establishing Manhattan Chinatown as "America's Chinatown." "The paradigm," the document states, "would no longer be Manhattan's Chinatown in relation to Flushing and Sunset Park but New York City's Chinatown in relation to those of San Francisco, Toronto and Vancouver" (p. 3). The 10-year, $500-million plan proposes new affordable housing, an arts and cultural center, linkages to an improved waterfront, and a Pacific Rim office complex with Class A office space, all of which would propel Manhattan Chinatown into the ranks of the world's premier destinations.

The plan seeks to sustain and strengthen Chinatown's linkage to the regional economy by upgrading the physical environment; commodifying Asian culture into marketable images, products, and events, and establishing a business gateway for American companies that seek Asian manufacturers. Affordable housing development will preserve Chinatown's authenticity as an Asian residential and social space, thereby preventing its (de)evolution into an ethnic theme park. AAFE's RCI plan calls for three implementation steps. The first is to form a local development corporation to undertake development projects like the office complex and waterfront park.[24] The second is to designate housing districts to initiate affordable housing design and development. The third is to establish a business and cultural improvement district to help local property owners and merchants tackle the problem of sanitation.

While these are important elements of a revitalized Chinatown, the RCI document is short on labor-centered strategies that address the outstanding needs and concerns of the immigrant working poor population. The economic development section of the RCI plan is subtitled "Industrious Chinatown" and highlights three components—the Pacific Rim office district, the preservation of manufacturing, and increased job mobility and training. The plan calls for improved physical linkages to the Wall Street area by extending a corridor of office development along the major thoroughfares of Broadway, Canal, and Bowery streets. Noting the need for a small production center to accommodate the rapid turnaround time and strict quality control of New York City's fashion manufacturers, AAFE predicted that Chinatown's garment industry will stabilize with a labor force of 4,000 workers employed in approximately 100 shops—a mere shadow of the industry's presence only a decade ago. To sustain this industry sector, RCI proposes the development of incubators and showrooms and the preservation of industrial districts through zoning regulations.

AAFE also proposes several industries that are "logical sources of employment" for immigrant workers—health care and hospitality for women and construction and hospitality for men (p. 19). An additional advantage of these industries is the opportunity for small business start ups. The RCI recommendations to "bolster" the heath care, hospitality, and construction sections are vague and call for partnering with medical institutions to develop a medical arts building, creating a full-service spa in a new waterfront hotel, and helping to foster networks with construction unions. Recognizing the limited human capital of immigrant workers, RCI notes the need for training in English as a second language; the plan concedes, however, that the "linkage to jobs is presently missing" (p. 20). Finally, RCI proposes to create a virtual community college for the adult population of Chinatown that lacks high school diplomas, but there is no detail on workforce development activities and linkages—although the potential to partner with institutions such as the City University of New York is great.[25]

RCI's emphasis on creating premier office space, an arts and cultural institution, and linkages to the waterfront is consistent with New York City's "symbolic economy" (Zukin 1995). As Jan Lin (1998) describes,

> Neighborhood preservation has been linked with heritage tourism as an economic development strategy and a source of local revenue. This evolving multicultural urban development policy that promotes the livelihood of ethnic communities takes place within a broader agenda of "world city" promotion among city managers and regional planners (p. 7).

Cultural tourism, by promoting the consumption of ethnic-themed goods and services and the production of ethnic spaces, helps to sustain immigrant economies. However, counting on tourism to generate a sustained economic boost is not always a reliable strategy. The pan-Asian neighborhood of Flushing, Queens, which has numerous hotels, restaurants, and shopping venues—including national chains such as Old Navy—is located a stone's throw away from two of New York City's premier tourist attractions: Shea Stadium and the National Tennis Center. Despite numerous major league baseball games and an annual worldwide tennis tournament (the U.S. Open, which draws nearly 3 million visitors from around the world) very few people spend any tourist dollars in Flushing (Polgreen 2004). A comparison with Los Angeles might be instructive at this point. Researchers find that Asian immigrant businesses in Los Angeles are not involved in tourism but are located in more-profitable sectors like technology, international trade, and producer services (Zhou 1998).

Emergent Asian enclave economies in New York City also seek to encourage tourism as an economic development strategy. Liberty Avenue in Richmond Hill, Queens, has evolved into the "cultural heart of the Indo-Caribbean immigrant community" (Abeles Phlips Preiss and Shapiro, Inc., 2001:3). Dotted with numerous ethnic specialty shops, reflecting the cultural products of the Indian diaspora in the Caribbean islands of Trinidad and Tobago and Guyana, Richmond Hill's Liberty Avenue offers sari shops, roti shops, bakeries, and shipping companies that serve a transnational immigrant market (Khandelwal 2002). To strengthen and broaden Liberty Avenue's market appeal and reach, a community organization founded by two Indo-Caribbean entrepreneurs participated with the Queens County Overall Economic Development Corporation to commission a retail study of "Richmond Hill's Main Street" that recommends the formation of a Business Improvement District (BID) to stimulate commercial revitalization and expansion.

New York City has the greatest number of Business Improvement Districts of any U.S. city. Currently numbering 50, BIDs are promoted by the Bloomberg Administration as a key economic development tool.[26] BIDs are designated commercial districts where property owners agree to impose an annual tax on themselves based on a percentage of their assessed property values. This self-imposed tax is collected by the New York City Department of Small Business Services to supplement city services in that area, such as street maintenance and beautification, security and public safety, façade improvement, visitor services, and promotional campaigns and materials. Under the leadership of the first elected Asian American public official, City Councilor John Liu, the Downtown Flushing Transit Hub BID was established in November 2003.[27] In addition to the Indo-Caribbean community's proposal for a Liberty Avenue BID, one RCI recommendation is to form a Manhattan Chinatown BID. But do BIDs represent good economic development policy for immigrant economies?

BIDs are a business-driven approach to neighborhood development. While improving the business environment and marketing commercial activity, BIDs, as organizations of property owners, do not necessarily promote a community-based agenda for economic development. As discussed earlier, escalating property rents are a key concern for many immigrant small businesses throughout New York City. Real estate pressures are fueling the subdivision of housing and commercial storefronts in numerous New York City immigrant neighborhoods. Renters are concerned that property owners will pass on the costs of the additional tax, thereby increasing the burden of running a small business. Some are critical that communities have to raise additional resources for services that should be provided for by city government. Moreover, not all BIDs have the same ability to raise money for services. While the annual budgets for BIDs can be as high as $11 million (for the mega-BIDs in the Times Square and Grand Central areas), most BIDs typically have much smaller budgets—ranging from $150,000 to $500,000 (O'Grady 2002). The annual budget for the Downtown Flushing Transit Hub BID is $380,000 (Virasami 2003).

BIDs narrowly promote community economic development through marketing and upgrading the physical environment and providing a forum for property owners to leverage collective interests. BIDs are not a venue for broader equity goals.[28] For example, a common issue of the Sunset Park BID is dealing with immigrant street vendors, who are viewed as unfair competitors and public nuisances because they don't pay overhead costs, crowd streets and block the entrances to stores, and sell goods at cheaper prices. The Sunset Park BID has actively engaged the New York Police Department to regulate this informal sector.[29] Through upgrading the business environment, BIDs may create trickle-down effects, but they fail to counter working poverty and economic marginalization. Asian community economic development needs to be multifaceted in promoting small businesses, especially since this sector anchors the immigrant labor market but the sustainability of immigrant economies also requires strategies to diversify tourist-based and downgraded manufacturing industries.

In light of the severe economic conditions that pervade immigrant workplaces and the wealth of technical expertise and political capital that community stakeholders and planners were able to draw from to envision the rebuilding of Chinatown, it is a missed opportunity that the plan for an "Industrious Chinatown" was not more substantive on best practices in economic and workforce development strategies. Kathyrn Wylde's advice to "think outside the box" was prescient, but the recommendations are squarely inside the box, and in the case of workforce development, the RCI plan substitutes one low-wage manufacturing industry with other low-wage, deskilled jobs in construction, health care, and hospitality. There is no reference to building the institutional capacity for worker advocacy or to making the case for a city industrial policy that recognizes the importance of entry-level unionized manufacturing jobs for immigrant incorporation and mobility.

WORKFORCE DEVELOPMENT

Immigrants are not well served by existing workforce development systems, which are largely defined by employer-provided job training for high-skilled workers and government-sponsored job training programs whose priority is to move welfare recipients into the labor force. With the implementation of the 1996 Welfare Reform and 1998 Workforce Investment acts, the shift in policy priorities and programmatic resources affected community-based organizations that serve as critical intermediaries in immigrant workforce development. Established in the 1970s, the Chinatown Manpower Project, Inc., (CMP) has been addressing the employment training and placement needs of Asian immigrants in Manhattan Chinatown for three decades. Its first executive director, Nora Wang Chang, was a former commissioner of the city's Department of Employment. Through the years, CMP successfully built numerous partnerships with both private and public institutions, including Cabrini Medical Center and CUNY Hunter College's School of Social Work, to provide job training.

The late 1990s, however, saw significant setbacks for CMP, as it lost federal grants in vocational training, workplace literacy, and specialized targeted workers' programs. In one year the losses totaled a million dollars. CMP faces increasing challenges in sustaining partnerships, "chasing the funding," and sustaining organizational leadership. To continue supporting workforce intermediaries in immigrant communities, the reauthorization of the 1998 Workforce Investment Act should provide states with greater resources to serve workers with limited English proficiency and to combine ESL, adult education, and job training services.

The recent restructuring of New York City's Department of Small Business Services presents an opportunity to comprehensively address the small business and workforce development needs of New York City's immigrant economies. Late last year, Mayor Michael Bloomberg dissolved the Department of Employment. He reassigned the adult workforce programs to the Department of Small Business Services and the youth employment programs to the Department of Youth and Community Development. The Department of Small Business Services has created a new Division of Workforce Development and expanded its staff to include a director of business partnerships and outreach management, who focuses on the six industry sectors that are strategic to New York City's economic growth: construction/small business, technology/bioscience and health, industrial and food manufacturing, retail/hospitality and tourism, aviation, and film/media.

This institutional restructuring would be greatly enhanced if the city also expanded the Department of Immigrant Affairs (and its jurisdiction) and then promoted interagency collaboration with the Department of Small

Business Services. Such a move would demonstrate a substantive approach to improving labor market prospects for immigrant New Yorkers. Currently, there is no formal or explicit policy position on immigrant businesses or workers. However, as the commissioner for the Department of Youth and Community Development recently noted, "we are not dealing with as many public assistance recipients as we had in the past so our workforce development really has to reflect that. What we are seeing are new immigrants—pretty much the working poor—who come to our offices or our contract agencies with a number of needs."[30] Despite this acknowledged demographic shift, the Department of Immigrant Affairs is not engaged in policy decisions regarding workforce or economic development—even though immigrant businesses and workers are an integral part of the city's economy.

Beyond immigrant outreach and information on city services and programs, the Department of Immigrant Affairs should be empowered to engage in policy decisions and to collaborate with other city agencies on economic development. One possibility is to form a group like the Toronto Region Immigrant Employment Council, which is "a multi-stakeholder council that is working to improve access to employment for immigrants in the Toronto region."[31] Immigrants and their community-based organizations should be part of a regionwide discussion on policy and strategies to effectively integrate immigrant economic activity in a way that ensures equity and economic benefit for all.

IMMIGRANT WORKER CENTERS

In an article published a decade ago, Peter Kwong (1994) documented the growing irrelevance of the garment workers' union—then the International Ladies Garment Workers Union (ILGWU)—in advocating for Chinese immigrants. This observation led him to argue that grassroots organizations such as the Chinese Staff and Workers Association (CSWA) were a more effective institution in the struggle for economic justice.[32] The historic exclusion of immigrant workers from mainstream labor unions helped facilitate the formation of community-based worker organizations or worker centers.[33] Although large trade unions, such as the AFL-CIO, have renewed their dedication to organizing immigrant workers, they are doing so at a time when union influence is waning. Nor are the unions' incentives to organize small immigrant businesses that great. Unions get limited returns from organizing workers employed in numerous small businesses because even a successful campaign may not generate a large dues-paying membership base (Gordon 2001).

Worker centers may be a good substitute for traditional unions. An ongoing Economic Policy Institute study found approximately 118 worker centers in 30 states with the greatest numbers in California and New York (Fine and Werberg, 2003). In New York City, these groups include CAAAV: Organizing Asian Communities; Desis Rising, United, and Moving (DRUM); Nodutdol for Korean Community Development;[34] New York City

Taxi Workers Alliance; Workers Awaaz; and the Restaurant Opportunities Center of New York (ROC-NY). The shared objective of these organizations is to reach out to and organize low-wage immigrant (including undocumented) Asians and Latinos who work in nonunionized sectors such as restaurants, garment production, and domestic work.

As worker centers are community-based, worker organizing is frequently tied to broader issues of civil rights, immigrant rights, and community development. For example, CAAAV formed the Chinatown Justice Project, which mobilized around land use issues and gentrification pressures in Manhattan Chinatown. The group has staged protests and produced educational materials including a video entitled "Chinatown is Not For Sale!" Worker centers combine service delivery—such as ESL classes, job placement and advocacy—with their organizing efforts. The CSWA, for example, offers ESL classes in its Sunset Park office. CSWA also protests unfair hiring practices; the organization advocated for the hiring of Chinese construction workers at a New York University dormitory construction site several years ago and staged protests at various public functions to call attention to the exclusion of Chinese workers.[35]

Worker centers in New York City frequently engage with civil rights organizations, such as the Asian American and Puerto Rican Legal Defense and Education Funds, to secure wages that have been withheld from workers. In fact, a coalition of worker centers was instrumental in formulating and lobbying for the passage of the Unpaid Wages Prohibition Act in 1997, which increased statutory penalties and fines for underpayment or nonpayment of wages. A more recent example of legislative change is the "Dignity for Domestic Workers" resolution, which was passed by the New York City Council in May 2003. Developed and promoted by CAAAV, this legislation promotes a standard contract for all domestic work, including basic rights to sick days and vacation and protection from discrimination and unjust firings. Worker centers also conduct industry studies. ROC-NY recently completed a survey of the restaurant industry and found poor conditions such as overtime, minimum wage violations, and lack of health insurance to be prevalent.[36]

By virtue of these activities, worker centers are essential in establishing a floor on employment standards for immigrant workers. They do this by securing wages that were withheld by employers and enforcing existing labor laws such as minimum wage, overtime pay, and a 40-hour workweek. Their fight for immigrant worker rights is not about achieving significant labor improvements for immigrants alone but about ensuring that existing labor laws genuinely protect *all* workers. While worker centers do not have the capacity to negotiate collective-bargaining agreements or protect workers from arbitrary firings as unions do (Gordon 2001), they frequently provide the sole recourse for workers laboring under exploitative conditions. Worker centers represent a new generation of grassroots institutions that are community-based. They cultivate immigrant leadership to organize for social and economic justice in the workplace and community at large.

CONCLUSION

Immigrant businesses are important sources of neighborhood revitalization and entry-level jobs, but they are typically concentrated in marginal retail, service, and downgraded manufacturing sectors. Small business development is an integral part of asset-based neighborhood development, and immigrant economies are frequently distinguished by high levels of economic activity and employment generation. However, the qualities of immigrant economies indicate that immigrant-owned small businesses typically generate marginal employment opportunities and contribute to working poverty. There is no question that immigrant small businesses provide an alternative strategy for addressing underemployment and unemployment for both risk-taking immigrant entrepreneurs and their low-wage labor force. But to harness this entrepreneurial energy in ways that promote viable economic and community development requires innovative and targeted policy efforts that better "connect" immigrant small businesses with public- and private-sector assistance and that regulate workplace practices and standards. As von Hoffman (2003:48) wrote, "the idea of nurturing small businesses once again became a central part of urban policy," but urban policy makers must address both the contributions and dilemmas posed by immigrant small business development.

Policy directives that address the supply and demand conditions of ethnic labor markets would help promote immigrant economies as viable economic engines. To mitigate the uneven levels of human and social capital among immigrant business owners, business roundtables or trade associations may help position immigrant businesses to advocate and engage in citywide and regional economic development discussions and access business assistance resources. Small business assistance, however, must be accompanied by policies that protect and advance immigrant worker rights. Enforcement of labor standards through codes of conducts and inclusion of labor organizations such as worker centers in economic development initiatives must be an integral part of sustaining the vitality of immigrant economies. Immigrant businesses are an integral and invaluable local asset, but to fully realize their potential for revitalizing local neighborhoods and contribute to regional growth, a first step is to appreciate both the opportunities and challenges that define the immigrant sector of New York City's economy.

NOTES

I wish to acknowledge Commissioner Robert Walsh of the New York City Department of Small Business Services for sharing his time and expertise.

1. Based on the 1997 Survey of Minority Owned Business Enterprises (SMOBE), New York City leads the nation with the greatest number of APA firms at 96,952. The city of Los Angeles follows with the second highest number at a distant 43,000.

2. See von Hoffman 2003, and Velazquez 2004.

3. According to the 1997 SMOBE, 114,577 of Los Angeles County's 778,577 firms (15 percent), 24,149 of San Francisco County's 90,599 firms (27 percent), and

44,840 of Orange County's 252,935 firms (18 percent) are owned by Asian Pacific Americans.

4. For an example of the concentration of APA firms in Queens, see Ahn 2003.

5. Unfortunately, SMOBE does not provide industry sector for ethnic groups except on the national level.

6. Examples of Asian niche in transportation include taxicabs, shuttle vans between Manhattan Chinatown and Sunset Park, and bus companies that serve popular New York City–Boston and Philadelphia routes, and casinos in Connecticut (Luo 2004a). The *New York Times* recently completed a series on the auction of taxicab medallions and featured several immigrant bidders (Luo 2004b, 2004c).

7. Of the 88,808 firms that were not classified in any industry, 56 percent were minority-owned businesses with APA firms accounting for the largest share (42 percent). The definition of industries not classified was clarified in a conversation with an Economic Census Bureau staff person on January 14, 2004.

8. Timothy Bates's (1998a) research finds that Asian immigrant self-employment is frequently a form of underemployment, and highly educated immigrants are most likely to exit from self-employment, especially those in traditional sectors such as retail and personal services.

9. Kim 2004, describes common discriminatory practices by Korean employment agencies such as providing detailed information on applicants' race, gender, and nationality to potential employers.

10. Lin conducted a survey of Chinatown street vendors (1998:76–78).

11. Kamber's photo essay is available on-line. See Kamber 2001.

12. Newspaper articles related to this incident include Chen and Kilgannon 2004 and Lueck and Chen 2004.

13. The Sunset Park Business Survey, conducted in 2000–2001, involved a business census and a mail survey translated into Chinese and Spanish. Of the 700 surveys sent out, 89 were returned, representing a 12 percent response rate. For a full discussion of the survey findings, see Hum 2002.

14. Another indication of this underrepresentation can be derived from a survey on computer use in Asian-owned firms conducted by New York City's Asian American Business Development Center, which showed a significant digital divide—a majority of surveyed firms do not use the Internet or computers at all (Curan 2000, Wang 2000b).

15. Refer to www.aaari.info for information on the Chinatown workshop series that culminated in this June 25, 2004, event.

16. The transcript for the March 11, 2004, forum, "Restarting NYC's Economic Engine: Tapping the Economic Potential of the City's Immigrant Entrepreneurs," is available online at www.nycfuture.org.

17. See Lii 1995.

18. For a summary of and the full Greengrocer Code of Conduct, refer to the New York State Attorney General's Web site at http://www.oag.state.ny.us/labor/index.html.

19. Refer to Berger 2004 and Chang 2002.

20. Comment made at a March 11, 2004, forum. A transcript is available online at www.nycfuture.org.

21. Comment made at a March 11, 2004, forum. A transcript is available online at www.nycfuture.org.

22. The Web site for this Aspen Institute program is http://www.fieldus.org/.

23. There is no conference transcript, but for a newspaper account of Ms. Wylde's comments, refer to Kalita 2002.

24. The recently formed Chinatown Partnership Local Development Corporation was searching in June 2004 for an executive director, and the job announcement

identified three responsibilities: (1) improve business conditions by making China-town a cleaner, safer, more attractive place; (2) strengthen connections between commerce and culture to enhance Chinatown's role in New York City; and (3) form new partnerships to increase public and private investment.

25. The Center for an Urban Future conducted a study on CUNY and workforce development which is available from its Web site, www.nycfuture.org.

26. Mayor Bloomberg appointed former Union Square–14th Street BID Director Robert Walsh to the post of commissioner of the Department of Small Business Services (O'Grady 2002).

27. See Bertrand 2003.

28. A provision to pay BID employees (e.g., street cleaners) a living wage was eliminated in the New York City Council's version of the living wage bill. See Greenhouse 2002.

29. Conversation with Renee Giordano, Executive Director, Sunset Park Business Improvement District, November 22, 2000.

30. From a transcript of the Summit on the Future of Workforce Development (Center for an Urban Future).

31. Refer to http://www.triec.ca/ for more information.

32. Recognizing CSWA's success in advocating for immigrant workers notably in the garment and restaurant industries, CSWA founder Wing Lam was recently awarded the prestigious Ford Foundation Leadership for a Changing World Award. For information about Mr. Lam's award, refer to http://leadershipforchange.org/awardees/awardee.php3?ID=18.

33. A notable exception includes the Service Employees International Union 1199 and 32BJ locals, which organize home health aides and janitors, but these campaigns to mobilize low-wage immigrant workers remain the exception.

34. According to the Web site www.nodutdol.com, *nodutduol* means stepping stone or entryway in Korean.

35. Refer to http://lists.village.virginia.edu/listservs/spoons/postcolonial-info.archive/postcolonial-info.9801 for a student's account of a CSWA protest at an inaugural event for New York University's Asian/Pacific/American Studies Program and Institute.

36. ROC-NY's restaurant industry study is available from its Web site, http://www.rocny.org/.

REFERENCES

Abeles Phillips Preiss and Shapiro, Inc. 2001. Liberty Avenue study: Richmond Hill's main street. A retail study. Unpublished document.

Ahn, Jun-yong. 2003. "Central Queens has more than 416 Korean businesses." *Korea Daily News*, September 19.

Appelbaum, Eileen, Annette Bernhardt, and Richard J. Murnane, eds. 2003. *Low-Wage America: How Employers Are Reshaping Opportunity in the Workplace.* New York: Russell Sage Foundation.

Asian American Federation of New York. 2002. Chinatown after September 11th: An economic impact study. Interim Report. www.aafny.org/research/dl/911study/001WholeRpt.pdf. Accessed December 2005.

Asian Americans for Equality. 2004. America's Chinatown: A Community Plan. Rebuild Chinatown Initiative. http://www.rebuildchinatown.org/doc/RCI_Part 1&2.pdf. Accessed December 2005.

Bagli, Charles V. 2002. "Seeking Security, Downtown Firms are Scattering." *New York Times*, January 29, B1.

Bates, Timothy. 1998a. Exiting self-employment: An analysis of Asian immigrant-owned small business. U.S. Census Bureau, Center for Economic Studies #98–13. http://ideas.repec.org/p/wop/censes/98–13.html.

———. 1998b. *Race, Self-Employment, and Upward Mobility: An Illusive American Dream*. Baltimore, MD: Johns Hopkins University Press.

Berger, Joseph. 2003. The overhead? Just a scaffold; For city's repairmen, shop may be the sidewalk. *New York Times*, September 10, B1.

Berger, Joseph. 2004. "As Manufacturing Shifts in Fashion Industry, Gritty Lofts Become Upscale Apartments." *New York Times*, August 23, B1.

Bertrand, Donald. 2003. "Big Time Scrubbing Coming to Flushing." *New York Daily News*, November 6.

Chang, Sophia Y. 2002. "Harsh Reality Hits Makers of Fairy Tale Gowns: China-town Factory Faces Eviction." *The Village Voice*, January 2–8. http://www.village voice.com/news/0201,chang,31206,5.html. Accessed December 2005.

Center for an Urban Future. 2002. "Summit on the Future of Workforce Development in New York City." December. http://www.nycfuture.org/content/forums_trans/forum_view.cfm?forumkey=13&area=workpol. Accessed January 2005.

Center for an Urban Future. 2003. "Engine Failure." September. http://www.city limits.org/images_pdfs/pdfs/engine_failure.pdf. Accessed January 2005.

Chen, David W. and Corey Kilgannon. 2004. "Chinese Builder's Death Reveals Anonymous Web of Risky Labor." *New York Times*, June 9, B1.

Chin, Margaret M. 2003. Moving on: Chinese garment workers after September 11. A Report for the Russell Sage Foundation Social Effects Working Group. Unpublished Report.

Community Development Technologies Center. 2001. The Southern California Minority Small Business Atlas. http://www.cdtech.org/atlas/index.html. Accessed December 2005.

Curan, Catherine. 2000. Asian American businesses struggle to reach e-speed. *Crain's New York*, August 7–13.

Dolfman, Michael L. and Solidelle F. Wasser. 2004. "9/11 and the New York City Economy: A Borough-by-Borough Analysis." *Monthly Labor Review*, 127(6):3–33.

Ettlinger, N. and S. Kwon. 1994. "A Comparative Assessment of the Role of Immigrants in U.S. Labor Markets: A Case Study of Asians in New York and Los Angeles." *Tijdschrift voor Economische en Sociale Geografie*, 85(5):417–433.

Fine, Janice, and Jon Werberg. 2003. Map of Worker Centers. http://www.labor notes.org/pdf/workercentermap-aug03.pdf. Accessed August 2003.

Gittell, Ross and J. Philip Thompson. 1999. "Inner-City Business Development and Entrepreneurship: New Frontiers for Policy and Research." In *Urban Problems and Community Development*, eds. Ronald F. Ferguson and William T. Dickens 473–520. Washington, DC: The Brookings Institution.

Gordon, Jennifer. 2001. Immigrants fight the power: Workers centers are one path to labor organizing and political participation. *The Nation* 270(1):16–21.

Greenhouse, Steven. 2002. Korean grocers agree to double pay and improve workplace conditions. *New York Times*, September 18, B1.

Greenhouse, Steven. 2002. "Council Offers Compromise on 'Living Wage' Measure." *New York Times*, October 30.

———. 2003. Job training that works, and it's free. *New York Times*, August 10.

———. 2004. Agencies sued over low-paying jobs. *New York Times*, June 16, 4.

Guest, Kenneth. 2003. *God in Chinatown: Religion and Survival in New York's Evolving Immigrant Community*. New York: New York University Press.

Hum, Tarry. 2002. Immigrant economies and neighborhood revitalization: A case study of Sunset Park. New School University ICMEC Working Papers, Project on Immigrants and New York City at the Turn of the Century: Essays on Employment, Education, Health and Public Policy. http:www.newschool.edu/icmec/lucepaper5.html. Accessed January 25.

Hum, Tarry. 2004. Asian immigrant settlements in New York City: Defining "communities of interest." *AAPI Nexus: Asian American & Pacific Islanders—Policy, Practice and Community* 2(2):20–48.

Kalita, S. Mitra. 2002. "Scarcity of Jobs, Housing Threatens Chinatown." *Newsday*, November 14.

Kamber, Michael. 2001. "On the Corner: New York's Undocumented Day Laborers Fight for their Piece of the Big Apple." Available on-line at http://www.villagevoice.com/issues/0130/kamber.php.

Khandelwal, Madhulika. 2002. *Becoming American, Being Indian*. Ithaca, NY: Cornell University Press.

Kim, Dae Young. 1999. Beyond co-ethnic solidarity: Mexican and Ecuadorian employment in Korean-owned businesses in New York City. *Ethnic and Racial Studies* 22(3):581–605.

Kim, Joo-Chan. 2004. "Employment Discrimination High Among Koreans." *Korean Times*, June 24.

Kwong, Peter. 1994. Chinese Staff and Workers Association: A model for organizing in the changing economy? *Social Policy* 25(2):30–38.

Kwong, Peter. 1996. *The New Chinatown*. New York: Hill and Wang, 2nd edition.

———. 1997. *Forbidden Workers: Illegal Chinese Immigrants and American Labor*. New York: The New Press.

Lee, Jennifer 8. 2002. Report says 10 percent of jobs lost post-Sept. 11 were in Chinatown. *New York Times*, April 5.

Lichtenstein. Gregg A. and Thomas S. Lyons. 2001. "The Entrepreneurial Development System: Transforming Business Talent and Community Economies." *Economic Development Quarterly* 15(1):3–20.

Lii, Jane. 1995. "Week in Sweatshops Reveals Grim Conspiracy of the Poor." *New York Times*, March 12.

Lin, Jan. 1998. *Reconstructing Chinatown: Ethnic Enclave, Global Change*. Minneapolis: University of Minnesota Press.

Lombardi, Frank. 2004. Job agencies taken to task, state settles with 5, sues 4 more. *New York Daily News*, June 16.

Lueck, Thomas J. and David W. Chen. 2004. "Construction Accident in Queens Kills Workers and Injures 2." *New York Times*, June 8.

Luo, Michael. 2004a. In Chinatown, a $10 trip means war; Weary owners struggle to stay afloat in cutthroat competition. *New York Times*, February 21.

———. 2004b. Medallions fetch $712,101 as taxi auction sets records. *New York Times*, April 17.

———. 2004c. With pride of a new taxi medallion, the gravity of new realities. *New York Times*, May 27.

Marcuse, Peter. 1997. The enclave, the citadel, and the ghetto: What has changed in the post-Fordist U.S. city. *Urban Affairs Review* 33(2):228–264.

O'Grady, Jim. 2002. Under Bloomberg, new life for business districts. *New York Times*, July 7.

Ong, Paul. 1984. "Chintatown Unemployment and the Ethnic Labor Market." *Amerasia*, 11(1):35–54.

Ong, Paul, and Doug Miller. 2002. Economic needs of Asian Americans and Pacific Islanders in distressed areas: Establishing baseline information. Department of Commerce, Economic Development Administration Report.

Ong, Paul, Dennis Arguelles, Susan Castro, Theresa Cenidoza, Bruce Chow, Chanchanit Martorell, Tarry Hum, Winnie Louie, Erich Nakano, and Roderick Ramos. 1999. *Beyond Asian American Poverty: Community Economic Development Policies and Strategies*. 2nd edition. Los Angeles: Asian Pacific American Policy Institute, LEAP.

Ong, Paul, and Karen Umemoto. 1994. Asian Pacific Americans in the inner-city. In *The State of Asian Pacific America: Economic Diversity, Issues, and Policies*, ed. Paul Ong, 87–112. Los Angeles: Asian Pacific American Policy Institute, LEAP.

Parrot, James A. 2001. Testimony on economic impact of the September 11 terrorist attacks and strategies for economic rebirth and resurgence. Hearing Before the New York State Assembly Standing Committee on Economic Development and the Assembly Standing Committee on Small Businesses, December 6. www.fiscal policy.org. Accessed January 2005.

Pastor, Manuel Jr., Peter Drier, J. Eugene Grigsby III, and Marta Lopez-Garza. 2000. *Regions That Work: How Cities and Suburbs Can Grow Together*. Minneapolis, MN: University of Minnesota Press.

Polgreen, Lydia. 2004. Ethnic food, anyone? After tennis, Flushing calls. *New York Times*, September 4.

Ponce de León, Juana. 2003. "A ray of hope for the street vendors in El Barrio," *Siempre*, April 8.

Porter, Michael. 1995. The competitive advantage of the inner city. *Harvard Business Review*, 73(3):55–72.

———. 1997. New strategies for inner-city economic development. *Economic Development Quarterly* 11(1):11–27.

Portes, Alejandro. 1995. "Economic Sociology and the Sociology of Immigration: A Conceptual Overview." In *The Economic Sociology of Immigration*, ed. Alejandro Portes, 1–41. New York, NY: Russell Sage Foundation.

Portes, Alejandro, and Robert Bach. 1985. *Latin Journey: Cuban and Mexican Immigrants in the United States*. Berkeley: University of California Press.

Portes, Alejandro and Ruben G. Rumbaut. 1990. *Immigrant America: A Portrait*. Berkeley, CA: University of California Press.

Portes, Alejandro, and Min Zhou. 1992. Gaining the upper hand: Economic mobility among immigrant and domestic minorities. *Ethnic and Racial Studies* 15(4):491–522.

Queens County Overall Economic Development Corporation. 2002. Queens global business outlook: Comprehensive economic development strategy. Fall/Winter, 3, 3 & 4. Special Edition.

———. 2004. Survey of new American business owners. Unpublished preliminary findings.

Russ, Hilary. 2002. SOLD OUT: What happens to the neighborhood when street vendors disappear? *City Limits*, September/October.

Schaller, Bruce. 2004. *The New York City Taxicab Fact Book*. http://www.schallerconsult.com/taxi/taxifb.pdf

Tietz, Michael. 1989. Neighborhood economics: Local communities and regional markets. *Economic Development Quarterly* 32:111–122.

Tilly, Charles. 1990. "Transplanted Networks." In *Immigration Reconsidered*, ed. Virginia Yans-McLaughlin, 79–95. Oxford, UK: Oxford University Press.

Urban Institute. 2000. *Building Capacity: The Challenges and Opportunities of Asian Pacific American Community Development*. A report to the National Coalition for Asian Pacific American Community Development Corporations. April.

Velazquez, Congresswoman Nydia. 2004. "Help Small Businesses, Not the Wealthy." http://www.gothamgazette.com/feds/velazquez_032904.php. Accessed August 2004.

Virasami, Bryan. 2003. Some merchants oppose Flushing BID. *Newsday*, April 15.

Virasami, Bryan, and Graham Rayman. 2004a. Advocates decry workers' deaths. *Newsday*, June 14.

Virasami, Bryan, and Graham Rayman. 2004b. The latest death of a day laborer prompts calls for better control of industries that rely heavily on immigrants. *Newsday*, June 15.

von Hoffman, Alexander. 2003. Small businesses, big growth. *New York Times*, September 4, A23.

Wah, Tatiana. 2003. Afro-Caribbean entrepreneurial development and minority business development programs in two counties: Brooklyn and Miami-Dade. Report to the Ford Foundation. Community Development Research Center, Robert J. Milano School of Management and Urban Policy, New School University.

Waldinger, Roger. 1993. The ethnic enclave debate revisited. *International Journal of Urban and Regional Research* 17(3):428–436.

Waldinger, Roger. 1996. *Still the Promised City? African Americans and New Immigrants in Post-Industrial New York*. Cambridge, MA: Harvard University Press.

Wang, John. 2000a. The boom that threatens Chinatown. *New York Times*, July 8.

———. 2000b. E-business and IT awareness survey report: New York City Chinatowns. Unpublished Report. July 25.

Yoon, In-Jin. 1995. The growth of Korean immigrant entrepreneurship in Chicago. *Ethnic and Racial Studies* 18:2.

Zhou, Min. 1992. *Chinatown: The Socioeconomic Potential of an Urban Enclave*. Philadelphia, PA: Temple University Press.

Zhou, Yu. 1998. How do places matter? A comparative study of Chinese ethnic economies in Los Angeles and New York City. *Urban Geography* 19(6):531–533.

Zukin, Sharon. 1995. *The Culture of Cities*. Cambridge, MA: Blackwell Publishers.

9   Indian Gaming as Community Economic Development

Ted Jojola and Paul Ong[1]

Introduction

American Indians constitute an indigenous people who have been repeatedly robbed of their land and resources by western encroachment and U.S. federal policies of removal and assimilation. Tribal peoples have endured centuries of racism and colonialism and today remain one of the most economically disadvantaged minority groups in the United States. Of the 1.8 million American Indians, over a quarter live below the poverty level, over twice the proportion for the total population and three times the proportion for non-Hispanic whites.[2]

American Indians share many of the same economic barriers with other people of color; consequently, they would also benefit from developing and implementing many of the community economic development strategies discussed in the other chapters of this book. Like other low-income communities, American Indian reservations suffer from a shortage of human, physical, and financial capital. Despite these similarities, Indian tribes are unique because they have a "nation-to-nation" or "country-to-country" relationship with the federal government. Federally recognized tribes maintain governments that are equal to or superior to those of the states where Indian reservations are located. This unique relationship is derived from the Constitution of the United States, which specifies that "Congress shall have the power to regulate Commerce with foreign nations, among the several states, and with the Indian tribes." The exercise of this authority is seen in the numerous treaties with Indian nations.[3] Because of this unique legal status, community economic development has taken a different trajectory than in other low-income minority communities.

The nation-to-nation relationship, however, is far from being one involving equal partners. Instead, it evolved into a special "trust relationship," where the United States government stated it had obligations to protect tribal lands and resources, honor the rights to self-government, and provide basic social, medical, and educational services. In practice, the federal government had, for much of history, used the trust relationship to subjugate, treating the population as wards of the state and providing limited support in a paternalistic fashion. Since the late 1960s and early 1970s, American Indians have fought for greater control over their own destiny, in part by reasserting their sovereignty rights over community and economic development.[4]

One promising, albeit controversial, community economic development approach in Indian Country is gaming, a strategy that dates back to the early 1970s and today includes activities ranging from bingo to high-stakes gambling. The impetus for transforming gaming from a marginal activity into a major economic enterprise in the 1990s came out of the failure of earlier efforts to redress the dire conditions faced by tribes. By 2002, gaming was a primary economic development strategy for 224 federally recognized tribes offering gambling, which took in billions in revenues and accounted for over one-fifth of the total revenue for the entire domestic gaming industry.[5] Despite this growth, not all Indian tribes have pursued gaming. A large majority of federally recognized tribes (338 out of 562) still does not have large-scale gambling operations. The ability and willingness to pursue gaming has real economic consequences for reservations. Advocates of gaming point to the jobs generated by casinos and other gaming operations for both Indians and non-Indians; however, there is little systematic information on how much reservations benefit.

This chapter examines the economic effects on reservations through a case study of gaming within a 50-mile radius of Albuquerque, New Mexico. While Indian gaming is a multifaceted phenomenon with numerous important issues, most are beyond the scope of this chapter.[6] Instead, the chapter focuses on the employment and income outcomes for reservation residents using census and noncensus information. Despite some data limitations, the analysis does provide key insights. The results from an assessment of gambling as an economic development enterprise have been decidedly mixed. While gaming promoted a greater degree of economic self-sufficiency for gaming tribes relative to those without gaming, it is not a panacea because even those on gaming reservations remain severely economically disadvantaged.

The rest of the chapter is organized into five parts. The first part critiques economic development efforts prior to gaming. These efforts involved federal agencies but proved to be ineffective. The second part examines the development of gaming at the national level. While the courts generally have ruled in favor of the tribes, Indian gaming has been regulated by federal law and has been subject to negotiation with states. Despite these limitations, gaming rapidly emerged as a major economic activity on reservations. The third part documents the development of gaming in New Mexico and Albuquerque. The negotiation with the state proved to be both protracted and highly political, which slowed but did not prevent the establishment of gaming on reservations, with a majority being located around Albuquerque. The fourth part evaluates the economic impact of gaming on reservations, with a focus on employment. The evidence shows an improvement in earnings and income for residents of gaming reservations relative to residents of nongaming reservations. The chapter concludes with some remarks about the limitations and challenges facing Indian gaming as a community economic development strategy. For numerous reasons, gaming has reached a plateau in some regions, and the benefits have not been able to eliminate the racial disparity facing American Indians. Ideally, gaming profits should be invested to enable tribes to move beyond a single industry to a more diverse and sustainable economy based on a better-educated population.

Economic Development before Gaming

The modern era of Native American economic development began when Congress passed the Indian Self-Determination and Education Assistance Act of 1975.[7] This landmark legislation changed how the Bureau of Indian Affairs (BIA) and other governmental units interacted with Indian tribes. Where once the official policy and practice was to force American Indians to assimilate (often with dismal results), the federal government acknowledged its obligation to "promote self-determination on behalf of Tribal Governments, American Indians and Alaska Natives."[8] The legislation affirmed the ability of tribes to contract social, health, and educational services that had principally been offered through the BIA, the Indian Health Service, and various Indian education offices. In response to the new policy, many supported programs were decentralized, and offices located on the reservations were substantially expanded. As tribal operations were consolidated, there was a push to remodel or construct larger building complexes. For the first time in the history of U.S. and Indian relations, native programs were accessible locally by tribal members. This effort coincided more or less with the implementation of Indian housing programs by the Department of Housing and Urban Development. The need for new infrastructure to meet the demands of this repatriated population led to the construction of new streets and site development.

By 1977, a succession of federal agencies began to comply with the self-determination mandate for greater local tribal governance. The Bureau of Sport Fisheries and Wildlife, the Department of Labor, the Economic Development Administration, the Farmers Home Administration, the Forest Service, the Rural Electrification Administration, the Small Business Administration, and the U.S. Geological Survey established "Indian Desks" to work with tribal programs that were being set up on reservations.[9] Indian desks not only served to maintain networks but also assisted tribes in navigating the myriad of new regulations and procedures.

Another benefit of self-determination was the implementation of Indian preference in tribal hiring. This practice was extended to "qualified persons of at least one-fourth degree or more Indian blood." Although this policy had been established in Section 12 of the 1934 Indian Reorganization Act, there had been little incentive to implement it. Once tribes took over their own contracts, they now had a vested stake in employing their own tribal membership. This helped to partially reverse the historical migration of professional white- and blue-collar workers who had trickled outward into urban centers. As some jobs were relocated back into reservation areas, the Office of Economic Opportunity retooled to take advantage of these changes.

The devolution of services and the increase in power of local tribes held considerable promise. The ability to contract and control federally funded programs ushered in an era of greater potential for economic self-determination. The shift created a chain of events that helped reshape the reservation economy. However, the changes were not always positive.

Despite what appeared as a promising start, economic development was soon hindered by legislative action anchored in a larger swing in political ideology to the right. Whereas Native American programs comprised only .04 percent of the total federal budget in 1982, the Reagan administration nevertheless reduced funding for Indian programs.[10] The impact on reservation economies was nothing short of catastrophic.[11]

With funding for self-determination curtailed, unemployment escalated as social services were reduced. Because many of these programs were part of the U.S. federal trust responsibility, they could not be eliminated entirely. Federal agencies like the Indian Health Service instead instituted strict eligibility criteria, thereby effectively stretching dollars by reducing the pool of qualified applicants. Patients first had to prove tribal residency before they were afforded access to a designated regional provider. This left thousands of Native Americans living off the reservation—the so-called Urban Indians—with no Indian health care.

With tribal government undercut, the only remaining economic sector was the extraction industry. In 1982, the U.S. Supreme Court upheld the right of tribes to impose severance taxes on the value of oil, gas, coal, and other minerals extracted on their reservations.[12] The legal victory, though, was far from being an economic victory. Lacking the capital to manage their own operations, the tribes depended on the U.S. Department of the Interior to negotiate oil, mineral, and timber leases for them. Unfortunately, many such leases proved to be noncompetitive and were grossly mismanaged. Moreover, the court ruling became a justification for implementing even more cutbacks under President Reagan's "bootstrap and safety net" initiatives.[13] Proactive tribal organizations whose work had leveraged the hard-fought concessions were dismantled. The Council of Energy Resource Tribes, for example, lost two thirds of its operating budget in 1984 as a result of federal funding cutbacks. The Native American Rights Fund suffered a similar fate. The reliance on extracting natural resources also placed reservations at the mercy of the world markets, hardly a formula for economic self-sufficiency.

The major community development efforts of the 1980s had done little to dramatically improve the economic capacity of reservations. Local tribal governments were ill equipped to inject the new dollars needed to keep local businesses afloat. There were no funds for research and development. Entrepreneurship was stifled due to the inability of a tribe or its residents to build investment collateral using tribally controlled property or trust lands. Although a few tribes had successes in local ventures, they did not have the resource base to tap into the outside markets. Marketing was limited to promoting a limited venue for tourism and outdoor recreation.[14] Reservation economies were hampered by geographic isolation.

By the end of the 1980s, the economic-development system on reservations was severely underfunded, with much of the available resources diverted to nonlocal expenditures and with an overdependence on a largely unresponsive federal government. The restructuring of services led to the employment of more people to oversee operations and the creation of a distinct "managerial class."[15] Both phenomena drained resources. By 1989, the BIA employed some 15,000 civil servants, and according to congressional sources, only 12 cents of every federal dollar designated for Indian programs had trickled down to the local level. At the same time, the failure to develop alternative economic opportunities created an unhealthy dependency on the meager federal funds that trickled down to the reservations. Nearly half of all American Indian income was attributed to federal and tribal employment.[16]

The failures were politically spun by the administration to point the blame elsewhere. James Watt, Ronald Reagan's Secretary of the Interior, stated, "If you want an example of the failures of socialism, don't go to Russia. Come to America and go to the Indian reservations." The President also chimed in. To add insult to injury, a few years later, President Ronald Reagan told a group of Soviet students in 1984, "Maybe we made a mistake. Maybe we should not have humored [Native Americans] in wanting to stay in that kind of primitive lifestyle. Maybe we should have said, 'No, come join us.' "[17] The ideological message was clear: promoting self-determination for American Indians was out, and a retreat back to the old and failed policy of forced assimilation was in. Unfortunately, the latter was a hollow commitment. The federal government had never been fully committed to ensuring full and equitable integration of Indians into the American mainstream, and there is no evidence that the President would do what was needed to ensure that American Indians would be able to "join us."

Because of the multiple shortcomings, economic development before gaming had at best only marginal positive impacts on American Indians. According to the 1990 census, 31 percent of this population lived below the federal poverty line, compared to only 13 percent for the total population.[18] The problem was even more severe on the reservation, where 51 percent lived below the poverty line. The one major accomplishment of this earlier era was a strengthening of the desire (and necessity) of American Indians to use their sovereignty rights and self-determination as a basis for community economic development.

INDIAN GAMING AT THE NATIONAL LEVEL

Burdened with serving their own populations and faced with the ineffectiveness of the federal government, tribes have been desperate to find alternative activities to support their populations. Gaming was one option, a strategy that has evolved over time. The earliest efforts were community-oriented bingo games offering limited prizes. This changed in 1979 when the Seminole Tribe of Florida instituted a high-stakes bingo game with the intent of tapping into the surrounding non-Indian market. Further expansion of Indian gaming proved to be controversial and generated political confrontations. State and local governments were among the most vocal in their objections, arguing that they had the right to determine whether gambling was legal. Indian tribes, on the other hand, argued that they had the right to establish and run gambling operations by virtue of their tribal sovereignty. In 1987, both arguments were put to the test by the U.S. Supreme Court in a case that pitted the state of California against a minscule gaming tribe, the Cabazon Band of Mission Indians. The Court ruled in favor of the tribe, stating that Indian tribes had the right to conduct gaming as long as the state government permitted similar activities.[19] Within a decade, scores of other trials followed suit, most favoring the tribes.[20] Although these decisions cleared the way for tribes to pursue gaming as an economic development enterprise, new obstacles materialized.

State and local governments did not have the power to curtail tribal gaming, but the federal government, through its fiduciary trust responsibility, did. An intensive lobby by both the state and local governments, along with the nontribal gaming industry, resulted in the passage of the Indian Gaming Regulatory Act (IGRA) in 1988.[21] The IGRA attempted to clarify both the rights and procedures for Indian gaming by dividing it into three distinct classes.:[22]

Class I is comprised of "social games played solely for prizes of minimum value or traditional forms of Indian gaming"

Class II operations include "the game of chance commonly known as bingo ... including (if played in the same location) pull tabs, lotto, punch boards, etc."

Class III is defined as casino-style gaming, including slot machines and video poker.

Class I activities are considered the exclusive jurisdiction of Indian tribes. Class II activities are regulated by a special National Indian Commission and are not subject to state regulation. Class III gaming, however, requires that a state and tribe enact an "Indian Gaming Compact," which include the rules, regulations, and conditions under which a tribe may operate casino-style gaming.

Unfortunately, negotiating compacts is inherently contentious. Compacts have become the major source of contention between states and their resident tribal communities. Although provisions allow the state to negotiate on an individual basis with each tribe, the dominant pattern has been to reach an accord that covers all tribes within its state boundaries with a uniform compact. This collective bargaining approach has both advantages and disadvantages. One major advantage has been the streamlining of negotiations into a unified set of accords. Foremost among these is the negotiation of a rate of return for the state from the casino's net profit. Another pertains to setting the number of slot machines allocated to each tribe, and yet another pertains to the amount of liability every tribe is expected to assume. In many states, the negotiations dragged on for years, a phenomenon that is discussed later in this chapter.

Despite the delays caused by legal suits and protracted negotiations with states, Indian gaming quickly took root in the early 1990s as the most important business enterprise pursued by many tribes. In a 1995 report to the U.S. Economic Development Administration, it was noted that

> The explosion of Indian gaming onto the economic map of Indian country has been the single largest phenomenon of the past twenty years. The rapid growth of this industry marks the first time that any reservation-based economic activity not only entered a market, but has actually captured a significant market share in a relatively few years, with some $4.1 billion of the $39.7 billion of the gross revenues generated annually by the legal gaming industry in this country.[23]

Since that beginning, total revenues have continued to grow rapidly, from $5.4 billion in 1995 to $16.7 billion in 2003.[24] In 2002, the most recent year with detailed figures, 224 tribal governments (40 percent of the 562 total) offered some type of Class II or Class III gambling, generating $14.5 billion in revenue and accounting for one-fifth of the total take for the domestic gaming industry as a whole. According to the National Indian Gaming Industry, Indian gaming generated 400,000 jobs in the early 2000s.[25]

As a community economic development tool, gaming proved extremely successful. IGRA provided provisions to ensure that the community would be its primary beneficiary. Tribal gaming needs approval by the Secretary of Interior (who reviewed all compacts between states and tribes) and is allowed only if it was conducted as a means of economic development and tribal self-sufficiency and if it would result in a strong tribal government. Specifically, gaming profits were to

- fund tribal government operations or programs,
- provide for the general welfare of the Indian tribe and its members,
- promote tribal economic development,
- donate to charitable organizations, or
- help fund operations of local government agencies.

Under certain situations an Indian tribe can petition the Secretary of the Interior to waive the above requirements and distribute gaming profits as taxable payments directly to tribal members. Only a quarter of the gaming tribes have distributed profits this way.[26] Such per-capita payments have often been the cause of internal dissent, however, because tribes can become involved in heated debates about who qualifies for tribal membership and thus is eligible for payments. After income generation, one of the major justifications for gaming by tribal governments is job creation. At the national level, approximately a quarter of the jobs created by gaming went to American Indians.[27] In some areas, the proportion is even higher. An analysis of Indian gaming operations in Oklahoma, for example, indicated that Indian gaming created over 3,800 jobs (directly) in 2000, with three-quarters of those jobs going to American Indians.

While gaming has become big business and provided new employment opportunities, it has also created problems. One is a growing inequality among tribes. Returns from gaming are not distributed equally among all Indian casinos. Two-thirds of all the revenues ($9.4 billion) are concentrated among just 41 tribes.[28] The tribes whose reservations are located near large population centers with little or no competition from other tribes have taken a lion's share of the revenues.[29] There is also an issue about how much gaming has improved the economic well-being of the residents of reservations with gaming, and this question is examined later in the chapter.

GAMING IN NEW MEXICO

Events in the state of New Mexico serve as a dramatic case in point of the difficulties in establishing Indian gaming compacts in the face of state and local opposition. In 1990, 134,000 American Indians lived in New Mexico, accounting for about 9 percent of the state's total population. Nearly half (46 percent) live below the poverty line, over twice the proportion for the total population and nearly three times the proportion for whites. For many tribes, gaming has become a central economic development strategy, but obtaining approval for gaming in New Mexico was a major battle, with Indian tribes suing the state for failing to engage in good faith negotiation and then injecting themselves in gubernatorial politics by funding a more supportive candidate.[30]

Gaming in the state began in 1983 with the introduction of a high-stakes bingo operation at the Acoma Pueblo reservation, located west of Albuquerque. Spurred on by its success, other New Mexico tribes quickly followed suit. By 1989, a few tribes had introduced electronic machine gambling into their bingo halls, anticipating that New Mexico laws that permitted the limited placement of coin slot machines in Veteran's Halls would pave the way for Class III gaming. In the same year Garrey Carruthers, New Mexico's Republican governor, informed the state's Office of Indian Affairs of his intent to close all tribal gaming operations unless a compact was negotiated. The threat, however, never materialized.

In 1991, the Mescalero Apache tribe and the Pueblo of Sandia presented compacts to the newly elected Democratic governor, Bruce King, who had previously held that office from 1971 to 1975. King, a gaming opponent, refused to endorse the compacts. With the legislative route blocked, the tribes turned to the federal court for relief. Because it was determined that the state's immunity prevented the case from proceeding, the parties reluctantly agreed to mediate the matter. But the impasse didn't stop tribal gaming operations from moving forward. Several more tribes expanded their casinos with the introduction of new electronic machines. Despite the posturing of federal and state enforcement agencies to shut down these "illegal" operations, little or no action was taken.[31]

In 1993, the New Mexico legislature passed a bill authorizing the state's Office of Indian Affairs to negotiate with tribes over gaming compacts. King, however, vetoed it. Frustrated, the gaming tribes organized their own gubernatorial slate in response, and poured over $190,000 into the campaign of a pro-gaming candidate.[32] On November 6, 1994, a pro-gaming Republican, Gary Johnson, defeated King. With Johnson presiding, New Mexico voters approved a constitutional amendment to allow video gaming, and the establishment of a statewide lottery offset declining tax revenues for education from other sources.

Early in 1995, using only the authority of the governor's office, Johnson signed compacts permitting 14 tribes to offer unlimited Class III gaming. By July, the U.S. Attorney General signed nonprosecution deals with eight of these tribes. In exchange for this freedom from federal lawsuits, the eight tribes agreed to limit the number of gambling devices pending further resolution of the matter. By November, however, the New Mexico Supreme Court invalidated all the governor's compacts, ruling that the state legislature, not the governor, was the proper authority for approving compacts.

In the meantime, state officials reversed their progaming support by seizing all electronic payoff games from charitable organizations.[33] The next calculated move was to shut down Indian casinos. Faced with this impending threat, Pueblo authorities strategically poised themselves to exercise their sovereign authority by restricting non-Indian access to Indian lands. The most effective ploy was a traffic slowdown by the Pueblo of Pojoaque; the tribe imposed a 15-mile-per-hour speed limit, which brought Santa Fe–to–Los Alamos commuters to a near-standstill. The Pueblo of Isleta, for its part, threatened a road blockade.[34] Confronted with these measures and with statewide rallies held by casino employees in support of Indian gaming, the state withdrew its plans to close down casinos. In the end, only the Mescalero Apache tribe, which had refused to be a party to the original state compact, had its casino shut down, in August of 1996.

In 1997, the New Mexico legislature reluctantly approved a statewide Indian Gaming Compact, which Governor Johnson signed into law. That year, there were 11 tribes operating casinos throughout the state of New Mexico.[35] In addition to making tribal casinos legal, the law also permitted a fixed number of slot machines at horse tracks. But this only laid the groundwork for further turmoil. The horse track casinos were required to pay 25 percent of their net winnings to the state, while some of the larger tribal casinos were required to pay only 16 percent. Moreover, the Mescalero Apache tribal casino was reopened under the terms of the new compact, although it refused to make any payments to the state until it could broker a separate agreement. The original signers then refused to submit payments, contending that the 16 percent revenue-sharing fee imposed by the compact was twice the rate designated under IGRA provisions.

The compact was eventually reworked and returned to the legislature, which gave its approval in 2001. The revenue-sharing fee was reduced to 8 percent—3 percent for smaller casinos—and the gaming tribes agreed to pay an additional $100,000 in annual regulatory fees to the state. In December of 2001, the Interior Department added its approval. The tribes and the New Mexico Attorney General settled out of court, and the state garnered a collective windfall of slightly over $90 million, owed since Class III gaming had begun.[36] The Mescalero Apache tribe continued to hold out for a separate compact and was later joined by the Pueblo of Pojoaque. Both

Table 9.1. Gaming reservations surrounding Albuquerque.

Tribe	Year Started	Number of Slots (2004)	Net Revenues (First Half of 2004)
Acoma	1984	800	$18.4m
Isleta	1990	1,700 (2 locations)	$45.0m
Laguna	Unknown	1,930 (3 locations)	$20.4m
San Felipe	1995	800	$10.5m
Sandia	1986	1,700	$65.5m
Santa Ana	1993	1,500	$20.4m

Sources: http://www.skycitycasino.com/, http://www.isletacasinoresort.com/about.html, http://www.sandiacasino.com/, http://www.sanfelipecasino.com/pages/facilities_games.html, http://www.santaanastar.com/gamingareas.htm

Note: Net revenue data are from the New Mexico Gaming Control Board and are equal to the amount wagered on gaming machines less the amount paid out in prizes less a deduction for regulatory fees.

contended that they were left out of direct negotiations. In 2004, the Mescalero tribe and the State Attorney General settled for a sum of $25 million.[37]

The tribes around Albuquerque were among the most active in pursuing gaming and dramatically expanded their facilities because they had the advantage of locations next to major interstates or the city. Table 9.1 lists the 6 gaming tribes in the Albuquerque region, along with information on when they were established, their size in 2004 as measured by the number of slot machines, and net gaming revenues for the first half of 2004. As mentioned early, Acoma Pueblo was a pioneer, starting in 1983 with high-stakes bingo. They were joined a few years later by Pueblo Sandia, and the other tribes started operating gaming in the following decade. The importance of proximity to the urban center is illustrated by the eventual growth of Sandia and the Isleta, two Pueblo tribes whose reservations hemmed the city in on the north and south, into the state's two largest casinos. The two have been in a building race to tap the nearby population. The Pueblo of Isleta opened its new casino in March 2001. The expansion was tagged at $55 million and comprised a 100,000-square-foot facility with 1,500 slot machines, 125 table games, 5 restaurants, and a 1,500-seat indoor performance stage. No sooner had the luster of this grand opening worn off that the Pueblo of Sandia opened its own $110-million casino.[38] In 2003, in a bid to become the tribe with the third largest casino, the Pueblo of Laguna constructed a $60-million gaming facility on Albuquerque's western edge.

Business development has not been limited to the casinos but has also extended through direct investments of gaming revenue to related businesses such as restaurants, hotels and resorts, golf courses, and shops. Some of these developments have been formed as joint ventures. The Pueblo of Santa Ana, despite its struggling financing situation, has developed the state's only 5-star luxury resort, Tamaya, which was built in partnership with the Hyatt Hotels.[39] Moreover, recreational tourism has spurred other casino-related operations, particularly concerts.[40] While these investments have helped diversify the reservation economy, these ventures are nonetheless dependent on the gaming industry.

EMPLOYMENT AND INCOME IMPACTS ON RESERVATIONS

This section examines the employment and income impacts of gaming on reservations. Job creation is the single most-important benefit of casinos that the tribes in New Mexico and around Albuquerque have touted. According to a 1999 monograph issued by the New Mexico Indian Reservation Economic Study Group, Indian gaming contributed 11,265 jobs and $226 million in salaries to the state.[41] Although the New Mexico Department of Labor does not publish employment data by individual tribe due to confidentiality agreements, the aggregate totals indicate that casino employment accounted for 42 percent of the tribe's total labor in 2003. Even the smallest operation, the Hollywood Casino of the Pueblo of San Felipe, claims that it has created 350 new jobs, with 60 percent of them held by Native Americans. On some reservations, many of the jobs have to be filled by non-reservation workers because of excess demand. In 1998, Sandia paid out an estimated $17 million in salaries for 1,300 employees, even though its total population was only about 500, according to the 2000 Census.

While the evidence on direct job generation by casinos is clear, the net economic impact on reservations is difficult to determine because of spillover and substitution effects. Spillover effects refer to the jobs generated by economic activities stimulated by the growth in gaming, such as investments in other businesses and greater public expenditures by tribal governments. On the other hand, the gross job gains could be offset by reservation residents leaving jobs outside the casino-related sector for jobs within the casino-related sector. Consequently, net employment and earnings gains for the reservation would be smaller than the jobs generated by casinos.

It is possible to get a first-order approximation of the overall impact of gaming by comparing the changes in employment and economic status of residents of reservations with and without gaming. In addition to the 6 tribal reservations with gaming in the Albuquerque region, there are another 5 that do not have gaming (Cochiti, Jemez, Santo Domingo, To'hajiilee, and Zia). Figure 9.1 shows the 11 reservations within a 50-mile radius of Albuquerque along with the location of the existing casinos.

The analysis draws heavily on U.S. Census data because the tribes exercise proprietary control over economic and labor force information for their gaming enterprises. The available information is used to compare changes between 1990 and 2000 for reservations with gaming and reservations without gaming. The classification by gaming and nongaming is based on the status in 2000. According to the census, 17,946 people lived in the gaming reservations in 2000, up from 16,360 a decade earlier. The population in the nongaming reservations increased from 7,748 to 8,821. The analysis also includes American Indians in the city of Albuquerque.

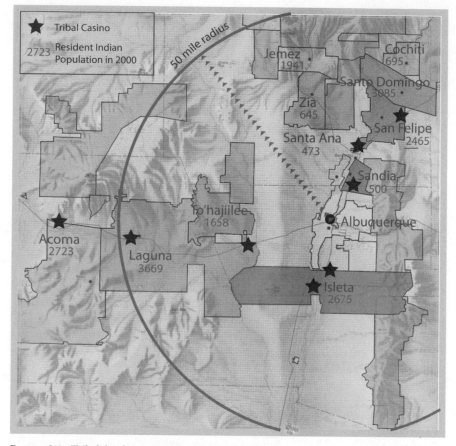

FIGURE 9.1. Tribal lands surrounding Albuquerque

Historically, American Indians relocated to cities in part because of the push of limited opportunities on the reservations and the pull of jobs in the urban areas. Because of these factors, urbanized American Indians fared better than those on the reservation.

The census data indicate three outcomes.[42] The first is that gaming communities have become more self-reliant than nongaming communities. This can be seen in the data on the place of work of reservation residents in Table 9.2. Unfortunately, the available data do not report the number of reservation residents working on the reservation. However, the data do report the number of reservation workers employed in the central city (Albuquerque) and outside the central city. Employment in the central city serves as a proxy measure for reliance on nonreservation jobs. In 1990, nearly half of all reservation workers in the Albuquerque area had to commute to the central city to work, and there is essentially no difference in the proportion for gaming and nongaming reservations. In 2000, the situation on nongaming reservations had not changed; the percentage is nearly identical to that for a decade earlier. The percentage for gaming reservations, however, did decline

TABLE 9.2. Place of work

	Reservations		
	All	Gaming	Nongaming
1990			
Total	7,774	2,129	5,645
In central city	3,533	969	2,564
Noncentral city	4,241	1,160	3,081
Percentage in central city	45.4	45.5	45.4
2000			
Total	7,883	2,368	5,515
In central city	3,143	1,070	2,073
Noncentral city	4,740	1,298	3,442
Percentage in central city	39.9	45.2	37.6
Change			
Total	109	239	−130
In central city	−390	101	−491
Noncentral city	499	138	361
Percentage in central city	−5.6	−0.3	−7.8

noticeably. This was due to an absolute number of workers commuting to the central city.

The second outcome was a noticeable increase in earnings. In real dollars, total earnings in the gaming reservations increased by 41 percent during the decade, compared with only 23 percent in the nongaming reservations. Much of this difference is due to differences in average earnings. According to the 2000 census, average earnings for all workers living in gaming reservations was about $21,000, about $4,000 more than the average for their counterparts living in the other reservations. Unfortunately, it is not possible to trace what proportion of the gains came from gaming, but it is very likely that casinos made both direct and indirect contributions to increasing earnings. One ironic consequence of the higher earnings potential was a decrease in the labor force participation rate among adults on gaming reservations, from 60 percent in 1990 to 51 percent in 2000. These rates are higher than the comparable rates for nongaming reservations (50 percent in 1990 and 49 percent in 2000) but are nonetheless a less-than-desirable outcome. The labor market response on gaming reservations appears to be a backward bending supply curve, an economic phenomenon where labor force participation decreases in response to an increase in average earnings. While this is not unknown for advanced economics, it is surprising for reservations. The net result is that more adults on the gaming reservations became unemployed as gaming became more established.

Not surprisingly, the increase in earnings has had a positive effect on two indicators of economic status. According to one Indian tribal administrator for the casinos, casino jobs "have helped many people out of poverty and toward leading themselves and their families into prosperity for the future."[43] This is supported by the data from the Bureau of the Census. The poverty rate was lower for gaming reservations than for nongaming reservations, and the

TABLE 9.3. Poverty rate and per capita income

	1990	2000	Percentage Difference
Poverty rate			
Gaming reservations	32.2%	23.6%	−8.6
Nongaming RESERVATIONS	35.7%	31.5%	−4.2
Albuquerque American Indians	28.7%	26.5%	−2.3
Per capita income			
Gaming reservations	$8,382	$10,242	22.2
Nongaming reservations	$7,323	$8,078	10.3
Albuquerque American Indians	$11,112	$11,735	5.6

decline in the rate during the 1990s was also greater for gaming reservations. Equally interesting, the poverty rate for residents of gaming reservations as reported in the 2000 census fell below the rate for American Indians in Albuquerque, eliminating some of the relative economic advantage enjoyed by those who sought their fortunes in the city. The statistics on per capita income tells a similar story. Those residing on gaming reservations enjoyed a significantly greater advantage relative to those on other reservations, with the advantage growing over time. While per-capita income on gaming reservations did not catch up with per capita income for American Indians in Albuquerque, the gap shrank dramatically.

Not only is average income higher in gaming reservations, living costs are lower because gaming revenues have been used to increase funding for local education and health programs.[44] In the instance of Sandia Peublo, for example, they included a health clinic, a gym and workout center, a library, and a preschool. There is also a renovated swimming pool, a new police station, a waste water treatment station, a new church, restoration of the bosque, in-home care for the pueblo's elderly, and a program to repair houses and create summer jobs for teens, to name a few. Half of the schoolchildren are sent to private schools by the pueblo, and those that go into postsecondary education have their tuition paid in full out of a scholarship fund. The same type of accomplishments, to varying degrees, are also being heralded among other gaming tribes.[45]

CONCLUDING REMARKS: LIMITATIONS AND CHALLENGES

Gaming has had mixed results as an economic development strategy. As we have seen, it is more effective in promoting self-reliance than earlier efforts under the 1975 Indian Self-Determination and Education Assistance Act. However, gaming is not a panacea. It is an approach that works only for the tribes on reservations near large urban centers, and this immutable difference in opportunity creates inequality among tribes. But even for the tribes that have gaming, the improvements have often fallen short of eliminating the racial disparity facing American Indians. In the Albuquerque area, the 2000 poverty rate for gaming reservations was still over three times as high as the poverty rate for non-Hispanic whites in Albuquerque (24 percent versus 8 percent), and the per capita income was far less than half ($10,200 versus $27,100). Gaming, by itself, is insufficient to achieve economic self-sufficiency.

Moreover, gaming is likely to become less effective because gaming tribes have experienced slow or no growth in recent years. A recent effort to expand the hotel at the Pueblo of Santa Ana stalled midway through construction. Interest rates used to finance the construction became too costly after the economic downturn that resulted from the September 11 terrorist attack. The growth problem is not isolated. From the fourth quarter of 2002 to the second quarter of 2004, 4 of the 6 gaming reservations around Albuquerque did not experience sustained secular growth. This indicates a more fundamental problem of market saturation. With limited room to grow, open cutthroat competition replaced cooperation. In 2003 the Pueblo of Isleta took out a three-quarter-page advertisement in the *Albuquerque Journal* that contained derisive remarks about its rivals.[46] In response to being chided publicly by others, the tribal governor fired the marketing manager and published another advertisement apologizing for the indiscretion. While this particular instance was resolved, the action inadvertently uncovered and jeopardized a secret pact among the gaming tribes to refrain from presenting anything but a cooperative public face. Reestablishing meaningful cooperation will be difficult given that any future growth for one tribe may have to come at the expense of another tribe.

Competition may also come from non-Indian sources. In most states, gaming has become a race-specific economic niche because of the sovereign status afforded to American Indians. The non-Indian public does not generally perceive gaming as a legitimate exercise of tribal sovereignty, but instead as an unfair monopoly. This leaves an opening for those who advocate breaking the perceived monopoly. In New Mexico, there is a push to allow non-Indians to expand their horse racetrack and casino operations. This has required the tribes to respond at a cost. For example, in a move intended to dampen the support of the Jemez off-reservation casino, New Mexico State University was made the beneficiary and half-owner of the enterprise that is most likely to be hurt, Sunland Park racetrack and casino.[47]

There are also challenges to the legitimacy of gaming. Economic gains notwithstanding, gaming raises some moral concerns. Segments of the non-Indian community have rallied around an anti-Indian gaming campaign on the basis of moral and ethical grounds. A paid political advertisement for a gubernatorial candidate appeared espousing the return to Christian principles in government, boldly proclaiming a "get gambling out of New Mexico" campaign.[48] Such a platform has also infiltrated the New Mexico legislative slate through the lobby of the New Mexico Anti-Gaming Coalition. The morals-based objections are not just external. Concerns are also encountered within the American Indian community. Nowhere is this more evident than in the Pueblo of Isleta after its religious leaders declared a moratorium on economic development projects that could adversely impact traditional ways of life.[49] While these attacks and concerns will not end Indian gaming, they will certainly add to the woes facing the tribes.

The limit on growth is forcing tribes to look for new markets. One strategy is to attract customers from a wider geographic area. In 2004, the Pueblo of Sandia, for instance, broke ground for a second-phase expansion of its casino. This is designated as a strategic move intended to transform its operation into a casino-resort for purposes of attracting and lodging out-of-state visitors. The other path is to invest in other regions. The nongaming Pueblo of Jemez proposed to enter the industry by locating a new casino hundreds of miles to the south near the New Mexico, Texas, and Mexican border.[50] Both strategies, however, are unproven because the moves would put the Albuquerque tribes in competition with a larger group of competitors outside the region.

Today, Indian gaming is at a crossroads. It has improved the overall economic status of the tribes, but it has not eliminated deep-seated social ills on the reservations. Many of these are related to long-term health impacts, disrupted family living patterns, and low educational attainment. Whereas Indian gaming only gained momentum in the 1990s, many of the chronic social conditions on reservations have persisted for generations. Tribal governments have begun systematically addressing these problems by improving capital infrastructure and contracting local services for their tribal members. This collective approach has significantly improved the overall welfare of the community but has not necessarily affected individual or household gains in employment and income.

Gaming provides the tribe with short-term advantages. As outside political pressure increases to regulate the growth of tribal casinos, the opportunity for more profit appears to be running out of steam. What is needed is a long-term economic development strategy that uses gaming as a launching pad, with a sizeable share of the profits being invested in diversifying the reservation economy and in enhancing tribes' own human capital.

As seen in New Mexico, gaming tribes are implementing efforts along these lines. Much of that success can be predicated on their new ability to supplement federal and state services that are tied to treaty reparations in health, education, and government. Self-generating tribal enterprises, however, are still in their infancy. The success of these will depend on an educated and trained labor force, especially if that force's own tribal members are expected to assume the key managerial positions.

Currently, most of the reservation workforce is non-Indian and still being imported from the outside. The tribal labor force, on the other hand, is small and tends to be unskilled. Tribes are forced to compete for their educated tribal members, who are attracted to wages and benefits provided by outside employers located in adjacent urban centers. These employees seek the amenities of reservation life but prefer to commute for gainful employment.

All of the above is symptomatic of a situation that can only be solved by providing sustainable and lasting employment in the reservation. Indian gaming has opened the door to such possibilities but by itself will not solve the greater need for economic self-determination.

NOTES

1. The authors are listed in alphabetical order, with each contributing equally to the research and writing.

2. The statistics are from the 2000 Census, and the figures are based on the single-race counts.

3. Vine Deloria and Clifford M. Lytle, *The Nations Within: The Past and Future of American Indian Sovereignty* (Austin, TX: University of Texas Press, 1998).

4. Troy Johnson, Joane Nagel, and Duane Champagne, eds., *American Indian Activism: Alcatraz to the Longest Walk* (Urbana: University of Illinois Press, 1997).

5. National Indian Gaming Commission, "Annual Report, 2003" (Washington, DC: National Indian Gaming Commission, 2003).

6. The issues include but are not limited to the impacts on tribal governance, adverse effects on gambling habits, the role of outside corporations, state and local fiscal impacts, and the restrictions on labor organizing.

7. The Indian Self-Determination and Assistance Act, Public Law 93-638, (1975): 88 stat. 2203.

8. Bureau of Indian Affairs, "Mission Statement," http://www.doiu.nbc.gov/orientation/bia2.cfm, downloaded November 18, 2004.

9. American Indian Policy Review Commission, *Task Force Seven: Reservation and Resource Development Protection*, Report on Reservation and Resource Development and Protection, vol. 1 (Washington, DC: U.S. Government Printing Office, 1976), p. 88.

10. "Reaganomics on the Reservation," The New Republic, November 22, 1982.

11. See C. Patrick Morris, "Termination by Accountants: The Reagan Indian Policy," in Fremiont J. Lyden and Lyman H. Legters, eds., *Native Americans and Public Policy* (Pittsburgh: University of Pittsburgh Press, 1992), 63-98.

12. *Merrion v. Jicarilla Apache Tribe*, 455 U.S. 130 (1982).

13. "Empty Promises, Misplaced Trusts," Empire Magazine, *Denver Post*, November 20, 1983.

14. Veronica Tiller, *American Indian Reservations and Trust Areas* (Washington, DC: Economic Development Adminstration, 1996).

15. Philip S. Deloria, *The Era of Indian Self-Determination: An Overview* from Indian Self-Rule. (Salt Lake City, UT: Howe Bros., 1986), p. 199.

16. Robert H. White, *Tribal Assets: The Rebirth of Native America* (New York: Henry Holt & Co., 1990), p. 274.

17. "Reaganomics on the Reservation."

18. U.S. Bureau of the Census, *We the...First Americans*, (U.S. Dept. of Commerce, Bureau of the Census, Washington, DC: U.S. Government Printing Office: , September 1993).

19. *California v. Cabazon Band of Mission Indians*, 480 U.S. 202 (1987).

20. William R. Eadington, ed., *Indian Gaming and the Law* (Reno: University of Nevada–Reno, 1990); Roger Dunstan, "Gambling in California," (Sacramento: California Research Bureau, January 1997); Angela Mullis and David Kamper, eds., *Indian Gaming: Who Wins?* (Los Angeles, CA: UCLA American Indian Studies Center, 2000).

21. Public Law 100-497, *U.S. Code* 1, Title 25, Section 2703 (1/22/02).

22. *Indian Gaming Regulatory Act Overview*, National Indian Gaming Commission, http://www.nigc.gov/nigc/laws/igra/overview.jsp.

23. Veronica E. Velarde Tiller, "American Indian Reservations And Indian Trust Areas," report to U.S. Economic Development Administration, Department of Commerce, October, 1995.

24. National Indian Gaming Commission, "Growth in Indian Gaming," NIGC Web page, http://www.nigc.gov/nigc/tribes/revenue-03–95.jsp, downloaded November 15, 2004.

25. *Indian Gaming Facts*, NIGA Library and Resource Center, http://www.indiangaming.org/library/index.html#facts.

26. *Final Report*, National Gaming Impact Study Commission, June 18, 1999, chapter 6, p. 18.

27. *Indian Gaming Facts*.

28. National Indian Gaming Commission, *Annual Report* (Washington, DC: National Indian Gaming Commission, 2003).

29. Eduardo E. Cordeiro, *The Economics of Bingo: Factors Influencing the Success of Bingo Operations On American Indian Reservations* (Cambridge, MA: The Harvard Project On American Indian Economic Development, John F. Kennedy School of Government Harvard University, 1989).

30. W. Dale Mason, "Tribes and States: A New Era in Intergovernmental Affairs," *Publius* 28 (Winter 1998):111–130.

31. "What's Next in Gaming Fray?" *Albuquerque Journal*, December 17, 1995.

32. "Gambling Industry N.M.'s 800-Gorilla," *Albuquerque Journal*, January 9, 2005.

33. "Kelly: Casinos Must Close," *Albuquerque Journal*, December 15, 1995.

34. "State: Indian Roadblocks Won't be Forced Open," *Albuquerque Journal*, January 6, 1996.

35. These were the Pueblos of Acoma, Isleta, Pojoaque, Sandia, Santa Ana, San Felipe, San Juan, Taos, and Tesuque in addition to the Jicarilla and Mescalero Apache tribes. The two additional tribes that joined later are the Pueblos of Laguna and Santa Clara.

36. "6 Pueblos Pay Gaming Fees," *Albuquerque Journal*, January 26, 2002.

37. "Tribe, AG Cut Slot Deal," *Albuquerque Journal*, April 21, 2004.

38. "Playing for Money," *Albuquerque Tribune*, February 25, 2001.

39. "Bond Deal with Pueblo Stagnant," *Albuquerque Journal*, June 4, 2004.

40. This is the promotion of affordable entertainment intended to woo music-goers into the casino. In 2001, more than 160 concerts were held in Santa Fe and Albuquerque. The vast majority were in casino performance halls. Most venues have halls that seat from 1,500 to 3,000. The Pueblo of Sandia has an outdoor amphitheatre and the Pueblo of San Felipe opened an 18,000-seat outdoor stadium for its concerts in 2001. This is in contrast to years past, when a successful concert season consisted of a half-dozen major shows. "Live and Well," *Albuquerque Journal*, December 28, 2001.

41. The monographs are reprinted in abbreviated form at the Sandia Pueblo Web site, www.sandiapueblo.nsn.us/gaming/car_gaimg.html. After deducting the costs for state public services used by tribal members, it was further estimated that the state received $77.6 million in net revenues. It should be noted that this report was not widely distributed, and, generally, the complete monographs are not available to the public.

42. The raw data come from the Bureau of the Census's American Fact Finder Web site and are taken from the Census 2000 Summary File 4 (SF 4) and the 1990 Summary Tape File 3 (STF 3). These files report detailed demographic, socioeconomic, and housing characteristics based on a sample of the population. The statistics for the reservations are based on all residence, regardless of race.

43. Frank Chaves, "Wall Street Lost Sight of Jobs," *Albuquerque Journal*, electronic edition, Saturday, August 3, 2002, http://www.abqjournal.com/opinion/guest_columns/guestb08–03–02.htm.

44. *Tribal Government Gaming: Ensuring Our Children's Future*, Sandia Pueblo Web site, from www.sandiapueblo.nsn.us/gaming/pueblo_gaming_benefits.html.

45. "Betting on the Future," *Albuquerque Journal*, July 8, 2001.

46. "New Mexico Casino Ad Irks Competitors," *Casino City Times*, 26 November 2003, http://www.casinocitytimes.com/news/article.cfm?contentID=139564ß.

47. "NMSU Give Would Be Big Boost," *Albuquerque Journal*, September 10, 2004.

48. "Mike Nalley For Governor, DEM, Paid Political Ad by Mike Nalley," *Albuquerque Journal*, February 3, 2002.

49. "Indian Gaming Brings Mixed Blessings," *Albuquerque Journal*, August 25, 2001.

50. "Anthony Residents Give Casino a 'Maybe,'" *Albuquerque Journal*, August 18, 2004.

IV COMPLEMENTARY STRATEGIES

MUCH OF THE traditional thinking in economic development for minority communities focuses on the economic isolation of residents and on the lack of employment and business opportunities. While addressing these problems is paramount, it is equally important to understand that labor market and business development efforts are not sufficient in themselves to address the multiple issues facing the residents of minority communities. Even the best programs to overcome spatial mismatch, increase human capital, and promote entrepreneurship cannot operate in a vacuum. This last part of the book gives a closer look at some of the complementary components of community economic development. The three chapters in this section discuss the importance of social capital and social networks, the need for affordable housing, and ways to improve social services (child care, transportation, food, education, etc.) for low-income communities of color.

There is a growing consensus among scholars and community activists that strong social networks and social capital constitute an important dimension of individual and community economic development. An individual's social network has an impact on job search outcomes and economic advancement. Especially for recent immigrants who are unaware of the particularities of the U.S. labor market, ethnic networks are extremely important in assisting them "connect" to the larger societal framework. In the absence of affordable or dependable social services, individuals often "get by" because of the offerings of food, childcare, and even rides to and from jobs from family, friends, and compatriots. Because of their lack of financial capital, low-income communities are more likely than higher-income communities to depend on neighborhood resources and kinship and friendship networks in their neighborhoods. The challenge from a policy perspective is to foster the development of social capital within the neighborhood but also develop its links with networks outside its confines. Networks linking individuals to the outside world help people "get ahead" by offering information, resources, and access to jobs and economic opportunities. The chapter by Anastasia Loukaitou-Sideris and Judy Hutchinson provides an example of the role of social networks and social capital through a case study of the Pico-Union neighborhood in Los Angeles.

Low-income people may be gainfully employed, but they cannot escape poverty if they must spend a large proportion of their income for housing. Rent or mortgage payments represent the most significant expenditures of American households. Unlike the situation in other countries (e.g., Great Britain, France, Sweden, Singapore) that have developed housing initiated by the public sector, in the United States the housing market is almost exclusively operated by the private sector. This has led to a significant undersupply of affordable housing, which negatively affects low-income households. This situation leads to the conclusion that housing should be an integral effort of economic development strategies in low-income communities. Giving an account of the dire results of a variety of policies seeking to address the housing hardship faced by low-income households in the Figueroa Corridor, a low-income inner-city neighborhood in Los Angeles, Jacqueline Leavitt argues for the necessity of a joint economic and housing strategy. Such a strategy is, however, inherently complex and requires the formation of collaborations and coalitions that cut across different sectors (public, private, and nonprofit) and community groups.

For some, jobs may be elusive because of lack of affordable and dependable support services, such as childcare, transportation, food, and education. Social services support entry to and sustainability of labor market participation. Low-income, minority, and female-headed households are much more dependent on social service provision than other households, but their varying needs are not always appreciated or understood by social service agencies and their funders. Lois Takahashi outlines the special needs encountered by low-income communities of color and argues for incorporating social service delivery in economic development strategies in low-income and minority communities.

Collectively, the chapters in this part of the book suggest that for community economic development to be effective, policy makers must address the underlying dynamics perpetuating the disadvantages of the poor in job seeking and gainful employment.

10 Social Networks and Social Capital
Latinos in Pico-Union

ANASTASIA LOUKAITOU-SIDERIS
AND JUDY HUTCHINSON

INTRODUCTION

The bonds among individuals and between individuals and communities have gained renewed attention as a wealth of scholars have emphasized the importance of social networks and social capital for employment and other important outcomes, from neighborhood security and public health, to the nurturing of children, to the successful integration of immigrant populations, to upward socioeconomic mobility. There is indeed a growing consensus that strong social networks and social capital constitute an important dimension of individual and community economic development. Local community is viewed as an ongoing system of social networks, some of which are internal to the locality or neighborhood, while others are external (Kasarda and Janowitz 1974). The assimilation and adaptation of newcomers (new residents and immigrants) to the neighborhood and its wider context depends, to a great extent, on their access to existing social networks. Scholars have also hypothesized that an individual's social network has an impact on job search outcomes and his/her economic advancement (Johnson et al. 1993; Lin 1982; Granovetter 1973). This assumption has both theoretical and conceptual appeal. Immigrants do not enter the United States and begin work within an asocial setting. Rather they obtain jobs, housing, and support through a close network of social ties (Massey 1986). Empirically, however, we know very little about how social capital operates at a micro-level (Putnam 1998). What is it about networks and reciprocity that enhances economic development? Is ethnicity an asset or a liability for the building of social capital and for economic development in ethnic communities? What types of social networks and ties exist in ethnic communities and do they lead to economic development? If access to social networks is important for economic advancement, how can we strengthen and support these networks, from a policy perspective?

This chapter addresses the previous questions by examining the social and survival networks of immigrant populations in the Pico-Union neighborhood of Los Angeles. Pico-Union is a poor inner-city neighborhood with very high concentrations of recent immigrants from Mexico and Central America. Despite an official neglect—demonstrated by poor municipal services, dilapidated and overcrowded housing, and lack of community programs—Pico-Union is a rather vibrant inner-city economy, with high rates of business formation and resident participation in the labor force. Our study assesses the contribution and effectiveness of the social and survival networks for the fostering of economic development opportunities in the neighborhood. It discusses the activities, alliances and collaborations among different social networks and examines the challenges and hurdles that immigrant communities are facing in adjusting to new physical and economic realities.

To set our empirical study in its larger theoretical framework, we first review the literature on social networks and social capital, examining the various types of networks and the different factors that contribute to social capital's formation and strength. Our focus is on ethnic neighborhoods, and for this reason we place particular emphasis on studies of ethnic networks and communities and their role in economic development. In the second part of the chapter we detail the findings of our empirical study, and conclude with a series of policy recommendations for building social capital in ethnic communities.

SOCIAL AND SURVIVAL NETWORKS

Social networks connote an individual's voluntary participation in associations that produce collective and individual goods. Networks imply social ties and interactions among participants and a sense of belonging in more or less defined social groupings (e.g., families and extended kinship networks, neighborhood associations, professional associations, church or advocacy groups, unions, etc.) (Chavis and Wandersman 1990). Social groupings and self-help grassroots activities that aim to protect and nurture extremely poor and vulnerable populations in their struggle for day-to-day survival are called *survival networks*.

The most basic social network is, of course, one based on family or kinship ties. It is far from the only one, however. Territorial community also often emerges as an important locus around which social networks can be built. Individuals sharing the same place of birth may be united by similar cultural characteristics and life experiences that bind them together even if they cease to reside in their birthplaces. This is evidenced in the many village and town associations whose members may be dispersed in different parts of the globe. Networks also arise in the neighborhood or locality in which one lives (neighborhood associations and clubs, neighborhood watch groups, etc.). People in these networks often share similar concerns and aspirations about improving neighborhood life, safety, or cleanliness. Networks can also form in places of work, motivated by the commonality of experiences and objectives that employees in the same environment share.

Local attachments constitute only one pattern of social networks and social life among others. In fact, some have argued that the importance of place has diminished, and local ties have become weaker in the late twentieth century, overlapping less frequently with ties of kinship, friendship, or leisure (Webber 1964; Willmott 1986).

As place has become less important, dispersed networks and communities of interest have arisen, which are not necessarily territorial or place-based.

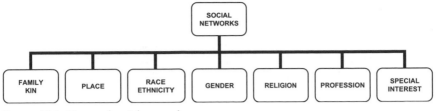

FIGURE 10.1. Types of social networks

As shown in Figure 10.1, the glue that ties people together in voluntary associations and networks can be that of race or ethnicity (e.g., ethnic associations), gender, religion, profession (e.g., professional associations), or some special interest (e.g., unions and advocacy groups). Networks are not always rigidly defined and are often overlapping. As scholars have pointed out, individuals often have to deal with the "competing claims and obligations of the complex networks in which they are enmeshed" (Wellman and Berkowitz 1988). Social networks can also be differentiated in terms of their size and density, the level of cohesiveness among their members, the preponderance of weak or strong ties (Light and Karageorgis 1994), and their structure (see Figure 10.2). As we will later explain, the particular type and content of ties in a network often determines the resources that it can provide.

Factors Influencing Network Formation

Early twentieth century sociologists faulted the industrial revolution for weakening communal bonds and creating new forms of social pathology (Durkheim 1911). Under the classic Tönnies-Wirth approach, the large populations and high densities of urban areas led to alienation and low partici-

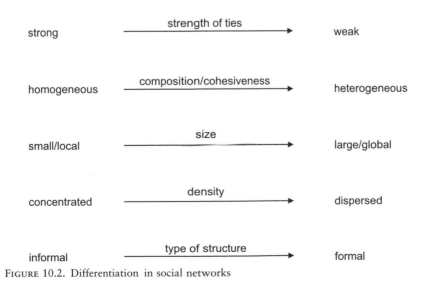

FIGURE 10.2. Differentiation in social networks

TABLE 10.1. Factors influencing formation of social networks

Positive	Negative
Exogenous	*Exogenous*
Long length of residence Stable, long-standing communities	Short length of residence Transient communities
Homogeneity Concentration of co-ethnics	
	Heterogeneity
Sociopetal urban form	Sociofugal urban form
Endogenous	*Endogenous*
Perceived control, sense of empowerment	Alienation
Perception of environmental problems, threats	

pation in social networks (Tönnies 1877; Wirth 1938). More recent empirical studies have, however, disputed this assertion, as community has been discovered in places where it had once been pronounced "lost," in slum and poor neighborhoods (Suttles 1968), among extended kin, and in workplaces and ethnic communities (Wellman and Berkowitz 1988). In light of these discoveries, scholars are now seeking to identify the factors that determine an individual's propensity to participate in place-based social networks.

Several exogenous and endogenous factors have been recognized as contributing positively to the development of social ties and networks (Table 10.1). A community attitudes survey in Great Britain, which examined population size and density, length of residence, socioeconomic position, and life cycle stage, found that people's length of residence in an area was the most important determinant of community attachment and local participation (Kasarda and Janowitz 1974). The authors found that urbanites tend to have more extensive social ties than people in rural communities. Wealthier individuals had smaller proportions of friends and relatives residing within their own communities or living nearby, but they also tended to belong to more formal associations (e.g., churches, clubs, and professional associations) and had more extensive reliance on formal social networks. In contrast to the arguments of early sociologists, the authors found that increased community size and density did not necessarily weaken bonds of kinship and friendship.

Neighborhood homogeneity, the concentration of people of the same socioeconomic background and at the same life-cycle stage, has been considered a positive factor for the formation of social bonds. In particular the concentration of co-ethnics in a neighborhood has been shown to result in higher levels of participation in social networks. Studies in Great Britain reported that it was ethnic minorities who felt most linked to friends in their districts and had more local attachment (Willmott 1986). Similarly, studies in the United States found that low-income ethnic communities were more likely than higher income white communities to depend on neighborhood resources and kinship and friendship networks (Banerjee and Bear 1984).

A neighborhood's physical form can support or discourage social association, and by extension the formation of social ties and networks (Low 2003). Certain kinds of neighborhood layout can be more conducive than others to neighborhood contact (Willmott 1988). Environmental psychologists have distinguished between *sociopetal* environments, which encourage social association and interaction, and *sociofugal* environments, which prevent or discourage such associations. Neighborhoods with parks, public buildings, and other public spaces, as well as neighborhoods with pedestrian-friendly streetscapes, are sociopetal. In contrast, neighborhoods with a preponderance of fences and gates, inwardly oriented private spaces, and lack of public environments are sociofugal.

Certain endogenous factors can also influence an individual's participation in voluntary associations. The perception of an external threat or environmental problem may serve as a motivator for participation in a local group or network (Fischer 1977); many neighborhood organizations are formed as a response to the threat or reality of physical deterioration (Lavrakas 1981). One's perceived level of control and empowerment within a community, as well as the anticipated costs and benefits of involvement in social networks, can also influence the decision to participate (Chavis and Wandersman 1990). The perception that participation in a local network can contribute to personal and group empowerment and that it may lead to desired outcomes in the neighborhood, shapes an individual's tendency to associate with neighbors.

Contribution of Networks

Social networks can offer a wide range of resources and support. Lewis and Juarez (1995) identify three major functions of networks: (1) as buffers protecting individuals from stress, (2) as providers of instrumental and social support, and (3) as sources for information and referrals. Briggs de Souza (1998) distinguishes between networks that help someone "get by" and networks that push him or her to "get ahead." The first type offers emotional and personal support—companionship, small services like child care, small loans of tools or food, and help in emergency situations. For newcomers in a neighborhood and particularly immigrant families, these networks can offer valuable survival functions and help them navigate the particularities of a different sociocultural system while they adapt to living conditions in their newfound homes (Chavez 1988). "Get-by" networks are tied closely to the local community and to relatives, friends, and neighbors. They are described as providing Band-Aids to help cope with the stresses and strains of everyday life (Wellman, Carrington, and Hall 1988).

By contrast, networks that help people "get ahead" typically link individuals to the outside world by offering access to jobs, economic gains, housing, and other resources and opportunities (Lang and Hornburg 1998). Rather than Band-Aids, these networks provide ladders—tools that help people change their situations, improve their economic conditions, and move up in the social hierarchy (Wellman, Carrington, and Hall 1988).

Scholars have connected the existence of social networks with the generation of *social capital*, an "intangible resource that exists in the relations among persons" (Coleman 1988:S100). Social capital has been described as a store of reciprocal, trust-based relationships that give those who have access to them an advantage over those who do not. These relationships include shared norms and sanctions that encourage communicative interaction and cooperation among group members. Social capital theory calls this type of social capital "bonding capital" (Gittell and Vidal 1998). Even more important for economic development is "bridging capital," which provides information channels as well as connections to others outside the social group. These outside linkages may provide access to jobs and resources (Gittell and Vidal 1998).

The resources that networks can provide depend upon the type and content of ties that bind their members together (see Figure 10.2). As Xavier de Souza Briggs argues,

> strong ties tend to be the best sources of emotional aid and other social support.... Such ties to kin and friends are known to be especially important to the survival or coping strategies of poor people. On the other hand, weak ties or acquaintances are often key sources of everyday favors, an important type of instrumental support, and for some people, such ties are the most important sources of job referrals and other forms of leverage resources. Where dense networks, in which everyone or almost everyone knows everyone else, are good for mobilizing social support, widely dispersed ties to many kinds of people, even if these ties are casual acquaintanceships, tend to be more crucial for job search and other processes that depend on advantage and influence beyond support." (1998:188).

As Johnson et al. (1993) explain, three structural elements of social networks seem to particularly influence outcomes: their size, composition, and strength. People with larger networks have been typically found to better position themselves in the job market (Boxman, de Graaf, and Hendrik 1991). Socially heterogeneous networks (in terms of class, race, gender, etc.) seem to offer more opportunities for economic advancement to their members than networks consisting of similar sociodemographic individuals (Braddock and McPortland 1987)—presumably because they give access to many diverse social worlds. And weak ties are often found to be beneficial because they are more likely than strong ties to provide valuable information about jobs (Granovetter 1973). Weak ties do not always, however, materialize into jobs or resources, and they are not constant across groups (Johnson et al. 1993).

SOCIAL NETWORKS AND SOCIAL CAPITAL IN ETHNIC COMMUNITIES

For many immigrant communities, social networks and their "product," social capital, are considered crucial for economic advancement and participation in the "American Dream." While there are many arguments about the cause/effect relationships between social capital and economic success, it is generally accepted that immigrant groups with abundant social capital are more successful economically than groups with less (Light, Bhachu, and Karageorgis 1993; Zhou 1992).

A major advantage of social capital is its accessibility (Light 2001). Whereas economic and human capital may be limited among the poor, social capital is still an accessible asset. Low-income immigrants being confronted with a shortage of financial and human capital often find themselves in undesirable neighborhoods. In such a situation ethnicity may be their only resource. Social capital, almost by necessity, becomes a substitute form of capital, which compensates to some degree for shortages of capital in its other forms (Light 2001; Zhou and Bankston 1994).

For some ethnic communities social support appears to be an integral part of their culture. Components of ethnic social support may include the extended family, religious institutions, ethnic associations, merchant associations, and social clubs. Latino cultures—the subject of our empirical study in Pico-Union—stress strong intergenerational family ties. Members of kinship networks feel a strong sense of obligation to each other for economic assistance, collaboration, encouragement, and support (Gomez 1987). Individuals and their families are integrated into a close-knit system of social relations that often evolves around the church (Patterson and Marsiglia 2000; Kayden 1996).

Scholars have found that ethnicity can work as an asset for some groups, as it creates "sources of adaptive advantages" that are based on trust, solidarity, and reciprocity among co-ethnics (Zhou and Bankston 1994:824). Light and Karageorgis (1994, 662) explain how social networks fuel the ethnic economy:

> By enhancing the scope of integrations of social networks, ethnic solidarity confers important business resources. First, ethnic networks carry business-related information, including business and trade secrets. . . . Social networks also encourage mutual aid, ranging from advice to preferential purchasing among business owners. . . . Ethnicity extends social trust; a key form of social capital. . . . Multiplex social networks permit ethnics to trust one another in business. . . . Social trust also contributes to the proliferation of entrepreneurs by reducing external transaction costs. Relying on informal social trust immigrant entrepreneurs transact business cheaply.

But social capital is not a panacea for overcoming economic problems and barriers in ethnic neighborhoods. Community-based economic development encounters some of its most serious challenges here. There are many reasons why this should not be so. America is, after all, a country of immigrants. The Statue of Liberty is recognition of the contribution that the "poor, tired, and hungry" can make to a country and its various communities. Immigrants come with dreams for a better future. They are often prepared to work hard to make those dreams come true. Many arrive with the broad range of work experience that is typical of rural people who must deal with all aspects of survival in limited circumstances. Most value education and have a strong desire to give their children more opportunities than they themselves enjoy. This is the kind of raw material with which community can be built.

However, immigrant neighborhoods face serious constraints. Even in the most favorable cases, the trauma and loss of dislocation combined with the anxiety of dealing with a strange environment and, in most cases, a strange language, create a situation of stress for both the arriving immigrants and the receiving community. The stress level is heightened when immigrants enter the new country illegally. Low levels of formal education and limited local networks put them further at risk. Social capital cannot always substitute for the severe lack of educational and economic resources faced by many immigrants. A third of current immigrants enter the United States as unskilled labor, with an average of 3–4 years of schooling. Fifty-three percent of immigrants from Latin America have less than a high-school education (Light 2001). In some inner-city areas, the numbers are even more daunting. A study published shortly after the Los Angeles riots revealed that over 80 percent of Latino immigrants in South Central Los Angeles over 25 years of age lacked a high school education (Pastor 1993).

The wages of workers in ethnic economies are appreciably lower than those prevailing in the mainstream economy, while the level of exploitation is considerably higher (Light 2001). Immigrants in urban centers typically work in unstable jobs in labor-intensive enterprises. Employers of immigrants in the ethnic informal economy frequently keep employees off official books—dealing strictly in cash, not paying taxes, and not conforming to minimum wage legislation (Massey 1986; Chapter 6 of this volume). Thus ethnicity can also act as a liability for certain immigrants who have to struggle for economic survival facing exploitation, language problems, and nonexistent economic and educational resources, and who live in transient inner-city communities (Skery 1993). The Pico-Union neighborhood in Los Angeles is one such community. In what follows we will detail the findings from our empirical study of social and survival networks in this neighborhood.

ETHNIC NETWORKS IN PICO-UNION, LOS ANGELES

The Context

If Los Angeles has truly replaced New York as the new "Capital of Immigrant America" (Waldinger and Lee 2001:43), then Pico-Union is the new Ellis Island. The area, just a couple of miles west of downtown Los Angeles, is a crowded and dilapidated inner-city neighborhood, where immigrants can find ways to survive and sometimes prosper in a new country. But Pico-Union's reputation as the port of entry for immigrants is not new. Since the early 1930s the neighborhood has received hundreds of thousands of newcomers.[1] The early immigrants were Europeans: Greeks, Norwegians, Swedes, Welsh, and Russian Jews. Most of them were merchants who opened small stores or established themselves as sidewalk vendors along Pico Boulevard, the major commercial thoroughfare of the neighborhood. From the 1930s to the 1940s, thousands of immigrants from different parts of the world added to the ethnic mix. An Armenian family owned a local grocery store; a Jewish family operated a Five and Dime; a Chinese family ran a vegetable market. Beginning in the 1950s, as many of the early immigrant residents moved out to more fashionable Los Angeles districts, other ethnic groups settled in, including Romanians, Lithuanians, Hungarians, Chinese, as well as also African Americans and American Indians.

In the 1950s and 1960s, L.A.'s population suburbanized at a rapid pace, and Pico-Union, once an enclave outside the urban core, became the "inner city." The disinvestment that accompanied suburbanization left its economic and social resources drastically diminished. A report of the early 1970s found that "the income of more than half of the residents is at, or below, the poverty level, and the median education attainment is well below that of Los Angeles County. In short, it is a poor, minority, high-density inner-city community" (Evansen 1972 in Cooper 1980).

Property values in the neighborhood fell, as did the demand for commercial space. Some shops were boarded up; others were simply razed. Physical desolation and a general deterioration of the urban form exacerbated the trend toward economic disinvestment. Housing became run down as landlords kept subdividing the units and renting them out to accommodate ever-larger numbers of immigrant families. Public facilities and infrastructure deteriorated. Barbed-wire fences and graffiti multiplied. The neighborhood was characterized by overcrowding and substandard housing conditions (Hutchinson and Loukaitou-Sideris 2001).

In the 1970s the character of immigration in the neighborhood changed, and large numbers of working-class Mexican immigrants began to settle in Pico-Union. In the early 1980s the immigrant demographics changed yet again, as the civil wars, social unrest, and economic downturns that roiled Central America resulted in an influx of migrants from El Salvador, Guatemala, Nicaragua, and Honduras. Today the neighborhood maintains a strongly Latino profile, with 85 percent of the residents from either Mexico or Central America, most of Indian descent. Other groups present are Asian and Pacific Islanders (8 percent), African Americans (3 percent), and Caucasian (3 percent) (U.S. Bureau of the Census 2000). Sixty-six percent of the population, according to the 2000 census, is foreign born. Of them, 24 percent have arrived within the last ten years.

Many of L.A.'s inner-city communities can be characterized as "multiple melting pots," which serve as incubators for new groups of workers and the development of a "new kind of economy" (Frey and DeVol 2000). The Pico-Union neighborhood—with its history as a portal for immigrants, and its mosaic of social groups with different backgrounds, values, and experiences with democracy—provides a window through which to observe the evolution of this "new kind of economy."

The Method

The study of social networks often requires a combination of research methods. We first compiled a demographic history of the area with data from the U.S. Census Bureau. Next, by administering questionnaires to community members and having semistructured interviews with community leaders connected to local institutions and associations, we were able to put a human face on these numbers. The combination of these data sources allowed us to create a broader framework within which to assess the type and content of networks, to understand the historical context for current social situations, and, to some extent, to provide insights regarding future potential and constraints to the economic development of the neighborhood and its people.

It is not easy to gain the trust of people living in the crowded inner city. For us, the task was made less difficult by our positions as co–project managers for a community revitalization project in the area. This gave us a unique opportunity to meet and work with residents and community leaders, attend meetings of the neighborhood watch and Parent Teacher Association (PTA) groups, and observe and participate in their struggles to maintain and improve the area. Although we were outsiders, our roles gave us a reason for being on the street, an *entrée* to public gathering places such as the churches and schools, and ultimately gained our admission into the homes of some residents.

For this study we conducted a "social networks survey" soliciting responses from 79 local merchants and residents participating in one local church group,[2] two neighborhood watch groups,[3] two athletic groups,[4] three Parent-Teacher Associations,[5] and a youth group from a local youth service organization.[6] Our intention was to assess the networks and community building strategies of people actively involved in their community. The weakness of this approach was that it primarily represented findings from individuals who belonged in one or more associations, leaving behind those who may be completely disconnected from the neighborhood's social networks.

To compare and contrast the survival and economic development strategies of two different ethnic groups in the area we also conducted focus group meetings with members of residents from Oaxaca as well as members from a local Salvadoran support organization.

Finally, observation of and participation in formal and informal gatherings—including meetings of neighborhood watch groups, local town hall meetings (organized by the district council office), meetings of the merchants' association, and neighborhood celebrations and festivals—enabled us to gain a sense of the community and to build the relationships of trust necessary for conducting our research.

The Findings

Social Networks Survey. The community survey gave us an indication of the neighborhood profile, as well as the type and role of social networks in Pico-Union. Fifty-five women and 24 men responded to a survey that sought to identify the type of networks present in Pico-Union and their role and contribution to the residents' economic and social well-being. Even though the sample was not random, it did provide a good ethnic representation of the neighborhood.[7] The overwhelming majority of residents were Latino, mostly from Mexico (48.7 percent), El Salvador (10.5 percent), Ecuador

(6.6 percent), Guatemala (6.6 percent), Honduras (2.6 percent), and Nicaragua (2.6 percent). Only 22.4 percent of the Latino respondents were born in the United States.

Pico-Union is a community of renters; data from the 2000 U.S. Census show that 90 percent of the housing units are renter-occupied. The survey respondents were mostly renters (63.2 percent), but homeowners were represented in higher numbers than in the general area population. This is not necessarily surprising: other studies have shown that property owners tend to get more involved in neighborhood-based networks because of their higher financial stakes in the neighborhood (Hutchinson 1999). The survey population also differed from the general area population in the longevity of its U.S. residence; respondents' residency tended to be significantly higher (22.85 years on average) than that of the general population. This finding clearly supports the previously stated argument that that length of residence is an important contributing factor in social network formation.

Pico-Union lags significantly behind the rest of the city of Los Angeles in average household income ($33,617 compared to $58,677). This is especially important considering that the average number of persons per household is higher than the citywide average (3.7 persons compared to 2.9 persons). Half of the households earn less than $20,000 (U.S. Census 2000). Recent immigrants coming into the Pico-Union area typically have little financial capital. A priest at St. Thomas Catholic Church told us that the majority of new immigrants arrive at the church doors with little more than the clothes they are wearing. Most of their other resources have gone to pay those who got them across the border. Many of the immigrants are subsistence farmers, fleeing from desperate poverty and having minimal formal education. Their farming skills, which constitute their human capital, are of little or no value in the urban environment of Pico-Union. According to the 2000 U.S Census, only 12 percent of the neighborhood's population has some college education, and 30 percent have not completed high school. This relative lack of education, combined, for many, with a lack of English language skills, limits them to working as laborers in low paying work requiring physical strength and endurance rather than formal skills. Although the income levels of survey respondents were somewhat higher that those of the area population, over one third (34.9 percent) reported an annual household income of less than $10,000, and 36.5 percent reported incomes of $20,000–$30,000. Only 12.7 percent had incomes exceeding $40,000.

A comparison of the current occupations of Pico-Union residents with citywide data shows that people in Pico-Union have fewer stable, high-wage jobs, and a higher proportion of low-wage jobs (Hutchinson 1999). While this is particularly true for recent immigrants to the area it is also partly reflected in our sample. The most prominent occupation category among survey respondents was low-wage personal services (housekeeping, babysitting, gardening, waitressing, etc.) (Figure 10.3). Unemployment in the neighborhood, according to the 2000 U.S. Census, is at 7.5 percent, higher than the city average of 3 percent, but quite a bit lower than the unemployment rates of many other inner-city neighborhoods. Focus group respondents

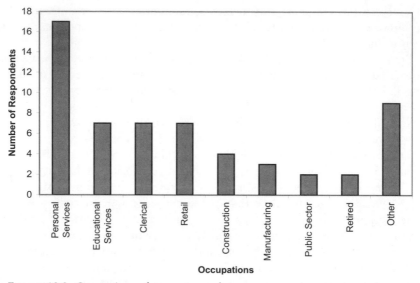

FIGURE 10.3. Occupations of survey respondents

tended to have even lower unemployment levels (6 percent) than the rest of the neighborhood. About 24 percent of them were self-employed, while 5 percent stated that they worked for a family member. Self employment rates in this group were significantly higher than in the neighborhood, where only 9.5 percent are self-employed, while the vast majority (81 percent) are wage earners and salaried employees in the private sector.

Community feelings and neighborhood attachment seemed to run high among respondents. The overwhelming majority (88 percent) identified Pico-Union as a "community," and 91 percent felt that they were a part of this community, while 64 percent were actively involved in community projects and networks. Respondents were aware of a number of associations and social networks in Pico-Union. These included church groups, neighborhood watch groups, PTA groups, social clubs, social service groups, ethnic groups, business groups (e.g., merchant associations), sports groups, and transportation cooperatives. While the existence of these groups was deemed helpful for individual and neighborhood welfare, not all networks are positive. Respondents also pointed to the existence of gangs and drug dealing rings as examples of networks with negative impact on their neighborhood.

Kinship and friendship networks seemed to be prevalent, as over half of the respondents stated that they live in Pico-Union because family members and friends live there. Another 18 percent claimed that they stay in the neighborhood because it has high concentrations of compatriots. Additional considerations that weighed heavily in respondents' decisions to live in Pico-Union included a perception of better opportunities for work and housing. In regards to the categories presented in Figure 10.2, networks in Pico-Union appeared to be internally homogeneous, informal, local, and highly

TABLE 10.2. Type of help offered

	General Information	Job Referrals	Social Support	Major Financial Support
Relatives	3.0%	32.3%	40.9%	30.3%
Friends/neighbors	68.7%	21.5%	25.0%	—
Church	30.3%	20.0%	18.2%	—
Compatriots	3.1%	1.5%	4.5%	—
Neighborhood associations	31.8%	10.8%	—	—
Business acquaintances	—	40.0%	4.5%	—
Merchants	20.0%	—	—	—
Newspapers/TV	36.9%	4.5%	—	—
Unemployment office	—	44.6%	—	—
Schools	39.4%	—	—	—
Council office	3.0%	1.5%	—	—
Bank/credit union	—	—	—	69.7%
Other	3.0%	4.5%	6.8%	—

concentrated in the Pico-Union neighborhood. They were also bonded by strong ties and had evolved around networks of kinship, religion, ethnic origin, and special interest (e.g., merchants, sports groups, neighborhood watch groups, and PTA groups).

The survey showed that a significant number of respondents (69 percent) rely on friends and neighbors for general information and to find out what is happening in the neighborhood (Table 10.2). The church, local merchants, and neighborhood associations also function as information networks for residents, complementing the local press, radio, and TV networks. For job referrals, however, respondents seemed to rely more on weak business ties ("other people at my job") and the unemployment office than they did on kinship and neighborhood-based networks. Respondents looked to neighbors, relatives, and friends for social and emotional support, help settling in the neighborhood, and other day-to-day needs, such as borrowing pieces of furniture and helping with children and transportation. While many respondents would not hesitate to request up to twenty-five dollars as a loan from neighbors and friends,[8] they would not go to them for more significant financial support. Almost one third of respondents stated that they would rely on relatives for a loan to start a business, but a significantly higher number said that they would turn to a financial institution for such a transaction.

Thus, networks in Pico-Union seem to accomplish at least two of the roles identified by Lewis and Juarez (1995); they act as sources of general information and referrals and as providers of instrumental and social support. However, residents have to rely primarily on outside agents (e.g., unemployment office, banks) for issues relating to economic development. In other words, local networks in Pico-Union seem to help people "get by" but not necessarily "get ahead." The importance of ethnicity was not confirmed in the survey, as "compatriots" were not credited with significant contributions for job referrals or social or financial support. This may be erroneous, however, as the category "compatriot" may have overlapped with the categories "relatives" and "friends/neighbors." One's friends and neighbors may well be one's ethnic compatriots as well, but may be more readily identified as "friends" than as co-ethnics. To better understand the importance of ethnicity in social networks, social capital, and economic development we conducted focus group research with representatives from two ethnic groups in Pico-Union, the Oaxacans and the Salvadorans.

Focus Groups. Outsiders might interpret the apparent ethnic homogeneity related to the high numbers of Spanish surnames in Pico-Union as a predictor of a certain level of ease in constructing social networks. And certainly there are commonalities in the immigrant experience, related to the disruption and stress of the immigration process and the adjustment in a new land. Beyond this, however, there is frequently more that divides ethnic groups than there is that unites them. The Oaxacans and the Salvadorans are a case in point. A comparison of the social organization of these two groups, as represented by their cohorts in Pico-Union, might be enough to finally disabuse scholars and citizens of the idea of a monolithic Hispanic ethnicity. The Oaxacans and Salvadorans who participated in this study[9] differed significantly in their purposes for coming to the United States, in their attitudes toward their new country, and in their expectations of those in the receiving country and community. These differing purposes, attitudes, and expectations have led each group to differing strategies and agendas fashioned and supported by their own authority structures, behavioral norms, survival, and social networks. These varied processes have socioeconomic impact not only for the individuals and the ethnic compatriots, but also for the receiving community. In this part of the study we will compare some of the social processes of these two groups, including their approaches to building and using social capital, as they seek to survive and prosper in Pico-Union.

Pico-Union remains the primary destination for new Oaxacan and Salvadoran immigrants to Southern California. For Oaxacans, Pico-Union is the place where they can be assured the welcome and support of an established and organized contingent of pioneers from previous waves of Oaxacan immigrants. The vast majority of immigrant Salvadorans also head for this neighborhood. As one Salvadoran participant in the focus group recounted, even in the most remote villages of El Salvador everyone knows about "el Pico."

The Oaxacan "Underground Railroad"

It was the local Catholic priest who first suggested the inclusion of the Oaxacans in our study: "If you want to see the next big success among an immigrant group, watch the Oaxacans." It turned out, however, that he was not referring to Oaxacans as a whole, but rather those Oaxacans who have migrated to Pico-Union from San Francisco, 1 of over 40 small villages in Oaxaca (further undermining any idea of monolithic ethnicity, each Oaxacan village has its own dialect, set of networks, and authority structures).

The economic advancement plan of the Oaxacans of Pico-Union is comprehensive. A close-knit and mutually supportive group, they have an effective individual and collective strategy for success in their pursuit of the American Dream. Oaxacans focus on creating economic capital, human capital, and bridging capital in their new environment, while also maintaining a strong commitment and connection to their home village of San Francisco. As new immigrants from San Francisco arrive in Pico-Union, those who have preceded them help them acclimatize, find places to stay, and get jobs. Due to the influence and support of the more established compatriots who train newcomers in the use of the tools of their new environment—social mores, business practices, and personal finance and networking skills—the Oaxacan immigrants have a disproportionate level of upward mobility. Many of them own their homes and businesses, and their children are educated, English speaking, and well integrated into the U.S. culture. New Oaxacan immigrants, because of this help from their compatriots, do not have to rely on social services or charity. The reputation of their predecessors as cooperative and hard working helps them find work readily even outside their compatriot networks.

The social networks of Oaxacans in Pico-Union are based on kinship, ethnicity, and religion. They maintain a social structure that revolves around families, and village values and norms. They are united in their commitment to provide help to compatriot newcomers while also supporting and sustaining their home village. The ties in their network represent a classical example of bonding capital. However, at the same time they work hard to build their bridging capital, through the development of a multitude of weak ties with other networks and organizations, both inside and outside the Pico-Union neighborhood. These weaker ties help Oaxacans to better integrate into the American society and gain the maximum benefit from its economic system.

The attitude of this immigrant group is one of general optimism and trust. They are trusting of each other, open to learning and getting to know others, and eager to get ahead economically and socially. The results are quite favorable. The Oaxacans' networks, skills, and attitudes allow them to quickly tap the local job market, expand their networks outside their own group, and take advantage of educational opportunities. However, their success does not cause them to lose sight of their other home; this juncture marks the beginning of an ongoing struggle to maintain their position in both worlds, the one they have entered and the one they have left behind. This is more than what the next group of our study, the Salvadorans, can afford.

The Salvadoran Flight to Sanctuary

Because of their different experiences with democracy, immigrants from countries divided by civil war are frequently faced with distinct challenges and may find it difficult to adjust to a nonrevolutionary context. Salvadorans who have fled the chaos of their homeland exemplify this problem. Like

Cambodian and Vietnamese refugees, their experiences with violence and war have preconditioned many Salvadorans to face new situations with suspicion and mistrust. And when criminals who have preyed upon them in their own country flee along with them—and still use them as prey in the new and strange environment—they find themselves in difficult circumstances indeed.

Hundreds of Salvadoran refugees who were able to reach their destination in Pico-Union, tired and without resources, found sanctuary in the St. Thomas Catholic Church, which attempted to garner resources for emergency aid. But the lives of many of these new immigrants are characterized by fear. Their inability to call on police protection (because of their illegal residency status) leaves them vulnerable to both local criminals and criminals who followed them from El Salvador. For the same reason they can make no complaints to or about negligent landlords, nor can they demand a reasonable wage for their work if they find employment. A self-protective isolationist mentality emerges as a result, evidenced by a lack of trust in each other and of the community. This has led the Salvadorans to format a rather exclusive social network, with few expectations for collaboration with other ethnic groups. Such exclusivity and pessimism becomes self-fulfilling; other Pico-Union residents and ethnic groups are insulted by the Salvadorans' apparent unfriendliness and so do not trust them either.

In situations of extreme vulnerability people tend to rely on the responses that have kept them safest in the past. Immigrants from revolutionary settings may fight or retreat. Neither choice is constructive. Both aggressive behavior toward and withdrawal from their new society make community unavailable to them. These immigrants find themselves in a strange environment where their lack of financial capital is exacerbated by the fact that their cultural capital—their understanding of how society operates and their ability to navigate through it properly—is off base. At the same time, because of their fear-based self-isolation, they also come ill equipped to recreate social capital in their new neighborhood.

Despite the bleak economic and social situation that many Salvadorans find themselves in, a political and religious leadership has emerged among the group. The Asociacion de Salvadorenos de Los Angeles (ASOSAL) has its base and headquarters in Pico-Union. It focuses exclusively on Salvadoran interests and has gained a considerable political base both externally and internally as it gains a platform to speak for an oppressed and growing constituency. The Salvadoran leadership has sought to emulate the Miami Cuban economic enclave suggesting the establishment of a "Little Salvador" in Pico-Union.[10] This could provide economic advantages for the group and help recycle Salvadoran dollars to support Salvadoran businesses. An ethnic enclave officially designated "Little Salvador" could also help create a sense of attachment for the neighborhood among Salvadorans, a major factor in community development. On the negative side, the creation of such an enclave in Pico-Union is likely to generate opposition from other local ethnic groups, who would feel left out of the strongly bonded and politically powerful enclave of another group.

POLICY IMPLICATIONS: BUILDING SOCIAL CAPITAL FOR ECONOMIC DEVELOPMENT

Building social capital for economic development in neighborhoods like Pico-Union, which are characterized by chronic official neglect, transience, and lack of human and financial capital among residents, may be particularly challenging. Still, our empirical research in the neighborhood did not necessarily confirm Robert Putnam's pessimistic assessment that "we are withdrawing from those networks of reciprocity that once constituted our communities" (Putnam 2000:184). Our survey showed that Latinos in Pico-Union engage in multiple informal associations, evolving around the family, the school, the church, or the recreation center. Admittedly, these associations serve more as survival networks that help people "get by" rather than as venues for major economic advancement. Nevertheless, the emotional and practical support provided by these networks—sometimes in the form of baby-sitting or transportation services—can help individuals enter the job market.

If we agree with the premise of many scholars that there is a relationship between social capital and economic development, then policy makers should try to help neighborhoods acquire more social capital. This is predicated on neighborhood stability. It is easier to promote social capital in close-knit neighborhoods than in areas characterized by transience and alienation (Wilson 1997; Temkin and Rohe 1998). Policy makers and lending institutions can contribute to neighborhood stability in minority and immigrant communities by identifying ways to ensure them an affordable housing supply and access to low-interest loans and mortgage credit. As Lang and Hornburg (1998:5) argue, "decent and affordable housing forms the core of connectedness: a secure home gives people roots and stabilizes communities." Additionally, social capital is formed easier when residents share feelings of attachment to their neighborhoods and a sense of pride about them. Such feelings are nonexistent in derelict and unsafe places where gangs are menacing the streets, and fear of crime permeates people's lives. In Pico-Union residents identified the existence of gangs and drug rings as having an extremely negative impact on their efforts to build community. As Temkin and Rohe (1998) argue, helping residents acquire neighborhood pride and a strong sense of place are not "soft variables to be neglected by policy makers." They recommend incorporating concerns for social capital into urban revitalization efforts.

The challenge is to link the strong social networks that frequently exist in ethnic communities to the larger matrix of networks and opportunities present in the outside world. In the case of Pico-Union we saw that the networks were strong among co-ethnics but often remained isolated from other entities and groups inside and outside the neighborhood. The role of local groups and coalitions, community-based organizations, and community development corporations is crucial in building these bridges between the neighborhood, its different constituent groups, the local government, the private sector, and philanthropic foundations. The successes of the Figueroa

Corridor Coalition for Economic Justice, detailed in Chapter 11, provide a good example of a local group that was able to successfully build bridges and negotiate with public agencies and the private sector.

Our focus group analysis showed that some ethnic groups are quite eager in their pursuit of alliances and coalitions, while others follow a more isolationist strategy. The Oaxacans in this study have followed much the same model of group socioeconomic development as the Greeks, Swedes, Lithuanians, and others before them in Pico-Union. The Oaxacans focus on training and supporting individuals and families of compatriots in getting ahead, making it "up and out" of the neighborhood, and having the ability and opportunity to participate fully in their new country's educational, social, and economic mainstream. They keep their linkages in the Los Angeles area through the maintenance of their Zapateco language and through reference to and support of their common home—the village of San Francisco in Oaxaca. At the same time, they are cultivating networks with associations and groups outside their ethnic cohort, thus expanding their economic opportunities.

The strategy of Salvadorans is quite different, as it evolves primarily around the formation of strong and very homogeneous social networks. Salvadorans in Pico-Union have tried to create a concentrated spatial and political ethnic enclave with its own internal power system (around a handful of political leaders), its own economic systems through exclusive merchandising (buying from and selling to co-ethnics), the creation of a Salvadoran financial institution (credit union El Rescate),[11] and the development of its own social service organization (ASOSAL) to advocate for the legalization of Salvadoran immigrants and the advancement of Salvadoran culture and interests. The Salvadorans appear to be one immigrant "pot" that has no intention of melting.

The case of Salvadorans highlights an underlying tension between community development, which encompasses the well-being of a spatially situated community composed of different groups, and localism, which focuses on the economic development of one particular group. Efforts for the latter may balkanize the former. For this reason the development of horizontal linkages among different neighborhood groups that foster intragroup collaboration around common goals and interests is very important. These can be in the form of merchant associations; Parent-Teacher Associations; local athletic teams; cultural, historic, music, or choral societies; and any other form of association that has a larger neighborhood appeal, can attract members from different groups towards a common goal, and thus counteract the tendency for isolationism.

For policy makers and urban planners, the call to support social capital formation among ethnic communities in order to improve their chances for economic development becomes quite challenging in "multiple melting pot" neighborhoods like Pico-Union. Policy responses for economic development strategies might differ significantly from one ethnic group to another. What would be of most help to the Oaxacans and their economic development might not fit the type of help wanted by the Salvadorans. In both cases, the strategies and the potential long-term consequences for the specific groups, other groups, the neighborhood, the broader area, and even the nation must be considered. Understanding how social networks and social capital operates can help policy makers evaluate the diversity and hierarchy of needs among different neighborhood groups (Saegert and Winkel 1998).

The challenge then becomes to strive for a model of economic development tailored to the specificities of one ethnic (or social) group in the neighborhood, which however, does not detract from the economic potential of another co-habitant group. This cannot happen if we balkanize neighborhoods and cities into small and disconnected patchworks of hostile enclaves. It can, however, begin to occur if we help build horizontal linkages among ethnic groups in the neighborhood and vertical linkages between ethnic groups and the larger American society.

NOTES

The authors wish to thank the UCLA Institute of American Cultures for partly funding this study, as well as Steve Moga and Michela Zonta, who provided research assistance. We also would like to thank the merchants, neighborhood watch groups, and Parent Teacher Associations in the Pico-Union neighborhood, as well as youth from Clean and Green and parishioners of St. Thomas Catholic Church who participated in our study.

1. Originally, the neighborhood was called Pico Heights and started as a fashionable suburb of Los Angeles at the turn of the twentieth century. But soon the wealthy families moved out to new, more fashionable districts and outlying suburbs. The name Pico-Union was given to the neighborhood in the mid-1960s by a group of seven community activists because Pico Boulevard and Union Street were two major cross streets at the heart of the area. This name stuck as local nonprofits and social service organizations started using it, and it was later picked up by the city and was "officiated" with signs.

2. St. Thomas Catholic Church is the major parish in the area attended by the vast majority of Latino residents and merchants.

3. These included the two local neighborhood watch groups, *Pico Pride* and *Pueblo Nuevo*.

4. These included an adult soccer and an adult softball team practicing at the local Normandie Recreation Center.

5. These included three neighborhood schools: Magnolia Elementary School, Berendo Middle School, and St. Thomas Catholic School.

6. The local service group Clean and Green offers part-time employment to neighborhood youth, involving them in a variety of tasks such as cleaning sidewalks, planting trees, and so on.

7. The overrepresentation of women in these social networks is explained by other studies that find women to be more actively involved in local social networks than men. Women play a larger role than men in PTAs, neighborhood watch, and church-related groups (Hutchinson 1999). Nevertheless, studies indicate that women's networks tend to be more local and truncated than men's, which diminishes their capacity to gain access to resources (Fernandez-Kelly 1995).

8. A significantly higher number of people were willing to lend twenty-five dollars to their neighbors than to request the same amount from them.

9. There is much variability within the Oaxacan community. Web information from Fresno would suggest that the Oaxacan leadership in that area may have a significantly more political agenda than the Oaxacans in this study.

10. Even Salvadoran church leaders were proponents of the Salvadoran enclave proposition. In interviews with Salvadoran pastors of two different congregations in Pico-Union (Methodist and Seventh Day Adventist), both pastors indicated that the name for the area should be "Little Salvador."

11. El Rescate Credit Union is located in the Pico-Union area at 1340 South Bonnie Brae. According to their website information, the organization, founded in 1981, was "the first agency in the United States to respond with free legal aid and social services to the mass influx of refugees fleeing the war in El Salvador. Institutions founded by El Rescate include Clinica Monsenor Romero, providing free medical care to the refugee community (1983) and El Refugio (1987), which served as a transitional housing shelter for newly-arrived refugees. The organization was also active in registering over 60,000 individuals in the first 6 months of its Temporary Protected Status Campaign in 1991 to secure political refugee status for Salvadorans."

REFERENCES

Banerjee, T., and W. Baer. 1984. *Beyond the Neighborhood Unit: Residential Environments and Public Policy*. New York: Plenum Press.

Boxman, E., P. De Graaf, and D. Hendrik. 1991. The impact of social and human capital on the income attainment of Dutch managers. *Social Networks* 13:51–73.

Braddock, J. H., and J. M. McPortland. 1987. How minorities continue to be excluded from equal employment opportunities: Research on labor market and institutional barriers. *Journal of Social Issues* 43:5–39.

Briggs de Souza, X. 1998. Brown kids in white suburbs: Housing mobility and the many faces of social capital. *Housing Policy Debate* 9(1):177–221.

Chavez, L. 1988. Settlers and sojourners: The case of Mexicans in the United States. *Human Organization* 47(2):95–108.

Chavis, D., and A. Wandersman. 1990. Sense of community in the urban environment: A catalyst for participation and community development. *American Journal of Community Psychology* 18(1):55–67.

Coleman, J. 1988. Social capital in the creation of human capital. *American Journal of Sociology* 94(Supplement):S95–S120.

Cooper, T. 1980. Bureaucracy and community organization: The metamorphosis of a relationship. *Administration and Society* 11(4):411–444.

Durkheim, E. 1911 [1893]. *The Division of Labor in Society,* trans. G. Simpson (4th edition). New York: The Free Press.

Fischer, C. 1977. *Networks and Places: Social Relations in the Urban Setting*. New York: Free Press.

Fernandez-Kelly, P. 1995. Towards triumph: Social and cultural capital in the urban ghetto. In *The Economic Sociology of Immigration*, ed. A. Portes, 213–247. New York: Russel Sage.

Frey, W., and R. DeVol. 2000. America's demography in the new century: Aging baby boomers and new immigrants as major players. Policy Brief No. 9. Santa Monica, CA: Milken Institute.

Gittell, R., and A. Vidal. 1998. *Community Organizing: Building Social Capital as a Development Strategy*. Thousand Oaks, CA: Sage Publications.

Gomez, R. 1987. Hispanic Americans: Ethnic shared values and traditional treatments. *Hispanic Journal of Behavioral Sciences* 7:215–219.

Granovetter, M. 1973. The strength of weak ties. *American Journal of Sociology* 78:1360–1380.

Hutchinson, J. 1999. Propinquity without community: A study of social capital, survival networks and community building in the Pico Union neighborhood of Los Angeles. Ph.D dissertation. Los Angeles: UCLA Department of Urban Planning.

Hutchinson, J., and A. Loukaitou-Sideris. 2001. Choosing confrontation or consensus in the inner city: Lessons from a community-university partnership. *Planning Theory and Practice* 2(3):293–310.

Johnson, J. H., Jr., E. J. Bienenstock, W. C. Farell Jr., and J. L. Glanville. 1993. Bridging social networks and female labor force participation in a multiethnic metropolis. In *Latinos in a Changing U.S. Economy,* ed. R. Morales and F. Bonilla. Beverly Hills, CA: Sage Publications.

Kasarda, J., and M. Janowitz. 1974. Community attachment in mass society. *American Sociological Review* 39(3):328–339.

Kayden, X. 1996. *The Mexican American Community in Los Angeles.* Unpublished report. Los Angeles: UCLA School of Public Policy and Social Research.

Lang, R., and S. Hornburg. 1998. What is social capital and why is it important for public policy? *Housing Policy Debate* 9(1):1–16.

Lavrakas, P. J. 1981. *Factors Related to Citizen Involvement in Personal, Household, and Neighborhood Anti-Crime Measures: An Executive Summary.* Washington, DC: U.S. Department of Justice, National Institute of Justice.

Lewis, E. A., and Z. E. Juarez. 1995. Natural helping networks. In *Encyclopedia of Social Work,* 19th edition. Silver Spring, MD: National Association of Social Workers, pp. 1765–1772.

Light, I., P. Bhachu, and S. Karagcorgis. 1993. Migration networks and immigrant entrepreneurship. In *Immigration and Entrepreneurship: Culture, Capital, and Ethnic Networks,* ed. I. Light and P. Bhachu, 25–49. New Brunswick, NJ: Transaction Publishers.

Light, I., and S. Karageorghis. 1994. The ethnic economy. In *The Handbook of Economic Sociology,* ed. N. J. Smelser and R. Swedberd, 647–671. Princeton, NJ: Princeton University Press.

Light, I. 2001. Immigrant neighborhoods as centers of commerce. Unpublished paper presented at Palmer House Hotel, Chicago, under the auspices of the Illinois Immigration Policy Project, October 18, 2001.

Lin, N. 1982. Social resources and instrumental action. In *Social Structure and Network Analysis,* ed. P. Marsden and N. Lin, 131–145. Beverly Hills, CA: Sage Publications.

Low, S. 2003. *Behind the Gates: Life, Security and the Pursuit of Happiness in Fortress America.* New York: Routledge.

Massey, D. 1986. The settlement process among Mexican migrants to the United States. *American Sociological Review* 51(5):670–684.

Pastor, M. 1993. *Latinos and the Los Angeles Uprising: The Economic Context.* Claremont, CA: Thomas Rivera Center.

Patterson, S., and F. F. Marsiglia. 2000. Mi casa es su casa: Beginning exploration of Mexican Americans' natural helping. *Families in Society: The Journal of Contemporary Human Services* 81(1):22–31.

Putnam, R. 1998. Social capital: Its importance to housing and community development. Foreword. *Housing Policy Debate* 9(1):v–viii.

————. 2000. *Bowling Alone: The Collapse and Revival of American Community*. New York: Simon & Schuster.

Saegert, S., and G. Winkel. 1998. "Social capital and the revitalization of New York City's distressed inner city housing," *Housing Policy Debate*, 9(1):17–60.

Skery, P. 1993. *Mexican Americans: The Ambivalent Minority*. New York: Free Press.

Suttles, G. 1968. *The Social Order of the Slum: Ethnicity and Territory in the Inner City*. Chicago: University of Chicago Press.

Temkin, K., and W. Rohe. 1998. Social capital and neighborhood stability: An empirical investigation. *Housing Policy Debate* 9(1):61–88.

Tönnies, F. 1877. *Gemeinschaft und Gesellschaft* (tr. *Community and Civil Society*, ed. J. Harris; 2001). Cambridge and New York: Cambridge University Press.

Waldinger, R., and J. Lee. 2001. New immigrants in urban America. In *Strangers at the Gates*, ed. R. Waldinger, 30–79. Berkeley: University of California Press.

Webber, M. 1964. The urban place and the non-place urban realm. In *Explorations into the Urban Structure*, ed. M. Webber, J. Dyckman, D. Foley, A. Guttenberg, W. Wheaton, and K. Bauer Wurster, 79–153. Philadelphia: University of Pennsylvania.

Wellman, B., and S. P. Berkowitz (Eds.) 1988. *Social Structures: A Network Approach*. Cambridge: Cambridge University Press.

Wellman, B., P. Carrington, and A. Hall. 1988. Networks as personal communities. In *Social Structures: A Network Approach*, pp. 130–184. Cambridge: Cambridge University Press.

Willmott, P. 1986. *Social Networks, Informal Care, and Public Policy*. London: Policy Studies Institute.

Wilson, P. A. 1997. Building social capital: A learning agenda for the 21st century. *Urban Studies* 34(5–6):745–760.

Wirth, L. 1938. Urbanism as a way of life. *American Journal of Sociology* 44(1): 3–24.

U.S. Bureau of the Census. 2000. Decennial Census: 2000 Summary Tape Files 1A and 3A. Washington, DC: U.S. Bureau of the Census.

Zhou, M. 1992. *Chinatown: The Socioeconomic Potential of an Urban Enclave*. Philadelphia: Temple University Press.

Zhou, M., and C. Bankston III. 1994. Social capital and the adaptation of the second generation: The case of Vietnamese youth in New Orleans. *International Migration Review* 28(4):821–845.

11 Linking Housing to Community Economic Development with Community Benefits Agreements

The Case of The Figueroa Corridor Coalition for Economic Justice

JACQUELINE LEAVITT

THE HIGH COST of housing has become a permanent financial hardship for people who earn low wages. The other chapters in this book rightfully stress the importance of increasing employment opportunities and improving human capital to increase earned income. Unfortunately, the gains are often marginal, and the small economic advancements can be eroded by escalating housing cost. Unless they receive subsidies, poor and working poor are paying 30 to more than 50 percent of their income on rent. They are primarily people of color, women, single parents, and immigrants who fill the increasing need for low-wage labor in restaurants and retail stores, as garment workers, janitors and day laborers. Many earn below the national minimum wage of $5.15 nationwide and fall below the federal poverty level, which is $18,884 for a family of four. Since 1994, activists' struggle to raise the minimum wage has also led to a higher visibility of the housing crisis. A full-time minimum-wage job does not pay for housing in any state in the United States.

For a few who happen to reside in the right jurisdiction and work for local government or their contractors, living wage ordinances improve the minimum to an average of about $9.00 (Fairris and Reich 2005).[1] Despite this higher wage, the living wage can still be two to three times below the housing wage that "a household must earn in order to afford a rental unit of a range of sizes at the area's Fair Market Rent (FMR), based on the generally accepted affordability standard of paying no more than 30 percent of income for housing costs" (NLIHC 2003).[2]

Fewer Section 8 housing subsidies are available to low-income families, elderly, and disabled persons. Section 8 vouchers allow recipients to rent from any property owner participating in the program at a rate consistent with the U.S. Department of Housing and Urban Development's (HUD) affordability guidelines. Tenants using Section 8 paid 30 percent of their income for housing in 2004, but in 2005 the program raised this to 40 percent.

The situation becomes even grimmer when an economically disadvantaged community faces developers with deep pockets who can acquire property, bulldoze affordable housing stock, and implement big plans. More tenants will compete for fewer units. Across the nation, grassroots "Davids" are using community benefits agreements (CBAs) in order to negotiate with the developer "Goliaths" and gain a community voice at the negotiating table. In return for community support, developers are signing CBAs that include a variety of provisions such as affordable housing, living wage jobs, card check neutrality permitting organizing in new developments (e.g., at hotels, airports, and sports and entertainment districts), local hiring or first-source hiring programs, on-site job training, parks, child care, youth centers, parking, environmental mitigation, neighborhood improvement funds, and revolving loan funds. The Figueroa Corridor Coalition for Economic Justice (FCCEJ)—which includes unions, religious groups, community-based organizations, citywide organizations, environmentalists, students, health groups, block groups, and worker centers—negotiated the 2001 "Staples Agreement" with the developers of a large sports arena in the City of Los Angeles.[3] This CBA is considered to be the first full-fledged comprehensive agreement (LAX Coalition for Economic, Environmental, and Educational Justice n.d.) and is an excellent example of combining housing and economic development.[4]

Impressive as it is, the CBA is only one tool in an overall FCCEJ strategy that combines changing policies, negotiating agreements, and developing alternative institutions. The FCCEJ vision includes planning inclusively, over time, and with a long-term commitment to the neighborhood. By using a variety of popular education tools, the coalition aims for full disclosure of information and to build leadership capacity among people in the community.[5] The result is that people who would otherwise have become victims of an unchallenged makeover of the community are more likely to remain in the neighborhood. Second, community involvement is more likely to be ongoing when residents feel empowered and able to question other development decisions affecting them.

This chapter evaluates the FCCEJ's use of the CBA as part of a comprehensive strategy, using multiple research methods and drawing from historical information, census data, and other public documents. Background information includes material from community development corporations, government agencies, and citywide and local technical assistance organizations. A review of the secondary literature cast a wide net and drew from histories of Los Angeles, labor studies, community development, and community organizing (e.g., Alinsky 1946; Chambers and Cowan 2003; Ferguson and Dickens 1999; Keil 1998; Pastor Jr., Dreier, Grigsby, and Lopez-Garza 2000; Gittel and Vidal 1998; Shaw 2001; and Stoecker 2003). The 2004 UCLA Community Scholars class produced a report that provided background information (Aparicio et al. 2004).[6] The nonprofit Strategic Actions for a Just Economy (SAJE), the convener and home to the FCCEJ, provided research reports and staff offered insight from their organizing activities over the course of several years. In-depth interviews were held with SAJE founder and Executive Director Gilda Haas.

I begin by describing the urgent reasons for linking housing to economic development in situations where poor tenants are concentrated. The second section of this chapter briefly summarizes ways in which grassroots groups have typically entered the housing and economic development field. In Los Angeles, nonprofit community development corporations (CDCs) stepped in to fill the vacuum left when the public sector reduced funding and withdrew from subsidizing housing and the private sector walked away from many poor communities. The third section reviews the history of organizing that led to the formation of the FCCEJ coalition. The fourth section defines the CBA and reviews its components. Finally, I present the Staples Agreement and analyze the reasons why it is important that the CBA be only one tool among many.

THE HOUSING-WAGE GAP: LINKING HOUSING AND COMMUNITY ECONOMIC DEVELOPMENT

Housing prices are increasing at a faster rate than income creating a phenomenon known as the housing wage gap. This gap continues to widen, leaving tenants competing for a limited supply of decent, safe, and affordable housing. As noted in the beginning of this chapter, the housing wage is a formula that highlights the relationship between the number of hours worked in relation to the cost of housing and the ability to pay the Fair Market Rent (FMR). In 2005, California is the second-least affordable state, following Hawaii (National Low Income Housing Coalition [NLIHC] 2005). In 2005, California's housing wage was $22.69. The state minimum wage at $6.75 per hour ($14,000 annualized wage) for full-time and year-round work is insufficient to meet the Los Angeles County FMR of $1,189. Even with lower housing wages, workers need to put in at least 130 hours per week, more than triple the 40-hour week, in order to afford rent (Southern California Studies Center 2001:20). At the state minimum wage of $6.75 an hour, a low-wage worker can afford a monthly rent of no more than $351; a worker earning 30 percent of the area median income of $19,327 can only afford a monthly rent of $483.

Building janitors, production workers in poultry processing, and cashiers at independent Latino supermarkets all earn the minimum wage. Construction day laborers bring in $9.00 an hour. Homecare workers earn a high of $8.50 as a result of union bargaining with the County of Los Angeles. Many others earn far less and face difficulties when employers withhold wages as with day laborers (see Chapter 6 in this book). Between 1992 and 2002 the total increase in service jobs was almost 2.5 million jobs, with an average annual wage in 2001 of $38,507. In comparison, over the same period the 1,069,500 jobs in the declining private sector had an average annual wage of $50,520. The average payroll for jobs in retail such as cashiering in clothing stores, sporting goods stores, and gasoline stations is below $18,500 and for jobs waiting tables in restaurants and drinking establishments, $15,116. The economic trends reveal that a growing population will be unable to afford housing at market prices on the wages that they bring home.

Simultaneously, a shortage of affordable housing exists. This exacerbates the situation for people who face forced evictions in gentrifying areas or where landlords have opted out of Section 8 housing. California experienced a loss of 24,000 housing units between 1995 and 2002. In the 1990s, an annual average need for over 200,000 new units was projected in California; just half were built, and of those, only 24 percent were for multifamily construction, down from 45 percent in the 1980s (State of California Department of Housing and Community Development 1999). The production deficit in Los Angeles is almost 8,000 units annually (Myerhoff 2004; L.A. Housing Crisis Task Force 2000, 16). In Los Angeles, one new house is built for every five jobs; in the state of California as a whole, one house is built for every 3.5 jobs (No end in sight to California's housing troubles 2003).

It becomes clear that in the private market and in the absence of government subsidies, acquiring decent housing is strongly linked to the amount of money a person earns. Attacking the problem of housing affordability must be accompanied by economic development.

After the 1960s, CDCs stepped into the breach when government policies stopped setting a targeted goal of low-income units and constructing public housing units. Such policies had never been popular to begin with and were beset with financial problems. But CDCs are limited in their funding and face an uphill battle; they have to prove themselves to financial institutions before each new project. In response to the need for neighborhood commercial facilities and jobs, some CDCs became involved in economic and workforce development.

COMMUNITY-DRIVEN INTERVENTIONS IN THE CITY OF LOS ANGELES

The CDC efforts are important to neighborhoods as much for being symbols of hope as for the delivery of housing and jobs. Compared to east coast cities, Los Angeles was slow to embrace the concept of CDCs, whose history is tied to a variety of bottom-up responses beginning with the response to the 1965 Watts Rebellion,[7] and to deteriorating conditions after a decade of urban renewal and redevelopment projects. After the rebellion, three CDCs were formed, one in Watts, a second in another section of South Los Angeles, and the third in East Los Angeles. Over the next four decades, the numbers of CDCs in L.A. grew. By 1996, the Southern California Association for Non-Profit Housing (SCANPH), a coalition of community development corporations, calculated that about 500 community corporations existed in the Southern California 6-county area (SCANPH 2004). The growth in CDCs was occurring up to and continued after 1992 when riots erupted, spurred by the not guilty verdict in the trial of policemen whose brutal actions toward Rodney King were captured on videotape (Leavitt 1996). The 1992 riot spread through the region, creating property damage that reached over a billion dollars, 55 people died, and 2,500 were injured. Ninety-four percent of the damaged buildings within city limits were concentrated on commercial streets and retail stores in Southeast Los Angeles.

Soon after the riot, the Coalition of Neigborhood Developers (CND), a group of non-profit organizations, many of which were located in the riot areas, formed. They had received training through the office of the Local Initiatives Support Corporation (LISC) LA is a Ford Foundation-sponsored financial intermediary for nonprofits. As part of its mandate, LISC builds organizational capacity and leadership through seminars that also provide opportunities for CDCs to come together (Gittel and Vidal 1998). Under the leadership of Denise Fairchild, a noted community development expert who was heading the LISC LA office at the time, a group of CDCs that had received training from LISC LA formed the Coalition of Neighborhood Developers (CND) soon after the 1992 riot. One objective was that the CDCs would lead a neighborhood planning process and a second was to attract local investment. The CND divided itself into 10 neighborhood clusters: Watts, Vernon/Central, Crenshaw, Broadway/Manchester, West Adams/Hoover, Pico Union, City Terrace/Lincoln Heights, Mid-City/Koreatown, Boyle Heights, and Vermont/Slauson. Each cluster member received funds to identify the needs of that area and plan for the area's future. Families in most of the ten clusters "were earning $20,000 to $35,000 a year although in enclaves of South L.A.—Watts, Vernon Central, and Adams-Maple—earnings were $20,000 or less" (Coalition of Neighborhood Developers 1994:17).

At the national level, and in the wake of the Los Angeles riots, the U.S. Congress had enacted an empowerment zone policy that would provide incentives for development and requested proposals (Leavitt 1996). Members of the CND participated in writing the city's proposal for an empowerment zone and advocated for their community's needs. This effort faltered when the city's proposal was turned down. Over time, the CND fell apart, but the CDCs have remained actively engaged in housing and other activities.

Notable examples of community development corporations that have successfully pursued economic development exist in Los Angeles. One main objective of the coalition was to identify investment funding needed for economic development projects. For example, in 2001 the Esperanza Community Housing Corporation (ECHC) later completed the rehabilitation of a building, Mercado de Paloma, including restaurants and cultural shops, as well as office space for nonprofit organizations. Concerned Citizens of South Central Los Angeles, in partnership with Regency Centers, developed plans for the Slauson Central shopping center with the Community Redevelopment Agency; in 2003, the city council approved the plan, considered to be the first in the community in over 20 years. In 1998, the Vermont Slauson Economic Development Corporation helped keep the city's promise to build one of the first new supermarkets in South Los Angeles since the 1992 civil unrest.

The Southern California Association for Non-Profit Housing has spearheaded broad coalitions including a community labor alliance for a city Housing Trust Fund. In 2000, the Los Angeles Housing Department committed seed funding for a $5 million budget, and the following year the budget increased to $10.5 million. In 2003, the city council approved general guidelines for allocating funds. In March of that year, the city "approved awarding Trust Fund dollars to thirteen affordable housing development projects seeking to leverage Proposition 46 state housing bond funds" (City of Los Angeles Housing Department).[8]

The CDCs continue to package proposals and seek funding from government and foundations. They remain significant actors in stabilizing neighborhoods, providing housing, offering jobs within their organizations, and job training. They frequently include other types of services from case management to child care to arts programming. Single CDCs, however, are vulnerable in fights over major development projects; alone they are less likely to have necessary resources, staff, capacity, and support from a mass base. The next section will discuss an alternative and more effective model of community action that is based on broad coalition building and negotiation.

History of the Figueroa Corridor Coalition for Economic Justice

The FCCEJ covers a 40-block area between the University of Southern California (USC) and the Staples Center, from Martin Luther King Boulevard on the south to 8th Street on the north, and from Western Avenue on the west to Alameda on the east. Figueroa Avenue is a major north-south artery and in this area includes institutions such as USC, a cluster of museums, and the Coliseum. Single room occupancies are concentrated in the part of the area known as Skid Row and sweatshops are cheek to jowl with the fashion and toy districts. Older residential neighborhoods are interspersed, some of which have experienced urban redevelopment and others of which were deteriorating and whose buildings were under-maintained.

The FCCEJ model is an example of what Appadurai calls "deep democracy" (2002). This term is used to describe partnerships "between traditionally opposed groups, such as states, corporations and workers" (2002:1). The FCCEJ strategy is multifaceted. Power usually lies with those who control land, money, and investment. In the case of FCCEJ, what might have been a standoff between community groups and the powerful Anschutz Entertainment Group, formerly the LA Arena Company, the developer-owner of the Staples Center, evolved into constructive negotiations and a CBA (Haas 2002).[9] The result has been to lessen one-sided, top-down development.

The history of the FCCEJ lies in an earlier community group known as the Committee for a Responsible USC. That group fought two main battles, one about the rights of 350 food service workers who were working at the University of Southern California without a contract, and the other about university expansion and displacement of existing residents.[10] In 1998, the Committee for a Responsible USC changed its name to FCCEJ. The winning of the contract for the USC workers laid the foundation for building a permanent community-labor organization—one that would serve worker and community needs over the long term.[11] The resulting strategy also acknowledged the fact that thousands of low-income workers and union members—food and service workers, home care workers, and janitors—lived in the neighborhood and shared the broader community's concerns, such as affordable housing, park space, and parking (Haas 2002:91).

The Figeroa Corridor community was increasingly anxious about the proposed sports and entertainment district. The community had experienced displacement when the Staples Center was constructed in a record 18 months and opened in 1999.[12] With the announcement that the Staples Center was an anchor for a new and larger development—a sports and entertainment district known as Staples Center Phase II—questions about what this meant and fear of displacement spread from household to household.

The LA Arena Company planned to build two hotels, one a convention hotel with 1,200 rooms that would also include 100 condominiums, and a smaller building with 300 rooms. Also in the plan for Staples Center Phase II were over 1.1 million gross square feet for retail, entertainment, office, and residential uses, which included medical offices, a sports medicine center, a health/sports club, an open-air plaza, a 7,400 seat theater, and 5,305 parking spaces.[13] SAJE convened a series of community meetings at the First United Methodist Church, and the planning process began. The FCCEJ evolved into an umbrella organization for other organizations. Strategic Action for a Just Economy (SAJE) became a membership organization with tenant committees. Gilda Haas, a well-respected activist with substantial practical experience in and out of the Los Angeles City Hall, had founded and become the executive director of SAJE in 1996. The mission of the organization was to provide resources for the working poor through a threefold policy of combining community organizing, coalition building, and grassroots policy. SAJE was already successful in creating the nation's first welfare-to-work bank account and, in collaboration with Esperanza Housing Development Corporation and St. John's Well Child and Family Center, has reduced blood lead levels in thousands of neighborhood children; generated repairs by landlords that remove exposure to lead, mold, mildew and other health hazards; and participated in generating new policy, such as California Senate Bill 460, which incorporates lead safety into local municipal building inspection programs. (SAJE 2002)

Haas had been through numerous other campaigns and was knowledgeable about the destruction that large-scale development leaves in its wake. Problems that the community faced in housing, jobs, health, and so on would escalate. She wrote that the development would further encroach on community businesses and residents "with virtually no consideration for the 200,000 working-class people who live[d] in the surrounding neighborhoods" (2002:92). Gentrification would mean that landlords would sell buildings at dramatically increased prices. Evictions would become the landlords' tool of choice to raise rents or convert single-room occupancy hotels (SROs) in nearby Skid Row into upscale housing.

Haas has emphasized that without the consolidated community and labor organization, residents would have been left with few options for either jobs or housing. She attributes the success of the coalition to its broad base of groups which were able to function with mutual reciprocity:

> When labor negotiations went sour, the coalition took up the issue so the developer would understand that workers' concerns were also community concerns. And, when the coalition's negotiations on affordable housing hit a brick wall, the unions took up that issue, letting the company know that

affordable housing was an important issue for union members as well. (Haas 2002:94)

If the early meetings were "venting sessions," as one reporter noted (Romney 2001), consider that the community was also recovering from the Democratic National Convention, held at Staples Center in August 2000. The combination of problems that residents had to deal with during the Convention included tear gas, rubber bullets, and police often preventing them from getting into their apartments. These incidents were accompanied by the neighborhood residents' experiences at the end of arena games when police left the neighborhood to sports fans leaving the Staples Center, who would create mayhem, stealing cars and smashing windows. The FCCEJ also had cause to be angry when an invited representative from the developer's office failed to show up for a meeting. In the aftermath, a senior vice president of Staples Center was assigned to work with the FCCEJ. Corporations do not like negative publicity. SAJE's mission to change public and private policy through a positive working relationship with the corporate sector required all parties at the negotiating table.

By March 2001, when formal negotiations occurred, the FCCEJ had crafted a number of demands. The practice of SAJE and other members of the coalition is building leadership capacity and through organizing, identifying key people. For example, Enrique Velazquez, an SAJE staff member, identified tenant leaders while organizing the neighborhood around the Staples Center's first move to the area. Neighborhood leaders were essential and played a role in negotiating the CBA, not used as token community representatives. These leaders were at the front lines in bringing up-to-date information back to residents in the buildings. Other coalition organizations brought different strengths to the table. The environmental defense attorney Jerilyn Lopez Mendoza, for example, "helped the group craft a 42-page comment to the developers' draft environmental impact report" (Romney 2001). The Los Angeles Alliance for a New Economy (LAANE) had spearheaded the living wage campaign in Los Angeles and had solid experience in negotiating accountable development (interchangeably used with CBA) in Hollywood, while Action for Grassroots Empowerment and Neighborhood Development Alternatives (AGENDA) brought similar credibility from its success in negotiating with Dreamworks Studios for jobs and training in the movie industry. At the same time, five unions[14] negotiated contracts with the developers, a move that could have split the coalition had the FCCEJ chosen a strategy that opposed the development.

The CBA is an important tool in negotiations with developers who have deep pockets and the ability to expedite their plans very quickly. The FCCEJ tried to cover every imaginable possibility to protect residents;[15] the agreement became attached to the city's agreement with the developers and afforded another layer of protection. At each development stage, the developers and the city are obligated to meet with the FCCEJ. Victor Narro, a lawyer who was at the time representing the Coalition for Humane

Immigrant Rights, noted, "If they don't comply with even one portion of the agreement, then the whole thing is void" (Romney 2001).

Each CBA is tailored to specificities of the local setting and political and economic context but they all share common characteristics. The next section discusses these.

WHAT IS A COMMUNITY BENEFITS AGREEMENT?

CBAS are legally enforceable contracts that result from a negotiation process whereby a developer will provide certain benefits in return for a community group's promise to support the project. This differs from a development agreement that is negotiated between the city or county and the developer. A CBA may be useful to a developer that has been subjected to negative press and, as was the case with the FCCEJ, a coalition building instrument when tactics among allies might conflict.[16] Advocates for accountable development who have been promoting CBAS nationwide are also trying other mechanisms. As of 2004, "at least 43 states, 41 cities, and five counties apply some sort of job-quality—wage, healthcare, or full-time employment—standards to subsidized economic development. Every type of subsidy, including tax credits, training programs, industrial revenue bonds, loan programs, enterprise zones, and tax increment financing, is affected by these standards" (Goodno 2004:9).

Greg LeRoy, director of Good Jobs First, based in Washington, DC, explains why the comprehensive CBAS have resonated around the country among disenfranchised communities: "They are best-practice models for any group seeking to make development dollars really pay off for workers, communities and taxpayers" (Good Jobs First 2002). Madeline Janis-Aparicio, executive director of the Los Angeles Alliance for a New Economy, explains that CBAS provide "the ability to make sure developers really follow through on their promises" (Good Jobs First 2002).

LAANE, the Center for Policy Initiatives, the East Bay Alliance for a Sustainable Economy, and the San Diego–based Working Partnerships are part of the California Public Subsidies Project and offer help on negotiation strategies for CBAS in an effort to "standardize the process of evaluating real estate development" (Gross, LeRoy, and Janis-Aparicio 2002). Julian Gross, a civil rights attorney that LAANE hired to work on the Staples CBA, and his colleagues Greg LeRoy and Madeline Janis-Aparicio give five reasons that CBAS are important: inclusiveness of community residents and businesses, enforceability, transparency that increases the ability of the community to monitor agreements and evaluate other developers, coalition building, and efficiency in a public process that otherwise has outcomes that can delay or reject development and not address either developers' or communities' concerns.

Table 11.1 summarizes the choices that community residents face in developing a CBA. The options include quality jobs, community services, first source/local hiring and job training, environmental improvements, affordable housing, and community involvement (Center on Policy Initiatives 2004). Each benefit category is a response to different goals and links to a

Table 11.1. Category of community benefit, goal, and selected methods

Benefit	Goal	Method
Jobs	Create quality jobs	Government body passes a living wage ordinance Developer provides seed money for locally owned operators and worker retention Criteria for hiring and staffing responsible contractor is developed
Community services	Childcare Filling gaps in neighborhood services Community/youth centersHealth clinics Neighborhood improvement fund	Developer provides space, free rent, seed money
First source/local hiring and job training	Link job opportunities to people in community	Employers agree to hire from a specified source (e.g., a community group) Employers agree to hire from certain zip codes surrounding development Developer agrees to provide seed money and space
Environmental improvements	Protect from environmental dangers and enhance improvements for a healthy community	Developer invests in parks, construction and traffic management, and mitigation of negative environmental impacts, and agrees to use green building practices
Affordable housing	Provide quality housing for those in need	Developer invests in affordable units through low- or no-interest housing loans, inclusionary zoning, linkage fee, land to build housing, responsible landlord policy, contribution to relocation benefits, establishing a revolving loan fund to nonprofit community development corporations
Community involvement	Involve communities affected by development process	Community input in all stages of development process

Source: Adapted from Center on Policy Initiatives, 2004. www.onlinecpi.org/campaigns_responsible_benefits.html, accessed on February 26, 2005.

variety of implementation methods. The Figueroa Corridor's CBA is important because it covers all the categories, its community involvement is deep, and it has an overall vision and strategy that avoids ad hoc and possibly conflicting decisions over development.

Gross, LeRoy, and Aparacio (2002:38) suggest that a CBA can improve existing requirements to achieve affordable housing. These include specifying

- the percentage of units that will be made affordable,
- the definition of *affordable*,
- the number of years after construction that units must remain affordable, and
- the number of bedrooms in affordable units.

In addition, CBAs can determine

- whether and how the required affordable units will be integrated with market-rate units;
- if the developer will apply for a waiver or reduction in affordability requirements, as is permitted in some jurisdictions;
- whether the developer will contribute money to an affordable housing fund rather than building affordable units, as is permitted in some jurisdictions; and
- if the affordable units must be built at the same time as the market rate units.

Even if a proposed project does not include new residential housing, community groups can ask the developer to fund local affordable housing programs. When a development is likely to increase rents in the area, as is the case in the Figueroa Corridor, mitigating the impact of increased rents is important, and the FCCEJ includes a number of different ways to increase housing supply in its CBA.

The following section summarizes the CBA the FCCEJ negotiated in the context of the coalition's overall strategy.

THE FCCEJ OVERALL STRATEGY: MORE THAN CBA

Table 11.2 sets forth the FCCEJ's negotiated agreement. Since its signing, the developer has moved forward on establishing preferential parking for residents, developing parks in the neighborhood, setting up a revolving loan fund and making loans to two nonprofit corporations, and holding a course on economic survival and setting up other courses with Los Angeles Trade Tech, located in the neighborhood. These courses include training in English as a second language (ESL) and computer literacy.

The CBA, comprehensive as it is, has flaws. It cannot halt landlords from continuing to evict tenants and selling property at prices that keep soaring. This would require fundamental shifts in thinking about policies to restrict speculation and strengthen security of tenure. A CBA by itself may not replace as many units as are demolished without other tools that apply to a broader area; for example, inclusionary zoning requiring citywide mandates can help to offset net losses of housing.

In the face of gentrification, the FCCEJ actively promoted and is pursuing financing for developing a "displacement-free" zone, that is, an area in which no displacement will happen. Designating the original displacement-free zone of 10 blocks was a defensive action; in this area, SAJE focused on educating tenants about their rights, organizing buildings, and building a

TABLE 11.2. FCCEJ: Community benefits agreement, negotiated settlement, and results prior to construction of sports and entertainment district

Type of Benefit	Settlement Agreement	Results
Living wage jobs	70 percent of new jobs will be unionized and/or pay a living wage.	2,500 jobs to be made available; $12 to $15 is wage goal
Local hiring/job training	50 percent of new jobs will be hired locally through a community-run job training and placement center funded with $100,000 in seed money from the developer.	An economic survival class, ESL classes, and computer literacy classes are available for local residents who need pre-employment education and support. Classes are produced in collaboration with the UCLA Downtown Labor Center and Los Angeles Trade Technical College with faculty support from the Downtown Labor Center; Garment Worker Center; Downtown Women's Action Center; and Korean Immigrant Workers Advocates. The Garment Worker Center will take the lead in training. Staples hired 30 students from the first economic survival class through SEIU Local 1877, the janitors' union, at $9.00 per hour, prior to establishing a job training program. Sixty-seven students graduated from the first economic survival class at Los Angeles Trade Technical College.
Affordable housing	A minimum of 20 percent of housing units must be affordable to low-income people. The developer will provide a $650,000 zero-percent interest revolving loan fund towards the building of new, affordable units by community nonprofits.	$650,000 in zero-interest loans were made to Esperanza Community Housing Corporation and 1010 Housing Corporation.
Parks and recreation	The developer will provide $1 million for parks and recreation facilities within a 1 mile radius, and between $50,000 and $75,000 to involve community members in site identification and planning.	Coalition members, the Environmental Defense Environmental Justice Office, Coalition L.A., and hundreds of local residents participated in a park planning process that helped guide investment of $1 million fund. A $500,000 commitment has been made for a free family recreation center and an approximate $415,000 commitment to Hope and Peace Park in the Pico Union neighborhood.

(*continued*)

TABLE 11.2. (Continued)

Type of benefit	Settlement agreement	Results
Environmental planning	Issues include: construction, traffic, pedestrian safety, waste management, air quality, and "green" buildings.	Establish ongoing Coalition Advisory Committee
Parking	The developer will help establish preferential parking and pay resident parking costs for 5 years.	Street signs for the city's first Poor People's Preferential Parking District are up, dedicating evening parking for local residents.

Source: SAJE-Net, http://www.saje.net/; see Publications, "LA Sports and Entertainment District Agreement," accessed on October 4, 2002; www.saje.net/programs/fccej.php, accessed on February 5, 2002.

support network of *pro bono* attorneys to limit illegal evictions and abuses. With expanding gentrification, other buildings and leaders joined the Displacement Free Zone Committee and expanded the zone to include the entire Figueroa Corridor. SAJE has been researching land trusts as one way to control growth and prevent speculation, and coalition partners are exploring financial resources to acquire property.

Even more direct action is required against evictions. SAJE and one of its partners, Esperanza Housing Development Corporation, were successful in their fight against the eviction of a tenant from a building that HUD was foreclosing. This sparked activity around changing HUD's practice of evictions on properties that the agency owns. More recently, SAJE brought together the Los Angeles Departments of Building and Safety, Housing, and the city attorney's office over the eviction of tenants from the Morrison Hotel. The case was presented to the office of the district attorney who is seeking jail terms for the owners of the Morrison Hotel following conviction on multiple counts of encouraging slum conditions. The case against the owners uncovered about 100 building violations, including lack of heat, locked fire doors, and vermin. SAJE is trying to secure relocation money for the tenants and assisting them with setting up bank accounts and finding other housing. Creating transparency about big landlords' holdings has the potential to restructure the ways in which landlords are held accountable to tenants; frequently when tenants require enforcement of Los Angeles's housing code, owners may not respond to complaints about heat, hot water, safety, and so on.

Another important aspect of the overall strategy is the premise of developing people as well as land. Allocation of jobs could become a sensitive issue if residents are not prepared to compete. Even before the application period opens, residents will need to fill prior requirements that include taking ESL and computer classes. SAJE and the FCCEJ developed a planning process to design a community jobs program and offered an "economic survival" class that included community residents and students from Los Angeles Trade Tech community college. The class was devoted to tenant, worker, and immigrant rights and to building individual skills such as opening checking accounts. The class is a prerequisite for the coalition's Community Jobs Program.

There are other complications that the FCCEJ will have to be vigilant about. Gross, LeRoy, and Janis-Aparicio (2002:9) note that an essential part of the CBA is building in leadership capacity and training for community groups who may be uncomfortable "giving up the right to express negative opinions on a public matter like a development project." Indeed, not all FCCEJ members agreed to give up the right to protest (Cummings 2005). AGENDA and the Association for Community Organizations for Reform Now (ACORN) declined to sign the agreement. Should they or other interested parties protest, the developer is released from adhering to the CBA. Nine groups signed the agreement and the others are referred to as "interested parties."

Legal scholar Scott L. Cummings offers insight into questions about "the enforceability of the benefits conferred ... [They] rely more on community persuasion than the coercive force of law" (forthcoming, 2006). Terms like *best efforts* and *flexible benchmarks* dot the CBA. Cummings says, "failure to comply with the 70 percent living wage goal does not breach the agreement. ... From a regulatory perspective, CBAs are therefore a second best solution reflecting the relative political weakness of accountable development action to enact change through conventional political channels" (48).

All of this emphasizes the importance of the CBA being incorporated into other strategies, as well as the importance of coalition building. In the case of FCCEJ, partnering has evolved with key players who are part of or join the coalition. Research projects are closely linked to day-to-day organizing. The lead organizer of SAJE, Andrea Gibbons, and Haas are developing a sophisticated research method about the practices of large-scale landlords, exposing the dense connections between their property holdings and financial institutions. The SAJE research helps in thinking through a broader strategy against big slum landlords. This might lead to a better way of holding landlords accountable for endangering tenants instead of a building-by-building process that relies on code enforcement. Each strategy used by the FCCEJ, whether setting policy (e.g., the Senate bill including lead-based paint in code enforcement regulations), entering into negotiations (the CBA), or establishing alternative institutions (cooperatives) reinforces each other and opens up new possibilities for research and organizing.

The overall strategy leads back to linking organizing to what some call "organic intellectuals," who draw from their everyday experiences, with college- and university-educated people, and with diverse people of all ages, races, and ethnicities. A synergy is created. The membership committees at SAJE are spaces in which leaders emerge who in effect become trainers of others. The process creates an openness between staff, members, community members-at-large, and organizations. This builds in what might be called an early warning system about infractions or problems that arise in the development process. The many items that are not covered by the CBA, such as evictions, can be integrated into the overall strategy. People are likely to buy in because the need arises from their own experiences or those of neighbors being evicted or losing a job or living in overcrowded conditions. The FCCEJ is not recreating a top-down structure at the community level but fostering structures that tap into the organic leadership, enhancing, bringing people together with different skills, and spawning collaborations that reinforce and stimulate each other.

CONCLUSIONS

Some characteristics of the FCCEJ's holistic approach are found in other community-based groups. In Montreal, Canada, a community-led effort transformed private development that was gentrifying a community into a community plan that retained existing buildings, converting some into co-operatives and others into rental properties (Helman 1995). The Dudley Street Neighborhood Initiative in the Roxbury section of Boston, Massachusetts, gained control of their land, acquiring the power of eminent domain through state legislation and developing an organizational structure to represent the diverse population (Medoff and Sklar 1994). As discussed in this book in Pastor et al., regional community development exists whereby CDCs or community-based organizations pursue projects that are geographically broader than one neighborhood and where people's lives are being directly affected by the shape of the regional economy.

Some theoretical proposals have been put forth that would return CDCs to their organizing roots. Sociologist Randy Stoecker has proposed different models where CDCs can add organizing and avoid becoming inundated with packaging developments that leave staff and boards disconnected from the community (2003). A CDC can join forces with an independent group of organizers in order to bridge the day-to-day, door-to-door work to recruit and sustain a constituency. A separate organizing arm can be started with more formal ties. In the FCCEJ, different types of organizations and organizing, whether by place, occupation, institution, or issue, are increasing the possibility of reaching more people and greater support from the bottom.

To a degree that was not previously possible, CBAs equalize the development playing field and provide an instrument for building a broader movement. In the Figueroa Corridor, they are linking housing to economic development. It is fortuitous that construction of the hotels has given way to prioritizing housing. The timeframe allows the FCCEJ to tackle economic development and affordable housing simultaneously. Because of the pressure to build housing and the CBA requirement that makes it impossible for a developer to market luxury units without affordable units, housing opportunities should open up for community residents. Because construction is a few years away, time is available for residents to acquire prerequisite skills before they look for jobs at a higher skill level. This is especially crucial in situations where housing prices keep increasing, the threat of eviction is real, and existing jobs do not pay well.

Goodno (2004:2–3) points out that CBAs emerged in response to three reasons. One was that "community groups seeking input in development were overpowered by developers, the business community, and in some cases construction unions, and they were being ignored by the redevelopment agencies." The second reason is the support of unions representing service workers whose low wages lead them to live in communities where redevelopment occurs. The third reason is the history of community organizations and labor unions working together in living-wage campaigns.

When the FCCEJ became a player, the community coalition provided a voice for the people who will clean the offices and cultural establishments in the area, wait tables and wash dishes in the restaurants, and park the cars in the sports and entertainment district. One day these people or their children may even become managers and owners of businesses. The community's vision is neither utopian nor unreasonable. They want to remain where they live and not experience dislocation. They want to see their children grow up with their neighbors. They want jobs that allow them to send their children to college. They want respect. They do not want to live in poverty that plagues virtually every census tract in the Figueroa Corridor. By organizing and creating a CBA, they are following a traditional American practice of self-help and creating a civil society based on collectively accessing property and resources. Should the CBA not live up to the community's expectations or if other problems arise, the accomplishments so far and the goals linking housing and economic development have a good chance of surviving as other organizing strategies take shape.

NOTES

I am grateful to the staff and tenant leaders of SAJE for their willingness to talk and share their work with me and the Community Scholars class of 2004. Over the years, discussions with Gilda Haas have clarified my thinking about connections between theory and practice. Scott L. Cummings was gracious in sharing his interpretation of events. Eric Schwimmer, a graduate of the UCLA Department of Urban Planning, provided valuable research assistance and insight. Mary Novak and Gigi Szabo, graduates of the UCLA Department of Urban Planning, assisted in the original research. The author thanks the editors of the volume for their input and the reviewers who read a version of an earlier of manuscript.

1. The Los Angeles City Council approved a living wage ordinance on March 18, 1997.

L.A. City's living wage ordinance represents a landmark achievement in the national effort to alleviate working poverty. Passed in 1997, the ordinance was only the county's third living wage law, and the first to include a provision for health care benefits. It was also the first piece of living wage legislation to bar retaliation by employers against their workers.

2. L.A. City's living wage ordinance applies to certain businesses in four categories: those which have service contracts with the city, lease land from the city, require city operating permits, or receive city financial assistance. The law mandates that workers at these businesses be paid $7.72 an hour if the company provides health benefits, or $8.97 an hour if no health coverage is provided. The wage level is indexed to the city employees retirement plan, and is adjusted accordingly.

More than 10,000 workers are covered by L.A. City's living wage ordinance, making it second only to San Francisco's law in scope. Through the persistent efforts of advocacy groups, an effective enforcement system has been created to ensure that employers abide by the ordinance and that workers have appropriate recourse when violations occur (http://www.laane.org/lw/legislation.html#1a_lwo).

2. Landlords who have the option of withdrawing from the program cite reasons of slow payments, meeting housing inspector demands, irresponsible tenants, and too much paperwork.

3. The numbers in the coalition range from a high of 29 to today's 25.

4. At least 16 other projects in the City of Los Angeles have development agreements, each with different provisions (LAX Coalition for Economic, Environmental, and Educational Justice n.d.). http://laane.org/lax/docs/About_CBAs.pdf

5. The Figueroa Corridor residents are 53 percent immigrants (26 percent compared in California); 67 percent speak Spanish at home (26 percent in California), and 42 percent have less than a ninth-grade education (11 percent in California); 38 percent of residents live in poverty (compared to 14 percent in California) (Schwimmer 2004).

6. Community Scholars is a program of the UCLA Department of Urban Planning and the Center for Labor Research and education in which community and labor activists work alongside students on an applied research project.

7. The 1965 rebellion covered eleven acres in Watts, causing forty million dollars worth of property damage, the death of 34 people, and injuries to 1,000 people over 7 days. When the 1992 riot happened, one comment given for Watts avoiding extensive damage was that nothing had been built up since 1965.

8. In 2002, California voters approved the $2.1 billion Housing and Emergency Shelter Trust Fund Act for construction, rehabilitation, and preservation of affordable rental housing, emergency shelters, and homeless facilities; down payment assistance to low- and moderate-income first-time homebuyers; and provisions for eligible credentialed teachers.

9. Subsequently, FCCEJ, seeking policy changes, asked for amendments to the Community Redevelopment Agency's City Center Redevelopment Plan, the Plan and Method of Relocation, and changes to the plan's percentages for affordability to comply with recommendations of the city's Housing Element: 47 percent of units would be for people with incomes less than 80 percent of the median income of about $55,000 per year for a family of four. Thirty percent of new construction would be affordable to people with incomes below 50 percent of the median income; the other 17 percent would be for people with incomes between 51 and 80 percent of median income (Gibbons and Haas 2002). This was not approved, but the principles contribute to the vision of the FCCEJ.

10. SAJE is conducting research on university-community partnerships. They are also continuing to talk with USC, although in 2003 the university declined to sign an agreement to negotiate exclusively with the FCCEJ. The coalition wanted to negotiate a community benefits agreement for housing and jobs; the immediate issue was the building of USC's new sports arena, which is expected to open in 2006.

11. In 1999, the LOS ANGELES City Council approved an amendment to the worker retention ordinance to include workers whose employees received city economic development grants. This broke the 4-year-old impasse between the union and USC.

12. According to Cummings, 130 families and individuals and about 35 businesses were relocated (forthcoming, 2006). Other figures put the total up to 200; in all likelihood the threat of displacement led some people to leave without gaining benefits.

13. Ground for this mega-project was broken at the end of 2004.

14. They were: Hotel Employees and Restaurant Employees (HERE) Local 11 of the Service Employees International Union (SEIU); SEIU Local 1877, representing janitors and security guards; Operating Engineers Local 501; the International Alliance of Local Stage Employees (IATSE) Local 33; and the Teamsters Local 911.

15. Other lawyers, recruited from the "CED [community economic development] attorneys from LAFLA [Legal Aid Foundation of Los Angeles], Public Council, and the pro bono office of the Los Angeles County," reviewed drafts of the proposal (Cummings 2005:40).

16. In October 1999, Staples Center's profit-sharing relationship with the *Los Angeles Times* was front-page news. The flare-up was over the newspaper's sharing the costs of a magazine supplement boosting the Staples Center, as well as over editorial reports' being unaware of this transaction. Although Staples deflected the negative publicity, its promise of being a space that promoted downtown development had yet to become a reality. The potential for community protest was building due to the earlier displacement of 200 households from the Staples site and the newer plans for redevelopment (Online NewsHour 1999).

REFERENCES

Alinsky, Saul D. 1946 [1991]. *Reveille for Radicals*. New York: Vintage Books.

Aparicio, Richard K., Roberto Bustillo, Davin Coronoa, Zabel Odabashian, Arturo Gartcia, Jeffery Henderson, et al. 2004. A "just" redevelopment: Lessons from the Figueroa Corridor Coalition for Economic Justice. Unpublished report prepared for the Community Scholars and Comprehensive Project class, University of California at Los Angeles.

Appadurai, Arjun. 2002. Deep democracy: Urban governmentality and the horizon of politics. *Public Culture* 14(1):21–47.

California Budget Project. 2001. Still locked out: New data confirms that California's housing affordability crisis continues. http://www.cbp.org/2001/r0102slo.html, Sacramento, CA, March 2001. Center on Policy Initiatives. 2004. Campaigns, Responsible Development. http://www.onlinecpi.org/campaigns_responsible_benefits.html. Accessed February 26, 2005.

Chambers, Edward T., and Michael A. Cowan. 2003. *Roots for Radicals: Organizing for Power, Action, and Justice*. New York: Continuum.

Coalition of Neighborhood Developers. 1994. From the ground up: Neighbors planning neighborhoods. Los Angeles: Local Initiatives Support Corporation.

Cummings, Scott L. Forthcoming 2006. "Mobilization Lawyering: Community Economic Development in the Figueroa Corridor." In Cause Lawyers and Social Movements, eds. Austin Sarat and Stuart Scheingold. Standford, CA: Stanford University Press.

Department of Housing of the City of Los Angeles. Los Angeles Housing Department. http:www.ci.la.ca.us/lahd/afhsgtrstfd.htm. Accessed October 7, 2004.

Fairriss, David, and Michael Reich. 2005. The impacts of living wage policies: Introduction to the special issue. *Industrial Relations* 44(1):1–13.

Ferguson, Ronald F., and William T. Dickens. 1999. *Urban Problems and Community Redevelopment*. Indianapolis: John Wiley.

Gibbons, Andrea, and Gilda Haas. 2002. Redefining redevelopment: Participatory research for equity in the Los Angeles Figueroa Corridor. Report prepared for the Figueroa Corridor Coalition for Economic Justice.

Gittell, Ross, and Avis Vidal. 1998. *Community Organizing: Building Social Capital as a Development Strategy*. Thousand Oaks, CA.: Sage Publications.

Good Jobs First. 2002. New model for economic development reform report offers guide for labor/community coalitions, highlighting recent agreements in Los Angeles that mandate living wages, other benefits. http://www.ctj.org/itep/cbar elease.htm. Accessed December 12, 2005.

Goodno, James B. 2004. Feet to the fire: Accountable development keeps developers and community groups talking—and walking. *Planning Magazine.* Page 16. Chicago: American Planning Association.

Gross, Julian, with Greg LeRoy and Madeline Janis-Aparicio. 2002. Community benefits agreements: Making development projects accountable. Prepared by the California Public Subsidies Project.

Haas, Gilda. 2002. Economic justice in the Los Angeles Figueroa Corridor. In *Teaching for Change: Popular Education and the Labor Movement,* ed. Linda Delp, Miranda Outman-Kramer, Susan J. Schurman, and Kent Wong, pp. 90–100. Los Angeles: UCLA Center for Labor Research and Education.

Helman, Clare. 1995. Montreal's Milton Park: After the opening fanfare. In *The Hidden History of Housing Cooperatives,* ed. Allan Heskin and Jacqueline Leavitt, pp. 42–46. Davis, California: University of California Center for Cooperatives.

Keil, Roger. 1998. Los Angeles: Globalization, Urbanization, and Social Struggles. Chichester, UK: John Wiley & Sons.

LAANE. Accountable Redevelopment Research, http://www.laane.org/ad/adresearch. html. accessed on October 4, 2004.

LAANE. Los Angeles Living Wage. http://www.laane.org/lw/legislation.html#1a_lwo. Accessed December 20, 2005.

LAX Coalition for Economic, Environmental, and Educational Justice. http://www. laane.org/lax/docs/About_CBAs.pdf. Accessed December 20, 2005.

Leavitt, Jacqueline. 1996. Los Angeles neighborhoods respond to the civil unrest: Is planning an adequate tool? In *Revitalizing Urban Neighborhoods,* ed. Dennis Keating, Norman Krumholz, and Phil Star, pp. 112–130. Kansas City: University of Kansas Press.

Medoff, Peter, and Holly Sklar. 1994. *Streets of Hope: The Fall and Rise of an Urban Neighborhood.* Cambridge, Mass.: South End Press.

Myerhoff, Matt. 2004. Families at various levels feel the housing pinch. www-scf .usc.edu/~jour556/issues/housing.shtml. Accessed September 26, 2004. National Low Income Housing Coalition. 2003. "Out of Reach 2003: America's Housing Wage Climbs." http://www.nlihc.org/oor2003. Accessed September 29, 2004.

National Low Income Housing Coalition. 2005. "Out of Reach 2005." http://www. nlihc.org/oor2005. Accessed December 20, 2005.

No End in Sight to California's Housing Troubles. 2003. *San Diego Union Tribune.* July 20, G-6.

Online NewsHour. 1999. Trouble at the *Los Angeles Times.* www.pbs.org/news hour/bb/media/july-dec99/la_times_12–16.html. December 16, 1999.

Pastor, Manuel Jr., Peter Dreier, J. Eugene Grigsby III, and Marta Lopez-Garza. 2000. Regions That Work: How Cities and Suburbs Can Grow Together. Minneapolis, MN: University of Minnesota Press.

Romney, Lee. 2001. Staples plan spotlights invisible communities. Copyright 2002. www.saje.net/programs/fccej.php. Accessed February 28, 2005.

Shaw, Randy. 2001. *The Activist's Handbook: A Primer.* Berkeley: University of California Press.

Schwimmer, Eric. 2004. The Figueroa Corridor in the regional economy. In *A "Just" redevelopment: Lessions from the Figueroa Corridor Coalition for Economic Justice,* ed. Aparicio et al., 36 pages, A1–A38. Unpublished report prepared for the Community Scholars and Comprehensive Project class, University of California at Los Angeles.

Social and Economic Trends in Los Angeles County and the Southern California Region. "Housing Affordability in LA."

Southern California Association for Non-Profit Housing. 2004. http://www.scanph.org/about_scanph/index.html. Accessed February 28, 2005.

Southern California Studies Center. 2001. Sprawl hits the wall: Confronting the realities of metropolitan Los Angeles. A report of the Southern California Studies Center (University of Southern California) and the Brookings Institution Center on Urban and Metropolitan Policy, Los Angeles, California.

State of California Department of Housing and Community Development. 1999. The State of California's Housing Markets 1990–1997. Prepared as part of the California Statewide Housing Plan Update. Sacramento, California.

Strategic Actions for a Just Economy. 2002. www.saje.net/programs/fccej.php. Accessed October 8, 2004.

Stoecker, Randy. 2003. Understanding the development-organizing dialectic. *Journal of Urban Affairs* 25(4):493–512.

12 Synchronizing Social Services with Labor Market Participation
Implications for Community Economic Development in Minority Neighborhoods

LOIS M. TAKAHASHI

INTRODUCTION

There is wide agreement among scholars that economic and welfare state restructuring at multiple spatial scales (metropolitan, regional, national, international) has had devastating impacts on low-wage, low-skilled workers and those seeking work. While the sources and particular impacts of restructuring have been widely debated, what is clear is that the combination of decreasing union membership and activity, vertical and horizontal disintegration of firms, declining manufacturing, and rising service sector employment—along with the retraction of welfare programs, changing eligibility requirements for income maintenance, and time limits on welfare program use—have drastically reduced the economic resources available to low-income communities of color. And even as economic resources have dwindled, low-income individuals, households, and communities of color have had to contend with rising housing prices, lack of medical insurance, child care expenses, and transportation challenges, all of which have forced them to make difficult choices about meeting their daily needs.

The social service delivery system (provided through the public, nonprofit and charitable, and private sectors) has been crucial in filling the gap between inadequate wages and daily living expenses. It provides for basic needs (food, clothing, shelter), facilitates access to physical and mental health care, and offers training and support to enhance employment opportunities. But the provision of social services has in recent years become increasingly complex. The population needing social services has diversified (with rising numbers of documented and undocumented immigrants, welfare recipients, and low-skilled workers); the low-wage labor market has become more turbulent (with increasing reliance on contract and temporary employment, growth in part-time employment, and more and more jobs that do not offer benefits); and the future of many social service programs has been cast into doubt as a result of retrenchment and shrinking funds.

This chapter argues that a comprehensive and effective economic development strategy for communities of color must include a social services component, and further, that this component must be designed to synchronize with the turbulence and vagaries in the contemporary labor market. To identify and begin to overcome the barriers to synchronization between the social service delivery system and local economies important to communities of color, the chapter proceeds in the following manner. First, I discuss the rising need for social services among low-income individuals and households in communities of color, and the ways in which labor market participation largely structures the daily lives of low-income workers of color. I turn next to a discussion of the social service delivery system. From there I highlight the barriers faced by agencies and their staffs (as both service providers and employers/employees) in trying to adjust to sometimes volatile client circumstances. Finally, I offer recommendations for better synchronizing social services with the needs and capacities of low-income communities of color; in this section I also suggest questions for future research. These recommendations are offered as a vital, but often overlooked, component of a broader set of strategies to enhance opportunities for economic development in communities of color.

Communities of Color in Need

Communities of color face increasing pressures as real wages fall and daily living costs rise. Economic marginality can be traced in large degree to global economic restructuring, which has created an expanding service sector that provides a growing number of low-wage jobs, many of them temporary and contractual, and many that also offer only limited benefits (Law and Wolch 1991; also chapters 4 and 7 of this volume). For communities of color, this has led to more competition for fewer and less-well-paid jobs, and this competition has contributed to a context of instability and uncertainty. In the past, public assistance programs could buffer the hardships wrought by economic downturns or periods of restructuring, but welfare reform—with its time limits and work requirements—has made these programs more difficult to access than they were in previous decades.

The implementation of welfare reform, and the restructuring of the welfare state more generally, has reduced income maintenance and in-kind services; reduced or eliminated the production of public housing and the provision of subsidized housing; tightened eligibility requirements; and placed a five-year time limit on lifetime use of welfare programs (Wolch and Dear 1993; Ong and Blumenberg 1998; Chapter 2 of this volume). And while there have been federal efforts to combat visible expressions of severe poverty, such as homelessness, most federal and state funding—when it exists—remains focused on emergency, short-term policies rather than longer-term comprehensive strategies. Those long-term policies that do exist, such as the Stewart B. McKinney Act of 1987 (which funds programs targeting homeless services), suffer from constant underfunding (Blau 1992).

The housing market, which has been extremely competitive across metropolitan areas in the United States, has also contributed to the expanding economic marginality of low-income households of color (chapters 1 and 11 of this volume). Affordable rental units for low-income households have been declining in number and quality. This forces many to live in overcrowded conditions, compels others to pay more than 30 percent of their income (the threshold recommended by the U.S. Department of Housing and Urban Development) in rent, and puts the most vulnerable onto the streets (Takahashi 1996). The reasons for the housing crisis are numerous: gentrification and urban renewal, demolition of affordable units (e.g., single-room occupancy hotels, multifamily units), and conversion of low-rent units into luxury apartments and condominiums (Wolch and Dear 1993).

All these circumstances have been exacerbated by the significant sociodemographic transformation in the U.S. population. Levels of income and wealth have diverged; divorce has increased and poverty has become increasingly feminized; and health care costs have risen even as the population has aged. These and other challenges, such as substance abuse and domestic violence, have created dire circumstances for many households of color and reduced their capacity to meet their basic, short-term, and longer-term needs. Even for those individuals and households who are participating in the labor force, contingent employment, economic uncertainty, and interpersonal challenges mean that individuals and households are trying to cope with interpersonal conflict, challenges to work performance, dual or multiple roles (e.g., parent, spouse, employee, caregiver to older relative), and a lack of preparedness to compete in a rapidly changing labor market (Perlman 1982).

For communities of color, in particular, to respond to rapidly changing employment, housing, child care, and other conditions, resilience[1] and adaptability are crucial. Greater labor market participation (e.g., holding multiple jobs, working longer hours) and reliance on social services (e.g., child care, housing assistance) have been common strategies to cope with increasing economic marginality (Law and Wolch 1991). However, these strategies come with high costs and often require that individuals and households make difficult choices about how best to cope with crises and longer-term issues. London et al. (2004) argue, for example, that while "[a]ll working mothers must find ways to 'weave' and 'balance' their work and family commitments in accordance with their cultural and familial preferences, values, and resources, ... low-income working mothers face particular constraints on the choices they can make and the strategies they can enact" (p. 149).

Populations of color participating in the labor force face additional challenges if they have chronic physical or mental disabilities. While some public and private programs seek to address work-related disabilities (e.g., injuries at the work site, conditions such as alcohol abuse that are linked to workplace conditions), such as workers' compensation or means tested benefits such as Supplemental Security Income (ssi) (Thomason, Burton, and Hyatt 1998), disabled persons still face significant hurdles to gain entry into the labor market. For those with non–work-related disabilities (which are not usually addressed by compensation policies), participation in the labor market depends on the ability to fit social and medical services into the already-constrained daily routines of family and work. This is also true more generally for individuals, households, and communities of color trying to balance low-wage work, family obligations, and individual needs.

Consequently, the need for social services that address a variety of complex issues has never been greater. Sosin (1986) describes the need for three types of social services: (1) emergency one-time assistance, or those needs that are "clearly beyond the control of individuals, such as need generated by a fire or flood that destroys a family's home" (p. 5); (2) special needs stemming from chronic conditions or specific health circumstances, including needs for specific furnishings, dietary needs, clothing for school; and (3) emergency basic needs, such as food, clothes, or fuel (p. 5). Orthner et al. (2004) further argue that "[f]amilies who are unemployed, under-employed, or employed at low wages are likely to experience hardship in one or more of the following areas: food insecurity, lack of access to health care, and lack of access to affordable quality child care" (p. 160). What is clear is that there are a myriad of needs that will emerge for different individuals, households, and communities of color in particular times, depending on their life cycle position (e.g., young children, caring for elderly parents), economic and working circumstances, housing conditions, and personal/individual challenges.

SOCIAL SERVICES

Traditionally, social service delivery has tended to focus on individuals and households receiving public assistance, but the contemporary vagaries of the low-wage labor market and the diversification of low-income populations have made more and different people dependent on social services for daily survival. According to Kamerman and Kahn (1976), the social service delivery system in the United States includes the following: child welfare; child care; elderly care (e.g., counseling, food, information); services for families (in-formation, referrals for employment, housing, health care, social work and family counseling, family courts); home health care/aides; veterans programs; correctional and penal services (juvenile delinquency prevention, probation, family court); community centers; access centers (for information, advice, referrals, advocacy); special programs for refugees, Native Americans, and migrant workers; and the community mental health care system.

Prior to the New Deal, social services were primarily, although not al-ways, provided through religious organizations. Sosin (1986) lists the major providers before the New Deal as the Salvation Army, Charity Organization Societies, St. Vincent de Paul, Catholic Charities, and settlement houses. These organizations retreated from service delivery after the New Deal, when the public sector made its visible and large-scale entry into social policy. The entry of the public sector brought with it a rise of profession-alism in the field, as well as an increasing focus on individual counseling (Sosin 1986:18). Welfare state restructuring, which has led to retrenchment and retreat of the public sector, began in the 1970s and continues today (Wolch and Dear 1993).

This service system, while clearly aiming to be comprehensive, is fraught with gaps and fragmentation. These gaps and fragmentations are largely the result of the system's ad-hoc development over time and drastic funding shifts—usually downward—in recent decades. The resulting patchwork of services is difficult to use, particularly for communities of color. To address these gaps and the fragmentation, researchers have long held that integration, coordination, and accountability are critical to service effectiveness (Kamerman and Kahn 1976). However, such integration, coordination, and accountability have in the past focused primarily on "effective meshing of the services offered by different units, bureaus, departments, agencies, programs, service systems with regards to the needs of consumers" (Kamerman and Kahn 1976:437). That is, integration has been sought through improved coordination and reduced duplication within varying service organizations. Less attention has been paid to integrating and co-ordinating social services with the daily realities of life for individuals, households, and communities in need. As a consequence, the organizational schedules, procedures, and practices of social service agencies have likely contributed to the difficult choices that households of color must make in coping with the multiple and often conflicting obligations stemming from work, family, and school (e.g., Wilton 1996). In other words, along with the obligations defined by the workplace(s), school, medical institutions, and other individual and familial responsibilities, the social service system, as a result of its fragmentation, has complicated—rather than made easier—the already complex lives of its clients, many of whom are juggling the competing demands of work, school, and family. There are four primary sources to this problem: distance, time, service mix, and acceptability.

Scholars have long argued that the distance between facilities and populations in need is one of the most important barriers to social service use (Dear and Taylor 1982). Simply put, the further individuals and households live from existing social service agencies, the less frequently they will use these agencies' services (Cunningham et al. 1996). Improved access to social services would therefore require either greater mobility by those populations needing services or shorter distances between social service agencies and the individuals and households needing them.

Linked to this spatial dimension of accessibility is the temporal character of social service delivery. Distance is important but so too is time; the clients of social service agencies, like most people, have busy schedules and numerous demands on their time. For individuals who are working multiple jobs, who are working in temporary, part-time, or contractual employment, or who have child care and other familial obligations, opportunities for traveling to and using social services can be severely constrained. Blumenberg (2002) has argued that low-income women with children in the labor force who travel via mass transit suffer from severe time constraints because they need to make multiple household-related trips in addition to work-related trips, and mass transit—with its long travel times, fixed routes and fixed schedules—is ill-suited to such a complex and unpredictable schedule. As more time during the day becomes consumed by both other obligations and traveling to those other obligations, less time is left to take advantage of available social services. Temporal scarcity means that for some households there is literally no time to use social services.

Another example of temporal constraints is drawn from a recent survey of individuals working and not working who are living with HIV/AIDS.[2] For these persons of color, there were significant differences in terms of the degree of daily flexibility. The survey showed that for a 10-hour day (8 A.M.– 6 P.M., the usual operating hours for service providers), between zero and 10 hours were assessed to be flexible by both nonworking and working respondents of color (Table 12.1). The flexible time was defined in the following way: respondents ranked each activity during the 10 hours in terms of whether it could possibly be rescheduled—that is, could a work shift be pushed back. The mean and standard deviation in flexible hours during the previous 10-hour day indicated that while a large number of hours may be considered flexible, there was wide variation in the availability of those flexible time blocks across the nonworking and working subgroups. In addition, while working respondents had lower mean and median flexible time blocks than nonworking respondents (this of course is not surprising because of their employment obligations), the standard deviation for working respondents was much higher, indicating that the range of flexible time blocks was larger than for nonworking respondents.

Similar patterns were indicated when the day was extended to 13 hours (8 A.M.–9 P.M.). That is, nonworking respondents had more flexibility in terms of mean and median time blocks that represented the ability to reschedule activities, which should not be surprising. Again, however, the standard deviation was larger for working than nonworking respondents, indicating a wider range of flexibility within the working respondent subgroup. The 13-hour day (8 A.M.–9 P.M.) offered many more flexible time blocks for employed respondents than the 10-hour day (8 A.M.–6 P.M.). The implication, of course, is that services provided during a longer daily time period would result in greater access.

The actual types of services offered, or service mix, is also crucial to understanding the usefulness of social services for communities of color in need. Service mix can be characterized by the availability of services and the types of services offered in particular communities. A lack of access to needed services may stem from a mismatch between needs and types of services offered. When social service agencies misread current individual, household, or community needs or do not adapt to the rapidly shifting needs of their community members, the existing service mix offered by these

TABLE 12.1. Daily activities inventory by employment

	Minimum (Hours)	Maximum (Hours)	Mean (Hours)	Median (Hours)	Standard Deviation (Hours)	F-value (p-value)
Flexible time—8 A.M.–6 P.M.						
Nonworking	0	10	7.5	8	2.90	9.05
Working	0	10	5.4	5	3.59	(p < .003)
Flexible time—8 A.M.–9 P.M.						
Nonworking	2	13	10.2	11	3.23	13.37
Working	0	13	7.4	6.5	4.09	(p < .001)

agencies will likely not address current community concerns. Consequently, although some communities of color may be service-rich, those services may not actually provide for the emergency, short-term, and longer-term needs of these residents (Takahashi, Weibe, and Rodriguez 2001).

Finally, the acceptability of social services both by communities of color in need and by the wider population strongly influences their potential use. There are two dimensions of acceptability: (1) suspicion or trust of the service agencies providing programs and (2) broader societal definitions and stigma of needy households and the services that serve them. Many communities of color are suspicious or distrustful of social service agencies. As Altman (2003) has argued, "[f]amilies of color often feel coerced, distrustful, or fearful of public social service systems" (p. 478). Many perceive a threat of deportation (if they are undocumented), seizure of young children (if they are seen as unfit parents), or the potential or actual penalties associated with noncompliance across a host of local, state, and federal regulations if they access social services and identify themselves (Takahashi, McElroy, and Rowe 2002). In addition to perceived sanctions associated with service use, there are also larger societal norms that discourage social service use. For individuals who do not self-identify as "needy" or who imagine social services to be only for those who are somehow different from the wider populace, proximity, temporal match, and appropriate service mix may be insufficient to overcome this stigma associated with social service use.

There is clearly a tension between self-identifying as "needy" and working toward self-sufficiency and economic independence. On the one hand, the self-identification as "needy" or as fulfilling specific social service definitions, such as "homeless," "indigent," or "living in poverty," are necessary to access social services (Takahashi 1998). On the other hand, such self-identification can lead to a self-fulfilling prophecy, as individuals and households begin to primarily define themselves using these social service labels, creating strong and reinforcing self-identities as service-dependent (Rowe and Wolch 1980), or to stigmatization and ostracization by the broader community (Takahashi, McElroy, and Rowe 2002). To deny the stigmatized labels as service-dependent that often come with social service use, individuals and household may believe that they do not need knowledge about or access to available social services (Takahashi, Wiebe, and Rodriguez 2001). And if they do use social services associated with stigmatized groups (e.g., welfare, food banks, housing vouchers), individuals may choose not to disclose, or may even deny, the use of these services and programs to potential/current employers, family members, and acquaintances (Takahashi, McElroy, and Rowe 2002).

Barriers to Synchronizing Social Services and Realities of Life for Communities of Color

The characteristics of the existing social service system comprise a set of diverse and complex challenges to communities of color. There are several reasons why these characteristics are difficult to address: (1) the lack of influence by workers and social service providers on workplace and other institutional (e.g., medical, school, probation, etc.) schedules, procedures, and usual organizational practices; (2) the uncertainty characterizing low-wage, low-skilled work in the twenty-first century, including temporary, part-time, and contractual employment and multiple job sites, and the lack of resources in communities of color in need to deal with meeting multiple obligations (e.g., dependence on mass transit, lack of control over institutional schedules and procedures); and (3) the temporal and geographic distance between where individuals, households, and communities of color in need are at any point in time, and the schedules and locations of social service providers.

There can be little doubt that economic restructuring and the decline in unionization have diminished worker power. Social service providers, however, have also long felt disconnected from the world of work. Perlman (1982) has argued that social workers "feel—not without reason—that they have little entrée into and little power in the world of industry or business" (p. 95). Consequently, workers and social service providers have little say, or at least limited influence, over work schedules, and this in turn has contributed to the lack of time that often prevents those in need from accessing services (Orthner, Jones-Sanpei, and Williamson 2004).

In part because of this lack of influence on the workplace, low-income communities of color have long had to juggle multiple obligations (e.g., work, school, child care, elder care). Scholars have clarified the complex and dynamic mechanisms defining temporal and spatial constraints to the labor market, housing, and social and medical services (e.g., Granovetter 1995; Ong and Blumenberg 1998). Individuals, households, and communities of color have devised creative and at times effective strategies to cope with these difficult obstacles (Dyck 1999; Gilbert 1998; Kearns 1997; Moss and Dyck 1996; Rowe and Wolch 1990). Often low-income households must strictly ration time and money. Roy et al. (2004), for example, have argued that "[t]ime obligations to jobs, family, children, transit, and institutional interaction keep the need for organized control over time high for working families" (p. 168).

Low-income individuals, households, and communities who are dependent on social services are also vulnerable to changing organizational practices and procedures by social service providers. If a social service agency decides to alter its program times and places and individuals and households cannot adjust their own schedules accordingly, their basic needs will likely not be met (Takahashi, Wiebe, and Rodriguez 2001). And as Roy et al. (2004) have similarly argued, "families without resources . . . are less able to purchase or negotiate for discretionary time" (p. 169), meaning that those who most need social services are often least able to adjust to changes in the way they are provided. As work becomes more flexible and temporally or spatially fragmented, family obligations shift (because of changes in the life cycle), and individual needs grow and change, individuals, households, and communities of color must cope with a shifting temporal and geographic separation between their varied obligations and the social services that might meet their basic, short-term, and longer-term needs. Synchronizing social service delivery with the life realities of communities of color would clearly address some of the disjunctures between daily life patterns and social service organizational practices. Cohen and McGowan (1982) have argued, for example, that "[k]nowledge of the community's work schedule in terms of the numbers of consumers available at various hours of the day would permit social agencies to schedule their time in such a manner as to create the greatest impact in the time zones that promote utilization, while maintaining sufficient service opportunities at less saturated but still necessary time slots" (p. 134).

But while this seems to be a straightforward solution to address the disjuncture between communities in need and social service delivery, social service agencies face multiple challenges in trying to design and implement such a strategy. The lack of decision making power in the workplace(s) by workers and social service providers, the increasingly fragmented and contingent conditions of contemporary labor market participation by low-wage workers, and as a consequence of these two factors, an increasing temporal and spatial separation between individuals and communities in need and the existing social service system, have created a context where social service agencies must more closely monitor the needs of communities, adjust and adapt program design and organizational practices to fit these changing needs, and implement programs and policies that address these needs.

Pressures on Social Service Agencies to Address Barriers

The social services sector changed significantly during the 1990s. Twombly (2001), in an analysis of human service agency growth and change from 1992 to 1996, found that "[t]he growth in the number of human service nonprofits between 1992 and 1996 was particularly pronounced in metropolitan areas ... [increasing] by more than 41 percent [and] nearly 25 percent greater than in the nonprofit sector as a whole in metropolitan regions" (p. 2). During the same period, however, Twombly also found a high degree of organizational volatility and churning, with many organizations leaving the social service system. This volatility is emblematic of contemporary social service delivery systems, where instability both across the organizations and within them (staff turnover, uncertain funding, and increasing competition for funds) has stymied efforts to synchronize social service delivery with community needs.

Researchers and practitioners have long argued that social services targeting varying populations should be better coordinated and integrated. Across public, private, and nonprofit organizations, significant time and resources have been focused on ensuring that individuals and households in need have current information about, and access to, available services. But the social service delivery system remains ill-equipped to cope with the turbulent and changing circumstances of many communities and ill-equipped to cope with the changing landscape of organizational funding. The contemporary pressures on social service agencies are enormous and challenge even the most competent and effective organizations. These pressures can be divided into three interrelated elements: (1) significant and rapid shifts in funding availability, creating the need to become more entrepreneurial; (2) the need for effective monitoring of the changing needs of individuals, households, and communities and adaptation of programs and services to meet those changing needs; (3) organizational volatility (e.g., rapid turnover in staff) and the need for culturally sensitive and multilingual staff to provide appropriate services.

Funding Shifts

Social service constituencies have rarely been mistaken for groups with influence and power. Low-income persons of color, immigrants, substance users, and homeless individuals lack the political connections to foundations and private sector corporations that might provide funding to support programs. In addition, changing political climates at the regional and national levels—where attention has shifted to economic stimulus, the remedying of budget deficits, and not least, geopolitical conflict—have placed low-income social service program funding low on the nation's and states' priority lists. An expansion of the population in need, along with budget crises and deficits at the federal, state, and county levels, have contributed to greater and more diversified needs and fewer resources for meeting those needs. And the downward trends in public sector and philanthropic funding have led to an increased need for private sector fundraising.

Especially in terms of providing services for employed persons, social service providers remain quite constrained because of the regulations governing eligibility for programs supported by varying streams of federal funding. Although many clients served by social service agencies are indigent or are characterized as the "working poor,"[3] there remain strict eligibility requirements that may prevent specific services aimed at employed persons, especially when the monies are tied to specific agencies (e.g., programs serving physically or mentally disabled).

There are also reporting and auditing obligations associated with publicly funded programs. Consequently, though nonprofit medical and service organizations have in the past relied heavily on public money, today many—especially in communities of color—have increasingly sought private funding sources (e.g., individual donations, endowments, corporate grants).

Rapid Changes in Community Needs

When social services focused on specific target populations, such as families on public assistance, homeless individuals living on Skid Rows, or physically or mentally disabled veterans, there was a sense that while there was likely diversity within each of these populations, social service agencies could confidently plan for and provide targeted services because the needs of these populations did not change. However, welfare reform, welfare state re-structuring, diversification in the population, and increasing economic marginality has expanded the population that might seek social services and changed the individuals, households, and communities that social service agencies had targeted for services in the past.

Social service providers, increasingly recognizing the diverse and ex-panding needs of their client populations and the obstacles facing those populations, have shifted service delivery times and places (such as pro-viding services during evenings and weekends in addition to weekdays, as well as in accessible locations, such as parks) to accommodate labor market participation and complex familial and social obligations. While difficult, accommodating the schedules of people with hectic work and family ob-ligations often works well, particularly if the many members of a target population have similar time or place constraints (i.e., a large number of people in a given area work at night, or cannot access a particular agency because of distance or transit schedules). However, as contemporary social service agencies are serving a diversifying and expanding population in need, such commonalities are becoming harder to find.

Organizational Volatility and Multicultural Services

Social service agencies have experienced frequent volatility over the past few decades, both in terms of the external funding and policy environment as indicated earlier in the chapter and in terms of internal organizational churning due to staff turnover, pressured work environments, and the need for services that accommodate the expanding and increasingly diverse needs of local communities. The decline in available funding has contributed to a highly pressured work environment where staff turnover and burnout are common. Hyde (2004) has argued that "workload issues, specifically com-peting agency priorities and high work demands with inadequate support"—along with funding reductions—have created more work for the same or less pay (p. 11). As Bednar (2003) has argued concerning child welfare workers, "[j]ob satisfaction, burnout, and staff turnover have been shown to be strongly correlated, and decreased satisfaction and increasing burnout may impair workers long before they decide to leave their positions" (p. 7). In addition, employees drawn to social service delivery may be younger and may, after a relatively short time, decide to return to school to obtain ad-ditional educational credentials or change jobs to pursue better career op-portunities.

The social service workplace is made even more challenging by the po-tential for violence directed at providers. While the professional perception of potential physical assault varies by client group, mental health providers in particular have long been concerned with potential violence in varying settings (including offices and homes) (Shields and Kiser 2003).

Even as funding opportunities are shrinking and becoming more com-petitive, there have been added administrative burdens placed on those agencies receiving grants and funds for performance and outcomes-based evaluation (often without funding to support such activities). Consequently, social service agencies must now, in addition to designing and implementing programs, also engage in frequent data collection, evaluation, and reporting to their funders (Salamon 1995).

To better serve a rapidly expanding and diversifying populace in need, more researchers and practitioners have called for cultural sensitivity and competence in social service program design, delivery, and evaluation. Culturally sensitive and appropriate social services requires more than the employment of staff with multilingual skills. Researchers have called for the "multicultural development" of social service organizations, incorporating the instrumental dimensions of communication (multilingual and ethnically diverse staff) along with more process and long-term organizational trans-formations aimed at power redistribution (e.g., from service agency staff to broader stakeholders, including clients or service users), antiracism and multicultural ideologies, and commitments to social justice (Iglehart and Becerra 1995). In the current severely constrained fiscal environment, however, efforts at "cultural competence"[4] will likely translate into awareness building and attempts to employ diverse staff (Nybell and Gray 2004) rather than longer-term strategies to realign power relations, em-power clients, aim at broader social justice goals, or include more stake-holders in decision making.[5] And even when the longer-term mission of cultural competence is a primary goal for social service providers, staffing challenges remain. Culturally competent programs require a relatively high level of skills from social service providers, but with relatively low pay and demanding work environments, retaining such employees is a daunting task.

CONCLUSION

Many social service organizations are aware that their client populations are changing; some have been quick to adapt to this new client diversity by offering services off-site, at night and on weekends, and with associated supportive services (child care, transportation, food). Others have been slower to change. Diversity and change, however, have become the preeminent characteristics of contemporary social service delivery. Unstable and insecure funding, lack of funding flexibility, and staff turnover and burnout contribute to a highly turbulent and unpredictable social service organizational climate.

Social service organizations have attempted to cope with this turbulent climate by diversifying their funding sources and collaborating with other agencies to leverage scarce resources. Such strategies require additional staff time and start-up resources, which are stretching local service providers to the limit (Takahashi and Smutny 2002). More entrepreneurial activities and coordinated action may constitute the predominant model for social service delivery in the twenty-first century, and social service agencies targeting communities of color will likely need to expand their capacities in these areas to survive. On a positive note, diversifying their funding sources may provide social service organizations the flexibility necessary to be responsive to the needs of their expanding and diversifying client base.

As this chapter has argued, in the context of this turbulent social service organizational climate, there are clearly substantial obstacles to synchronizing social service delivery with the realities of life for low-income communities of color. The uncertainty and temporal/spatial impermanence defined by low-wage labor markets, the rising costs of housing, transportation, and child and elder care, and the lack of social and economic resources to deal with these issues have placed many individuals, households, and communities of color in dire need of social services.

The realities of life in communities of color call for social service agencies and planners to devise creative new strategies to design and implement effective and sustainable community economic development programs. Social service agencies must continue to monitor and adapt to the changing needs and capacity of communities of color to generate an integrated, coordinated, and accountable service delivery system. As a first step, social service agencies should recognize that communities of color are juggling multiple obligations and that many of these obligations are contradictory and outside community control. To facilitate the use of existing services, social service providers must investigate and understand the temporal and spatial characteristics of these work, family, community, and individual obligations and offer programs that accommodate and fit—in terms of time and location—within the busy schedules being balanced by these communities.

Second, social service providers should understand that the social services funded by public and charitable sources may or may not mesh well with the current needs of communities or with the communities' desire for self-sufficiency and self-determination. That is, while social service funding is driven largely by funder mandates and priorities, community needs for economic and social support may be derived from a distinctly different set of assumptions and trade-offs. To address this potential disjuncture, social service providers should seek out funding sources that can accommodate a multicultural or empowerment model even as they pursue more traditional client service program support.

Finally, though social service providers have tended to focus their efforts on individual and household interventions, the contingent nature of the labor market, welfare state, housing market, and other socioeconomic structures makes a more structural approach a necessary element to any long-term community building endeavor. A structural approach would require that social service providers partner with groups, organizations, and agencies working to change the economic, political, social, and environmental conditions affecting communities of color. This longer-term approach is critical to understanding the potentials and pitfalls of incorporating social service delivery in economic development strategies in communities of color. What this chapter has argued is that the economic and social futures of communities of color have largely been driven by structural forces that have severely marginalized them. A longer-term approach that addresses these structural constraints lies in the coordination of economic development and social service delivery in addressing the fundamental challenges to communities of color in their quest for empowerment, self-sufficiency, and self-determination.

For planners and policy makers engaged in economic development strategies, a fundamental component should be the socioeconomic safety net that will enable communities of color to be long-term active participants in local, regional, and global economies. To ensure this sustainable future, planners and policy makers should (1) increase their awareness and knowledge about existing social services and particularly how these social services support the entry to and sustainability of labor market participation by communities of color—such efforts might include passive activities (such as using Internet and other information sources to identify social service agencies in the region of interest) or proactive approaches (joining existing partnerships, inter-agency groups, or consortia involved in social service delivery); (2) identify and implement coordinated or collaborative efforts to bridge the divide between economic development and social service delivery and to work toward temporal and spatial synchronization among the work, family, and community lives of persons of color—these efforts could include revamping administrative or procedural issues (such as greater communication among public sector departments) and material projects (such as designing small business incubators with job training and child care facilities on site).

Researchers are increasingly exploring the time-space constraints and opportunities experienced by low-income communities of color in their quest to meet their varying—and at times conflicting—obligations. Future research should continue to investigate the pressures placed on resource-poor communities as they negotiate difficult and inflexible institutions (such as work, school, and other institutions) and how they have developed creative strategies to cope with these marginalizing circumstances. In addition, scholars should continue to explore the increasingly pressured world of social service delivery, and identify those innovations and practices that have addressed not only the expanding and changing needs of the community, but also the organizational turbulence so common in social service employment. Researchers focusing on social service delivery and economic development should work together to develop cross-disciplinary and multimethod analyses to better understand and address these complex issues. Through creative strategies and innovative research that work to synchronize the temporal and spatial obligations of communities of color, social service delivery, and economic development, a longer-term future of self-sufficiency and self-determination in communities of color is a realizable goal.

NOTES

The survey data analyzed in this chapter was supported by a grant from the University of California's university-wide AIDS Research Program (R97-I-116).

1. Resilience can be defined as "the remarkable capacity of individuals to withstand considerable hardship, to bounce back in the face of adversity, and to go on to live functional lives with a sense of well-being" (Turner 2001:441).

2. A survey of 206 respondents living with HIV/AIDS was conducted between June 21 and July 9, 1999 (Takahashi, Wiebe, and Rodriguez 2001). The convenience sample was contacted at agencies providing medical or social services to persons

living in HIV/AIDS in Orange County, California. Potential survey participants were selected using a quota sampling technique to obtain a purposive sample to maximize the number of persons of color and women. To contact potential respondents, a trained survey team (many of whom were bilingual in English and Spanish), with the permission of the executive directors and staff, waited in the lobbies of the service organizations. As individuals entered the facilities, they were asked whether they would be willing to participate in the survey, and were provided with a short description of the project and its objectives. Twenty-six persons were unwilling to participate (resulting in a response rate of 89 percent). If individuals were willing to participate, the survey team obtained verbal consent (anonymity and confidentiality were assured). Surveys were administered by research team members in English or Spanish depending on the preference of the respondent. Each survey took twenty minutes to complete, and participants upon completion of the survey received a five-dollar food voucher.

3. The definition of "working poor" remains in dispute; see for example Acs et al. (2000).

4. Sue and Sue (1990) outline the characteristics of a culturally competent counselor as constant re-evaluation of assumptions and biases concerning human behavior, exploring and comprehending the culturally distinct worldview of the person seeking help, and developing appropriate and sensitive strategies.

5. Transforming power relations to create greater self-determination for communities in need is a substantial challenge given the client-provider hierarchical relationship and individually oriented therapeutic model still prevalent among service providers and social workers (e.g., Jacobson 2001).

REFERENCES

Acs, Gregory, Kathrin Ross Phillips, and Daniel McKenzie. 2000. *Playing by the Rules but Losing the Game: America's Working Poor*. Research Report prepared for the Assessing the New Federalism Project and Jobs for the Future. Washington, D.C.: The Urban Institute.

Altman, Julie Cooper. 2003. A qualitative examination of client participation in agency-initiated services. *Families in Society: The Journal of Contemporary Human Services* 84(4):471–479.

Bednar, Susan G. 2003. Elements of satisfying organizational climates in child welfare agencies. *Families in Society: The Journal of Contemporary Human Services* 84(1):7–12.

Blau, Joel. 1992. *The Visible Poor: Homelessness in the United States*. New York: Oxford University Press.

Blumenberg, E. 2002. On the way to work: Welfare participants and barriers to employment. *Economic Development Quarterly* 16(4):314–325.

Cohen, Jerome, and Brenda G. McGowan. 1982. 'What Do you Do?' An Inquiry into the Potential of Work–Related Research. In *Work, Workers and Work Organizations: A View from Social Work*, eds. Sheila H. Akabas and Paul A. Kurzman, pp. 117–146. Englewood Cliffs, NJ: Prentice Hall.

Cunningham, W. E., D. M. Mosen, R. Hayes, R. M. Andersen, and M. F. Shapiro. 1996. Access to community-based medical services and number of hospitalizations among patients with HIV disease: Are they related? *Journal of aids and Human Retrovirology* 13(4):327–335.

Dear, M., and S. M. Taylor. 1982. Not on Our Street: Community Attitudes toward Mental Health Care. London: Pion.

Dyck, I. 1999. Using qualitative methods in medical geography: Deconstructive moments in a subdiscipline? *Professional Geographer* 51:243–253.

Gilbert, M. 1998. Race, space, and power: The survival strategies of working poor women. *Annals of the Association of American Geographers* 88(4):595–624.

Granovetter, M. 1995. *Getting a job: A study of contacts and careers* (2nd ed.). Cambridge: Harvard University Press.

Hyde, Cheryl A. 2004. Multicultural development in human services agencies: Challenges and solutions. *Social Work* 49(1):7–16.

Iglehart, A., and R. Becerra. 1995. *Social Services and the Ethnic Community*. Boston: Allyn & Bacon.

Jacobson, Wendy B. 2001. Beyond therapy: Bringing social work back to human services reform. *Social Work* 46(1):51–61.

Kamerman, Sheila B., and Alfred J. Kahn. 1976. *Social Services in the United States: Policies and Programs*. Philadelphia: Temple University Press.

Kearns, R. 1997. Narrative and metaphor in health geographies. *Progress in Human Geography* 21(2):269–277.

Law, R., and J. R. Wolch. 1991. Homelessness and economic restructuring. *Urban Geography* 12(2):105–136.

London, Andrew, Ellen K. Scott, Kathryn Edin, and Vicki Hunter. 2004. Welfare reform, work-family trade-offs, and child well being. *Family Relations* 53(2): 148–158.

Moss, P., and I. Dyck. 1996. Inquiry into environment and body: Women, work, and chronic illness. *Environment and Planning D: Society and Space*,14:737–753.

Nybell, Lynn M., and Sylvia Sims Gray. 2004. Race, place, space: Meanings of cultural competence in three child welfare agencies. *Social Work* 49(1):17–26.

Ong, P., and E. Blumenberg. 1998. Job access, commute and travel burden among welfare recipients. *Urban Studies* 35(1):77–95.

Orthner, Dennis K., Hinckley Jones-Sanpei, and Sabrina Williamson. 2004. The resilience and strengths of low-income families. *Family Relations* 53(2):159–167.

Perlman, Helen Harris. 1982. The client as worker: A look at an overlooked role. In *Work, Workers and Work Organizations: A View from Social Work*, eds. Sheila H. Akabas and Paul A. Kurzman, pp. 90–116. Englewood Cliffs, NJ: Prentice Hall.

Rowe, S., and J. Wolch. 1990. Social networks in time and space: homeless women in skid row, Los Angeles. *Annals of the Association of American Geographers* 80(2):184–204.

Roy, Kevin M., Carolyn Y. Tubbs, and Linda M. Burton. 2004. Don't have no time: Daily rhythms and the organization of time for low income families. *Family Relations* 53(2):168–178.

Salamon, L. 1995. *Partners in Public Service: Government-Nonprofit Relations in the Modern Welfare State*. Baltimore, MD: Johns Hopkins University Press.

Shields, Glenn, and Judy Kiser. 2003. Violence and aggression directed toward human service workers: An exploratory study. *Families in Society: The Journal of Contemporary Human Services* 84(1):13–20.

Sosin, Michael. 1986. *Private Benefits: Material Assistance in the Private Sector*. Orlando, FL: Academic Press.

Sue, D. W., and D. Sue. 1990. *Counseling the Culturally Different: Theory and Practice*. New York: Wiley.

Takahashi, Lois M. 1996. A decade of understanding homelessness: From characterization to representation. *Progress in Human Geography* 29(3):291–310.

Takahashi, Lois M. 1998. *Homelessness, AIDS, and Stigmatization: The NIMBY Syndrome at the End of the Twentieth Century*. Oxford: Oxford University Press.

Takahashi, Lois M., Jaime McElroy, and Stacy Rowe. 2002. The role of networks in socio-spatial stigmatization: Homeless women with children in Orange County, California. *Urban Geography* 23(4):301–322.

Takahashi, Lois M., and Gayla Smutny. 2002. Collaborative windows and organizational governance: Exploring the formation and demise of social service partnerships. *Nonprofit & Voluntary Sector Quarterly* 31(2):165–185.

Takahashi, Lois M., Douglas Wiebe, and Rigoberto Rodriguez. 2001. Navigating the time-space context of HIV and AIDS: Daily routines and access to care. *Social Science and Medicine* 53:845–863.

Thomason, Terry, John F. Burton Jr., and Douglas E. Hyatt. 1998. *New Approaches to Disability in the Workplace*. Madison, WI: University of Wisconsin-Madison, Industrial Relations Research Association Series.

Turner, Sandra G. 2001. Resilience and social work practice: Three case studies. *Families in Society: The Journal of Contemporary Human Services* 82(5):441–448.

Twombly, Eric C. 2001. *Human Service Nonprofits in Metropolitan Areas during Devolution and Welfare Reform*. Brief No. 10 in a Series by the Center on Nonprofits and Philanthropy. Washington, D.C.: The Urban Institute.

Wilton, R. D. 1996. Diminished worlds? The geography of everyday life with HIV/AIDS. *Health and Place* 2:69–83.

Wolch, Jennifer, and Michael Dear. 1993. *Malign Neglect: Homelessness in an American City*. San Francisco: Jossey-Bass.

Conclusion
Lessons for Community Economic Development

ANASTASIA LOUKAITOU-SIDERIS
AND PAUL ONG

THE LAST 15 YEARS have brought opportunities and challenges for urban neighborhoods in America. The robust and protracted economic expansion of the 1990s coupled with significant policy initiatives is credited for an overall reduction and deconcentration of poverty. The progress, although far from solving all of the problems of low-income minority neighborhoods, offers a glimpse of what is possible. Unfortunately, the gains, like the economic expansion, proved to be transitory. The burst of the dot-com bubble and the deepening trend of outsourcing have hit domestic jobs hard. While different labor market segments have suffered the pain of decreased employment opportunities and diminished earnings, the impact has been particularly hard on low-income and minority communities, which are in the weakest position to cushion the financial blows. The job of community economic development (CED) for these neighborhoods remains largely unfinished, and for it to be effective in the decades to come, new approaches and strategies are needed.

The preceding chapters have provided insights into the challenges facing CED through case studies and quantitative analyses of a diverse set of neighborhoods across the country. But the objective of this book is to not only document and explain the varying circumstances affecting community economic development but also to outline a policy framework and normative guidelines for such development to happen. With that objective in mind, the book's contributors have discussed the policy implications of their studies. Rather than repeating the chapter-specific strategies and recommendations, this concluding chapter extracts the "collective wisdom" of the previous writings to identify crosscutting lessons that often come from two or more chapters. Collectively, the chapters tell a story about the complexity of the problems facing low-income minority communities, and one of the most repeated conclusions is that there is no panacea. The other lessons in this concluding chapter are organized into two parts. The first contains five recommendations about how community economic development should be structured and practiced, and the second contains recommendations about the role of three key actors.

FIVE CED RECOMMENDATIONS

The demographic and economic changes that American cities have experienced in recent decades have been massive. Of course, not all the changes have been negative, but nonetheless, there are new realities that make existing practices outdated. These changes coupled with significant shifts in public policies for the poor call for a serious rethinking of the strategies and processes that constitute our collective efforts for community economic development. We have identified five ways that CED should be practiced in today's environment.

First, *ced should be linked to the larger social, political, economic, and policy framework that fundamentally shapes outcomes at the neighborhood level.* To respond to problems facing low-income minority communities we have to adopt a broader vision that encompasses the fundamental dynamics perpetuating poverty. This means tackling deeply embedded problems of economic, social, and political injustices and changing the societal institutions that produce and replicate inequality. We need public policies that create opportunities and at the same time provide an adequate safety net when things go wrong. Today's disjointed and fragmented approaches to urban development and redevelopment may lead to economic and social imbalances, with gentrification chasing poor residents out of revitalized neighborhoods or successful job development leading to the abandonment of old neighborhoods by some residents. To prevent this, we should be careful that our policies and practices do not balkanize neighborhoods and regions into disconnected and competing enclaves. As noted in chapters 3, 10, and 11, this requires greater linkage with the world beyond the neighborhood.

Second, *ced must reach beyond inner-city neighborhoods because the traditional divisions between central cities and suburbs are no longer valid.* As chapter 1 by Evelyn Blumenberg clearly shows, the conventional dichotomy of wealthy suburbs versus desolate central cities and impoverished reservations are seriously tested by new demographic realities, which show that almost half of the low-income families now live in the suburbs, and wealthy households may be encountered in central cities and on reservations. Even while pockets of concentrated poverty dot many central cities, the last decade has also experienced selective revitalization as affluent residents moved back to newly built lofts and condos. At the same time that we are considering ways to link central city residents to suburban job opportunities, we also have to improve the economic opportunities offered in central cities, reservations, and suburban neighborhoods.

Third, *ced approaches should be tailored to the particularities of specific neighborhoods and populations.* A number of authors drawing from empirical evidence make the point that "one size does not fit all" because of the enormous economic, demographic, and spatial diversity among and within metropolitan areas and among different labor market segments (chapters 2, 6, 8, and 9). This heterogeneity produces equally significant variations in the outcomes from economic development policies and job creation strategies. For this reason, economic development strategies should differ significantly across minority groups and neighborhoods. What would be of most help to one neighborhood or group may not fit the type of help needed by another neighborhood. Nevertheless, the strategies and the potential long-term consequences for the specific neighborhoods and groups, the broader area, and even the region must be considered before choosing what kind of strategy or mix of strategies to be followed.

Fourth, *ced must address the needs in both the formal and informal sectors*. Low-wage jobs in the formal economy may not be sufficient to ensure the livelihood of households, thus household members may operate in the informal economy to supplement their income. While undocumented workers make up a disproportionate share of the informal economy, even native-born minorities participate. As argued by Abel Valenzuela in Chapter 6, in some cases, the informal economy may even provide entrepreneurial opportunities for minority households. Others may seek or be forced to accept sporadic, part-time, and contingent informal work that pays under the table. For many neighborhoods, the informal economy is a significant share of the local economy, and many of the residents move back and forth between the two sectors. CED must find ways to address the informal sector—and the solution is not simply to eliminate it.

Fifth, *multiple strategies focusing on people and place are needed to promote economic and employment development*. Increasing opportunities requires working on both the demand side and the supply side of the labor market. We need to break down the barriers that limit residents from finding and holding jobs that pay a decent wage with decent benefits, and we need to improve the residents' educational and skill levels so they can successfully compete for better jobs throughout the regional labor market (see chapters 4 and 5). As Thomas Boston argues in chapter 7, while local residents should be better linked to economic opportunities well beyond their immediate neighborhoods, it is also desirable to enhance the neighborhood economy through business development. Clearly, a major benefit of revitalizing businesses is the creation of jobs, but having a vibrant neighborhood economy also helps meet the residents' demand for goods and services and makes the area more livable. The focus on jobs and businesses needs to be part of a holistic approach to community economic development and will need to incorporate goals for affordable housing, transportation, health, and childcare services (see chapters 11 and 12).

THE ROLE OF KEY CED ACTORS

To tackle a problem as structural and long-standing as poverty, combined strategies and efforts of different actors are necessary. The combined responses and efforts of the state, the private sector, and the nonprofit sector are necessary to pull communities out of poverty and generate jobs and income. The failures of the past have shown that we cannot simply rely on a market-driven model of economic development.

The impact of welfare reform in reducing poverty attests to the power of federal policy. While welfare reform may be a step in the right direction, federal policies need fine-tuning and better outreach efforts to respond to the needs of those that they leave behind: the marginal workers, the workers of the informal economy, those who never apply for tax credits, and those who despite their efforts cannot enter the labor force. Beyond welfare reform, the role of the state is crucial in offering an enabling environment through tax incentives and regulatory frameworks that nurture and support ethnic entrepreneurship, business investment in minority areas, and the hiring of minority workers. The role of the federal government is crucial in fostering these businesses by providing funds to the states for job training programs, English as a Second Language and adult education, skill enhancement for low-income workers, and business assistance to advance the capacity of minority-owned firms. At the same time, federal and state legislation should also do a better job of enforcing labor standards, minimum-wage ordinances, and worker rights.

The private sector should be a very important partner in any CED effort in minority, low-income communities. As the federal block grants for low-income communities have consistently decreased over the last decades, the major financial investment in business development comes from the private sector. CED in minority, low-income communities is in desperate need of the private sector to offer jobs and investment, support training programs for workers, and plant the seeds for neighborhood revitalization. As chapters 7 and 8 indicate, minority entrepreneurs are among the most committed to low-income minority communities, so they should play a major role in revitalizing these neighborhoods. Because many small ethnic businesses are characterized by high turnover rates due to meager starting capital, the role of banking and financial institutions is essential in offering them loans with low interest rates and enabling them to operate and grow. The challenge in the next decade is to break the spatial, social, and structural barriers that separate low-income communities from private-sector jobs. This challenge is twofold: to persuade the private sector to locate and invest in low-income communities and to make businesses a responsible partner in revitalizing neighborhoods and providing upward mobility to workers.

The nonprofit sector has been proven to be an important partner in neighborhood revitalization efforts. In addition to foundations that have selectively funded projects in minority and low-income neighborhoods, recent decades have witnessed the emergence of different types of grassroots and community organizations. These organizations have been very active in the provision of affordable housing and social services, and some have also been involved in job training programs. More recently, some community groups have played an important role in spearheading coalitions around community economic development efforts in specific neighborhoods.

As argued in chapters 10, 11, and 12, social networks, collaborations and coalitions among community groups, labor unions, social service providers, and the private sector can help link communities to a larger pool of resources and have a better impact in bringing about economic and physical change in neighborhoods. One of the main obstacles that has in the past crippled low-income communities of color is their social and political isolation. Poor households in such communities often remain cut off from the larger framework of economic opportunities, and their neighborhoods remain desolate and neglected by policy makers and politicians. To address this important hurdle, economic development in low-income minority communities should work hand-in-hand with community development. Policy makers should try to help neighborhoods acquire more social capital and strengthen their ties to the outside world of political, financial, and civic institutions. The role of local groups—community-based organizations, community development corporations, and comprehensive community initiatives—is crucial in developing coalitions and building bridges between the neighborhood, the local government, the private and nonprofit sectors, and labor interest groups. As Pastor, Benner, and Matsuoka argue in Chapter 3, these groups should proceed with caution because effective regional strategies require an evaluation of both opportunities and challenges.

We are not under any naive illusion that any of the above recommendations will be easy to implement. In fact, our collective professional and academic experiences tell us that progress is often slow and subject to setbacks. The history of community economic development for low-income minority communities is one of very mixed results. And things have gotten more challenging given the demographic, economic, and policy changes described earlier. Simply tinkering with existing approaches would only provide Band-Aids for wounds that may get deeper if left unattended. Instead, we need to update and adapt our CED tools to the new social and economic realities. We hope that this book represents a step towards this direction.

Contributors

CHRIS BENNER
Professor Chris Benner, Department of Geography, 302 Walker Building,
The Pennsylvania State University, University Park, PA 16802

Books

BENNER, CHRIS. 2002. *Work in the New Economy: Flexible Labor Markets in Silicon Valley.* Oxford: Blackwell.

Book Chapters

BENNER, CHRIS. 2003. Information technology, employment and equity in South Africa: The role of national ICT policy. In *Technology and Development in Africa*, ed. I. Adesida, I. Kakoma, and P. Zeleza, 127–156. Trenton, NJ: Africa World Press.

BENNER, CHRIS. 2004. Labor in the network society: Lessons from Silicon Valley. In *The Network Society: A Global Perspective*, ed. Manuel Castells, 174–197. Cheltenham: Edward Elgar.

Journal Articles

BENNER, CHRIS. 2003. Computers in the wild: Guilds and next generation unionism in the information revolution. *International Review of Social History* 48:S11.

BENNER, CHRIS. 2003. Learning communities in a learning region: The soft infrastructure of cross-firm learning communities in Silicon Valley. *Environment and Planning A* 35(10):1809–1830.

EVELYN BLUMENBERG
Professor Evelyn Blumenberg, Department of Urban Planning,
University of California, Los Angeles, School of Public Affairs,
Box 951656, Los Angeles, CA 90095-1656

Book Chapters

ONG, PAUL, AND EVELYN BLUMENBERG. 1996. Income and racial inequality in Los Angeles. In *The City: Los Angeles and Urban Theory at the End of the Twentieth Century,* ed. A. Scott and E. Soja, 311–335. Berkeley: University of California Press.

Journal Articles

BLUMENBERG, EVELYN, AND PAUL ONG. 2001. Cars, buses, and jobs: Welfare recipients and employment access in Los Angeles. *Journal of the Transportation Research Board* 1756:22–31.

BLUMENBERG, EVELYN 2002. On the way to work: Welfare participants and barriers to employment. *Economic Development Quarterly* 16(4):314–325.

BLUMENBERG, EVELYN 2002. Planning for the transportation needs of welfare participants: Institutional challenges to collaborative planning. *Journal of Planning Education and Research* 22(2):152–163.

BLUMENBERG, EVELYN, AND DANIEL BALDWIN HESS. 2003. Measuring the role of transportation in facilitating the welfare-to-work transition: Evidence from three California counties. *Journal of the Transportation Research Board* 1859:93–101.

BLUMENBERG, EVELYN. 2004. En-gendering effective planning: Transportation policy and low-income women. *Journal of the American Planning Association* 70(3):269–281.

BLUMENBERG E., AND K. SHIKI 2004. Spatial mismatch outside of large urban areas: An analysis of welfare recipients in Fresno County, California. *Environment and Planning C—Government and Policy* 22(3):401–421.

THOMAS D. BOSTON

Professor Thomas D. Boston, Georgia Institute of Technology, School of Economics, Atlanta, GA 30318

Books

BOSTON, T. D., ed. 2002. *Leading Issues in Black Political Economy*. New York: Transaction Press.

BOSTON, T. D. 1999. *Affirmative Action and Black Entrepreneurship*. New York: Routledge. Book research supported by the 20th Century Fund.

BOSTON, T. D., AND CATHERINE L. ROSS, eds. 1997. *The Inner City: Urban Poverty and Economic Development in the Next Century*. New York: Transaction Press.

Journal Articles

BOSTON, T.D. 2005. The effects of revitalization on public housing residents: A case study of the Atlanta Housing Authority. *Journal of the American Planning Association* 71(4):393–407.

BOSTON, T.D. 2005. Black patronage of Black-owned businesses and Black employment. C. Conrad, J. Whitehead, et al. (eds.). *African Americans in the U.S. Economy*. New York: Rowman & Littlefield Publishers, Inc: 373–377.

BOSTON, T.D. 2000. Minority business trends. N. Smelser, W.J. Wilson, and F. Mitchell (eds.). *America Becoming: Racial Trends and Their Consequences.* Washington, DC: National Academy of Science Press: 190–221.

DOUGLAS HOUSTON

Douglas Houston, University of California, Los Angeles,
The Ralph and Goldy Lewis Center for Regional Policy Studies,
School of Public Affairs, Los Angeles, CA 90095-1656

Journal Articles

HOUSTON, DOUGLAS, JUN WU, PAUL ONG, AND ARTHUR WINER. 2004. Structural disparities of urban traffic in Southern California: Implications for vehicle-related air pollution exposure in minority and high-poverty neighborhoods. *Journal of Urban Affairs* 25(5):565–592.

MILLER, DOUGLAS, AND DOUGLAS HOUSTON. 2003. Distressed Asian American neighborhoods. *AAPI Nexus; Asian Americans & Pacific Islanders Policy, Practice and Community* 1(1):67–84.

ONG, PAUL, AND DOUGLAS HOUSTON. 2002. Transit, employment, and women on welfare. *Urban Geography* 23(4):344–364.

LEJANO, RAUL, BILL PIAZZA, AND DOUGLAS HOUSTON. 2002. Rationality as social justice and the spatial distributional analysis of risk. *Environment and Planning C: Government and Policy* 20:871–888.

TARRY HUM

Professor Tarry Hum, Urban Studies Department, Queens College,
City University of New York, Flushing, NY 11367

Book Chapters

HUM, TARRY. 2004. Immigrant global neighborhoods in New York City. In *Race and Ethnicity in New York City*, ed. Jerry Krase and Ray Hutchison, 25–55, vol. 7, *Research in Urban Sociology*. Kidlington, UK: JAI Press.

HUM, TARRY. 2002. Asian and Latino immigration and the revitalization of Sunset Park, Brooklyn. In *Intersections and Divergences: Contemporary Asian Pacific American Communities*, ed. Linda Vo and Rick Bonus, 27–44. Philadelphia: Temple University Press.

HUM, TARRY. 2000. The promises and dilemmas of immigrant ethnic economies. In *Asian and Latino Immigrants in a Restructuring Economy: The Metamorphosis of Southern California*, ed. Marta Lopez-Garza and David R. Diaz, 77–101. Palo Alto, CA: Stanford University Press.

Journal Articles

HUM, TARRY. 2003. Mapping global production in New York City's garment industry: The role of Sunset Park, Brooklyn's immigrant economy. *Economic Development Quarterly* 17(3):294–309.

Judy Hutchinson

Dr. Judy Hutchinson, Director, Center for Academic Service
Learning and Research, Azusa Pacific University,
901 East Alosta Avenue, PO Box 7000, Azusa, CA 91702—7000

Book Chapter

HUTCHINSON, JUDY, DEBRA FETTERLY, AND KRISTIN GURROLA. 2005.
"Service Learning in Faith-based Higher Ed: An Interfaith Dialogue." In
Spirituality, Social Justice, and Service-Learning, ed. John W. Eby, 23–40.
Grantham, PA: Messiah College Press.

Journal Articles

HUTCHINSON, JUDY, AND VIDAL, AVIS, eds. 2004. Using social capital to
help integrate planning theory, research, and practice. *Journal of the
American Planning Association* 70(2):142–192.

HUTCHINSON, JUDY. 2004. Introduction. *Journal of the American Planning
Association* 70(2):143–145.

HUTCHINSON, JUDY. 2004. Social capital and community building in the
inner city. *Journal of the American Planning Association* 70(2):168–175.

HUTCHINSON, JUDY, AND ANASTASIA LOUKAITOU-SIDERIS. 2001. Choosing
confrontation or consensus in the inner city: Lessons from a community-
university partnership. *Journal of Planning Theory and Practice* 2(3):293–310.

HUTCHINSON, JUDY. 2002 Citizen participation. *Journal of the American
Planning Association* 68(2):226–227.

Theodore Jojola

Professor Theodore Jojola, School of Architecture and Planning,
Community and Regional Planning Program, University of
New Mexico, Albuquerque, NM 87106

Book Chapters

JOJOLA, THEODORE. 1994. Public image: American Indian stereotypes, In
Native America in the 20th Century: An Encyclopedia, ed. Mary B. Davis.
Garland Publishers, NY.

JOJOLA, THEODORE. 1997. Indians in the movies. In *The Encyclopedia
of American Indians,* ed. Frederic E. Hoxie, pages. Location: Houghton
Mifflen.

JOJOLA, THEODORE. 1998 Indigenous planning: Clans, intertribal con-
federations and the history of the All Indian Pueblo Council. In *Making the
Invisible: Insurgent Planning Histories,* ed. Leonie Sandercock. Berkeley:
University of California Press.

Journal Articles

JOJOLA, THEODORE. 1995. A Zuni artist looks at Frank Hamilton Cushing. *Exhibition Reviews, Museum Anthro* 19(1).

JOJOLA, THEODORE. 1996. On revision and revisionism: American Indian representations in New Mexico, *American Indian Quarterly* 20(1):41–47.

JOJOLA, THEODORE. 1998. Guest Editor, Special Edition on Technology and Culture. Wacaso Sa Review: *Journal of Native American Studies.*

JACQUELINE LEAVITT

Professor Jacqueline Leavitt, Department of Urban Planning, University of California, Los Angeles, School of Public Affairs, Los Angeles, CA 90095-1656

Books

HESKIN, ALLAN, AND JACQUELINE LEAVITT, eds. 1995. *The Hidden History of Housing Cooperatives.* Davis, CA: Center for Cooperatives, University of California.

LEAVITT, J., AND S. SAEGERT. 1990. *From Abandonment to Hope: Community-Households in Harlem.* New York: Columbia University Press.

Book Chapters

LEAVITT, JACQUELINE, AND KARA HEFFERNAN. 2005. Multiplying knowledge: Service learning × activism = community scholars. In *From the Studio to the Streets: Service-Learning in Architectural and Planning Education,* ed. William Zeisel. Washington, DC: American Association for Higher Education.

LEAVITT, JACQUELINE. 2002. The struggle to struggle together: The case of women, housing, and labor. In *Housing Policies, Gender Inequality, and Financial Globalization on the Pacific Rim,* ed. Gary Dymski and Dorene Isenberg, 320–348. Amonk, N.Y.: M.E. Sharpe.

LEAVITT, JACQUELINE. 1996. Los Angeles neighborhoods respond to the civil unrest: Is planning an adequate tool? In *Revitalizing Urban Neighborhoods,* ed. Dennis Keating, Norman Krumholz, and Phil Star, 112–130. Kansas City: University of Kansas Press.

Journal Articles

LEAVITT, JACQUELINE, AND TERESA LINGAFELTER. 2005. Low Wages and High Housing Costs, *Labor Studies Journal* 30(2):41–60.

LEAVITT, JACQUELINE. 2005. "Art and the Politics of Public Housing." *Planners Network, the Magazine of Progressive Planning.* Fall 2005. 165:10–12, 17.

LEAVITT, JACQUELINE. 2003. "Where's the Gender in Community Development?" *SIGNS* 29(1):207–231.

Anastasia Loukaitou-Sideris

Professor Anastasia Loukaitou-Sideris, Department of Urban Planning, University of California, Los Angeles, School of Public Affairs, Los Angeles, CA 90095–1656

Books

Loukaitou-Sideris, A., and T. Bannerjee. 1998. *Urban Design Downtown: Poetics and Politics of Form.* Los Angeles and Berkeley: University of California Press.

Book Chapters

Loukaitou-Sideris, A., E. Blumenberg, and R. Ehrenfeucht. 2005. Sidewalk democracy: Municipalities and the regulation of public space. In *Regulating Place: Standards and the Shaping of Urban America*, ed. E. Ben-Joseph and T. Szold, 141–166. New York: Routledge.

Journal Articles

Loukaitou-Sideris, A. 2000. Revisiting inner city strips: A framework for community and economic development. *Economic Development Quarterly* 14(1):165–181.

Loukaitou-Sideris, A. 2002. Regeneration of urban commercial strips: Ethnicity and space in three Los Angeles neighborhoods. *Journal of Architectural and Planning Research* 19(4):334–350.

Loukaitou-Sideris, A. 2003. Children's common grounds: A study of intergroup relations among children in public settings. *Journal of the American Planning Association* 69(2): 130–144.

Loukaitou-Sideris, A., and C. Grodach. 2004. Displaying and celebrating the 'other': A study of the mission, scope, and roles of ethnic museums in Los Angeles. *Public Historian* 26(4): 49–71.

Kamel, N., and A. Loukaitou-Sideris. 2004. Residential recovery following the Northridge earthquake. *Urban Studies* 41(3):533–562.

Martha Matsuoka

Martha Matsuoka, Adjunct Assistant Professor, Department of Urban and Environmental Policy, Occidental College, Los Angeles, CA 90041, and Assistant Researcher, Center for Justice, Tolerance, and Community, US Santa Cruz, Santa Cruz, CA 95064

Book Chapters

Matsuoka, Martha. forthcoming. Economic development in Latino/a communities: Facing the challenges of shifting federal policy and community development. In *Latino Economic Development*, ed. David Diaz. New York: Routledge.

Fukumura, Yoko and Martha Matsuoka. 2002. "Redefining Security: Okinawa Women and their Resistance to U.S. Militarism." In *Women's*

Resistance to Globalization, eds. Nancy Naples and Manisha Desai, 239–263. New York: Routledge.

Journal Articles

MATSUOKA, MARTHA. 2004. From Mega to Micro: A Conversation with Manuel Pastor, Jr. *Critical Planning* 11: 113–21.

MATSOUKA, MARTHA. 1997. "Reintegrating the Flatlands: A Regional Approach to Base Closures in the SF Bay Area." *Capitalism Nature & Socialism: A Journal of Socialist Ecology* 8(29):109–124.

Reports

PASTOR, MANUEL JR., CHRIS BENNER, RACHEL ROSNER, MARTHA MATSUOKA, AND JULIE JACOBS. 2003. *Learning from the Neighborhoods: Community-based Regionalism and Comprehensive Community Initiatives in the San Francisco Bay Area.* A report to the William and Flora Hewlett Foundation.

MATSUOKA, MARTHA. 2003. *Building Communities from the Ground Up: Environmental Justice in California.* Completed with the Asian Pacific Environmental Network, Communities for a Better Environment, Environmental Health Coalition, People Organizing to Demand Environmental & Economic Rights, and the Silicon Valley Toxics Coalition/Health and Environmental Justice Project for the California Endowment.

PAUL ONG

Professor Paul Ong, The Ralph and Goldy Lewis Center for
Regional Policy Studies, University of California, Los Angeles,
School of Public Affairs, Los Angeles, CA 90095-1656

Books

ONG, PAUL, EDNA BONACICH, and LUCIE CHENG, eds. 1994. *The New Asian Immigration in Los Angeles and Global Restructuring.* Philadelphia: Temple University Press.

ONG, PAUL, ed. 1999. *Impacts of Affirmative Action: Policies and Consequences in California.* Walnut Creek: Alta Mira Press.

ONG, PAUL M., ed. 2000. *The State of Asian Pacific America: Transforming Race Relations.* Los Angeles: Asian Pacific American Public Policy Institute, LEAP and UCLA AASC.

Journal Articles

ONG, PAUL. 2001. Set-aside contracting in S.B.A.'s 8(A) program. *Review of Black Political Economy* 28(3):59–71.

ONG, PAUL M. 2002. Car ownership and welfare-to-work. *Journal of Policy Analysis and Management* 21(2):255–268.

Manuel Pastor

Professor Manuel Pastor, University of California, Santa Cruz,
Latin American & Latino Studies, Casa Latina, Merrill College,
1156 High Street, Santa Cruz, CA 95064

Books

Pastor, Manuel, Angela Glover-Blackwell, and Stewart Kwoh. 2002. *Searching for the Uncommon Common Ground: New Dimensions on Race in America*. New York: W.W. Norton.

Pastor, Manuel, Peter Dreier, Marta López-Garza, and Eugene Grigsby. 2000. *Regions That Work: How Cities and Suburbs Can Grow Together*. Minneapolis: University of Minnesota Press.

Journal Articles

Pastor, Manuel, Jim Sadd, and Rachel Morello-Frosch. Forthcoming. Waiting to inhale: The demographics of toxic air releases in 21st century California. *Social Science Quarterly* E5(2):420–440.

Up Against the Sprawl: Public Policy and the (Re-)Making of Southern California, 2004, edited volume, co-editors are Jennifer Wolch and Peter Dreier, Minneapolis: University of Minnesota Press.

Pastor, Manuel, Jim Sadd, and Rachel Morello-Frosch. 2004. Reading, writing, and toxics: Children's health, academic performance, and environmental justice in Los Angeles. *Environment and Planning C: Government and Policy* 22(1):27–290.

Pastor, Manuel, Laura Leete, Chris Benner, and Sarah Zimmerman. 2003. Labor market intermediaries in the old and new economies: A survey of worker experiences in Milwaukee and Silicon Valley. In *Workforce Intermediaries for the 21st Century*. Philadelphia: Temple University Press.

Michael Stoll

Professor Michael Stoll, Department of Public Policy,
University of California, Los Angeles, School of Public Affairs,
Los Angeles, CA 90095–1656

Books

Stoll, Michael A. 2004. *African Americans and the Color Line*. New York: Russell Sage Foundation and Population Reference Bureau.

Holzer, Harry J., and Michael A. Stoll. 2001. *Employers and Welfare Recipients: The Effects of Welfare Reform in the Workplace*. San Francisco, CA: Public Policy Institute of California.

Stoll, Michael A. 1999. *Race, Space and Youth Labor Markets*. New York: Garland Publishing, Inc.

Book Chapters

STOLL, MICHAEL A. 2005. Workforce development in the information technology age. In *Communities and Workforce Development*, ed. Edwin Melendez, 191–212. Kalamazoo, MI: W.E. Upjohn Institute.

Journal Articles

STOLL, MICHAEL A., AND HARRY J. HOLZER. 2003. Employer demand for welfare recipients by race. *Journal of Labor Economics* 21(1):210–241.

LOIS TAKAHASHI

Professor Lois Takahashi, Department of Urban Planning, University of California, Los Angeles, School of Public Affairs, Los Angeles, CA 90095-1656

Books

TAKAHASHI, LOIS M. 1998. *Homelessness, AIDS, and Stigmatization: The NIMBY Syndrome at the End of the Twentieth Century*. Oxford: Oxford University Press.

DANIERE, AMRITA, AND LOIS M. TAKAHASHI. 2002. *Rethinking Environmental Management in the Pacific Rim: Exploring Local Participation in Bangkok, Thailand*. London: Ashgate Publishing.

Journal Articles

TAKAHASHI, LOIS M., AND SHARON LORD GABER. 1998. Controversial Facility Siting in the Urban Environment: Resident and Planner Perceptions in the United States. *Environment and Behavior* 30(2):184–215.

TAKAHASHI, LOIS M., AND GAYLA SMUTNY. 1998. Community Planning for HIV/AIDS Prevention in Orange County, California. *Journal of the American Planning Association* 64(4):441–456.

TAKAHASHI, LOIS M., AND GAYLA SMUTNY. 2001. Collaboration Among Small Community-Based Organizations: Strategies and Challenges in Turbulent Environments. *Journal of Planning Education and Research* 21:141–153.

TAKAHASHI, LOIS M., DOUGLAS WIEBE, AND RIGOBERTO RODRIGUEZ. 2001. Navigating the Time-Space Context of HIV and AIDS: Daily Routines and Access to Care. *Social Science and Medicine* 53(7):845–863.

ABEL VALENZUELA

Professor Abel Valenzuela, Department of Chicana and Chicano Studies and the Chavez Center, University of California, Los Angeles, Los Angeles, CA 90095

Books

BOBO, LAWRENCE, JAMES JOHNSON JR., MELVIN OLIVER, and ABEL VALENZUELA JR. eds. 2000. *Prismatic Metropolis: Inequality in Los Angeles*. New York: Russell Sage Foundation.

Journal Articles

VALENZUELA, ABEL JR. 2001. Day laborers as entrepreneurs? *Journal of Ethnic and Migration Studies* 27(2):335–352.

STOLL, MICHAEL, EDWIN MELENDEZ, AND ABEL VALENZUELA JR. 2002. Spatial job search and job competition among immigrant and native groups in Los Angeles. *Regional Studies* 36(2):97–112.

VALENZUELA, ABEL JR., JANETTE A. KAWACHI, AND MATTHEW D. MARR. 2002. Seeking work daily: Supply, demand, and spatial dimensions of day labor in two global cities. *International Journal of Comparative Sociology* 43(2):192–219.

VALENZUELA, ABEL JR. 2003. Day-labor work. *Annual Review of Sociology* 29(1):307–333.

MICHELA ZONTA
Professor Michela Zonta, L. Douglas Wilder School of Government and Public Affairs, Virginia Commonwealth University, Richmond, VA 23284

Book Chapters

ONG, PAUL, AND MICHELA ZONTA. 2001. Trends in earnings inequity. In *The State of California Labor*, ed. Paul M. Ong and Jim Lincoln. Los Angeles and Berkeley: University of California, Institute of Industrial Relations.

HUM, TARRY, AND MICHELA ZONTA. 2000. Residential Patterns of Asian Pacific Americans. In *The State of Asian Pacific America: Transforming Race Relations*, ed. Paul Ong, 191–242. Los Angeles: LEAP, Asian Pacific American Public Policy Institute and UCLA Asian American Studies Center.

Journal Articles

ZONTA, MICHELA. 2005. Housing policies and the concentration of poverty in urban America. Review Essay. *Social Service Review* 79(1):181–185.

Reports

ZONTA, MICHELA. 2004. The state of Southern California's housing. Los Angeles: The Ralph and Goldy Lewis Center for Regional Policy Studies, UCLA School of Public Affairs.

2003. *The Economic Cycle and Los Angeles Neighborhoods: 1987–2001*. Report prepared for the John Randolph Haynes and Dora Hayines Foundation. Los Angeles: The Ralph & Goldy Lewis Center for Regional Policy Studies, UCLA School of Public Policy and Social Research.

2000. *Place and Economic Status Among Section 8 Vouchers and Certificates Recipients: Evidence from Los Angeles*. Los Angeles: The Institute for the Study of Homelessness and Poverty at the Weingart Center.

Index

Action for Grassroots Empowerment and Neighborhood Development Alternatives (AGENDA), 70, 264

affordable housing: lobbying, 75; shortage, in California, 260; shortage, for households of color, 278–79; shortage, in metropolitan areas, 24–25. *See under* African Americans; Hispanics; Pico Union neighborhood, in Los Angeles

African Americans: access to cars, 98; access to public transit, 98–99; applicant rates, 129–30, 133; black-owned businesses, 162–68, 171–73; census tract clusters, 124; communities, 80, 161; firm accessibility, 128, 133; home ownership rates, 81; population growth, 80; poverty, 46, 51–52, 56; spatial distribution of jobs, 97–98; unemployment, 91–92, 172

Aid to Families with Dependent Children (AFDC), 40, 42

American Indians: extraction industry, 216; poverty, 217, 225–26; tribal hiring, 215; trust relationship, 213

Asian American Federation of New York (AAFNY), 193

Asian American Legal Defense and Education Fund, 188

Asian Americans for Equality (AAFE), 199–200

Asian-owned businesses, in New York: average sales and receipts of, 179; concentration of, 183; employee earnings of, 179; and "enabling environment," 197–98; growth in, 179, 183; industrial mix of, 179, 183; "macro" perspective of, 194, 196; and networks, 192; share with paid employees, 179

Asociacion de Salvadorenos de Los Angeles (ASOSAL), 250, 252

Atlanta Housing Authority (AHA), 169–72

Bates, Timothy, 186
Bethel New Life, Inc., 70–71
blacks. *See* African Americans
Bloomberg, Michael, 203
breadbasket, 46
Bridges to Work Initiative, 103–4
Brown, Jerry, 77

Bureau of Indian Affairs (BIA), 215
Bush, George, 45, 102
Business Improvement Districts (BIDS), in New York, 201–2

camionetas, 152–53
Carruthers, Garrey, 220
cars, access to, 27–28, 98, 132. *See also* modal isolation
Center for Employment and Training (CETA), 154
Chang, Nora Wang, 203
Chicago: earnings, 48, 57; EITC usage, 49, 58; federal poverty level, 50–51; labor force participation, 48, 57; poor areas, 52; poverty rates, 50–51, 55; public housing, 57; welfare usage, 47–48, 57
Chinatown Justice Project, 205
Chinatown Manpower Project, Inc. (CMP), 203
Chinatown, in Manhattan, 177–178, 192–94, 199–200, 203
Clinton, William, 40, 45, 102
Coalition of Neighborhood Developers (CND), 260–61
community-based organizations (CBOs), 63, 68, 83
community-based regionalism (CBR), 64, 67, 69–70, 82–83
community benefits agreements (CBAs), 258, 264–67, 271–72
community development corporations (CDCs), 68–69
comprehensive community initiatives (CCIS), 64, 83
Comprehensive Employment and Training Act (CETA), 104–105
Coulton, Claudia, 52

Earned Income Tax Credit (EITC), 40–41, 44–46, 49, 54–55, 58, 155
economic development: community-based strategy, 152–53; definition, 147–49; employment and training programs, 154; entrepreneurial-based strategy, 149–151; recommendations, 296–97; traditional and nontraditional labor-based strategies, 155–56